The Hebrew Revelation

James and Jude

ספר אלה הסודות
אגרת יעקב ואגרת יהודה

Transcripts + translations of authentic Hebrew manuscripts of Revelation, James and Jude. Based on Ms. Oo.1.16 and Ms. Oo.1.32 from the Cambridge University Library. Also supported by Ms. Gaster 1616 from the Manchester University Library.

Version 2.2 © April 2024

Acknowledgments:

Michael J. Van Rensburg prepared initial transcripts and translations of James and Jude.

Various family members helped with proofreading and checking transcripts and translations.

Several friends helped with proofreading and suggestions, and various other readers also provided useful feedback.

We give all honor to Yahweh through Yeshua the Messiah!

Hardcover ISBN: 9780648639701   E-Book ISBN: 9780648639725

Softcover ISBN: 9780648639718   PDF ISBN: 9780648639732

iv

Page v shows a folio from one of the authentic Hebrew manuscripts of the Book of Revelation (Cambridge University Library Oo.1.16, folio 106v). This folio contains Revelation 21:18-22:21. The manuscript was discovered in 1806 by Buchanan, in a synagogue in Cochin, India, where it was preserved by the local Jewish community.

Refer to pp. 1-4 for more information about the Hebrew manuscripts used for this translation of Revelation, James and Jude.

One of the very important differences compared to the Greek Revelation is found in lines 22-23 of this folio. See our video "Who is the Morning Star, Yeshua (Jesus) or Satan?" for more information on this variant: HebrewGospels.com/videos-revelation/2

Visit our website HebrewGospels.com for:

- Color photos of all translated manuscript folios.
- Translations of the Hebrew Gospels.
- In-depth videos on the Hebrew Revelation.
- Free Hebrew Gospels mobile app.
- Video series on the Tetragrammaton, and much more!

Contact information:

www.HebrewGospels.com/contact

HebrewGospels@gmail.com

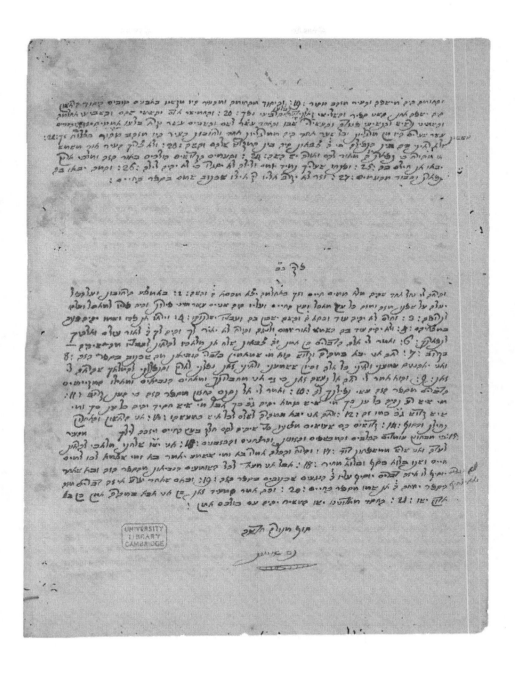

Manuscript Oo.1.16, folio 106v. Reproduced with kind permission from the
Cambridge University Library. Contains Revelation 21:18-22:21.

Table of Contents

Footnote Symbols and Abbreviations

The following list is not exhaustive, but includes important abbreviations and symbols that readers might find useful.

" "	Double quotation marks are used for direct quotations, literal meanings, non-paraphrase alternative translations, etc.
' '	Single quotation marks are used for quotes within quotes, alternative translations which are paraphrased, or transliterated words, etc.
E.g.	For example
Ed.	Edition or editor(s)
Ibid.	Same as previous reference
I.e.	That is
Lit.	Literally
Ms(s).	Manuscript(s)
MT	Masoretic Text (O.T.) or Majority Text (N.T.)
Pl.	Plural
P(p).	Page(s)
V.	Verse(s)
Vol.	Volume number
Vs.	Versus

Hebrew Transliteration Key

The transliteration of Hebrew words used in this book follows a simplified system which does not show all details of pronunciation. However, the following explanations will help the reader to pronounce the transliterated Hebrew words with reasonable accuracy.

'	Used to transliterate the Hebrew letters Ayin and Aleph. Simply start a new syllable when you see this symbol, e.g. 'Micha'el' is pronounced as 'Micha-el.'
a	Pronounced like the 'a' in 'father', but shorter. Similar to the 'u' in 'up' or 'under.'
b	As in English.
ch	Not pronounced as in English, but with a guttural sound as in the names 'Bach' or 'Lachlan.'
d	As in English.
e	Pronounced like the 'e' in 'egg' (sometimes also pronounced like the 'e' in 'cafe').
ei	Similar to the 'ei' in 'eight.'
g	Pronounced like the 'g' in 'go.'
h	Pronounced like the 'h' in 'house' at the start or in the middle of a word, but usually silent at the end of a word.
i	Pronounced like the 'i' in 'is,' or longer (like the 'ee' in 'bee').

k	As in English.
l	As in English.
m	As in English.
n	As in English.
o	Pronounced like the 'o' in 'or.'
p	As in English.
ph	As in English (also commonly transliterated as 'f').
q	Guttural 'k' sound (though commonly pronounced like the English 'k').
r	Rolled 'r' as pronounced in Spanish, but may also be pronounced more gutturally as in French.
s	As in English.
sh	As in English.
t	As in English.
ts	Pronounced like the 'ts' in 'pants.'
u	Pronounced like the 'ui' in 'fruit.'
v	As in English.
w	As in English.
y	Pronounced like the 'y' in 'yes.'
z	As in English.

About the Hebrew Manuscripts

In the year 1806, Claudius Buchanan found two Hebrew New Testament manuscripts in a Jewish Synagogue in Cochin, India.[a] Together, these two manuscripts contain all the books of the New Testament in Hebrew, compiled from various different sources.[b] Today these are known as Ms. Oo.1.16[c] and Ms. Oo.1.32[d] of the Cambridge University Library.

The first part of Oo.1.16 is written in a semi-cursive script and contains Acts to Ephesians. The second part is written in a very small cursive script and fits the whole Revelation on only five folios![e] Oo.1.32 is written in several different variations of cursive script (by two or more scribes) and contains nearly the whole New Testament (Matthew to Jude). Throughout the manuscripts there are various Hebrew notes by past readers. The notes are generally either neutral[f] or negative,[g] but there are also some positive[h] comments! It should also be noted that the scribes of the Cochin Hebrew New

---

[a] As recorded on the inside covers of mss. Oo.1.16 and Oo.1.32. Unfortunately, these two manuscripts have not received much attention over the past 200 years since they were brought to the U.K.

[b] As explained below, only Revelation, James and Jude show clear evidence of authenticity. The rest of the New Testament books contained in these two manuscripts were compiled/translated from at least three different sources.

[c] A sample image has been reproduced on page v. See HebrewGospels.com/revelation to view color photos of the applicable folios of Oo.1.16.

[d] See HebrewGospels.com/james to view color photos of the applicable folios of Oo.1.32.

[e] Written on both sides – ms. Oo.1.16, folios 102r - 106v.

[f] E.g. notes containing a summary of several verses, a reference to similar passages in the Tanach (Hebrew 'Old Testament'), or notes correcting mistakes (genuine or apparent).

[g] E.g. at Rev. 7:10, a reader commented, "קשה" (Difficult!).

[h] E.g. at Rev. 21, a reader commented, "זה פרק טוב מאד" "טוב" "טוב" (This chapter is very good! Good! Good!). Rev. 15:3 has the following note: "זה הרבה טוב שהקדים למשה" ('This is very good as it is zealous for Moses,' or possibly 'It is very good that he was zealous for Moses').

Testament manuscripts did not delete the instances where the original authors referred to Yeshua as the Messiah.[a]

Internal evidence indicates that not all the books in these two manuscripts derive from the same source. Most of the books in Oo.1.16 and Oo.1.32 do not contain the indications of authenticity expected in faithful copies of original Hebrew documents. Rather, many[b] of the books are similar to the Aramaic (Syriac) Peshitta,[c] and also contain Peshitta-based Aramaic or Aramaic-like words, not properly translated into Hebrew.[d]

---

[a] Although the word 'Messiah' is at times less frequent in the Cochin Hebrew New Testament manuscripts than 'Christ' in the Greek New Testament, there was no attempt to entirely obliterate the instances where the original authors referred to Yeshua as the Messiah (See e.g. Rev. 1:1; James 1:1; Jude 1:1). In contrast, the Shem Tov version of Matthew (as part of an anti-missionary book) omits every instance where **the writer** Matthew himself calls Yeshua the Messiah. In the Greek version of Matthew, the author refers to Yeshua as the Messiah in: Mat. 1:1,17,18, 11:2. The Shem Tov Matthew **never once** refers to Yeshua as the Messiah **from the author's own perspective**.

[b] Matthew to Ephesians fall into this group of translations from Aramaic (Syriac). Philippians to Philemon, as well as the epistles of Peter and John are from a different source text, but also lack evidence of authenticity. The Epistle to the Hebrews was copied from the translation of Friderico Alberto Christiano (published 1734). Only Revelation, James and Jude show clear evidence of authenticity (discussed below in Evidence of Authenticity section).

[c] For examples where Oo.1.32 (and Oo.1.16 where applicable) agrees with the Peshitta against other versions, see Mat. 18:22 (Peshitta: "seventy times seven seven"); Mat. 28:18 (Peshitta adds "as the Father sent me..."); Mark 3:6 (Peshitta: "house of Herod"); Mark 4:38 (Peshitta adds "they came"); Mark 15:38 (Peshitta: "the door of the temple"); Luke 1:11 (Peshitta adds "to Zechariah"); Luke 1:17 (Peshitta adds "prophet"); Luke 1:42 (Peshitta adds "to Mary"); John 3:2 (Peshitta: "you were sent"); Act. 2:30 (Peshitta: "I will cause to sit"); Act. 8:9 (Peshitta: "I, I am great"); Act. 8:25 (Peshitta: "word of God"); Rom. 5:7 (Peshitta: "die for the wicked"); 2 Cor. 6:2 (Peshitta uses "life" for 'salvation'); Gal. 1:1 (Peshitta: "the house of the dead"); Eph. 4:29 (Peshitta: "hateful word"); etc.

[d] Post-exilic Hebrew (e.g. in the biblical books Ezra & Nehemiah) does contain Aramized words, but see the following list of unusual Peshitta-based

In contrast, the Hebrew Revelation, James and Jude in these manuscripts contain many differences when compared to the Greek, Latin, and Aramaic versions. They also show the numerous linguistic evidences of authenticity expected in genuine copies of original Hebrew documents: gapping of explicit subjects and objects; Hebrew wordplays; inversed word order; Hebrew keywords linking sections together; and differences which indicate mistranslations in the Greek version.[a]

The Hebrew Revelation, James and Jude do not contain the many Peshitta-based Aramaisms found in most of the other books of Oo.1.32 and Oo.1.16,[b] and they can in no way be seen as translations from the Greek, Latin or Aramaic versions.

A second manuscript copy of the Hebrew Revelation, James and Jude is preserved in ms. Gaster Hebrew 1616 from the Manchester University Library.[c] It was copied directly from Oo.1.32 and Oo.1.16,

---

Aramaisms in Oo.1.32 (and Oo.1.16 where applicable) which suggest an Aramaic sub-text and incomplete translation: "משיחא" for "המשיח" (Mat. 1:1,16); "להון" for "להם" (Mat. 2:8); "מריה" for "יהוה" or "אדני" etc. (Mat. 2:13); "טובתהון" for "אשריהם" (Mat. 5:3); "מרי מרי" for "אדני אדני" (Mat. 7:21); "ליה" for "לו" (Mark 1:13); "לן" for "לנו" (Mark 1:24); "מלאכה" for "המלאך" (Luke 1:11); "בפרצופו" for "לפני" (Luke 2:31); "ליה" for "לו" (John 2:3); "מעמד" for "מטביל" (John 3:22,23); "הטביל" for "העמיד" and "תעמדו" for "תטבלו" (Act. 1:5); "קודסא" for "הקודש" (Act. 1:5, 1:8); "כהנא" for "הכהנים" (Act. 9:2); "ידעינן" for "אנחנו יודעים" (1 Cor. 8:4); "אכסנא" for "נכרים" (Eph. 2:12); "מרן" for "אדונינו" (Eph. 6:21,23), etc.

[a] Examples will be explained for each individual book in the Evidence of Authenticity sections. See pp. 21, 243, 304.

[b] Post-exilic Hebrew did use some Aramized words. Unlike the Peshitta-based books contained in these manuscripts, the few Aramaic words that do occur in this Hebrew Revelation, James and Jude, do not correspond to the forms used in the Peshitta. For example, Rev. 8:1 uses the Biblical Aramaic expression "כשעה חדא" which indicates 'a moment' rather than 'an hour.'

[c] To view color photos of the applicable folios of Gaster 1616, see HebrewGospels.com/revelation (or /james or /jude).

and thus contains virtually the same text as the older two manuscripts.

About the Transcripts

The Hebrew transcript of Revelation is based on the Cambridge University Library manuscript Oo.1.16, folios 102r – 106v,[a] while James and Jude are based on ms. Oo.1.32, folios 158a – 160b.[b] We have carefully transcribed the Hebrew text using digital color photographs of the actual manuscripts. The current transcripts have been thoroughly checked and revised.

The applicable manuscript folio numbers were referenced throughout the transcripts, e.g. (102r) or (158a). Note that all folio numbers ending in "r" or "v" are from Oo.1.16, while those ending in "a" or "b" are from Oo.1.32.

The following standardizations and corrections were made in the Hebrew transcripts:

- Vowel points were added to every word in the Hebrew text to accommodate easier reading. The few vowel points that do occur in the Hebrew manuscripts were not copied into the transcripts. (The vowel points used in the manuscripts were mostly added to help with the pronunciation of Greek proper nouns.[c] Also, they are based on the Ashkenazi pronunciation and could easily confuse the modern reader.) Rather, all vowel points in the transcripts were

---

[a] To view color photos of the applicable folios of Oo.1.16, refer to HebrewGospels.com/revelation.
[b] To view color photos of the applicable folios of Oo.1.32, refer to HebrewGospels.com/james.
[c] E.g. Rev. 9:10[11], "his name in the Hebrew tongue is Avadon, and in the Greek tongue, Apollyon (אַפְּלְלִיאָן)."

determined by context; vowel letters in the Hebrew manuscripts; and traditional pronunciation.[a]

- As far as possible, the vowel points in the transcripts follow the vowel letters which are present in the Hebrew manuscripts. This includes 'pausal'-like pronunciations in various places throughout the text, and using vowel points which match the full spellings (rather than deleting vowel letters or leaving them obsolete).[b]

- The accentuation of verses was not considered with regards to the use of Dagesh or 'pausal' forms. Thus, a 'Begadkephat' (בגדכפת) letter will always have a dagesh at the beginning of a word, and 'pausal' pronunciations (with special vowel points) are only used when explicitly indicated by vowel letters. However, quotes from the Tanach (Hebrew 'Old Testament') are pointed according to the Masoretic Text, (unless vowel letters in the Hebrew manuscripts indicate otherwise).

- All abbreviations in the Hebrew manuscripts were spelled out for easier reading. If the exact meaning of an abbreviation is ambiguous, there will be a footnote stating the Hebrew abbreviation.

---

[a] Except for the Creator's name which was provided with its true vowels and not with traditional replacement vowels. (See HebrewGospels.com/yhwh for more information.) The main source used to determine the traditional pronunciation of Hebrew words is the Masoretic Text. However, other traditional Jewish Hebrew sources were also consulted, e.g. the Mishnah, vowel-pointed Hebrew fragments of Ben Sira, and the Hebrew Midrashim.
[b] For example, "לרעיך" is pointed "לְרֵעֶיךָ" and not "לְרֵעֶיךְ"; "המקודשים" is pointed "הַמְקוּדָשִׁים" and not "הַמְקוּדְשִׁים"; "חופשים" is pointed "חוֹפְשִׁים" and not "חָפְשִׁים"; "בכתונות" is pointed "בְּכֻתֳּנוֹת" and not "בְּכֻתֳּנוֹת".

- Introductory scribal headings were replaced with book names, and concluding statements were omitted from the transcripts.

- Certain word(s) or letters were placed in [square brackets] to show that they have been corrected based on the context.

- Empty square brackets [   ] were used where a word or phrase in the manuscript has been crossed out or marked as a mistake by the scribe/proofreader.

- The abbreviation "הֹ" was replaced with the full name "יהוה".[a]

- The short Rabbinic spelling "ישו"[b] was replaced with the full spelling "ישוע".[c]

---

[a] See pp. 62-69 for more information.

[b] The spelling "ישו" (Yeshu) was commonly used by many Jews in the Middle Ages instead of the fully spelled out "ישוע" (Yeshua) – similar to "ה" or "השם" instead of "יהוה". The spelling "ישו" has a negative connotation and was generally used by non-messianic Jews. However, one **cannot** conclude that all Jews who used this spelling were non-Messianic Jews. E.g. next to Heb. 7:3 (Oo.1.32), a reader commented " מלכי צדק בלא אב ואם לא נברא ולא מת עדין הוא ישו" (Malki Tsedeq (Melchizedek) – without father or mother, he was not created and does not die – he is still Yeshu!) Also, there is no indication that any anti-messianic alterations were made in this Hebrew Revelation. The fact that Yeshua is the Messiah was not at all undermined by the scribe. (See Rev. 1:1,2,5,9, etc.)

[c] Note that the spelling "ישוע" has been used since the time of Ezra – long before the birth of Yeshua the Messiah! (See e.g. Ezra 2:2,6,36, etc. and especially Neh. 8:17 where Joshua the son of Nun is even called "ישוע" (Yeshua), using the shorter spelling.) Thus the pronunciation 'Yeshua' was not invented by anti-messianic Jews as some have claimed.

- In Revelation, the spellings "יאהנניס" and "אפרטס" were replaced with their proper spellings "יוחנן" and "פרת".

- In Jude, the spellings "יקבוס" and "יודס" were replaced with their proper spellings "יעקב" and "יהודה".

- All other names were transcribed as written in the Hebrew manuscripts (except for vowel points, as explained above).

The grammar, syntax, and vocabulary of the Hebrew Revelation, James and Jude are not exactly the same as either Classical or Mishnaic Hebrew. Although similar to Mishnaic Hebrew, it also overlaps with Classical Hebrew.

In order for Hebrew readers to become familiarized with the grammar and syntax used in these Hebrew New Testament manuscripts, we recommend reading the transcript alongside the English translation.

The correct meaning of most of the Hebrew vocabulary used in the Hebrew Revelation, James and Jude can be found amongst the following lexicons:

- Earnest Klein, *A Comprehensive Etymological Dictionary of the Hebrew Language for Readers of English.*[a]

- Marcus Jastro, *A Dictionary of the Targumim, the Talmud Babli and Yerushalmi, and the Midrashic Literature*, volume 1 + 2 (A Hebrew + Aramaic to English dictionary).[b]

- David J. A. Clines, *The Concise Dictionary of Classical Hebrew.*[c]

---

[a] Carta Israel Map and Publishing Company Ltd., 1987.
[b] Luzac and Co., 1903.
[c] Phoenix Press, 2009.

- William L. Holladay, *A Concise Hebrew and Aramaic Lexicon of the Old Testament*.[a]

Ben Yehuda's dictionary series[b] would also be useful for those who are very experienced in Hebrew – as explanations are given in Hebrew (only very basic meanings are given in English).

About the Translations

As with the transcripts, the manuscript used for this translation of Revelation is from the Cambridge University Library, ms. Oo.1.16, folios 102r – 106v, while James and Jude are based on ms. Oo.1.32, folios 158a – 160b. We have accurately and literally translated the Hebrew text, using digital color photographs of the actual manuscripts. Photos of the applicable folios are available via our website.[c] The translation is focused on accuracy rather than flowing English, as it is very easy to create contradictions with a paraphrase-type translation. In the current translation:

- Certain word(s) were placed in [square brackets] to show that they have been corrected based on the context.

- The spellings of all names and titles were standardized.

- Only Names and Titles were capitalized. Personal pronouns ('you,' 'he,' etc.) are not capitalized (even when referring to Yahweh or Yeshua) as this is sometimes based merely on the translator's interpretation. The reader should rather use the context to determine whom the pronoun is referring to.

---

[a] Eerdmans, 1971 (15th impression, 2000).
[b] Eliezer Ben Yehudah, *Complete Dictionary of Ancient and Modern Hebrew* (17 volumes), Hozaa-La'Or Le Zecher Eliezer Ben-Yehuda, 1908-1958. (Reprinted by T. Yoseloff in 8 volumes, 1960).
[c] See HebrewGospels.com/revelation and HebrewGospels.com/james.

- *Italic words* were added to help the English reader understand what the Hebrew text implies by context.

- Certain words were marked in **bold** according to emphasis in the Hebrew text – based on special word order etc. – and are not our own emphasis or interpretation.

- Chapter and verse numbering in the manuscripts are generally the same as in standard English translations. When chapter and/or verse numbers differ, the standard English equivalent is added in [square brackets].

- Introductory scribal headings were replaced with book names, and concluding statements were omitted from the translations.

10

The Hebrew Revelation

ספר אלה הסודות

Based on Ms. Oo.1.16 from the Cambridge University Library. Also supported by Ms. Gaster 1616 from the Manchester University Library.

Version 2.2 © April 2024

Introduction

Every author of the New Testament was either a Jew or a proselyte of the Jews.[a] So, is it really possible that the entire New Testament was originally composed in Greek? Scholars used to teach[b] that Hebrew was a 'dead language' in New Testament times, but the Dead Sea Scrolls[c] together with the Mishnah[d] provide ample evidence that Hebrew was still a living[e] language around the first century C.E.!

---

[a] The only possible proselyte was Luke (the author of Acts and the Gospel of Luke), but there are also reasons to believe that he was a Jew.

[b] E.g. "...Hebrew was a dead language in the time of Christ, as already stated... The world little realizes the importance of the Greek influence in shaping the destiny of Christianity..." – Dr. Jacob Elon Conner, *Christ was not a Jew*, independently published, 1936, pp. 13, 43.
"...Hebrew had long been a dead language to the Jewish people in general... Biblical Hebrew was then as unintelligible to an ordinary Jew as German is at the present day to an Englishman who has never studied that language." – Professor Alexander Roberts, *A Short Proof that Greek was the Language of Christ*, Alexander Gardner Publishers, 1893, pp. 46-47.
"...one of the main traditional arguments... was that Jesus spoke Aramaic because there was nothing else for him to speak unless he spoke Greek." – James Barr (Professor of Semitic Languages), *Which Language did Jesus Speak? – Some Remarks of a Semitist*, University of Manchester, John Rylands Library, 1970, p. 21.

[c] "Indeed, it is generally believed that the Dead Sea Scrolls, specifically the Copper Scroll [50-100 C.E.] and also the Bar-Kokhba letters [< 135 C.E.], have furnished clear evidence of the popular character of MH [Mishnaic Hebrew]." – Miguel Pérez Fernández, *An Introductory Grammar of Rabbinic Hebrew*, Brill, 1997, pp. 2-3.

[d] "...what was the language of ordinary life of educated native Jews in Jerusalem and Judea in the period from 400 B.C.E. to 150 C.E.? The evidence presented by MH [Mishnaic Hebrew] and its literature leaves no doubt that that language was MH [Mishnaic Hebrew]." – M. H. Segal, *A Grammar of Mishnaic Hebrew*, Clarendon Press, 1980, p. 13.

[e] E.g. "Far from being an artificial scholastic jargon, MH [Mishnaic Hebrew, 400 B.C.E. – 150 C.E.] is essentially a popular and colloquial dialect... Its vocabulary and its grammar both bear the stamp of colloquial usage and popular

Not only was Hebrew a living language, but it was also the most commonly used[a] language in Judea at that time. Hebrew was more frequently used in writing than both Aramaic and Greek.[b] Even in Galilee[c] and the rest of the world, "Hebrew survived as a language

---

development." – M. H. Segal, *A Grammar of Mishnaic Hebrew*, Clarendon Press, 1980, p. 6. (Compare ibid. p. 13 for dates.)

"Since the discovery of the non-biblical Dead Sea Scrolls manuscripts, about eighty percent of which are written in Hebrew... [and] the Hebrew Bar-Kokhba letters... a reassessment of the language situation in the 1st century C.E. has taken place. It now appears that Hebrew was alive and well as both a written and spoken language... Hebrew served as the language of the Jewish community..." – David N. Bivin, *Hebraisms in the New Testament,* in *Encyclopedia of Hebrew Language and Linguistics*, Ed. Geoffrey Khan, Brill, 2013, vol. 2, p. 198.

[a] E.g. "...the events described in the New Testament took place when Hebrew was still strong and dominant..." – Chaim Rabin, *Hebrew and Aramaic in the first Century*, in *The Jewish People in the First Century*, Fortress Press, 1976, vol. 2, p. 1036.

"...the majority of the Dead Sea Scrolls were written in Hebrew... [*and*] include biblical texts, non-biblical literary works, and documents such as deeds and letters. ...These texts illustrate the vitality of the Hebrew language in ancient Judea." – www.deadseascrolls.org.il/learn-about-the-scrolls/languages-and-scripts (accessed 2023).

[b] "...Of course, those educated Judeans [400 B.C.E. – 150 C.E.] also understood Aramaic, and used it even in writing, but only occasionally, and not habitually... Thus, for a number of generations, the Judean Jews remained Hebrews in their language," – M. H. Segal, *A Grammar of Mishnaic Hebrew*, Clarendon Press, 1980, pp. 13-14.

"The Qumran Caves Scrolls ...dates range from the third century B.C.E... to the first century [C.E.]... While Hebrew is the most frequently used language in the Scrolls, about 15% were written in Aramaic and several in Greek." – www.deadseascrolls.org.il/learn-about-the-scrolls/introduction (accessed 2023).

[c] "Those who, like Jesus, took part in the discussions in the synagogues (Mark 1:21 [in Galilee]) and in the Temple in Jerusalem... no doubt did so in mishnaic Hebrew..." – Chaim Rabin, *Hebrew and Aramaic in the first Century,* in *The Jewish People in the First Century*, Fortress Press, 1976, vol. 2, p. 1036.

spoken and written... in most diaspora communities in synagogue worship and religious texts." [a]

Besides the fact that the Hebrew language was actively used in Israel in the first century C.E., many evidences also show that the average Jew in the land of Israel in the first century did not speak [b] Greek: Less than 8% of the Dead Sea Scrolls were written in Greek, roughly 15% in Aramaic, and about 75% in Hebrew. [c] The New

---

[a] "...until its 20th-century revitalization... Hebrew survived as a language spoken and written... in most diaspora communities in synagogue worship and religious texts." – J. F. Elwolde, *Hebrew, Biblical and Jewish*, in *Encyclopedia of Language and Linguistics*, ed. K. Brown, Elsevier, 2006, vol. 5, p. 260.
"R. Joseph's saying proves that MH [Mishnaic Hebrew] was known as a spoken language [along with Aramaic and other languages] in Babylon in the fourth century C.E." – M. H. Segal, *A Grammar of Mishnaic Hebrew*, Clarendon Press, 1980, p. 15 (footnote).

[b] Hundreds of years of Greek influence did result in some Greek loanwords being used in first century Hebrew, but the average Jew in Israel in the first century did not speak and understand the Greek language. Some Jews (e.g. Josephus) learned and studied Greek to be able to work for the Graco-Roman government of the day. Only a minority group called 'Hellenistic Jews' were native Greek speakers.

[c] Of all the Qumran manuscript compositions, about 80% are in Hebrew, while 15% of the manuscripts are in Aramaic, and only 2.9% in Greek. Although the percentage of Greek compositions vary greatly from site to site, the combined statistics of all the manuscripts discovered around the Judean desert (including Qumran) is that about 7.3% were written in Greek, roughly ten times less than Hebrew. (These percentages exclude the later medieval Arabic manuscripts). See e.g. Emanuel Tov, *Hebrew Bible, Greek Bible, and Qumran, Collected Essays*, Mohr Siebeck, 2008, p. 340; Daniel Machiela, *A Handbook of the Aramaic Scrolls from the Qumran Caves*, Brill, 2023, p. 1; Martin G. Abegg, *Hebrew Language*, in *Dictionary of New Testament Background*, Ed. Craig A. Evans and Stanley E. Porter, InterVarsity Press, 2000, p. 461 (col. 2).
"More than 75 percent of the scrolls were written in Hebrew. Most of the others were written in Aramaic, but a small number of them were written in Greek." – The NIV Bible website: www.thenivbible.com/blog/15-surprising-facts-about-the-dead-sea-scrolls/ (accessed 2023).
"About 80 to 85 percent of the Dead Sea Scrolls are written in one of three dialects of Hebrew... some scrolls are written in Aramaic and a few in Koine

Testament mentions a minority of 'Hellenistic' or 'Greek' Jews in Israel, clearly indicating that the rest of the nation did not speak Greek.[a] Even Josephus had to make a great effort to learn the Greek language, and although he mastered Greek grammar, he was so used to speaking his own language that he could not pronounce Greek very well.[b]

Furthermore, there is internal[c] evidence in the Greek text of a number of New Testament books that the original autograph was

---

Greek." – www.newworldencyclopedia.org/entry/Dead_Sea_Scrolls (accessed 2023).

[a] In Act. 6:1 we read that the 'Hellenistic Jews' complained against the 'Hebraic Jews.' This shows that the multitude of believers included only a small number of Greek speakers – these Hellenistic widows did not receive sufficient support, and wanted the multitude of Hebrew speaking Jews to help them! Act. 9:29 states that Paul argued with the 'Hellenistic Jews,' but they planned to kill Paul. Apart from proving that most of the Jews did not speak Greek, this also suggests that Paul's ability to argue in Greek was an unusual threat – why would they try to kill Paul now, if all the apostles could speak and reason with them in Greek all along?

[b] "I have also taken a great deal of pains to obtain the learning of the Greeks, and understand the elements of the Greek language, although I have so long accustomed myself to speak our own tongue, that I cannot pronounce Greek with sufficient exactness..." – Flavius Josephus and William Whiston, *The Works of Josephus: Complete and Unabridged*, Hendrickson, 1996, Antiquities, Book 20, section 263 [chapter 11:2].

[c] "Translations of Hebrew syntactic structures and literary phrases are found in the narrative framework of these [Greek synoptic] gospels; while direct speech exhibits wordplays and idioms that are typical of post-biblical, spoken Hebrew." – David N. Bivin, *Hebraisms in the New Testament,* in *Encyclopedia of Hebrew Language and Linguistics*, Ed. Geoffrey Khan, Brill, 2013, vol. 2, p. 201. (See ibid. pp. 198-201 for several good examples.)

One very clear example is the explanation of the name "Yeshua" (ישוע) with "He will save" (יושיע) in Mat. 1:21, which shows a word connection only in Hebrew, not in Aramaic, Greek or Latin. Even the first verse of the New Testament incorporates an obvious Hebrew idiom "the book of the generations" – an expression known from the Tanach (Gen. 5:1), but unattested in the vast collections of over 600 Greek works in the *Perseus Digital Library*. Other well-known Hebraisms in the New Testament include

written in Hebrew.[a] More specifically, scholars of the Greek text of
Revelation have long recognized and acknowledged that it
abounds with Hebrew influence.[b] Some of these indications are
even clearly visible in Greek-based English translations! Let's discuss
one example:

"by the hand of" instead of "by means of"; "hand" instead of "power/
authority"; the extremely frequent use of simple conjunctions ("and," "but,"
etc., often eliminated in English translations); "in the days of" (very frequent in
Hebrew O.T. and N.T., very rare in other Greek writings); "he answered and
said" instead of "he answered" (frequent in Hebrew O.T. and N.T. [often
eliminated by translations], very rare in other Greek writings); indications of
the superlative by Hebrew idioms like "king of kings," "lord of lords," etc.
In fact, many scholars mention Hebraisms or Semitisms in their commentaries
on the Greek N.T. to explain awkward and/or confusing Greek grammar,
including: A. T. Robertson (*Word Pictures in the New Testament*); I. H.
Marshall, C. A. Wanamaker (*The New International Greek Testament
Commentary Series*); R. G. Bratcher, B. M. Newman, E. A. Nida, J. Reiling, J. L.
Swellengrebel (*UBS Handbook Series*); H. B. Swete (*The Gospel according to St.
Mark*); J. Bond (*The Gospel According to St. Luke*); D. L. Bock (*Luke: Baker
Exegetical Commentary on the New Testament*), etc.
[a] Jean Carmignac – whose conclusion was based solely on the Greek version of
Mark and how it facilitated easy translation back into Hebrew – said, "I was
convinced that the Greek text of Mark could not have been redacted directly
in Greek, and that it was in reality only *the Greek translation of an original
Hebrew*..." (Emphasis added, quoted from *The Birth of the Synoptic Gospels*,
translated from French by Michael J. Wrenn.) Claude Tresmontant believed
that all four Gospels were originally written in Hebrew. Hugh J. Schonfield
suggested the Hebrew or Aramaic origin of Matthew, Mark, John and
Revelation in his introduction to his translation of the Du Tillet version of
Matthew.
[b] E.g. "The Greek of the Apocalypse is marked by a series of most striking
peculiarities which, as has long been recognized, are due in large part to the
influence of the Hebrew idiom." – L. Cowden Laughlin, *The Solecisms of the
Apocalypse*, C. S. Robinson and Co., 1902, p. 4.
Dr. Robert B. Y. Scott documented numerous indications of Hebrew influence
in the Greek Revelation, and concluded that Revelation was originally written
in Hebrew (*The Original Language of the Apocalypse*, 1928).

"And the twenty-four elders and the four living creatures fell down and worshiped God who was seated on the throne, saying, '**Amen. Hallelujah**!'" [a, b]

How did these two Hebrew words – 'Amen' and 'Hallelujah' – end up in the Greek Bible? Most Christians have grown so accustomed to these two Hebrew words as part of their Christian terminology, that they unintentionally assume that it is normal for anyone and everyone to know only these two Hebrew words.[c] They do not even realize that these two words were part of the native Hebrew language of the original Jewish authors of the New Testament!

Let's pause to ask the question: "If John used Hebrew words like 'Amen' and 'Hallelujah', why are we taught that the entire Book of Revelation was originally written in Greek?" Below are three typical, hypothetical excuses (see if you agree or not):

1. "Perhaps Revelation was given in Hebrew, but John mentally translated everything into Greek[d] 'on the fly' and only retained two Hebrew words, 'Amen' and 'Hallelujah.'"

---

[a] Rev. 19:4, ESV.

[b] All emphasis throughout introductory sections was added for clarity. However, in the transcript/translation section, emphasis in the English translation reflects emphasis in the Hebrew text.

[c] Except for a few Hebrew names, of course.

[d] E.g. "His book abounds in grammatical solecisms which are clearly Hebraic… It does not necessarily follow that Revelation was originally written in Hebrew… for some reason he wrote in Greek…" – Nigel Turner, *Grammatical Insights into the New Testament*, T. and T. Clark, 1965, pp. 159-160.
"It has long been recognized that the Apocalypse contains a multitude of grammatical… irregularities… 'while [John] writes in Greek, he thinks in Hebrew…' a judgment that has met with subsequent agreement, especially recently." – G.K. Beale, *The Book of Revelation: A Commentary on the Greek Text*, Eerdmans, 1999, p. 96.
"Revelation… the Semitisms reflect an author who thought in Hebrew and wrote in Greek…" – John R. Yeatts, *Revelation, Believers Church Bible Commentary*, Herald Press, 2003, p. 446.

2. "John could not speak Hebrew[a] and only knew these two Hebrew words (just like most Christians) – and thus Revelation was graciously given to him in Greek!"

3. "Perhaps John could actually speak Hebrew, but the heavenly beings who praised Yahweh[b] in Revelation 7:11-12 and 19:4 do not speak Hebrew. In fact, everything in heaven is spoken in Greek[c] while only two Hebrew words are used, 'Amen' and 'Hallelujah.'"

Doesn't this sound ridiculous? Well, this is the dilemma which many scholars of the Greek New Testament face. To advocate that Revelation was originally written in Greek, they would have to believe one of these (or similar) excuses.

---

[a] This view was especially popular before the discovery of the Dead Sea Scrolls, e.g. "...for centuries before the birth of Christ, their native Hebrew had been entirely supplanted... [The Biblical Hebrew] literary treasures... were... as much sealed up to the common people as if they had been written in the Latin or Egyptian languages... Greek was in reality the reigning language of Palestine in the time of our Saviour." – Professor Alexander Roberts, *Greek, the Language of Christ and His Apostles*, Longmans, Green and Co., 1888, pp. 435-436. "...Hebrew was not a living language any longer." – A. T. Robertson, *A Grammar of the Greek New Testament in the Light of Historical Research*, Broadman Press, 1934, p. 94.

[b] The Hebrew name of the Creator. See HebrewGospels.com/yhwh for more information.

[c] Dr. William Mounce writes: "Don't be shy! There is too much at stake in learning the heavenly language. Oh, didn't you know that Greek is the heavenly language? It's true. We will all speak Greek in heaven (1 Cor 13:1) [the language of angels]. So while everyone else is learning Greek, we get to speak with Jesus!" – William D. Mounce, *Basics of Biblical Greek Grammar*, 3rd ed., Zondervan, 2009, p. 110.

"George Horton, the famous U.S. Consul General... [and Greek scholar, said:] 'God speaks Greek in Heaven.' ...I am inclined to side with Horton. Why else would God choose to communicate His message of salvation in Greek?" – Prof. Ismini Lamb, *Why learn Greek? Is it spoken in Heaven?*, The National Herald, Feb. 2nd, 2023. Available online at www.thenationalherald.com/why-learn-greek-is-it-spoken-in-heaven (accessed 2023).

It would make much more sense to acknowledge that John spoke Hebrew; that Yahweh and Yeshua,[a] as well as the heavenly beings in heaven speak Hebrew;[b] that John wrote the original autograph of Revelation in Hebrew; and that a Greek translation was only made afterwards,[c] using the original Hebrew text.[d] If the inspired message of Revelation was given in Hebrew, why would John record only a second-hand Greek translation, allowing the original Hebrew prophecy to be lost forever?

In the sections to follow, we will discuss technical, linguistic proofs from this Hebrew manuscript which confirm the Hebrew origin of the Book of Revelation.

---

[a] The Hebrew name for 'Jesus.'

[b] Even the names of the heavenly messengers/angels (e.g. Michael and Gabriel) are Hebrew names, not Greek! See also Acts 26:14.

[c] One should keep in mind that there were Messianic Jews throughout the Mediterranean region and the Middle East who were able to read such an original Hebrew version, and translate that into Greek, Latin or Aramaic as needed by non-Jewish believers in the assembly/synagogue.
Take note that the gospel message initially spread from synagogue to synagogue, where Hebrew remained the common language used by the Jewish people: "...until its 20th-century revitalization... Hebrew survived as a language spoken and written... in most diaspora communities in synagogue worship and religious texts." – J. F. Elwolde, *Hebrew, Biblical and Jewish*, in *Encyclopedia of Language and Linguistics*, ed. K. Brown, Elsevier, 2006, vol. 5, p. 260. Various other secondary languages were also used in synagogues, in addition to Hebrew, which also resulted in translations of the Bible into other languages.

[d] This would aptly explain why Hebrew words are present in the Greek Revelation: it has a Hebrew subtext! E.g. "Charles unconsciously gives away his case when he says: 'the chief Hebraisms in the Apocalypse... are sufficient to prove that it is more Hebraic than the LXX itself.' There is only one thing that is more Hebraic than a translation from Hebrew, and that is a translation that is more literal [than the LXX]... We come to the conclusion, therefore, that the Apocalypse as a whole is a translation from Hebrew..." – Robert B. Y. Scott, *The Original Language of the Apocalypse*, The University of Toronto Press, 1928, p. 6.

Evidence of Authenticity and Interesting Readings

Compared to all other textual traditions of Revelation, the Hebrew Revelation from Cochin, India,[a] is the most important and authentic version known to us.[b] In this section we will discuss a few of the many interesting differences between the Hebrew and Greek traditions,[c] as well as linguistic indications of authenticity in this particular Hebrew version.

We will present abundant evidence that the Hebrew text of Revelation preceded the Greek text, and that the Greek text is a translation from the original Hebrew.

Hebrew title of the Book of Revelation

One doesn't need to search very far to find interesting differences in the Hebrew Revelation. In fact, the first interesting difference is in chapter one, verse one!

---

[a] See pp. 1-4 for more information about the applicable manuscripts.

[b] We have also investigated other Hebrew versions of Revelation: Sloane 237 from the British library; Neofiti 33 from the Vatican Library, Hébreu 131 from the National Library of France; Ms. 314 from the Freiburg University Library; none of which proved to be linguistically authentic.

[c] Other textual traditions like the Latin Vulgate and Syriac Peshitta will also be discussed where relevant.

> "These are the **confidential counsels** (*sodot*) *which* Yahweh[a] gave to Yeshua[b] Ha-Mashiach..."[c,d]

The very word from which the title 'Revelation' is usually obtained, is different in this Hebrew version! Rather than the expected 'revelation' which would be '*chazon*'[e] in Hebrew, we find '*sodot*' instead.

'*Sodot*' is the plural form of '*sod*' and does not mean "revelation," but rather "confidential counsels" or "secrets." Thus, the Hebrew title for the Book of Revelation should really be *Eleh Ha-Sodot*[f] meaning '*These are the Confidential Counsels.*' To some people this might sound like a meaningless variant, but interestingly, this Hebrew word '*sod*' is repeated in several passages throughout the book.

Authentic Hebrew documents often contain such repeated keywords, which can link together some seemingly unrelated verses

---

[a] The manuscript uses the Hebrew abbreviation 'הֹ' (*he*) for "*Ha-Shem*," which literally means 'The Name.' For further discussion on this abbreviation 'הֹ', see pp. 62-69. Our translations employ 'The Name' Yahweh in every instance indicated by the Hebrew manuscripts. The only grammatically possible pronunciation of יהוה, from which all other abbreviations/contractions of the Name can be formed, is "*Yah-weh*" – with emphasis on the second syllable. For more information, see HebrewGospels.com/yhwh.

[b] The Hebrew name for 'Jesus.'

[c] Or "The Messiah."

[d] Rev. 1:1, translated from Oo.1.16.

[e] "חזון" or "חזיון" (vision/revelation) are generally used in Hebrew translations, e.g. those by Franz Delitzsch and by Salkinson/Ginsburg. Other translations also use "התגלות", "התגליות" or "גלוי" (revealing/revelation) – see e.g. Hébreu 131 from the National Library of France.

[f] This title could also be shortened to '*Sodot*' (*Confidential Counsels*). Compare the Hebrew title for Deuteronomy, '*Eleh Ha-Devarim*,' shortened to '*Devarim.*' Hebrew titles for Bible books are often formed from a keyword or phrase in the first verse of the applicable book.

or passages. Let's consider an example from the Tanach (Old Testament):

> "'What do you see Yirmeyahu?'[a] Then I said, 'I see an **almond branch**.' Then Yahweh said to me, 'You have seen well, for I am **watching** over my word to do it.'"[b]

In most English translations it is very difficult to see any connection between this vision and its interpretation. What does an 'almond branch' have to do with 'watching'?

Well, in Hebrew this makes perfect sense, as a key root-word is repeated in the vision as well as in the interpretation! The Hebrew word for "almond" is '*shaqed*' and the Hebrew word for "watching" is '*shoqed*.' Both words are formed from the same root-word, as shown below:

Root-word:	שקד	*Shaqad*
Almond:	שָׁקֵד	*Shaqed*
Watching:	שֹׁקֵד	*Shoqed*

Sadly, such keyword connections in the original Hebrew are nearly always lost in translation, not only in English but even in Greek! The Greek Septuagint translators rendered the Hebrew words '*shaqed*' and '*shoqed*' as two Greek words which sound **very different**: '*karuinen*' and '*egregora*.'[c]

---

[a] The Hebrew name for 'Jeremiah.'

[b] Jer. 1:11-12, Translated from the Masoretic Text. In Hebrew:

"...מֶה־אַתָּה רֹאֶה יִרְמְיָהוּ וָאֹמַר מַקֵּל **שָׁקֵד** אֲנִי רֹאֶה: וַיֹּאמֶר יהוה אֵלַי הֵיטַבְתָּ
לִרְאוֹת כִּי־**שֹׁקֵד** אֲנִי עַל־דְּבָרִי לַעֲשֹׂתוֹ:"

[c] Jer. 1:11-12 in Septuagint Greek: "τί σὺ ὁρᾷς ιερεμια καὶ εἶπα βακτηρίαν **καρυίνην**. καὶ εἶπεν κύριος πρός με καλῶς ἑώρακας διότι **ἐγρήγορα** ἐγὼ ἐπὶ τοὺς λόγους μου τοῦ ποιῆσαι αὐτούς."

Because most languages do not use similar words for 'almonds' and 'watching,' **only** the original **Hebrew** version **fully preserves** this beautiful keyword link.[a]

Now, with this background, let's get back to Revelation and the Hebrew word '*sod.*' Not only does this word occur in chapter 1:1, but also in:

Revelation 1:20: "Now the **confidential counsel** (*sod*) of the seven stars"[b]

Revelation 10:7: "all these **confidential counsels** (*sodot*) of Yahweh will be completed"[c]

Revelation 17:5: "the **secret** (*sod*) of the great city Bavel"[d]

Revelation 17:7: "I want to tell you the **secret** (*sod*) of the woman"[e]

Thus, in the Hebrew version there is a clear theme throughout the book, starting in chapter one, verse one!

However, the Greek version of Revelation uses '*apokalupsis*'[f] (meaning 'uncovering' or 'revelation') in chapter 1:1, probably to interpret or explain to the reader that the secrets are now revealed. But just as we saw in the above example from Jeremiah, part of this

---

[a] Second-hand translations (i) can use "almond" and "watching" which do not have any similarities in sound or meaning in most languages, or (ii) could be overly literal and translate both words as "watching." Either way, half the original meaning is lost. In Hebrew, the words '*shaqed*' and '*shoqed*' perform **double** duty: they mean "almond" and "watching" **while at the same time** they have similar sounds **and** similar literal meanings.

[b] Rev. 1:20, translated from Oo.1.16.

[c] Rev. 10:7, translated from Oo.1.16.

[d] Rev. 17:5, translated from Oo.1.16.

[e] Rev. 17:7, translated from Oo.1.16.

[f] Greek: "Ἀποκάλυψις."

keyword-based theme is lost in the Greek translation. The Greek word '*apokalupsis*' only occurs once in the entire Greek Revelation – with zero repetition! Also, reconstructed Hebrew translations which follow the Greek reading, all use words related to 'reveal' or 'appear'[a] in this verse, unlike this Hebrew manuscript.

We can therefore conclude that the Hebrew reading of Oo.1.16 for Revelation 1:1 is linguistically authentic, and not a second-hand translation, because:

1. The Hebrew reading enables a keyword-based theme throughout the book, and

2. the Hebrew reading differs[b] from the Greek, Latin, and Aramaic versions by not using any form of 'reveal' or 'uncover' in chapter one, verse one.[c]

If the Hebrew Revelation of Oo.1.16 derived from any Greek-based version, the above difference should not have existed.

Hebrew keyword repetition

Another example of section linking is found in the letter to the assembly of Smyrna, in Revelation 2. Even in standard English

---

[a] "חזון" and "חזיון" (vision/revelation) are generally used in Hebrew translations, e.g. those by Franz Delitzsch and by Salkinson/Ginsburg. Other translations use e.g. "התגלות", "התגליות" or "גלוי" (revealing/revelation) – see e.g. Hébreu 131 from the National Library of France.

[b] Some other keyword-based themes can also be seen in the Greek and Greek-based translations, and such keyword themes which are visible in **all versions** cannot indicate authenticity for any particular version.

[c] The Hebrew manuscript does have the word "revealed" in an introductory scribal heading, but not in the actual text of Rev. 1:1, where it would be expected if it were a translation from any Greek-based version of Revelation.

translations we can see that some form of the word 'die' is repeated in the introduction, exhortation, and promise sections:

> Introduction: "The words of the first and the last, who **died** and came to life." [a]

> Exhortation: "Be faithful unto **death**" [b]

> Promise: "The one who conquers will not be hurt by the second **death**." [c]

Although the above theme with the keyword "die" is visible in any translation of Revelation, a **second** keyword is also repeated in this Hebrew version of Revelation, in the same letter:

> Acknowledgment: "I know your works and your **sufferings**" [d]

> Exhortation: "you will have **suffering** *for* ten days" [e]

> Promise: "Whosoever overcomes will not have **suffering** from the last[f] death." [g]

The Hebrew word repeated three times is "צער" (*tsa'ar*) or "צערות" (*tse'arot*) in the plural.

---

[a] Rev. 2:8, ESV.

[b] Rev. 2:10, ESV.

[c] Rev. 2:11, ESV.

[d] Rev. 2:8[9], translated from Oo.1.16.

[e] Rev. 2:9[10], translated from Oo.1.16.

[f] Or "latter" or "second."

[g] Rev. 2:10[11], translated from Oo.1.16.

Although the Greek and Latin versions use the same word for 'suffering/tribulation' twice,[a] the Hebrew version repeats the same word a third time in the concluding section, to tie the whole message together!

Following the Greek tradition, the Aramaic Peshitta[b] and Greek-to-Hebrew translations do repeat the word for 'suffering/tribulation' in verses 9 and 10, **but not** in verse 11.[c] Why can't any Greek-based Hebrew translations repeat the same word again in verse 11? Because the Greek subtext of these translations uses a very different word in verse 11 than earlier in verses 9 and 10, and thus all subsequent translations follow suit.

Thus, the repeated keyword in this Hebrew manuscript (in verses 9, 10 **and** 11) is one piece of clear evidence that it cannot be a translation from Greek, Latin or Aramaic. This suggests that the Oo.1.16 manuscript of Revelation derives from the original Hebrew version, as it preserves keyword themes which were lost in the Greek version and subsequent translations.

Hebrew wordplay

Hebrew wordplay, like Hebrew keyword themes, is also an important indication of the original language of the Book of

---

[a] See below, the Greek and Latin words used in Rev. 2:9-11 which correspond to the repeated Hebrew word *Tsa'ar.*
Greek: "θλῖψιν... θλῖψιν... ἀδικηθῇ"
Latin: "*tribulationem... tribulationem... lædetur*"
[b] References to, and quotations from the Peshitta are based on the SEDRA 3 database by George A. Kiraz, except where specified otherwise.
[c] Aramaic Peshitta: "ܐܘܠܨܢܟ... ܐܘܠܨܢܟ ܗܘ ... ܢܗܪ"
Dalman/Delitzsch: "צרתך ... בצרה... ינזק"
Salkinson/Ginsburg: "צרתך... צרה ... יפגע בו"
National Library of France, Hébreu 131: "צרתך... צרה ...ינזק"

Revelation. A good example of Hebrew wordplay is found in Revelation 3:

> "Thus says... he who has the **key** of Dawid,[a] who **opens** and no one is able to shut, who shuts and no one is able to **open** – 'I know your works. Look, I have given[b] before you an **open door** and no one is able to shut it...'"[c]

This Hebrew wordplay involves the words 'key,' 'open' and 'door.' Although one can see a logical or functional connection between these three words in any language, this Hebrew manuscript uses the same root-word in each of these words, which results in a beautiful wordplay with internal rhyme:

Root-word:	פתח	*Patach*
The key:	המפתח	*Ha-Maphteach*
Who opens:	הפותח	*Ha-Poteach*
To open:	לפתוח	*Liphtoach*
Open (adjective):	פתוח	*Patuach*
Door:	פתח	*Petach*

This internal rhyme between the words 'key,' 'open' and 'door' is not found in the Greek, Latin, or Aramaic versions of Revelation. So, in what language was Revelation originally dictated? This Hebrew wordplay in Revelation chapter 3 clearly indicates that it was **originally** spoken by Yeshua **in Hebrew**, as this wordplay is only possible in Hebrew! The table below shows that in Greek, Latin and

---

[a] Hebrew name for 'David.' For a discussion on the original pronunciation of the Hebrew letter Waw/Vav, see HebrewGospels.com/yhwh/video-15.
[b] Or "I have set."
[c] Rev. 3:7-8, translated from Oo.1.16.

Aramaic, three different root words are used for 'key,' 'open' and 'door.' Only the Hebrew uses the same root word for all three words.

English	Hebrew (Oo.1.16)	Greek MT	Latin Vulgate	Aramaic Peshitta[a]
the key	המפתח	τὴν κλεῖν	clavem	ܡܩܠܝܕܐ
who opens	הפותח	ὁ ἀνοίγων	qui aperit	ܕܦܬܚ
door	פתח	θύραν	ostium	ܬܪܥܐ

Furthermore, most translations from Greek, Latin and Aramaic back to Hebrew, did not fully reclaim this original Hebrew wordplay. The majority of these translations do not use the word '*petach*' for 'door,' but rather '*sha'ar*' or '*delet*.' As a result, only the words for 'open' and 'key' do rhyme in most Hebrew translations derived from Greek, whereas the word for 'door' does not form part of the rhyme.

Because this wordplay does not exist in the Greek, Latin or Aramaic versions of Revelation, one cannot escape the conclusion that the Book of Revelation was originally penned in Hebrew, not in Greek, Aramaic, or Latin.

Will the day-night cycle cease on the new earth?

Many people perceive the Book of Revelation as a difficult prophetic book, partly because it can be challenging to reconcile certain prophecies in the Old Testament with those given in Revelation. For example, Revelation 22:5 translated from Greek says:

---

[a] References to, and quotations from the Peshitta are based on the SEDRA 3 database by George A. Kiraz, except where specified otherwise.

"**Night** will **no longer exist**" [a]

And chapter 21:25 states:

"...its gates will never be shut **by day**, for there will be **no
night** there." [b]

Based on the above verses translated from the Greek version of
Revelation, many scholars [c] have concluded that the day-night cycle
will cease on the new earth, and that it will always be day, as "its
gates will never be shut **by day**, for there will be **no night** there." [d]

However, even the Greek Revelation mentions "**day and night**" in
chapter 20:10, which could only be possible if day and night
continued as before.

Yahweh himself also declared in Isaiah chapter 66, that the Sabbath
will be kept on the new earth:

"For as the **new heavens and the new earth** which I will
make, will remain before me, declares Yahweh, so will your
offspring and your name remain. And it will be, *that* on

---

[a] Rev. 22:5, Holman Christian Standard Bible. Some translations: "night will be
no more."

[b] Rev. 21:25, translated from Greek.

[c] E.g. "the cessation of night... ... ...in the new creation the cosmic division of
night and day will have ceased to function" – Simon J. Kistemaker, *Exposition
of the Book of Revelation, Baker New Testament Commentary*, Baker Book
House, 2001, pp. 579-583. See also Grant R. Osborne, *Revelation: Baker
Exegetical Commentary on the New Testament*, Baker Academic, 2002, p. 764;
G. K. Beale, *The book of Revelation: A Commentary on the Greek Text, New
International Greek Testament Commentary*, Eerdmans, 1999, p. 1096, etc.

[d] Rev. 21:25, translated from Greek.

every New Moon and on every **Sabbath**,[a] all flesh will come to bow down before me, says Yahweh."[b]

Without a day-night cycle, the counting of days and the subsequent observance of the Sabbath day is impossible.

In Jeremiah chapter 33, it is stated that the day-night cycle is just as permanent as Yahweh's covenant with David!

"Thus says Yahweh, 'If you can break my covenant with the **day**, and my covenant with the **night**, so that **daytime** and **night-time** will not be in their time; *then* my covenant will also be broken with **Dawid**[c] my servant, that he will have **no son** ruling as king upon his throne..."[d]

Yeshua Messiah is the ultimate fulfilment of this prophecy about the 'Son of David.' He will return again and rule forever on the throne of David. So, how can we, on the one hand, believe that the day-night cycle will cease, but on the other hand still think that the covenant with David regarding the Messiah will never be broken?

Based on the above-mentioned verses from Isaiah and Jeremiah, there is absolutely no way that the day-night cycle will cease. So, why does the Greek Revelation **only** mention **daytime** in chapter 21:25 as if there will be no night at all?

"...its gates will never be shut **by day**, for there will be **no night** there."[e]

---

[a] Or "from New Moon to New Moon, and from Sabbath to Sabbath." The Hebrew text uses both "from," and an idiom for "every" – it is difficult to express both of these in a single English translation. Could also possibly translate 'every month on the New Moon, and every week on the Sabbath.'

[b] Is. 66:22-23, translated from the Masoretic Text.

[c] Hebrew name for 'David.'

[d] Jer. 33:20-21, translated from the Masoretic Text.

[e] Rev. 21:25, translated from Greek.

Remarkably, the Hebrew version of Revelation quotes from the Old Testament both in chapter 21:25 and 22:5, and this clears up most of the confusion caused by these verses in the Greek version! Revelation 21:25 (mostly quoted from Isaiah 60:11):

Oo.1.16:

"ופתחו שעריך תמיד יומם ולילה לא יסגרו כי לא יהיה לילה"

= "And your gates will be open continually, **day and night** they will not be shut, for there will **not be night**."

In this Hebrew version of Revelation there is no hint that the day-night cycle will cease as it clearly mentions both "**day and night**."

But how is it possible that "**day and night**..." "there will **not be night**"? How can there be night, and at the same time, no night? This is only a seeming contradiction. In Hebrew, 'night' and 'darkness' are synonymous.[a] The very first mention of 'night' in the Bible (Genesis 1:5), is where Elohim calls 'the darkness' 'night'!

"Then Elohim called the light day, and the darkness he called **night**."[b]

Thus, the correct understanding of Revelation 21:25 is that during **day and night**, there will be no **darkness** in the New Jerusalem!

Conversely, in the Greek translation, the first occurrence of "night" in Revelation 21:25 is **omitted**, possibly to avoid the seeming contradiction of 'night' and 'no night' at the same time. Regrettably, this omission in the Greek version only increases the possibility for confusion, as it suggests that **only day** will exist but no night.

---

[a] For examples where "night" refers to darkness and not to a specific time of the day, see Ps. 139:11, Mic. 3:6, etc.

[b] Gen. 1:5, translated from the Masoretic Text.

Now, let's discuss Revelation 22:5. In the Hebrew Revelation this verse is mostly[a] quoted from Isaiah 60:19!

Revelation 22:5:

Oo.1.16:

"ולא יהיה עוד בה השמש לאור יומם ולנגה והירח לא יאיר לך והיה לך הֿ לאור עולם ואלהיך לתפארתך"

= "And in it the **sun** will no more be for light by day, neither for brightness will the **moon**[b] shine for you,[c] but Yahweh will be an eternal light for you, and your Elohim will be your[d] glory."

This verse again implies both daytime and night-time, as both the **sun** and the **moon** are mentioned! During daytime and night-time, the New Jerusalem won't need any light except that of Yahweh!

It is noteworthy that the Greek version attempts to simplify the Hebrew readings, and 'correct' the seeming contradictions of 'night' and 'no night' at the same time:

---

[a] A careful comparison will show that these quotes in the Hebrew Revelation occasionally differ slightly from the Masoretic Text (e.g. in this verse, "בה" vs. "בך"; "והירח" vs. "הירח"). This clearly shows that these phrases were **not** merely inserted into the Hebrew Revelation by a medieval scribe, just to conform it to the Tanach. If that were the case, then why would there be any differences from the Masoretic Text? For more examples, see Rev. 2:25-26[26-27] vs. Ps. 2:8-9; Rev. 18:21 vs. Jer. 51:64; Rev. 21:25 vs. Is 60:11; Rev. 22:2 vs. Ezek. 47:12.

[b] Could also be translated: "And in it the sun will no more be for light by day, and for brightness; neither will the moon shine for you..."

[c] Feminine singular throughout this verse, referring to the city.

[d] Lit. "as your glory" or "for your glory."

"**Night** will **no longer exist**, and people will not need lamplight or sunlight, because the Lord God will give them light. And they will reign forever and ever."[a]

This is typical of **translations**,[b] and indicates that the Hebrew reading is the original while the Greek reading is a **translation** which attempts to superficially 'fix' the problem.[c]

However, careful study shows that the more difficult[d] Hebrew reading is perfectly understandable. It matches the Old Testament

---

[a] Rev. 22:5, Holman Christian Standard Bible.

[b] "...it is usually true that the more difficult reading is probably the original one, because it was the tendency of scribes to make the text easier to read." – Eldon Jay Epp and Gordon D. Fee, *Studies in the Theory and Method of New Testament Textual Criticism,* Eerdmans, 1993 p. 14.
"When a text was particularly difficult, there was a tendency for ancient scribes and translators to simplify the text... some "difficult" readings were indeed replaced by scribes with simpler ones" – Emanuel Tov (partly quoting Barthelemy), *Textual Criticism of the Hebrew Bible*, 3rd ed., Fortress Press, 2012, p. 275.
It is important to clarify that the "more difficult reading" does not refer to a nonsensical reading nor to a clear mistake, but rather to an authentic reading which might be difficult to grasp right away. At first glance, the Hebrew reading of Rev. 21:25 is confusing and difficult. Only upon an in-depth investigation does one find that the difficult Hebrew reading is understandable and correct in light of the larger context of the Bible.

[c] "Scribes were inclined to modify anything that seemed to them difficult or faulty..." – Leon Vaganay, *An Introduction to New Testament Textual Criticism*, 2nd ed., Press Syndicate of the University of Cambridge, 1991, p. 81.

[d] It is well known in Textual Criticism of the Bible, that the superficially more difficult reading (the reading which is most likely to confuse scribes and/or translators in terms of grammar, context or logic), which subsequently does make sense after a careful investigation, is clearly the original reading – rather than the reading which at first looks simple and easy to understand, but after investigation proves to be incorrect. The same principle is also applied in situations of lawsuits and court investigations. A seeming contradiction which can be explained and verified preserves the truth of the matter; but a smooth and simple statement which can be proved wrong is either erroneous or corrupted.

prophecies about the permanence of the day-night cycle as well as the Hebrew meaning of 'night.'

How can the tree of life be on both sides of the river?

The "tree of life" in Revelation 22 is another controversial topic. Translated from Greek, Revelation 22:2 reads:

> "On **both sides** of the river was **the tree of life** bearing **twelve kinds of fruit**... The leaves of the tree are for healing the nations..." [a]

How can the "tree of life" be on both sides of the river at the same time? This question has intrigued many people. Without the essential knowledge of the Hebrew meaning of "tree," many erroneous interpretations have been proposed.

Some have suggested that the tree of life grows in the middle of the river with branches extending to both sides.[b] Others think that the tree of life has a split trunk extending across the river, so that the tree literally grows on both sides at the same time.[c] It has even been speculated that the tree of life is **not** on both sides of the river, but rather the river flows on both sides of the tree![d]

---

[a] Rev. 22:2, Holman Christian Standard Bible.

[b] "Durham suppose[d], *the tree* was in the midst of the river, and extending its branches to both banks" – Robert Jamieson, A. R. Fausset, and David Brown, *A Commentary, Critical and Explanatory on the Whole Bible*, The S. S. Scranton Company, 1871, vol. 2, p. 603.

[c] "...artists have represented a split-trunk tree, with one half on either side of the river of life, meeting up in the middle..." – J. Kluttz, *The Spirit World*, independently published, 2009, p. 55.

[d] "Mede suppose[d]... in the midst of the plain, which itself is in the midst of the river's branches, stood the tree" – Robert Jamieson, A. R. Fausset, and

Others say there will be three trees, one in the middle of the river, and one on either side.[a]

Further confusion is caused by the statement that this tree will bear **twelve** kinds of fruit! Biblically speaking, it is absolutely impossible for any tree to bear more than one kind of fruit. Consider the following passages in Genesis:

"Let the earth cause to sprout... fruit trees bearing fruit **according to their kind**..."[b]

"So the earth brought forth... trees bearing fruit with their seed inside them, **according to their kind**."[c]

The same pattern of "according to their kind" is repeated over and over throughout Genesis chapter 1. The New Testament also confirms that it is impossible for one tree to bear various kinds of fruit:

David Brown, *A Commentary, Critical and Explanatory on the Whole Bible*, The S.S. Scranton Company, 1871, vol. 2, p. 603.
"This would mean... ...in the middle of the city's street is a single tree of life, located between either side of the river, 'which at this point has diverged into two branches.'" G. K. Beale, *The book of Revelation: A Commentary on the Greek Text, New International Greek Testament Commentary*, Eerdmans, 1999, p. 1104 (partly quoting from: Beasley-Murray, *Revelation*, p. 331).
"Others say that the river of life is narrow and that it flows on both sides of the tree" – J. F. Walvoord and R. B. Zuk, *The Bible Knowledge Commentary: An Exposition of the Scriptures*, Victor Books, 1983, vol. 2, p. 987.
[a] "for there were **three trees**; one in the street, and one on each side of the river" – B. Blayney et al., *The Treasury of Scripture Knowledge*, Macdonald Publishing Company, 1982, p. 187 (New Testament section).
[b] Gen. 1:11, translated from the Masoretic Text.
[c] Gen. 1:12, translated from the Masoretic Text.

"By their deeds you will recognize them – for a man is **not** able to gather grapes from a bramble,[a] **neither** figs from thorn bushes."[b]

"Or is a tree of dates[c] able to give oil,[d] or a vine – figs? So[e] the fountain is not able to give salt and sweet waters."[f]

Is it really possible that after all, Yahweh is going to change his mind and create one tree which produces various kinds of fruit? One tree with a split trunk across the river? One tree with enough leaves to provide all the nations with medicine?

Remarkably, the Hebrew Bible again holds the key to understanding this passage! Did you know that in the above verses from Genesis 1:11 and 1:12, every occurrence of the English word "trees" (plural) is actually singular in the original Hebrew? The Hebrew word "עץ" ('ets) in the singular form is very often used to refer to **many** trees collectively. However, when this Hebrew word is used in the plural "עצים" ('etsim), it often refers to hewn down trees or wood, and not to growing trees! For example:

---

[a] Hebrew "סנה." According to some sources, a brambleberry or blackberry bush.

[b] Mat. 7:16, translated from Hebrew, ms. Vat. Ebr. 100.

[c] Or "a date palm." The word for "dates" in the Hebrew ms. is crossed out and replaced with "figs" (in the same/similar script as original scribe).

[d] Most seeds contain a low percentage of oil, which is hard to extract. However, olive oil is easily extracted from the flesh of the fruit, which contains a large percentage of oil. Is. 41:19 and Neh. 8:15 also refer to olive trees as "עץ שמן" ('ets shemen) – "tree of oil," with the same Hebrew word used here for 'oil.' Thus, it is evident that James is speaking of olive oil specifically. The Greek translation even replaced the term 'oil' with 'olives' to avoid confusion.

[e] Or "Thus" or "Even so."

[f] Jas. 3:12, translated from C.U.L. Oo.1.32.

Genesis 22:7: [a]

"הִנֵּ֤ה הָאֵשׁ֙ וְהָ֣עֵצִ֔ים וְאַיֵּ֥ה הַשֶּׂ֖ה לְעֹלָֽה:"

> = "Here is the fire and the **wood**, but where is the lamb for a burnt offering?"

Thus, in Hebrew one does not generally [b] refer to living/growing trees by using the plural noun "עצים", but rather by using the singular noun "עץ" collectively. Therefore, the **singular** form "tree" in Revelation 22:2 does not even hint at one single tree, but rather refers to **many** trees as implied by the immediate context – they grow on **both sides** of the river!

Also, the Hebrew Revelation confirms that the "tree of life" refers to various kinds of fruit trees, not to one kind bearing twelve different kinds of fruit!

Revelation 22:2:

<u>Oo.1.16:</u>

"באמצע הרחובות ועל הנחל יעלה על שפתו מזה ומזה כל
עץ מאכל ועץ החיים ועליו היה שניים עשר מיני פירות
והיה פריו למאכל ועלהו לתרופה"

> = "In the midst [c] of the plains, [d] even [e] beside the stream, there grew up on its bank – on this side and on that side –

---

every tree of food,[a] even[b] the **tree of life**. And on it were twelve kinds of fruit, and its fruit was for food, and its foliage for healing."[c]

Take note that "every tree of food" is collectively referred to as "the tree of life."[d] Thus, "tree" in this context means "trees" (plural). Also, the above verse in the Hebrew Revelation is mostly quoted from Ezekiel 47:12!

Ezekiel 47:12 confirms that fresh fruit will be produced **every month** (12 times), and Ezekiel 47:7 establishes the fact that there will be **many** trees, not just one!

"...on the banks of the stream were **exceedingly many trees**, on this side and on that side."[e]

Thus there is no reason for creative speculation about the tree of life. The Hebrew Old Testament and the Hebrew Revelation are in perfect agreement. There will be **many** trees growing on both sides

---

[a] An idiom meaning "all kinds of fruit trees."

[b] Or "that is."

[c] For easier understanding in English, the Hebrew collective use can be translated as plural (most English translations do that with Ezek. 47:12). "And among the plains, even beside the stream, there grew up on both sides of its banks, all kinds of fruit trees, namely, the trees of life. And on them were twelve kinds of fruit, and their fruit was for food, and their foliage for healing."

[d] Such parallel constructions (where the definition/description is given first, then followed by a term/title) is also found in the Tanach, e.g. 1 Sam. 17:40 "in the vessel of shepherds which he had, even in the Yalqut" ('Yalqut' is the term used for a 'shepherd's vessel/pouch'); Is. 45:11 "concerning my sons, even concerning the work of my hands" (the 'work of my hands' is a term for 'my sons'); Is. 55:5 "because of Yahweh your Elohim, even because of the Qadosh of Yisrael" ('Qadosh of Yisrael' is a title for 'Yahweh your Elohim'); Dan. 8:10 "some of the host of the heavens, even some of the stars" ('stars' is a term for the 'host of heaven').

[e] Ezek. 47:7, translated from the Masoretic Text.

of the river, all kinds of fruit trees, not just one tree or one kind of tree.

Is Yeshua the 'Alpha and Omega'?

It is common knowledge that Alpha and Omega are the first and last letters of the **Greek** alphabet. Having already discussed some logical and linguistic evidence for the **Hebrew** origin of Revelation, it is rather obvious that this Greek expression 'Alpha and Omega' is not the original expression used in Revelation, but just the Greek translation thereof.

The question thus arises – what is the original Hebrew phrase which was translated into Greek as 'Alpha' and 'Omega'? Most people think it should be 'Aleph' and 'Taw,' the first and last letters of the Hebrew alphabet. But note that the expression "אלף ותו" (Aleph and Taw) or similar, never occurs in the Hebrew Old Testament – not even once!

There is a common misunderstanding that the expression 'Aleph and Taw' is the same as the Hebrew object marker "את" (*et*), which is spelled with an Aleph and a Taw, but compare the difference below:

"את" = marker of object in a sentence.[a]

"אלף ותו" = "Aleph and Taw" or 'first and last.'

In Hebrew, the word "את" (*et*) is never used with the same meaning as the expression 'Aleph and Taw.' The phrase 'Aleph and Taw' indicates 'first and last,' while the object marker '*et*' merely indicates the object(s) in a sentence, or occasionally it places

---

[a] There are several other Hebrew words also spelled "את" but none of these mean "first and last."

emphasis on a certain word. Below are some examples – the position of the Hebrew word *'et'* will be indicated by "(object:)" in each translated phrase:

Genesis 1:1:[a]

"בְּרֵאשִׁית בָּרָא אֱלֹהִים אֵת הַשָּׁמַיִם וְאֵת הָאָרֶץ:"

= "In *the* beginning Elohim created (object:) the heavens and (object:) the earth."

Exodus 2:1:[b] "וַיֵּלֶךְ אִישׁ מִבֵּית לֵוִי וַיִּקַּח אֶת־בַּת־לֵוִי:"

= "Then a man from the house of Lewi went and took (object:) the daughter of Lewi."

Often this object marker "את" (*et*) is essential to avoid confusion between the subject and object of a verb. In Hebrew, when a finite verb is directly followed by a name, the named person is the subject (performing the action); but if the word *'et'* is inserted between the verb and the following name, the named person is the object of the verb (the one to whom the action is done).[c] Compare the following two phrases for an example:

Genesis 5:32:[d] "וַיּוֹלֶד נֹחַ" = "then Noach begot"

Genesis 5:25:[e] "וַיּוֹלֶד אֶת־לָמֶךְ:" = "then he begot (object:) Lamech"

---

[a] Quoted from the Masoretic Text.
[b] Quoted from the Masoretic Text.
[c] This is a general rule with thousands of examples of verb > name (subject), and hundreds of examples of verb > et > name (object), throughout the Tanach. However, the object marker 'et' may occasionally be omitted, especially in poetry.
[d] Quoted from the Masoretic Text.
[e] Quoted from the Masoretic Text.

The difference between the above translations is indicated (and required) by the presence or absence of the marker "אֵת" (*et*). Below is another clear example:

Joshua 7:24:[a] "וַיִּקַּח יְהוֹשֻׁעַ" = "then Yehoshua took"

Numbers 27:22:[b] "וַיִּקַּח אֶת־יְהוֹשֻׁעַ" = "then he took (object:) Yehoshua"

The grammatical use and function of the object marker '*et*' can be seen when comparing the two Hebrew phrases above. Unlike English, the Hebrew word order is the same in both phrases. The only way to know whether Yehoshua is the subject or object of the verb is by the presence or absence of the object marker '*et*.' Thus it is clear from the above examples that '*et*' does not at all mean 'first and last,' but only marks the object. In fact, there is no single example of "אֵת" in the entire Old Testament with the meaning 'first and last.'[c]

Seeing that the expression 'Aleph and Taw' does not occur in the Old Testament at all, and the various Hebrew words spelled "אֵת" never mean 'first and last' – does it make sense that the original Hebrew Revelation would have used the expression 'Aleph and Taw'? Or could it be that the expression 'Alpha and Omega' in the Greek Revelation is just a fancy translation of a different original Hebrew phrase?

---

[a] Quoted from the Masoretic Text.

[b] Quoted from the Masoretic Text.

[c] Those who insist that – despite its grammatical function – the Hebrew word "אֵת" has a 'divine' or 'hidden' meaning because it is spelled with an Aleph and a Taw, should also consider the other Hebrew words spelled "אֵת". E.g. "אֵת" (*at*) which means "you" (feminine singular). Is every mention of "אֵת" – "you" divine? Does each occurrence of this spelling really mean "first and last"? See e.g. Gen. 12:11, 12:13, 24:23, 24:47, 24:60, 39:9; Num. 5:20; Judg. 9:10, 9:12, 11:35, 13:3; 1 Kin. 2:15, etc.

Let's compare the Hebrew and Greek versions of Revelation – there are four verses in the Greek Majority Text which use 'Alpha and Omega:'

Revelation 1:8:

Byzantine Greek:[a] "ἐγώ εἰμι τὸ ἄλφα καὶ τὸ ὦ"

= "I am the Alpha and the O(mega)"

Oo.1.16:[b] "אני הוא הראשון והאחרון"

= "I am the **first** and the **last**"

The Hebrew Revelation uses 'first and last' instead of 'Alpha and Omega'! This is very unique, as reconstructed Hebrew **translations** from Greek, Latin or Aramaic use either 'Aleph and Taw' or 'Alpha and Omega.'[c] This unique difference suggests that the Hebrew Revelation is not merely a second-hand translation from Greek. Below are the three other applicable verses:

---

[a] Note that some mss. (e.g. Codex Sinaiticus, 424, 1854) add "αρχη και τελος" (beginning and end), which is also found in the Hebrew Revelation in this verse.

[b] The Hebrew Revelation continues with "תחילת והסוף" (beginning and the end), as also found in some Greek mss. (e.g. Codex Sinaiticus, 424, 1854).

[c] Dalman/Delitzsch: "הָאָלֶף וְהַתָּו"

Salkinson/Ginsburg: "אָלֶף וְתָו"

British Library, Sloane 237: "הָאָלֶף וְהַתָּו"

National Library of France, Hébreu 131: "אַלְפָא וְאוֹמֶגָה"

Vatican Library, Neofiti 33: "אָלְפָא אוֹמֵיגָא"

Freiburg University Library, Ms. 314 omits every occurrence of 'Alpha and Omega,' and only translates the phrase 'first and last / beginning and end' when already present in the Greek.

Revelation 1:11:

<u>Byzantine Mᴬ Greek</u>:[a] "ἐγώ εἰμι τὸ α καὶ τὸ ω"

= "I am the A(lpha) and the O(mega)"

<u>Oo.1.16</u>: "אני הראשון והאחרון"

= "I am the **first** and the **last**"

Revelation 21:6:

<u>Byzantine Greek</u>:[b] "ἐγώ ἄλφα καὶ τὸ ὦ, ἡ ἀρχὴ καὶ τὸ τέλος."

= "I am the Alpha and the O(mega), the beginning and the end"

<u>Oo.1.16</u>: "אני הראשון והאחרון תחילת והסוף"

= "I am the **first** and the **last**, *the* beginning and the end"

Revelation 22:13:

<u>Byzantine Greek</u>: "ἐγώ τὸ ἄλφα καὶ τὸ ὦ, ὁ πρῶτος καὶ ὁ ἔσχατος, ἡ ἀρχὴ καὶ τὸ τέλος."

= "I am the Alpha and the O(mega), the first and the last, the beginning and the end."

<u>Oo.1.16</u>: "אני הראשון והאחרון תחילת והסוף"

= "I am the **first** and the **last**, *the* beginning and the end."

---

[a] This reading comes from a subdivision of Byzantine Greek manuscripts of Revelation, designated as Mᴬ in NA28. It is also found in the Textus Receptus. Many other Greek mss. omit this phrase entirely.

[b] Some Byzantine mss. omit "εγω," other Greek mss. read "εγω ειμι."

It is fascinating that the Hebrew Revelation does not use 'Aleph and Taw' nor 'Alpha and Omega' even once. Instead, it uses the phrase 'first and last,' which is also found in the Old Testament!

Isaiah 44:6:[a]

"כֹּה־אָמַר יהוה מֶלֶךְ־יִשְׂרָאֵל וְגֹאֲלוֹ יהוה צְבָאוֹת אֲנִי רִאשׁוֹן
וַאֲנִי אַחֲרוֹן וּמִבַּלְעָדַי אֵין אֱלֹהִים:"

= "Thus says **Yahweh** the king of Yisrael, and his Redeemer **Yahweh** Tseva'ot, **I am *the* first, and I am *the* last,** and except for me there is no Elohim."

It is very important to note that in Revelation 22:13, **Yeshua himself** said, "I am the **first** and the **last**." When compared with the above verse from Isaiah 44 it is clear that Yeshua claimed that he himself is Yahweh[b] (and not the Greek 'Alpha and Omega')!

---

[a] Quoted from the Masoretic Text.

[b] Apart from the Father being called Yahweh, the mediator between the Father and man is often called Yahweh in the Tanach. For example, Ex. 33:11 first says that "Yahweh spoke to Mosheh face to face," and then later in the same chapter (33:20), Yahweh said, "You cannot see my face, for no man will see me and live." What is the solution to this seeming contradiction, that no one can see Yahweh and live, yet Yahweh speaks to Moses face to face just like a man speaks with his friend? It is very clear that whenever Yahweh/Elohim appeared face to face, throughout the entire history of the world, it was not the Father; but rather the Son (Yeshua), who can be seen, who is the mediator between Yahweh the Father and man, and who is also called Yahweh and Elohim. Yahweh (the Son) appeared to Adam and Eve, walking with them in the garden, he appeared to Abraham, Isaac and Jacob, to Moses, Aaron, Nadab and Abihu together with 70 elders of Israel on Mount Sinai. Yeshua also said in John 8:58, "Before Abraham existed, I am!" – Clearly claiming that he was there at the time of Abraham! See footnote on p. 302 for a related discussion.

Isaiah 48:12-13:[a]

"...אֲנִי־הוּא אֲנִי רִאשׁוֹן אַף אֲנִי אַחֲרוֹן: אַף־יָדִי יָסְדָה אֶרֶץ
וִימִינִי טִפְּחָה שָׁמָיִם"

= "...I am he: **I am** *the* **first, also I am** *the* **last**, also my hand founded the earth, and my right hand spread out *the* heavens."

By claiming to be the **first** and the **last**, Yeshua claimed that he is Yahweh, and the Creator[b] of heaven and earth!

As shown above, the Hebrew Revelation clearly matches the Old Testament phrase 'first and last,' and neither uses the Greek 'Alpha and Omega' nor the non-Biblical Hebrew expression 'Aleph and Taw'!

Inversed word order

Inversed word order is one of the frequent differences between the original Hebrew and the second-hand Greek Septuagint translation of the Old Testament.

Possibly for stylistic reasons,[c] or otherwise simply because of carelessness, the Greek translators of the Septuagint often reversed the order of two words or phrases when they translated from the original Hebrew text.

This phenomenon should not be confused with differences in syntactical order, which is required by Greek vs. Hebrew grammar.

---

[a] Quoted from the Masoretic Text.

[b] See e.g. John chapter 1 in the HebrewGospels.com version. See also Col. 1:16.

[c] The changes in word order discussed below could also be for reasons of harmonization or cultural preference, but there is no grammatical requirement for these changes.

For example, the Greek word *'gar'* (meaning 'for,' etc.) usually stands in the 'second position' (as the second word in a clause), but the Hebrew equivalent *'ki'* is normally in the 'first position' (similar to English). When scholars revert a Greek translation back to Hebrew, they can easily move the Hebrew equivalent *'ki'* to the correct position in the clause, as this difference is simply required by Hebrew grammar as opposed to Greek grammar.

Below is an example where the Septuagint Greek translation has two words in the opposite order than the Hebrew Masoretic Text, without any grammatical requirement:

Genesis 30:43:

<u>Hebrew Masoretic Text</u>: "שְׁפָחוֹת וַעֲבָדִים וּגְמַלִּים וַחֲמֹרִים:"

= "**female** servants and **male** servants and camels and asses"

<u>Greek Septuagint</u>: "παῖδες καὶ παιδίσκαι καὶ κάμηλοι καὶ ὄνοι"

= "**male** servants and **female** servants and camels and asses"

The order of the words is clearly different in the Greek translation, compared to the original Hebrew. There is no grammatical reason for the change, rather, the Septuagint translators placed "male servants" first for stylistic reasons.

Now let us look at an example where two **phrases** are in the opposite order:

Ezekiel 5:12:

<u>Hebrew Masoretic Text</u>:

"בַּחֶרֶב יִפְּלוּ סְבִיבוֹתָיִךְ ... לְכָל־רוּחַ אֱזָרֶה"

= "**will fall round about you by the sword**... I will scatter to every wind"

Greek Septuagint: "εἰς πάντα ἄνεμον σκορπιῶ αὐτούς... ἐν ῥομφαίᾳ πεσοῦνται κύκλῳ σου"

= "I will scatter them to every wind... **will fall round about you by** *the* **sword**"

In this example it is clear that the two phrases are in the opposite order in the Greek, compared to the Hebrew. This phenomenon is very common when comparing the Greek translation vs. the Hebrew text of the Old Testament. In fact, there are at least eighty[a] verses in Genesis alone, where the Greek Septuagint uses a different[b] order than the Hebrew, without any grammatical requirement!

To reiterate, it is evident that Greek translators/editors **very often** made these changes in word/phrase order, even where grammar does not require it to be done.

---

[a] Manually confirmed Accordance search using the MT-LXX parallel. Some of these changes in the Septuagint are clearly to smooth out the text stylistically, but words which are required to be in a different position by Greek grammar are not listed here. See Gen. 1:11, 2:4, 4:15, 4:22, 6:16, 7:8, 8:18, 8:19, 8:21, 11:8, 11:12, 11:14, 12:20, 14:16, 14:24, 17:16, 18:6, 18:8, 18:11, 19:6, 19:20, 20:12, 22:3, 22:6, 23:6, 24:7, 24:43, 24:47, 25:7, 26:28, 26:29, 28:14, 29:24, 30:7, 30:10, 30:12, 30:30, 30:43, 31:16, 31:17, 31:32, 31:33, 31:48, 31:50, 31:51-52, 32:1, 32:8, 32:29, 33:4, 33:7, 33:16, 34:12, 35:13, 35:21, 37:4, 37:24, 41:8, 41:12, 41:18, 41:20, 41:35, 41:38, 41:56, 42:22, 42:24, 42:32, 42:34, 43:7, 43:15, 44:9, 45:1, 45:12, 45:16, 45:19, 45:20, 45:21, 47:6, 47:23, 50:10, 50:12, 50:17, 50:24, 50:25. (References given with standard Hebrew verse numbering.)

[b] Mostly, two words or phrases are placed in the opposite order (as shown in the above examples), but some differences are more complicated. Though these differences are often invisible in **English translations** of the Masoretic Text vs. the Septuagint, they are very clearly visible in the actual Greek vs. Hebrew texts.

Scholars have attempted to translate the Greek Septuagint back to Hebrew in an endeavor to reclaim the Hebrew text on which the Septuagint was based. However, except where grammar requires a different order, even scholars[a] **do not know** in which instances the word order needs to be changed, and in which the word order needs to remain the same as in the Greek text.

Similarly, Greek-based Hebrew translations of Revelation leave e.g. lists of nouns in the **exact same order** as in the Greek, because grammar does not demand a specific order for such lists of nouns.[b]

So, if this Hebrew version of Revelation is simply a translation, we should never see non-grammatical inversed word order when compared to the standard versions – but we do. Below are some[c] examples where the word order in the Hebrew Revelation is different than the Greek, without any grammatical requirement:

Revelation 4:5:

Oo.1.16: "קולות ורעמים וברקים"

= "voices and thunders and lightnings"

Byzantine Greek:[d] "ἀστραπαὶ καὶ φωναί καὶ βρονταὶ"

---

[a] "…the study of the word order in the LXX is a complicated issue. Soisalon-Soininen even regards this investigation as one of the most complicated and problematic issues in Septuagint research." – Staffan Olofsson, *Studying the Word Order of the Septuagint: Questions and Possibilities*, in *Scandinavian Journal of the Old Testament,* vol. 10 no. 2, 1996, p. 217.

[b] See e.g. translations by Franz Delitzsch and by Salkinson/Ginsburg in Rev. 4:5 and other examples discussed in this section.

[c] Apart from the examples to be discussed, see also Rev. 1:4, 2:23[24], 5:13, 7:3, 10:9, 13:17[16], 14:11, 16:19[20], 19:2, 19:18, 20:4, 21:9, 22:17. (Be sure to compare Hebrew vs. Greek texts as translations may sometimes obscure these differences).

[d] Textus Receptus "ἀστραπαὶ καὶ βρονταί καὶ φωναὶ" – still in different order than Oo.1.16.

= "lightnings and voices and thunders"

Revelation 3:12:

<u>Oo.1.16</u>: "השם מירושלים החדש העיר אלהי"

= "the name of the new Yerushalayim,[a] the **city of my Elohim**"

<u>Byzantine Greek</u>: "τὸ ὄνομα τῆς πόλεως τοῦ θεοῦ μου, τῆς καινῆς ἱερουσαλήμ"

= "the name of the **city of my God**, the new Jerusalem"

Revelation 5:1:

<u>Oo.1.16</u>:

"וזה שישב על הכסא ראיתי ביד ימינו ספר אחד"

= "**And he**[b] **who sat on the throne** – I saw in his right hand a scroll"[c]

<u>Byzantine Greek</u>: "καὶ εἶδον ἐπὶ τὴν δεξιὰν τοῦ καθημένου ἐπὶ τοῦ θρόνου βιβλίον"

= "And I saw in the right hand of **him who sat on the throne** a book"

---

[a] The Hebrew name for 'Jerusalem.'
[b] Lit. "this *one*," but means 'he' or 'him.'
[c] For comparison of word order, this verse is rendered more literally here than in the main translation.

Revelation 9:15:

Oo.1.16:

"להמית השליש מבני אדם בשעה וביום ובחודש ובשנה
אחד"

= '**to kill a third**[a] **of** *the* **sons of man** in an hour and in a day and in a month and in a year."

Byzantine Greek: "εἰς τὴν ὥραν καὶ εἰς τὴν ἡμέραν καὶ μῆνα καὶ ἐνιαυτόν, ἵνα ἀποκτείνωσιν τὸ τρίτον τῶν ἀνθρώπων."

= "...in an hour and in a day and a month and a year, **to kill the third of men**."

Revelation 14:9:

Oo.1.16: "להפסל ולההחיה"

= "to the carved **image**[b] and to the animal"

Byzantine Greek: "τὸ θηρίον καὶ τὴν εἰκόνα αὐτοῦ"

= "the animal and its **image**"

From the above examples, it is evident that the Hebrew Revelation often has a different word order than the Greek translation, just as the Hebrew Masoretic Text often has words or phrases in an order which differs from the second-hand Septuagint translation.

In each of the above examples from the Hebrew Revelation:

---

[a] Or "the third part."
[b] Or simply "the image."

1. There is no grammatical requirement for the Hebrew text to have a different order than the Greek, and

2. the scholarly Greek-based translations to Hebrew have each of these phrases in the same order as the Greek, and

3. the Hebrew word order in Oo.1.16 is also different than that of the Aramaic Peshitta and Latin Vulgate.

These differences in word order in this particular Hebrew Revelation are clear indications that it is linguistically authentic. It has to derive from the original Hebrew version and cannot be obtained from the Greek, Aramaic, or Latin versions.

Gapping

Word 'gapping'[a] is frequent in the Hebrew Old Testament as well as in other authentic Hebrew documents. Gapped words are **understood** in the Hebrew text without being explicitly written out. Greek translators often inserted these 'gapped' words into their translations,[b] and once that is done, we have a problem. When such a Greek translation is reverted back to Hebrew, it is often impossible

---

[a] 'Gapping' is also known by the term 'ellipsis.'

[b] "Translators... often make[ ] features explicit which are implicit [gapped] in the original... even this procedure makes a translation less literal." – Staffan Olofsson, *The LXX Version, A Guide to the Translation Technique of the Septuagint*, Almqvist and Wiksell International, 1990, p. 16.

"...the translator might insert [explicitly] into the translation any idea the source text called to mind [implied by context, etc.]." – Emanuel Tov, *The Text-Critical Use of the Septuagint in Biblical Research*, 3rd ed., Eisenbrauns, 2015, p. 50.

to know which of these words were originally gapped, and which were part of the original text.[a]

Thus, Greek-based Hebrew translations of Revelation simply have the Greek text translated into Hebrew with virtually no gapping of explicit subjects and objects, compared to the Greek.[b] Below we will focus on specific examples of 'gapping' in the Hebrew Revelation of Oo.1.16, which **cannot** be reclaimed from the Greek, Aramaic, or Latin versions, and are thus evidence of linguistic originality. In these examples, Hebrew grammar and syntax **do not require** gapping, and thus reconstructed Hebrew translations from Greek (e.g. by Franz Delitzsch and by Salkinson, etc.) do not have these words gapped.

Gapping of explicit subject:

Explicit subject gapping is very common in the Hebrew Old Testament. A sentence (or paragraph) will often only define the subject once (or perhaps twice), and afterwards simply refer to the subject as "he," "she" or "they," etc. We even do this in English, but

---

[a] "This example illustrates the difficulty in evaluating additions and omissions of personal names in the LXX [Septuagint Greek translation] (and, for that matter, in all ancient versions [translations])... In the verse under investigation, it cannot be determined whether the [Septuagint] translator added the personal name [explicit object] or whether this name was already found in his *Vorlage*... The LXX [Septuagint Greek translation] of Joshua thus reflects an expanded text, but it is impossible to determine whether the expansions derived from the Greek translator or from his Hebrew Vorlage." – Emanuel Tov, *The Text-Critical Use of the Septuagint in Biblical Research*, 3rd ed., Eisenbrauns, 2015, pp. 97-98.

[b] There are some words which are regularly written in Greek but gapped in Hebrew, e.g. "εχω," and the definite article (used as personal pronoun) in phrases like "ο δε ειπεν." Such words may/will be gapped in any Hebrew translation, depending on the context. However, in this section we will focus on examples of gapping (e.g. explicit subject gapping) which cannot be reclaimed from the Greek, Latin, or Aramaic versions, and therefore show authenticity.

not to the same extent as found in Classical/Biblical Hebrew. Below is an example of explicit subject gapping in the Tanach:

Genesis 3:1:

Hebrew Masoretic Text: "וַיֹּאמֶר אֶל־הָאִשָּׁה"

= "then **he** [*the serpent*] said to the woman"

In the above example, the explicit subject [*the serpent*] has been **supplied** (added) in square brackets, but it is not actually written in the Hebrew Text! We say that the explicit subject is '**gapped**,' or 'understood by context.' Only by reading the **context** can we know that the '**he**' in Genesis 3:1 refers to the serpent and **not** to Yahweh, nor to Adam.

In cases where confusion might occur, **translators** often insert the **implied** explicit subject to help their readers understand the text without any difficulty.[a] (In most translations, this is done without any indication – no brackets or font change is used!) For example, in the above verse from Genesis chapter 3, the Greek Septuagint translation **inserts** the Greek word for 'serpent' to eliminate any ambiguity:[b]

Genesis 3:1:

Greek Septuagint: "καὶ εἶπεν ὁ ὄφις τῇ γυναικί"

---

[a] "The [Septuagint Greek] translators added various elements to the translation that served to improve its readability from a linguistic and contextual point of view, clarifying Hebrew or Greek words and explaining their content." – Emanuel Tov, *The Text-Critical Use of the Septuagint in Biblical Research*, 3rd ed., Eisenbrauns, 2015, p. 50.

[b] "The brevity of the style of the biblical narrative created many situations in which... translators felt the need to add names that were implicit in the biblical text, but were not mentioned explicitly..." – Emanuel Tov, *The Text-Critical Use of the Septuagint in Biblical Research*, 3rd ed., Eisenbrauns, 2015, p. 97.

= "then **the serpent** said to the woman"

Because translators frequently added the implied subject explicitly, we can actually use such differences to determine which textual version is closer to the original![a]

If we compare two texts of the Bible in different languages, and find multiple and consistent examples[b] of **gapping** in the one, and **supplied** subjects/objects in the other, we know that the less interpretive version is closer to the original. This argument is especially strong in contexts where confusion is likely to occur if the subjects/objects are not stated explicitly.[c] Translators always strive to remove any possible ambiguity from their translations. If the resultant translation could cause confusion, translators would not leave out the explicit subject if it existed in the original text.

---

[a] "Explicit mention of the sentence subject or object was often lacking [gapped] in the original. As the text was… translated into other languages, proper names were inserted or substituted for pronouns. Occasionally, different subjects or objects were included in separate manuscripts." – Ralph W. Klein, *Textual criticism of the Old Testament, the Septuagint after Qumran*, Fortress Press, 1981, p. 81.

[b] Apart from the examples discussed in detail, further examples of gapping of explicit subjects/objects in the Hebrew Revelation (which were not reclaimed by Hebrew translations from Greek) may be found in e.g. Rev. 4:8 ("they" vs. "the four living creatures"); Rev. 10:4 ("them" vs. "what the seven thunders have said"); Rev. 11:5 ("them" vs. "their enemies"); Rev. 11:9b ("them" vs. "their bodies"); Rev. 14:1 ("them" vs. "their foreheads"); Rev. 15:8b ("it" vs. "the temple"); Rev. 16:10 ("it" vs. "its kingdom"); Rev. 16:20b[21b] ("they" vs. "the men"); Rev. 17:2 ("those" vs. "the inhabitants of the earth"); Rev. 18:5 ("her" vs. "her iniquities"); Rev. 19:20 ("him/it" vs. "its image").

[c] It can be argued that an explicit subject/object could be accidentally lost in a context where the implied subject/object is so obvious that neither the scribe/translator nor proofreader would even notice that a word has been omitted. But whenever the context would be ambiguous without the explicit subject/object, the chance that a scribe/translator could accidentally omit it is very small, and any proofreader would instantly recognize and correct such a mistake.

Now, let's look at such an example of explicit subject gapping in the Hebrew Revelation:

Revelation 18:3:

Oo.1.16: "כי כולם שתו מיינה"

= "For **all of them** have drunk of her wine"

Greek Textus Receptus:[a] "ὅτι ἐκ τοῦ οἴνου... πέπωκεν πάντα τὰ ἔθνη"

= "For **all the nations** have drunk of the wine"

If we read the beginning of verse 3 together with the last part of verse 2, we can see the reason for the addition in the Greek translation:

> "And it became a dwelling of **satans**,[b] and to hide all the unclean ones of the **birds** and **creeping things**. 3 For **all of them** have drunk of her wine..."[c]

At a first glance, one might think that "all of them" refers to the just-mentioned creatures in verse 2, or else the "satans" – but the larger context makes it clear that "**all of them**" refers to the "**nations**" as stated four chapters earlier in Revelation 14:8, and not to demons nor animals. Thus, to avoid confusion, the Greek translation **supplies** or **adds** the explicit subject "**nations**" – but without indicating that it is an addition.

The gapping of the explicit subject in this context is very good proof that the Hebrew Revelation contained in Oo.1.16 derives from the

---

[a] Very similar in NA28. Byzantine MT uses a different verb (πέπτωκασιν) but still supplies the explicit subject (πάντα τὰ ἔθνη / all the nations).

[b] Or 'demons.'

[c] Rev. 18:2-3, translated from Oo.1.16.

original Hebrew version and is not a second-hand translation from Greek, Aramaic or Latin.[a]

Gapping of explicit object:

Explicit **object** gapping works just like explicit **subject** gapping, but the words in question are objects (direct or indirect), rather than subjects.[b]

Revelation 1:13 is a good example of explicit object gapping in the Hebrew version. Let's compare the Greek tradition vs. Oo.1.16.:

Revelation 1:13:

Oo.1.16: "ובניהם"

= "and among **them**"

Byzantine Greek:[c] "καὶ ἐν μέσῳ τῶν ἑπτὰ λυχνιῶν"

= "and among **the seven candlesticks**"

As explained earlier, translators always strive to clarify and explain any difficulties in the text they are translating. Thus the Greek translation replaces the object "them" with the explanation "seven candlesticks" to avoid any ambiguity. The Greek version **supplies** or **inserts** the explicit object.

In the above example, Hebrew grammar does not **demand** this phrase to be gapped, therefore translations from Greek to Hebrew

---

[a] Neither the Greek, Latin nor Aramaic versions of Revelation has the explicit subject "nations" gapped in Rev. 18:3.

[b] See pp. 312-314 for an example from the Hebrew O.T. vs. Greek Septuagint.

[c] Note that some Greek manuscripts, e.g. the Alexandrian Codex, and also the Peshitta Aramaic version, do not include the word for 'seven,' though they still supply the word for 'lampstands.'

do not change "the seven candlesticks" to "them."[a] There is **no way** to know from the **Greek text** whether this phrase was originally gapped or written. So, the fact that it is gapped in this Hebrew manuscript is strong evidence that the Hebrew reading is authentic, as it could not have derived from the Greek, Aramaic or Latin versions. It also shows that the Greek reading is the interpreted second-hand translation, while the Hebrew reading is the original. Below we will discuss a few more examples:

Revelation 2:10:

Oo.1.16: "אל תירא מהם"

= "Do not be afraid **of them**"

Byzantine M^A Greek:[b] "μηδὲν φοβοῦ ἃ μέλλεις πάσχειν"

= "Do not fear **what you are about to suffer**"

The Hebrew "them" probably refers to the people who persecuted the believers of Smyrna, but the Greek translation **interprets** "them" to refer to the sufferings ("what you are about to suffer").

Revelation 4:10a:

Oo.1.16: "לפניו"

= "before **him**"

Byzantine Greek: "ἐνώπιον τοῦ καθημένου ἐπὶ τοῦ θρόνου"

---

[a] Franz Delitzsch: "וּבְתוֹךְ שֶׁבַע הַמְּנֹרוֹת"
Salkinson/Ginsburg: "וּבְתוֹךְ הַמְּנֹרוֹת" (Following other Greek manuscripts and not the Byzantine MT).
[b] This reading comes from a subdivision of Byzantine Greek manuscripts of Revelation, designated as M^A in NA28. It is also found in the Textus Receptus and NA28. Other mss. read "παθεῖν" for "πάσχειν", with similar meaning.

= "before **the one sitting on the throne**"

Revelation 4:10c:

<u>Oo.1.16</u>: "לפניו"

= "before **him**"

<u>Byzantine Greek</u>: "ἐνώπιον τοῦ θρόνου"

= "before **the throne**"

The Hebrew language uses the same word (or suffix) for 'him' and 'it.' The Greek translators interpreted that the first "him" refers to "the one sitting on the throne," and that the second "him" refers to "the throne" – thus they inserted these explanatory phrases into their translation. Although the Greek explanation is not entirely impossible, the most likely meaning in both cases is that the "him" simply refers to Yahweh.

Although in these examples the Hebrew readings could mean the exact same thing as the Greek translation, these are important indications that this Hebrew manuscript is authentic. It cannot derive from the Greek, Aramaic, or Latin versions. Rather, the Hebrew text preserves the uninterpreted original readings, which were interpreted and expanded in the Greek translation.

Mistranslation in the Greek version

Revelation 18:13 contains a very interesting variant between the Hebrew and Greek versions:

Revelation 18:13:

<u>Byzantine Greek</u>: "...καὶ οἶνον, καὶ ἔλαιον, καὶ σεμίδαλιν, καὶ σῖτον, καὶ πρόβατα, καὶ κτήνη· καὶ ἵππων, καὶ ῥαιδῶν, καὶ σωμάτων· καὶ ψυχὰς ἀνθρώπων."

= "...and wine and oil and fine flour and wheat, and sheep and animals and horses and **chariots**, and slaves – even souls of men."

<u>Oo.1.16</u>:

"ויין ושמן ולחם לבן וחיטים ובקרים וכשבים וסוסים ועגלים ונשמות אדם"

= "And wine and oil and white bread[a] and wheat and bulls and sheep and horses and **calves** and neshamot[b] of man."

In the above verse, the Greek version reads "horses and chariots" while the Hebrew reads "horses and calves." So, how did this difference come about? The Greek word "ῥαιδῶν" (*raidon*)[c] is not ambiguous and cannot be mistaken for 'calves' which is "μόσχων"[d] (*moschon*) in Greek. In the Latin and Aramaic versions, the meaning "chariots" is equally clear, and thus they provide no solution as to the source of this variant reading.

But what if the Hebrew reading is the original? Could the Greek be a mistranslation of the Hebrew? Unlike Greek, Hebrew uses similar words for chariots and calves!

---

[a] Could also mean "fine flour."
[b] Plural of "נשמה" (*neshamah*) – the Hebrew word for "blowing/breath," "soul" or "spirit." (See glossary for more information.)
[c] Also spelled "ῥεδῶν" (*redon*).
[d] Lexical form: "μόσχος." Inflected above to match context with same case, gender and number as "ῥαιδῶν."

| Calves: | עגלים | 'agalim |
| Chariots: [a] | עגלות | 'agalot |

The only difference in consonantal spelling between the two Hebrew words above is the masculine plural ending "ים" vs. the feminine plural ending "ות". Could the Greek translator have mistranslated 'agalim' as if it were 'agalot'? Note that the preceding word in Revelation 18:13 is "horses." Horses and chariots often go together, and this might have been the cause of confusion.

At closer inspection we find that the Hebrew reading "calves" is actually very suitable – the other objects mentioned around this word in verse 13b are not man-made objects but rather living creatures.

Considering that the only difference between "עגלים" ('agalim) and "עגלות" ('agalot) is their gender, and that the preceding word "horses" has a strong connotation with chariots, it is not unlikely that a translator could have rendered "עגלים" as if it were "עגלות".

On the other hand, it is not possible at all that the Greek word "ραιδῶν" (chariots) could have been translated into Hebrew as "עגלים" (calves) – in the Greek version there is no ambiguity or any scope for possible confusion in translation.

Thus, if the Hebrew is the original, this variant reading is possible in the Greek translation and subsequent versions. But if the Greek, Aramaic or Latin version is the original, this difference should never have existed.[b]

---

[a] Reading "עגלות" with different vowels could yield either "chariots" or "heifers" – but "עגלים" means "calves" and cannot mean "chariots."

[b] See also HebrewGospels.com/videos-revelation/5 for more examples of linguistic mistranslation in the Greek version of Revelation.

Was 'The Name' Yahweh translated as 'Theos'?

Another interesting variant between the Hebrew and Greek versions of Revelation is the frequent use of Yahweh (The Name) in the Hebrew version. More specifically, we want to investigate the instances[a] where the Greek version uses "θεος" (Theos) while the Hebrew version does **not** use the equivalent title "אלהים" (Elohim), but rather uses the Tetragrammaton[b] – indicated by an abbreviation.

The abbreviation used in this manuscript is the Hebrew letter "הֹ" with two dots above it – shortened from "השם" (Ha-Shem) which literally means "The Name."[c] The fact that the abbreviation "הֹ" really represents 'The Name' Yahweh is evident[d] when the Old Testament is quoted in the Hebrew Revelation, e.g.:

Isaiah 6:3:

Hebrew Masoretic Text: "קָדוֹשׁ | קָדֹושׁ קָדוֹשׁ יהוָה צְבָאֹות"

Oo.1.16 (Revelation 4:8):   "קדוש קדוש קדוש הֹ צבאות"

---

[a] Apart from the examples discussed below, see also Rev. 1:2, 1:6, 1:9, 2:17[18], 3:1, 3:2, 4:5, 7:3, 7:15, 8:2, 8:4, etc.

[b] The Tetragrammaton refers to the Creator's four-letter name "יהוה" (Yahweh), often represented by various abbreviations.

[c] To this day many Jews will use 'Ha-Shem' as a euphemism for 'The Name' Yahweh.

[d] Occasionally in the Hebrew Revelation, this "הֹ" also corresponds to "אדני" (Adonai) when quoting from the Tanach, but never to "אלהים" (Elohim).

Psalm 113:1:

<u>Hebrew Masoretic Text</u>:

"הַלְלוּ יָהּ | הַלְלוּ עַבְדֵי יהוה הַלְלוּ אֶת־שֵׁם יהוה:"

<u>Oo.1.16</u> (Revelation 19:5):

"הללויה הללו עבדי הֹ הללו את שם הֹ"

Isaiah: 60:19:

<u>Hebrew Masoretic Text</u>:

"וְהָיָה־לָךְ יהוה לְאוֹר עוֹלָם וֵאלֹהַיִךְ לְתִפְאַרְתֵּךְ:"

<u>Oo.1.16</u> (Revelation 22:5):

"והיה לך הֹ לאור עולם ואלהיך לתפארתך"

The above examples clearly show that the abbreviation "הֹ" actually represents the name Yahweh. It was common practice for many scribes to write Ha-Shem or some abbreviation rather than writing out the full name "יהוה" (Yahweh). Various abbreviations for the Tetragrammaton are used in traditional Jewish writings such as the Mishnah, Talmud, Midrash, and most of the Targums.[a]

Below are some examples where the Hebrew Revelation indicates '**Yahweh**' but the Greek version uses '**Theos**':

---

[a] "Targum manuscripts differ on the way to abbreviate the Tetragrammaton (e.g., יי , ייי , יוי , הֹ)." – Leeor Gottlieb, *Targum Chronicles and its Place Among the Late Targums*, Brill, 2020, p. 9.
In the Mishnah and Talmud, the name "יהוה" is usually replaced with "ייי" in the manuscripts, and with "הֹ" in the printed versions. Most other traditional Jewish writings will also use an abbreviation rather than the full "יהוה" whenever quoting from the Tanach.

Revelation 1:1:

<u>Oo.1.16</u>: "‎הֹ נתן‎"

= "**Yahweh** gave"

<u>Byzantine Greek</u>: "ἔδωκεν αὐτῷ ὁ θεὸς"

= "**Theos** gave to him"

Revelation 5:6:

<u>Oo.1.16</u>: "‎הֹ ואילו השבעה רוחות‎"

= "and these are the seven Ruchot of **Yahweh**"

<u>Byzantine Greek</u>: "ἃ εἰσιν τὰ ἑπτὰ πνεύματα τοῦ θεοῦ"

= "which are the seven spirits of **Theos**"

Further examples are found in Revelation 1:2, 1:6, 1:9, 2:17[18], 3:1, 3:2, 4:5, 5:6, 7:3, 7:15, 8:2, 8:4, etc.

So, how did this difference originate? Interestingly, the Septuagint Greek translation shows numerous[a] examples where 'Yahweh' was translated as 'Theos':

Genesis 4:4:

<u>Hebrew Masoretic Text</u>: "‎וַיִּשַׁע יהוֹה‎"

---

[a] Apart from the examples given here, this phenomenon also occurs in: Gen. 4:9, 6:6, 6:7, 12:17, 13:14, 15:7, 16:5, 18:1, 25:21b, 30:24, 30:27, 31:49, 38:7b, Ex. 4:11b, 4:30, 4:31, 5:21, 9:5, 13:21, 19:3, 19:7, 19:8, 19:21, 35:30, 36:2, and many other places throughout the Old Testament.
See also Emanuel Tov, *The Harmonizing Character of the Septuagint of Genesis 1-11*, in *Die Septuaginta – Text, Wirkung, Rezeption*, vol. 4, Mohr Siebeck, 2014, pp. 323-329.

= "Then **Yahweh** looked"

Greek Septuagint: "καὶ ἐπεῖδεν ὁ θεὸς"

= "Then **Theos** looked"

Exodus 4:1:

Hebrew Masoretic Text: "לֹא־נִרְאָה אֵלֶיךָ יהוה:"

= "**Yahweh** did not appear to you"

Greek Septuagint: "οὐκ ὦπταί σοι ὁ θεός"

= "**Theos** did not appear to you"

Although the above information would suggest that the Hebrew Revelation is the original, and that the Tetragrammaton was frequently replaced with 'Theos' when translated into Greek; some might argue conversely, that 'Theos/Elohim' was rather replaced with "הֹ" (for 'Yahweh') by the scribe (or translator) of the Hebrew Revelation. However, this is not the case! Firstly, this Hebrew version of Revelation does also use the Hebrew word Elohim,[a] so it is clear that the title Elohim was **not** simply removed from the Hebrew Revelation and replaced with this "הֹ" (for 'Yahweh').

Secondly, even in those Jewish Bible translations which did generally replace 'Elohim' with the Tetragrammaton,[b] there were specific cases in which they did **not** make this substitution. For example, it was extremely unlikely for any Hebrew translator to

---

[a] See Rev. 3:12 (x3), 7:12, 7:17, 11:4, 11:13, 12:15[10], 19:17, 21:3, 21:4, 21:7.
[b] The Jewish Targums (Aramaic translations of Tanach) often substituted the Tetragrammaton (though in abbreviated forms like "ייי", etc.) for "אלהים", with some important exceptions (as explained below).

render 'his God,' 'our God,' etc.[a] as 'Yahweh.'[b] The reason for that is simple: The Tetragrammaton is a proper name, and cannot be qualified by possessive suffixes in Hebrew. In other words, one cannot translate 'my Elohim/Theos' as 'my Yahweh,' because that would give the impression that 'Yahweh' is not a name but a generic title. Therefore, 'our Elohim/Theos,' etc. is never replaced by the Tetragrammaton in Greek-to-Hebrew Translations of Revelation, e.g. those by Franz Delitzsch, Salkinson/Ginsburg, and the modern translation by The Bible Society in Israel.

Surprisingly, the Hebrew Revelation contained in Oo.1.16 does show multiple examples where the Greek reads 'our Theos,' etc., but the Hebrew version reads "הֹ" (for 'Yahweh'):[c]

Revelation 7:10:

Oo.1.16: "לֹהֹ הישועה"

= "The salvation belongs to **Yahweh**"

---

[a] In Hebrew, this would include any occurrence of Elohim with a pronominal suffix; and in Greek, any occurrence of 'Theos' followed by a genitive personal pronoun (rarely also when preceded by a genitive personal pronoun).

[b] Targum Onkelos, Targum Pseudo Johnathan, and Targum Fragments never replaced Elohim with pronominal suffix ('our Elohim,' etc.) with the Tetragrammaton. Targum Neofiti has only one example of Elohim with pronominal suffix, changed to the Tetragrammaton, in order to avoid confusion in Deu. 31. This passage (Deu. 31:16-17) describes what would happen when Yahweh's people turn away from him and follow other 'elohim' (idols). To ensure that "my elohim" in verse 17 is understood to refer to Yahweh and not to any other 'elohim' (or idol), they substituted "the glory of the presence of יוי" for "my elohim." (Statistics are from manually confirmed searches with Accordance Bible software, utilizing the *Targums WordMap*.)

[c] The two given examples are also valid with regard to the Latin Vulgate and the Aramaic Peshitta. There are a few more examples which occur in Greek and Latin but not in the Peshitta: Rev. 3:2 (most Greek mss. and Vulgate), 7:3 (Greek and Vulgate), 19:6 (most Greek mss. and Vulgate).

Byzantine Greek: "ἡ σωτηρία τῷ θεῷ ἡμῶν"

= "The salvation belongs to **our Theos**"

Revelation 19:5:

Oo.1.16: "הללו את שם הֿ"

= "praise the name of **Yahweh**"

Byzantine Greek: "αἰνεῖτε τὸν θεὸν ἡμῶν"

= "Praise **our Theos**"

The only logical conclusion is that the use of 'Yahweh' (הֿ) in this Hebrew Revelation cannot be obtained from any Greek or Greek-based version, because 'our Theos,' etc. cannot be translated into Hebrew as 'Yahweh.' But what if the Hebrew text is the original? Would Greek translators occasionally have rendered 'Yahweh' as 'our Theos,' etc.?

Surprisingly, yes! The Greek Septuagint translation contains multiple instances in which 'Yahweh' was translated as 'Theos' followed by a genitive personal pronoun:

Exodus 5:17:

Hebrew Masoretic Text: "נֵלְכָה נִזְבְּחָה לַיהוָה:"

= "Let us go, let us sacrifice to **Yahweh**!"

Greek Septuagint: "πορευθῶμεν θύσωμεν τῷ θεῷ ἡμῶν"

= "Let us go, let us sacrifice to **our Theos**!"

Leviticus 21:21a:

Hebrew Masoretic Text: "לְהַקְרִיב אֶת־אִשֵּׁי יהוָה"

= "To offer the fire-offerings of **Yahweh**"

Greek Septuagint: "τοῦ προσενεγκεῖν τὰς θυσίας τῷ θεῷ σου"

= "To offer the sacrifices to **your Theos**"

Jeremiah 4:4:

Hebrew Masoretic Text: "הִמֹּלוּ לַיהוָה"

= "Be circumcised to **Yahweh**"

Greek Septuagint: "περιτμήθητε τῷ θεῷ ὑμῶν"

= "Be circumcised to **your Theos**"

Because Greek translators often translated 'Yahweh' as 'Theos,' and even rendered 'Yahweh' as 'our Theos,' 'your Theos,' etc.[a] – but on the contrary, Hebrew translators do not translate 'our Theos,' 'your Theos,' etc. as 'Yahweh'[b] – we can conclude that this Hebrew version of Revelation cannot be a translation from the Greek

---

[a] Apart from the above three examples, see also Ex. 23:17; Deu. 12:11; 1Sam. 2:1, 4:3b; 1 Kin. 20:3 (LXX 21:3); Is. 36:18, 58:13; Jer. 2:19b, 46:10 (LXX 26:10); 1Chr. 16:26.

[b] Besides the clear evidence from the Targums (explained above), even modern scholars did not make any such change in their Hebrew translations of Revelation from Greek. Contrast Oo.1.16 vs. Greek and Greek-based translations below:

Ref.	Greek MT	Delitzsch/ Dalman	Salkinson/ Ginsburg	Bible Society in Israel	Oo.1.16
3:2	τοῦ θεοῦ μου	אֱלֹהָי	אֱלֹהָי	אֱלֹהַי	ה
7:3	τοῦ θεοῦ ἡμῶν	אֱלֹהֵינוּ	אֱלֹהֵינוּ	אֱלֹהֵינוּ	ה
7:10	τῷ θεῷ ἡμῶν	לֵאלֹהֵינוּ	לֵאלֹהֵינוּ	לֵאלֹהֵינוּ	לה
19:5	τὸν θεὸν ἡμῶν	אֶת אֱלֹהֵינוּ	אֶת אֱלֹהֵינוּ	אֶת אֱלֹהֵינוּ	את שם ה
19:6	ὁ θεὸς ἡμῶν	אֱלֹהֵינוּ	אֱלֹהֵי	אֱלֹהֵינוּ	ה

version,[a] however, the Greek version could have originated from the Hebrew.

Harmonizing additions in the Greek Revelation

To avoid possible confusion, and to ensure a smooth reading experience, translators utilize a number of techniques to clarify the Biblical text when they translate it into another language.[b] One of the well-known translation techniques used in the Greek Septuagint is called "harmonizing addition."[c]

The Hebrew Bible was not simply translated into Greek, but the context was consulted, and extra information was gleaned from the

---

[a] Neither could the Hebrew text of Oo.1.16 be a translation from the Aramaic Peshitta or Latin Vulgate, as these versions agree with the Greek use of 'Theos' in the examples explained above.

Again, it should be remembered that the Hebrew Revelation did not simply replace 'Theos/Elohim' with 'Ha-Shem/Yahweh.' The Hebrew word 'Elohim' appears with a pronominal suffix in 3:12 (x3), 7:12, 12:15[10], 19:17; in the construct state without a suffix: 11:4, 11:13; and in the absolute state: 7:17, 21:3, 21:4, 21:7. Thus, 'Elohim' was not systematically replaced with 'Yahweh' in the Hebrew Revelation, but rather the Hebrew Revelation preserves intricate details in the text which cannot be reclaimed from the Greek version.

[b] "Translations contain many harmonizations, but often it cannot be determined whether these harmonizations derived from the translator himself or from his Hebrew sources." – Emanuel Tov, *The Nature and Background of Harmonizations in Biblical Manuscripts*, in *Journal for the Study of the Old Testament*, vol. 31, 1985, p. 4.

[c] "Among the known textual sources of Genesis most instances of harmonization are found in the LXX [Septuagint Greek translation of O.T.]." – Emanuel Tov, *The Harmonizing Character of the Septuagint of Genesis 1-11*, in *Die Septuaginta – Text, Wirkung, Rezeption*, vol. 4, Mohr Siebeck, 2014, p. 315.

"Quite surprisingly, the LXX and not the SP [Samaritan Pentateuch] includes the largest number of harmonizations in these chapters [Gen. 1-11], especially pluses [additions]." – ibid. p. 321.

preceding and following sections.[a] Such extra snippets of information were filled into various applicable passages to ensure that readers of the Greek translation would get the full picture right away.[b]

---

[a] "The harmonizations are usually adapted to verses occurring earlier in the text, but sometimes to verses occurring later…" – Emanuel Tov, ibid p. 317.

[b] "Almost all the numerous pluses of the LXX [Septuagint Greek translation of O.T.], against MT [Masoretic Text] and SP [Samaritan Pentateuch], in these chapters [Gen. 1-11], are harmonizing." – Emanuel Tov, ibid. p. 317. Although several scholars (including Tov) attribute many of these additions to the Hebrew *Vorlage* [source text] of the LXX (due to differences in the details of the Greek wording in the harmonized passage vs. base passage), such a hypothesis does not explain why the Greek LXX translation would contain more harmonizations than any text in the original language (MT, DSS [Dead Sea Scrolls], SP). It is obvious that the LXX translation contains more harmonizations exactly because it is a translation, with numerous changes made by the translators. If it can be claimed that Hebrew copyists (whose job was simply to copy every word) added harmonizations, why would it be unlikely for the LXX translators (whose job was to produce a clear translation) to make such harmonizations?! The difference in wording between Greek passages could simply be a matter of translation: The translators would obviously refer back to the Hebrew text as their base for harmonization, which would yield the exact same results as having a Hebrew *Vorlage* with the added harmonizations. Quite obviously, it would be easier to keep the Greek scroll being written as a translation open in position, and to roll the Hebrew scroll to find the parallel passage; rather than rolling away from the passage being written to a different location in the Greek scroll, sometimes even further ahead (not translated yet)! Another possibility is that the translators would sometimes add harmonizations from memory, especially if they could not quickly find the parallel verse, which would also give rise to similar though not identical wordings. Finally, even if some of these harmonizations already existed in the Hebrew vorlage of the LXX, such harmonizations would still indicate that the LXX vorlage was the smoothed-out and edited version, while the MT preserved the original wording in each example where the LXX contains a harmonization. As Tov rightly remarks: "most of the pluses [in the Greek Septuagint and Samaritan Pentateuch] consist of harmonizing elements which are by definition secondary." – Emanuel Tov, *The Greek and Hebrew Bible: Collected Essays on the Septuagint*, Brill, 1999, p. 287.

A good example of a harmonizing addition in the Greek Septuagint translation can be seen in Genesis chapter 8:

Genesis 8:7:

Hebrew Masoretic Text: "וַיְשַׁלַּח אֶת־הָעֹרֵב"

= "Then he sent out the raven"

If one reads the Hebrew text of Genesis 8:7 for the first time ever, one might wonder exactly why Noah sent the raven out of the ark, as no explanation is given in verse 7, nor in the preceding verses. Only if you continue reading, you will find out later in the narrative that Noah sent out the birds as an experiment to learn whether the water had subsided yet. The Septuagint translation avoids the uncertainty and possibility of confusion by giving their readers the answer right from the start – **adding** an explanation found elsewhere in the context:

Genesis 8:7:

Greek Septuagint: "καὶ ἀπέστειλεν τὸν κόρακα τοῦ ἰδεῖν εἰ κεκόπακεν τὸ ὕδωρ"

= "Then he sent the raven **to see if the waters had abated**"

The Greek Septuagint translation added the explanation highlighted above, based on a later verse in the Hebrew Bible (Genesis 8:8), to harmonize the passage:

Genesis 8:8:

Hebrew Masoretic Text:

"וַיְשַׁלַּח אֶת־הַיּוֹנָה מֵאִתּוֹ לִרְאוֹת הֲקַלּוּ הַמַּיִם מֵעַל פְּנֵי הָאֲדָמָה:"

> = "Then he sent out the dove from him, **to see if the waters had abated** from the surface of the ground."

Because the raven was the first bird which Noah sent out from the ark and because no explanation for this is given in the Hebrew text of Genesis 8:7, the Septuagint Greek translation had the explanation inserted (as found later on in the narrative) to ensure that any reader would instantly understand why Noah sent out the raven.

Professor Tov (an expert in the Hebrew Tanach, Dead Sea Scrolls and Greek Septuagint) described more than 40 harmonizing additions in the Greek Septuagint translation of Genesis chapters 1-11 alone.[a] This type of addition is also found in the remaining chapters of the book of Genesis (though less frequently), and throughout the rest of the Septuagint translation of the Tanach. In fact, the Septuagint Greek translation contains more harmonizing additions than any other textual tradition of the Tanach.[b]

If the book of Revelation was indeed written in Hebrew (like the Tanach), and then translated into Greek, we would expect to see similar additions in the Greek text of Revelation compared to the Hebrew – and we do! Let's study one example found in Revelation chapter 1:

Revelation 1:10:

Oo.1.16: "שמעתי מאחרי קול גדול"

> = "I heard behind me a great voice"

---

[a] Emanuel Tov, *The Harmonizing Character of the Septuagint of Genesis 1-11*, in *Die Septuaginta – Text, Wirkung, Rezeption*, vol. 4, Mohr Siebeck, 2014, pp. 316-317.

[b] "The mentioning of the LXX as the main source for harmonizing pluses in all Scripture books... causes some surprise... However, the data are quite clear in this regard." – Emanuel Tov, *Textual Criticism of the Hebrew Bible, Qumran, Septuagint: Collected Essays*, vol. 3, Brill, 2015, p. 167.

<u>Byzantine Greek</u>:[a] "ἤκουσα φωνὴν ὀπίσω μου μεγάλην ὡς σάλπιγγος"

= "I heard a great voice behind me **like a trumpet**"

The Hebrew text does not contain the explanation "like a trumpet," but interestingly, we can glean from the context later on, that this voice did sound like a trumpet (shophar)![b]

Revelation 4:1:

<u>Oo.1.16</u>:

"והקול הראשון ששמעתי המדברת עימי כקול שופר"

= "and the first voice which I had heard – **that spoke with me like the sound of a shophar**"

So, we learn in Revelation 4:1 that the first voice which was mentioned in chapter 1:10 did in fact sound like a shophar. Thus a harmonizing addition was made in Revelation 1:10 in the Greek translation, to ensure that we get the full picture right away, the first time.

Keep in mind that no one translating the Greek Revelation back to Hebrew would have any way to know which phrases in the Greek Revelation were harmonizing additions, and which were part of the original text.

Therefore, no translation from Greek to Hebrew omitted the explanation "like a trumpet/shophar" in Revelation 1:10, because

---

[a] Greek mss. vary in word order in this phrase, but all known Greek mss. include "ὡς σάλπιγγος."

[b] A 'shophar' is the Hebrew word for a 'ram's horn' or 'trumpet.'

the translators had no idea that this information was originally postponed till later in the context.[a]

Apart from showing which version is the interpreted translation, and which version is the original, unedited and uninterpreted text,[b] it is also significant that the Hebrew Revelation postpones mentioning the shophar until chapter 4, where Yochanan is called up to heaven! Compare some verses below which show that the blowing of the shophar is directly connected with Yeshua's return, and the time when Yahweh will gather his people to himself:

Isaiah 27:12-13:[c] "...and you will be gathered one by one, o children of Yisrael![d] And it will happen on that day – there will be **blown with a great shophar**, and those who are lost in the land of Ashur[e] will come, and those who are

---

[a] The harmonizing addition is marked in bold in the table below. Neither older translations found in manuscripts, nor traditional translations, nor modern translations to Hebrew could reclaim the non-harmonized reading of Oo.1.16:

Oo.1.16	ושמעתי מאחרי קול גדול
Greek MT	καὶ ἤκουσα φωνὴν ὀπίσω μου μεγάλην **ὡς σάλπιγγος**
Vulgate	et audivi post me vocem magnam **tamquam tubæ**
Peshitta	ܘܫܡܥܬ ܒܬܪܝ ܩܠܐ ܪܒܐ، ܐܝܟ ܕܐܝܬ ܩܠܐ ܕܩܪܢܐ
Sloane 237	ושמעתי קול גדול אחרי **כמו חצצרה**
Neof. 33	ואשמע אחרי קול גדול **כשופר**
BnF Hebr. 131	ואשמע אחרי את קול גדול **כקול שופר**
Freiburg 314	ושמעתי אחרי קול גדולה **כאילו קול [ח]צוצרה**
Delitzsch	וָאֶשְׁמַע אַחֲרַי קוֹל גָּדוֹל **כְּקוֹל שׁוֹפָר**
Ginsburg	וָאֶשְׁמַע אַחֲרַי קוֹל גָּדוֹל **כְּקוֹל שׁוֹפָר**
Modern	וְשָׁמַעְתִּי מֵאַחֲרַי קוֹל גָּדוֹל **כְּקוֹל שׁוֹפָר**

[b] "By definition, all harmonizing additions are secondary [i.e. non-original]." – Emanuel Tov, *Textual Criticism of the Hebrew Bible, Qumran, Septuagint: Collected Essays*, vol. 3, Brill, 2015, p. 188.

[c] Translated from Hebrew Masoretic Text.

[d] Hebrew name for 'Israel.'

[e] Hebrew name for 'Assyria.'

scattered in the land of Mitsrayim,[a] and they will bow down to Yahweh on the set-apart mountain in Yerushalayim."[b]

1 Corinthians 15:51-52:[c] "...we will all be changed, in a moment, in the twinkling of an eye, at the last **trumpet**. For **the trumpet will sound**, and the dead will be raised incorruptible..."

Thus, it is evident that the mention of the shophar in Revelation 4:1 is purposeful, because it points to the future event when believers will be taken to Yahweh,[d] just like Yochanan was taken to Yahweh's presence in heaven, in Revelation 4.

Not only does the harmonizing addition in the Greek version of Revelation 1 obscure the significance of mentioning the shophar in chapter 4, but it also matches the Greek translation tendencies found in the Greek Septuagint. The translator(s) found extra information elsewhere in the context, and inserted this in related verses to harmonize the text.

Another good example of harmonizing addition is found in Revelation 3:22. Unfortunately, this Greek addition also obscures an important feature in the original Hebrew text.

Revelation 3:22:

Oo.1.16: "מי שיש לו אזנים שומע מה שהרוח אומר"

= "Whosoever has ears must hear what the Ruach says."

---

[a] Hebrew name for 'Egypt.'

[b] Hebrew name for 'Jerusalem.'

[c] Quoted from the Legacy Standard Bible. (We do not currently know of any **authentic** Hebrew manuscripts of Paul's epistles.)

[d] See e.g. 1 Thes. 4:16-17.

Byzantine Greek: "ὁ ἔχων οὖς ἀκουσάτω τί τὸ πνεῦμα λέγει ταῖς ἐκκλησίαις."

= "He who has an ear must hear what the Spirit says **to the assemblies**."

The phrase "to the assemblies" in the Greek version is a harmonizing addition based on the first six letters to the elders/ assemblies, where the Hebrew text also includes this phrase, e.g.:

Revelation 2:6[7]:

Oo.1.16:

"מי שיש לו אזנים שומע מה שהרוח אומר להעדה"

= "Whosoever has ears must hear what the Ruach says **to the assembly**."

The Greek version harmonized the wording of this command in the last of the seven letters with the wording found in the other six letters, by adding the seemingly 'missing' phrase: "to the assembly(ies)."

However, in the Hebrew Revelation there is a progressive shift, ending in a climax which emphasizes that all who have ears must hear, even if they are not part of the specific assembly:

1. The first three letters (1-3) end with the exhortations "Whosoever has ears must hear what the Ruach says **to the assembly**. Whosoever overcomes..." (Take note that the phrase "Whosoever has ears must hear..." is the **second to last** exhortation in letters 1-3.)

2. The next three letters (4-6) end with "Whosoever overcomes... Whosoever has ears must hear what the

Ruach says **to the assembly**." ("Whosoever has ears must hear..." is the **last** exhortation in letters 4-6.)

3. Finally, the climax where the whole series of letters ends with "Whosoever has ears must hear what the Ruach says." (The exhortation "Whosoever has ears must hear..." is placed last, and "the assembly" is **not mentioned**.) This sets the stage for Revelation 4:1 where Yochanan himself hears Yahweh's voice speaking to him, and he must hear – even though he was in Patmos and not in one of the seven assemblies.

Thus, it is not a coincidence or mistake that the Hebrew text does not mention "the assembly" at the end of the seventh letter. This is a purposeful feature of the original text, which explicitly makes the repeated exhortation to hear/obey applicable to every single person.

The Greek version's harmonization only obscures this important shift in wording, which was intended to be the culmination of the seven letters as well as the bridge to the next chapter where Yochanan is called up to heaven.

This is yet another indication that the Hebrew Revelation preserves the original unedited text, while the Greek version preserves an interpreted and harmonized translation.

Below we will list numerous[a] examples of harmonizing addition in the Greek vs. Hebrew Revelation, with only brief explanations where needed. Each of these differences helps to show that the Hebrew Revelation preserves the original unedited text, whereas the Greek version is an interpreted translation, just like the Greek Septuagint, with multiple harmonizing additions.

---

[a] This list is nearly exhaustive, but doubtful cases and some of the more complex instances were excluded.

The harmonizing addition(s) which are present in the Greek version [a] of Revelation but absent from the Hebrew version, will be indicated below in **bold**, followed by a reference to the probable source(s) for the harmonization: [b]

Revelation 1:3 (from Greek): "**words of** this prophecy" – Harmonization based on Revelation 22:7.

Revelation 1:3 (from Greek): "**for the time is near**" – Harmonization based on Revelation 22:10 (and less clearly 1:1).

Revelation 1:20 (from Greek): "messengers **of the**... **assemblies**" – Harmonization based on Revelation 2:1, 2:7[8], etc., where each of the seven messengers is referred to as "the messenger of the assembly."

Revelation 2:14 (from Greek): "**to eat things sacrificed to idols and** to commit fornication" – Harmonized to match the narrative in Numbers 25:1-2, which explains that the Israelites were trapped in fornication when the Moabites invited them to eat of their idol sacrifices.

---

[a] All examples are valid when compared with NA28, Byzantine MT, and Textus Receptus.

[b] We have listed passage(s) from the Hebrew Revelation (and from the Tanach, where applicable) which are most likely the basis for the harmonizing addition under discussion. Take note that if some (or many) of the harmonizing additions were derived from source passages in the Greek Bible (and not from the Hebrew), the argument remains unaffected. The point is that the non-harmonized version preserves the primary, unedited text, while the version which contains numerous harmonizing additions is secondary (interpreted and therefore non-original). As professor Tov remarks, "By definition, all harmonizing additions are secondary [i.e. non-original]." – Emanuel Tov, *Textual Criticism of the Hebrew Bible, Qumran, Septuagint: Collected Essays*, vol. 3, Brill, 2015, p. 188.

Revelation 2:20 (from Greek): "to commit fornication **and to eat things sacrificed to idols.**" – Same as in 2:14, harmonized based on Numbers 25:1-2.

Revelation 3:17 (from Greek): "you are... poor **and blind and naked**" – Harmonization based on Revelation 3:18, which exhorts the assembly of Laodicea to "...clothe yourself with white garments, and anoint your eyes with oil, that you may be able to see."[a] The implied blindness and need of clothes in verse 18 are expressed in the Greek translation of verse 17 to harmonize the rebuke with the exhortation.

Revelation 4:11 (from Greek): "glory and honor **and power**" – Harmonization based on Revelation 7:12.

Revelation 5:3 (from Greek): "on the earth **or under the earth**" – Harmonization based on Revelation 5:13.[b]

Revelation 5:11 (from Greek): "the throne **and the living creatures and the elders**" – Harmonization based on Revelation 5:6, 14:3.

Revelation 5:13 (from Greek): "and the sea **and all that are in them**" – Harmonization based on Revelation 10:6.

Revelation 7:10 (from Greek): "**who sits on the throne**" – Harmonization based on Revelation 5:13, etc.

Revelation 7:11 (from Greek): "the **four** living creatures" – Harmonization based on Revelation 5:8, 6:1, 14:3, etc.

---

[a] Translated from Oo.1.16.

[b] Interestingly, this harmonization is not present in Codex Sinaiticus. See p. 98.

Revelation 7:17 (from Greek): "the lamb **who is in the midst of the throne**" – Harmonization based on Revelation 5:6.

Revelation 8:5 (from Greek): "and lightnings **and an earthquake**" – Harmonization based on Revelation 12:5 [11:19].

Revelation 9:3 (from Greek): "**like the scorpions**" – Harmonization based on Revelation 9:5.

Revelation 9:14[15] (from Greek): "the four messengers **were released**" – Harmonization based on Revelation 9:13[14], which commands that these messengers should be released.

Revelation 9:18 (from Greek): "a third of men were killed, **by the fire and the smoke and the sulphur which came out from their mouths**" – Harmonization based on Revelation 9:16[17].

Revelation 9:21 (from Greek): "they did not repent **of their murders nor** of their sorceries" – Harmonization based on Revelation 21:8, 22:15.

Revelation 11:12 (from Greek): "a voice **from heaven**" – Harmonization based on Revelation 10:4, 14:2, etc.

Revelation 11:12 (from Greek): "come up **here**" – Harmonization based on Revelation 4:1.

Revelation 11:13b (from Greek): "were killed **in the earthquake**" – Harmonization based on Revelation 11:13a.

Revelation 13:4b[3b] (from Greek): "**deadly** wound" – Harmonization based on Revelation 13:4a[3a].

Revelation 13:13b[12b] (from Greek): "**deadly** wound" – Harmonization based on Revelation 13:4a[3a].[a]

Revelation 14:1 (from Greek): "on their **foreheads**" – Harmonization based on Revelation 7:3.

Revelation 14:11 (from Greek): "the **beast and its** image" – Harmonization based on Revelation 20:4.

Revelation 14:15 (from Greek): "**for the harvest of the earth is ripe**" – Harmonization based on Revelation 14:18.

Revelation 17:2 (from Greek): "the wine of her **fornication**" – Harmonization based on Revelation 14:8.

Revelation 17:4 (from Greek): "**of her fornication**" – Harmonization based on Revelation 14:8, 19:2.

Revelation 17:8 (from Greek): "**whose names were not written in the book of life from the foundation of the world**" – Harmonization based on Revelation 13:9[8].

Revelation 18:3 (from Greek): "the wine **of her fornication**" – Harmonization based on Revelation 14:8.

Revelation 18:15 (from Greek): "will stand afar off **because of the fear**" – Harmonization based on Revelation 18:10.

Revelation 18:18 (from Greek): "the smoke of her **burning**" – Harmonization based on Revelation 18:9.

Revelation 19:9 (from Greek): "**Write:** Blessed are those who" – Harmonization based on Revelation 14:13.

---

[a] Interestingly, this harmonization is not present in Codex Alexandrinus. See p. 91.

Revelation 20:4 (from Greek): "I saw... **the souls of**" – Harmonization based on Revelation 6:9.

Revelation 20:4 (from Greek): "because of the testimony of Jesus and **the word of God**"[a] – Harmonization based on Revelation 1:2 and 1:9, where the testimony of Yeshua and the word of Yahweh are mentioned together.

Revelation 20:4 (from Greek): "the mark on their forehead **or hand**" – Harmonization based on Revelation 13:17[16], 14:9.

Revelation 21:2 (from Greek): "new Jerusalem coming down from heaven **from God**" – Harmonization based on Revelation 3:12.

Revelation 21:8 (from Greek): "sorcerers **and idolaters**" – Harmonization based on Revelation 9:19-20[20-21], which mentions idol worship in a similar list of sins.

Revelation 21:9 (from Greek): "**seven** bowls" – Harmonization based on Revelation 15:7, 17:1.

Revelation 21:10 (from Greek): "Jerusalem coming down from heaven **from God**" – Harmonization based on Revelation 3:12.

Revelation 21:11 (from Greek): "jasper **as clear as crystal**" – Harmonization based on Revelation 22:1.

Revelation 21:18 (from Greek): "pure gold **like pure glass**" – Harmonization based on Revelation 21:21.

Revelation 21:27 (from Greek): "book of life **of the Lamb**" – Harmonization based on Revelation 13:9[8].

---

[a] See pp. 62-69 for a discussion on 'Yahweh' vs. 'Theos' (God).

Revelation 22:2 (from Greek): "**yielding its fruit every month**" – Harmonization based on Ezekiel 47:12, which explains that the trees growing beside the 'river of life' will produce fresh fruit each month.

Revelation 22:15 (from Greek): "murderers **and idolaters**" – Harmonization based on Revelation 9:19-20[20-21], which mentions idol worship in a similar list of sins.

Revelation 22:19 (from Greek): "words of the book **of this prophecy**" – Harmonization based on Revelation 22:7, 22:18.

Take note that Greek-to-Hebrew translations of Revelation cannot and did not reclaim the Hebrew readings in any of the passages shown above. There is no way to know – based on the Greek text – which phrases/words are additions and which were written in the original text. Therefore, all the harmonizing additions shown above are also found in Greek-to-Hebrew translations of Revelation.[a]

Based on the numerous examples shown above, it is clear that the Hebrew Revelation preserves the original uninterpreted text; while the Greek version of Revelation is an interpreted translation with numerous harmonizing additions, just like the Greek Septuagint translation of the Tanach.

Surprising agreements with ancient Greek manuscripts and papyri

So, how old is the Hebrew textual tradition of the Book of Revelation? Proponents of the Greek primacy of the Book of Revelation may argue that all known Hebrew manuscripts of Revelation are more than 1000 years younger than the oldest Greek

---

[a] See e.g. the translations by Franz Delitzsch; Salkinson/Ginsburg; Bible Society in Israel, etc.

fragments. However, in this section we will present clear evidence that this Hebrew version of Revelation can be traced back, at the very least, to the time of the earliest Greek papyrus fragments!

Agreements between this Hebrew version of Revelation and the oldest Greek manuscripts will be divided into two main sections:

1. Agreements with ancient Greek mss. which cannot be reclaimed from late Greek mss., and therefore show a direct connection between the Hebrew Revelation, and the oldest Greek mss.

2. Agreements which derive specifically from Hebrew influence in the oldest Greek mss., showing that the ancient Greek text of Revelation was influenced by Hebrew, and later partly standardized into better Greek.

Agreements that cannot be reclaimed from late Greek mss.

Scholars will often gauge the value of medieval manuscripts by comparing their text with that of the most ancient manuscripts and fragments of the applicable book. If any particular manuscript shows multiple agreements with ancient sources, against the popular texts of the day, the manuscript clearly preserves an ancient version of the text.[a]

---

[a] Ms. 1739 for example, is considered a Category I text in the Aland classification system, despite the fact that it was written in the 10th century. It is believed to be a copy of an accurate 4th century manuscript, based on agreements with ancient manuscripts and papyri fragments.
"Minuscule 1739... written in the tenth century... is one of the most important Greek New Testament manuscripts... Zuntz argues that... 1739 is a faithful witness to an old tradition also attested in P46 and 03." – George Gabel, *The Text of Hebrews in GA 1739 in Selected Other Greek Manuscripts and in Works*

Now, if a particular reading is shared by e.g. Papyrus no. 47[a] (P47), plus dozens of minuscules[b] and the Textus Receptus, it would prove nothing about the age of any particular text with the same reading, because the reading in question was well known throughout the Middle Ages.

On the other hand, if a specific reading is unattested in all known medieval manuscripts of Revelation, and only found in one of the most ancient and respected Greek manuscripts, as well as in the Hebrew Revelation, this agreement is significant. Neither the ancient papyrus fragments nor the oldest majuscule[c] manuscripts of Revelation were available to translators in the Middle Ages.[d]

We will begin with specific agreements between this Hebrew version of Revelation and the oldest and most acclaimed Greek

---

of Origen: Preliminary Quantitative Assessments, in *The New Testament in Antiquity and Byzantium*, De Gruyter, 2019, pp. 147-148.

[a] One of the oldest Greek fragments of the Book of Revelation.

[b] Greek minuscules are manuscripts written in lowercase letters, mostly later than the 9th century C.E.

[c] Also known as 'uncials' or 'uncial manuscripts.' Greek majuscules are manuscripts written in capital letters, mostly before the 9th century C.E.

[d] Oo.1.16 was copied in the 1700's, when neither the Chester Beatty Papyri, nor the Oxyrhynchus Papyri, nor the oldest Greek majuscule manuscripts were publicly available for study.
See e.g. "It was not until the early 1930s that the scholarly public would welcome the first discovery of extensive biblical papyri… the now famous Chester Beatty biblical papyri" – Peter Malik, *P. Beatty III (P47): The Codex, its Scribe, and its Text*, Brill, 2017, pp. 2-3.
The first volume of the first facsimile edition of Codex Ephraemi was published in 1843 as: *Codex Ephraemi Syri Rescriptus*, ed. Constantin Tischendorf.
The first volume of the first facsimile edition of Codex Sinaiticus was published in 1862 as: *Bibliorum Codex Sinaiticus Petropolitanus*, ed. Constantin Tischendorf.
The first facsimile of the New Testament books of Codex Alexandrinus was published in 1879 as: *Facsimile of the Codex Alexandrinus, New Testament and Clementine Epistles*, ed. E. Maunde Thompson.

manuscripts of the Book of Revelation – unique readings which are not shared by medieval Greek manuscripts.[a]

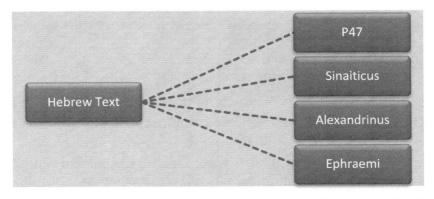

The Hebrew Revelation shares unique agreements with ancient Greek manuscripts – against later Greek, Latin and Aramaic versions.

Our first example is a unique agreement between the Hebrew Revelation and the esteemed Codex Alexandrinus from the fifth century C.E.:

Revelation 12:19[16]:

Oo.1.16: "המים שהשליך התנין"

= "**the waters** [b] which the dragon cast"

Alexandrinus: "το υδωρ ο εβαλλεν ο δρακοων"

= "**the water** which the dragon cast"

Other Greek mss.: "τον ποτομον ον εββαλεν ο δρακων"

= "**the river** which the dragon cast"

---

[a] Some examples discussed later do overlap with a few medieval manuscripts (out of hundreds), but we will note such instances below, one case at a time.
[b] Note that 'water' is always plural in Hebrew, but usually rendered as singular

It is astounding that the only known[a] Greek manuscript in the world to agree with the Hebrew Revelation is such an ancient one as the Alexandrinus – the oldest complete copy of Revelation which is highly regarded by scholars of the Greek New Testament.[b] Because this reading was not known in medieval Greek manuscripts, neither in the Peshitta nor in the Vulgate, we have clear evidence that this reading in the Hebrew Revelation is very ancient.[c]

The question whether the Hebrew Revelation was translated from the earliest Greek manuscripts, or whether the Greek was originally translated from Hebrew, will be addressed later. For now, it is important to understand that the above agreement between

---

in Greek. Compare e.g. Gen. 1:2, 1:6-7; Ex. 2:10, 4:9; Is. 1:22,30, etc. in the Hebrew Tanach vs. Greek LXX.

[a] Investigation based on NA28 [with variants from the Byzantine text and from 29 other important Greek mss. of Revelation] and the CNTTS apparatus [with data from 126 papyri (2nd–8th cent.), 47 majuscules (3rd–10th cent.), 165 minuscules (9th–15th cent.), some Latin witnesses, and three printed editions (MT SBL TR)]. Unique agreements were also checked against an even more comprehensive list of Greek manuscript transcripts of Revelation, available online via the INTF website (https://ntvmr.uni-uenster.de).
We have manually verified alleged agreements between the Papyri fragments and majuscule mss. with the Hebrew Revelation, using photos of the Greek mss. online. However, the minuscule mss. were not always available online, and readings for minuscules were often based on the above-mentioned sources.

[b] "Codex Alexandrinus [was] recognized since the nineteenth century as the best witness to the Greek text of Revelation... Sinaiticus certainly preserved an "old text," but... it was a secondary witness relative to Alexandrinus and Ephraemi for the book of Revelation." – Juan Hernández Jr., *The Greek Text of Revelation,* in *The Oxford Handbook of the Book of Revelation*, Oxford University Press, 2020, p. 346.

[c] Keep in mind that Oo.1.16 was copied in the 1700's, before Codex Alexandrinus was publicly available for study. A facsimile of the New Testament books of Codex Alexandrinus was first published in 1879 as: *Facsimile of the Codex Alexandrinus, New Testament and Clementine Epistles*, ed. E. Maunde Thompson.

Oo.1.16 and Codex Alexandrinus suggests that the text of the Hebrew Revelation can be traced back as far as the most acclaimed complete Greek manuscript of Revelation!

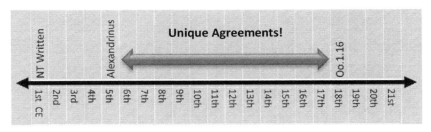

Unique agreements with ancient manuscripts show the antiquity of the Hebrew text of Revelation.

One example of agreement is obviously not enough for a firm conclusion, but below we will list more agreements between the Hebrew Revelation and ancient Greek majuscules and papyri, against the later, popular Byzantine Greek text and Textus Receptus:

Revelation 4:11:

<u>Oo.1.16</u>: "וע"י רצונך נעשה הכל"

= "and by your will everything **was made**" (or "and by your will everything **existed**")

<u>Alexandrinus</u> "και δια θεληματι σου ησαν"

= "and by your will they[a] **existed**"

---

[a] The omission of the second occurrence of 'everything' in Rev. 4:11 in Greek is not a real variant vs. the Hebrew, but simply due to a translational technique. The Hebrew Bible will often repeat the word "כל" (every/all/everything) two or more times in close proximity (e.g. in two parallel phrases or two sub-sections of a phrase), while the Greek LXX often eliminates the 'redundant' second occurrence. Compare e.g. the following verses in the Hebrew Tanach vs. Greek LXX: Gen. 7:19, Gen. 23:17, Gen. 37:35; Ex. 24:3a, 35:24a, 36:4; Lev. 20:22, 23:38; Num. 3:36, 18:29a, 30:15, 31:10; Deu. 4:19b; Josh. 11:12; Jud. 7:18; 1 Sam. 11:2; 1 Kin. 12:20, 19:1; Is. 53:6; Ezek. 23:23b, 38:4b.

<u>Other Greek mss.</u>: "και δια το θελημα σου ησαν[a] και εκτισθησαν"

= "and by your will they **existed and were created**"

The only known Greek manuscript which agrees with the Hebrew Revelation, by **not** adding the phrase "and were created," is the Codex Alexandrinus (from the 5th century C.E.). Take note that the Greek rendering of "they were/existed" in Codex Alexandrinus is not a real variant compared to the Hebrew, it is simply a translational interpretation (though inappropriate for this context): The Hebrew word "עשה" in the Niphal conjugation (to be made) was used in post-exilic Hebrew as a synonym of "היה" (to be/become/exist), as also seen in the Hebrew Gospels and Hebrew Revelation.[b]

We can now begin to answer our important question: Why does the Hebrew Revelation contain important and unique agreements with the ancient Greek manuscripts? Was the Greek text translated from the Hebrew, or was the Hebrew text translated from the ancient Greek text?

In this particular case, it is very clear that the Greek text stems from the Hebrew: The Hebrew reading "נעשה", as preserved in Oo.1.16, was misinterpreted by the Greek translator(s), based on the popular use of "עשה" (in the Niphal) as synonym of "היה" in the Hebrew

---

[a] The Byzantine M[A] reads "εισιν" (exist/are) for "ησαν" (existed/were).

[b] "היה" and "עשה" (in the Niphal) are even occasionally used synonymously in the Tanach, e.g. Eccl. 1:9, though not very often. This use is mentioned in Clines Concise Dictionary of Classical Hebrew and in Jastrow's Hebrew and Aramaic Dictionary (note that "be," "become" and "happen/occur" are all possible meanings of "היה" which can overlap with "עשה"). Such occurrences of "עשה" can be seen in the Hebrew Gospels and Revelation, e.g. Rev. 12:12[7]; Mat. 9:27; Luke 3:21; Mark 1:9; John 6:16, etc.

N.T. manuscripts.[a] Most probably, the initial Greek translation "they were/existed" (as preserved in Codex Alexandrinus) seemed ambiguous to later readers/copyists, and thus the subsequent explanation "and were created" was added, and perpetuated in all other surviving Greek manuscripts.

On the other hand, translations of the Greek Revelation into Biblical or Modern Hebrew do not employ "עשה" in the Niphal conjugation to translate the Greek word "ησαν," but rather various forms of the root "היה".[b] Therefore, the chance that the Hebrew reading "נעשה" derived from the Greek version is extremely small.

---

[a] In Rev. 12:12[7], "נעשה" (was made) was correctly translated into Greek as "ἐγένετο" (was/happened). Such occurrences of "עשה" can also be seen in the Hebrew Gospels, e.g. Mat. 9:27; Luke 3:21; Mark 1:9; John 6:16, etc. Similar examples may be found in the Mishnah, e.g. in Terumot 6:6, some versions (e.g. Kaufman, Munich) read "להעשות" while others (e.g. Parma, Eshkol) read "להיות". See also Terumot 6:1; Nedarim 9:10; Negaim 7:2, etc.

[b] Compare below, multiple Hebrew translations from Greek (and/or Latin and Syriac etc.) versus Oo.1.16 – the only Hebrew version which uses "נעשה":

	And were created	They were made / existed
Oo.1.16		נעשה
Peshitta	ܐܬܒܪܝ̈,	ܗܘ̈,
Neof. 33	ויהיו נבראים	היו
BnF Hebr. 131	ונבראו	היו
Freiburg 314	ונבראו	יהיו
Delitzsch	וְנִבְרָאוּ	הָיוּ
Ginsburg	וְנִבְרָאוּ	נִהְיוּ
Modern	וְנִבְרָאוּ	הָיוּ

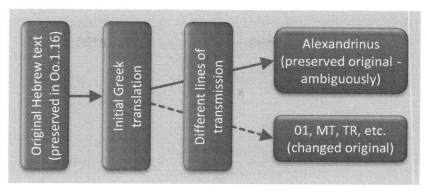

The initial, cryptic translation "they existed" (as preserved in Codex Alexandrinus) probably did not make sense to later Greek readers/copyists, and thus the gloss "and were created" was added and perpetuated in nearly all Greek manuscripts.

Further unique[a] agreements between Oo.1.16 and the Alexandrinus are:

Revelation 5:10, "to our God" omitted.

Revelation 13:13b[12b], "deadly" omitted.

Revelation 21:6, "fountain of" omitted.

The reason why many of these variants show a shorter text in the old Greek mss., is that Greek scribes (as well as translators) often made harmonizing additions which expanded the Greek text over time. (See pp. 69-83 for more information about harmonizing additions.)

Let us now consider some unique agreements between the Hebrew Revelation and codex Sinaiticus. Although Sinaiticus is often viewed

---

[a] We have specifically selected agreements which are not known in medieval Greek manuscripts, and thus show a direct connection between the oldest Greek manuscripts and the Hebrew text of Revelation.

as a secondary source for Revelation, it is nevertheless agreed that it preserves an ancient version of the text.[a]

Revelation 6:14:

Oo.1.16: "וכל ההרים וגבעות"

= "and all the mountains and **hills**"

Sinaiticus: "και παν ορος και βουνος"

= "and every mountain and **hill**"

Other Greek mss.: "και παν ορος και νησος"

= "and every mountain and **island**"

It is significant that the only known Greek manuscript to agree with this reading in the Hebrew Revelation is the Codex Sinaiticus.[b]

It is also important to take note that, in this instance, the Hebrew Revelation agrees with the Sinaiticus against the Alexandrinus. This is significant because it shows that the Hebrew Revelation is not simply a translation from the Alexandrinus, nor from any other known Greek manuscript for that matter.

---

[a] "Sinaiticus certainly preserved an "old text," but... it was a secondary witness relative to Alexandrinus and Ephraemi for the book of Revelation." – Juan Hernández Jr., *The Greek Text of Revelation,* in *The Oxford Handbook of the Book of Revelation*, Oxford University Press, 2020, p. 346.
Although the Sinaiticus is generally dated to the 4th century C.E., some have suggested the 5th century instead. Others have even argued that the Sinaiticus manuscript may be a 19th century copy, partly based on ancient Greek manuscripts available at Mt. Athos. See e.g. W. R. Cooper, *The Forging of Codex Sinaiticus*, Creation Science Movement, 2016.
[b] Mss. 367 and 2495 include both "island" and "hill," only Sinaiticus reads "hill" instead of "island."

Rather, various ancient Greek manuscripts preserve a variety of unique agreements with the Hebrew Revelation, often in different places. These peculiarities were lost over time as the Greek text was smoothed out and standardized.

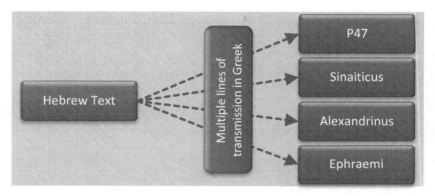

The oldest surviving Greek manuscripts and fragments show unique agreements with the Hebrew Revelation.

Further unique agreements between the Hebrew Revelation and the Sinaiticus are as follows:

Revelation 2:16[17], second occurrence of the verb "give" is gapped (omitted): Oo.1.16, Sinaiticus.

Revelation 9:10a[11a], "their king" (not "king **over** them"): Oo.1.16, Sinaiticus.

Revelation 10:3, "seven **voices**"[a] (not "seven **thunders**"): Oo.1.16, Sinaiticus.[b]

---

[a] In Hebrew, "voice" is a synonym of "thunder." See e.g. Ex. 9:29, 19:16, 20:18, etc.

[b] In some of the examples listed here, a corrector/proofreader altered the original reading of the Sinaiticus to bring it into harmony with other Greek manuscripts. However, in each of the listed examples the original reading of the Sinaiticus is still clearly visible and evident.

Revelation 12:5[11:19], "there **was**" (not "**were**"): Oo.1.16, Sinaiticus.

Revelation 17:2, "committed fornication" written as two separate words; "they did" (verb) and "fornication" (noun): Oo.1.16, Sinaiticus. Other versions use a verb only which means "to fornicate."

Revelation 19:13, "sprinkled upon/around with blood": Oo.1.16, Sinaiticus.[a]

Revelation 20:14, "**And** this is the second death": Oo.1.16, Sinaiticus.

We will now show that the Hebrew Revelation may indeed be traced back further than Codex Alexandrinus and Codex Sinaiticus, to Papyrus no. 47 from the third century C.E! P47 is the oldest known surviving copy for large parts of the Book of Revelation.

In Revelation15:4, the Hebrew version uses a singular verb with a plural subject:

---

[a] Sinaiticus uses a compound verb "περιρεραμμενον" for "sprinkled upon/around." According the Metzger's Textual Commentary, this reading is also confirmed by Irenaeus. Take note that multiple other manuscripts also employed a Greek verb meaning 'sprinkled' (instead of 'dipped'), but without the prefixed preposition "περι." The same is true for the Peshitta version. The Hebrew Revelation uses a passive verb plus preposition "על". The Septuagint Greek translation also shows examples of combining a Hebrew verb plus "על" into a compound Greek verb beginning with "περι," e.g. Num. 8:7 "הִזֵּה עֲלֵיהֶם" = "περιρρανεῖς αὐτούς." Thus, the Greek reading found in the Sinaiticus could be a direct translation of the Hebrew reading preserved in Oo.1.16.

Revelation 15:4:

Oo.1.16: "כי משפטיך נתגלה"

= "for your judgments **is** revealed" [a]

Although this is not standard in Hebrew, it is possible to use a singular passive verb with a plural subject, even in the Tanach.[b] This time, the only Greek manuscript which has a singular verb in this very passage is Papyrus 47!

Revelation 15:4:

P47: "οτι τα δικαιωματα σου εφανερωθη"

= "for your righteous judgments **is** revealed"

Despite the fact that Greek often uses a singular verb with a neuter plural subject,[c] in this particular case all but one of the surviving Greek mss. employ a plural verb, most likely to emphasize the plurality of Yahweh's judgments described in Revelation.[d]

---

[a] This phrase is rendered more literally here than in the main translation, to show the details of the Hebrew text.

[b] See e.g. Ex. 13:7; Num. 28:17; 2 Sam. 21:10; Jer. 6:7b, 46:15, 48:41 (x2); Ezek. 26:2, 32:25d, 45:21; Mic. 6:16; Ps. 87:3; Job 21:34, 22:9b, 42:15; Dan. 9:24, 9:26d; 1 Chr. 26:6.

[c] "Greek often uses a singular verb when the subject is neuter plural." – William D. Mounce, *Basics of Biblical Greek Grammar*, Zondervan, 2nd ed., 2003, p. 68.

[d] "When a subject is neuter plural, the verb is normally singular... The plural form of the verb may, however, be used to emphasize that the subject consists of various individual members." – Evert Van Emde Boas et al., *Cambridge Grammar of Classical Greek*, Cambridge University Press, 2019, p. 322.

It is very significant that the only [a] known Greek manuscript which agrees with the Hebrew singular verb in Revelation 15:4, is Papyrus 47, the oldest remaining Greek fragment which preserves this verse!

In Revelation 14:12 there is an intriguing agreement in word order between Oo.1.16, P47 and the Peshitta:

Revelation 14:12:

Oo.1.16: "בכאן יש תקוה מקדושים"

= "Here **is** *the* hope of *the* set-apart ones"

P47: "ωδε εστιν η υπομονη των αγιων"

= "Here **is** the hope of the holy ones"

Although the difference is lost in English translations, all other known Greek mss. of Revelation place the Greek verb "εστιν" as the last word in the phrase.

Revelation 14:12:

Other Greek mss.: "ωδε η υπομονη των αγιων εστιν"

= "Here the hope of the holy ones **is**"

Why would the Hebrew Revelation show such agreements with P47? This is actually a surprising example, because very often in Hebrew, the verb 'to be' is not written, but implied by context. But in this particular case it is indicated in the Hebrew text as "יש"

---

[a] Neither can this reading with a plural noun and singular verb be obtained from the Peshitta nor from the Vulgate. The SEDRA 3 Peshitta has a very different syntax (*you are righteous*), while other Syriac manuscripts and the Vulgate use a plural verb. The Salkinson/Ginsburg translation uses a singular noun and singular verb (*your righteousness is revealed*).

(*yesh*), and the oldest surviving Greek papyrus manuscript containing this verse has the verb in the same place as the Hebrew!

Revelation 12:5[11:19] shares an interesting agreement with Papyrus 115, which dates from the third century C.E. The Hebrew text of Oo.1.16 and the Greek text of P115 place the word "voices" (קולות/φοναι) first in the list of synonyms for 'thunder,' while nearly all[a] other Greek mss. place it as the second word in the list.[b]

Furthermore, the Hebrew Revelation also shows agreements with the Ephraemi Codex which dates to the sixth century C.E.:[c]

Revelation 14:4:

Oo.1.16: "המה נקנים לבכורת הֿ והשה"

= "they are bought as first fruits of Yahweh and the Lamb"

Ephraemi: "ουτοι ηγορασθησαν απαρχη τω θεω και τω αρνιω"

= "they are bought as firstfruits for God and the Lamb"

Other Greek mss.: "ουτοι ηγορασθησαν απω των ανθρωπων απαρχη τω θεω και τω αρνιω"

= "they are bought **from among men** as firstfruits for God and the Lamb"

---

[a] Only one other known manuscript (1854) places "voices" first.
[b] Only the first letter of the word "φονη" is recognizable in the Papyrus fragment, and the following two words are unfortunately lost. Thus, it is not known whether Papyrus 115 had all three words in the same order as the Hebrew, or only the first one.
[c] "Together with Codex Alexandrinus, Codex Ephraemi would represent one of the two best witnesses for the text of Revelation." – Juan Hernández Jr., *The Greek Text of Revelation,* in *The Oxford Handbook of the Book of Revelation*, Oxford University Press, 2020, p. 346.

In the above verse, most Greek manuscripts add an explanation to remind readers that these "firstfruits" are not literal fruit picked from plants or trees, but they are firstfruits of humans. This explanatory addition is not found in the Hebrew Revelation, and the only agreeing Greek manuscript is the Codex Ephraemi,[a] written more than a thousand years prior to the Oo.1.16 copy of the Hebrew Revelation. The only logical conclusion is that the Hebrew Revelation indeed preserves an ancient text.

The following agreements with ancient Greek manuscripts are also intriguing. These readings in the Hebrew Revelation are shared with several sources, against the Textus Receptus and Byzantine MT:

Revelation 2:1, "right hand" spelled out with two words ("δεξια" vs. "δεξια... χειρι"): Oo.1.16, Sinaiticus,[b] 250, 1828, etc.[c]

Revelation 2:12[13], "in which / wherein" (εν αις) omitted: Oo.1.16, Alexandrinus, Ephraemi, 2080, 2053, some editions of the Vulgate, Peshitta.

Revelation 3:7, "who shuts" (not "**and** who shuts"): Oo.1.16, Alexandrinus, 2080, some editions of the Vulgate.

Revelation 5:3, "and under the earth" omitted: Oo.1.16, Sinaiticus, 218, 1854, 2344, etc.

---

[a] According to NA 28, Beatus of Liébana also confirms this reading in his commentary on the Book of Revelation.

[b] In some of the examples listed here, a corrector/proofreader altered the original reading of the Sinaiticus to bring it into harmony with other Greek manuscripts. However, in each of the listed examples the original reading of the Sinaiticus is still clearly visible.

[c] Not all supporting manuscript witnesses are indicated in this list of agreements. Although these readings are found in some medieval mss., they differ from the Textus Receptus and the Byzantine Majority Text, and trace back to the oldest surviving Greek manuscripts.

Revelation 6:1, "say(ing)" (plural verb): Oo.1.16, Sinaiticus, 620, 2053.

Revelation 6:4, "was given" (not "was given **to him**"): Oo.1.16, Alexandrinus, Sinaiticus Corrector,[a] 2344, 2495.

Revelation 9:7, "like" (masculine):[b] Oo.1.16, Sinaiticus, 792, 2026, etc. (Locusts are masculine in Hebrew, but feminine in Greek.)

Revelation 9:10b[11b], "whose name / and his name"[c] (not simply "his name"): Oo.1.16, P47, Sinaiticus, 2344.

Revelation 9:11[12], "The" omitted ("η ουαι" vs. "ουαι"): Oo.1.16, P47, Sinaiticus, 792, 2053, Vulgate, Peshitta.

Revelation 13:8[7], "peoples" (plural): Oo.1.16, Ephraemi, Peshitta.

Revelation 14:13, "that" (not "**in order** that" – "ινα" vs. "οτι"): Oo.1.16, P47, 2019, 2429, and possibly Peshitta.

Revelation 15:2, a preposition (עם/εκ) is employed before "animal/beast," but the preposition is gapped (not repeated) before "it's image": Oo.1.16, P47, Sinaiticus, 104, 620.

Revelation 16:6a, "blood" (plural): Oo.1.16, Sinaiticus, 620, 2019. This agreement is significant, because the plural form

---

[a] Noted as א[2] in NA28 and 01c in the CNTTS apparatus.

[b] In Greek the gender is included in the adjective ("ομοια" vs. "ομοιοι"); but in Hebrew the gender is indicated by the pronoun accompanying the preposition ("המה כמו").

[c] Hebrew often uses literally "and his/her name" for "whose name." See e.g. Gen. 22:24, 25:1; Josh. 2:1; Judg. 13:2; Ruth 2:1; 1 Sam. 9:1; 2 Sam. 3:7, etc.

of "blood" is often used in the Hebrew Tanach for "bloodshed" or "shed blood," or "bloodguilt."[a]

Revelation 17:6, "testimony(ies)"[b] (not martyrs/witnesses): Oo.1.16, Alexandrinus, 2350.

Revelation 17:11, "**this** is **the** eighth" (not "**and he** is **an** eighth"): Oo.1.16, Sinaiticus, 452, 506.

Revelation 17:17, "and to do one purpose" omitted: Oo.1.16, Alexandrinus, 2329, Vulgate.

Revelation 18:9, "and lived luxuriously with her" omitted: Oo.1.16, Sinaiticus,[c] 456.

Revelation 20:9, "from God" omitted: Oo.1.16, Alexandrinus, 2845, some Vulgate mss. and some ancient commentaries. Most Greek mss. add an explanation for the Hebrew expression "heavens" which was sometimes used as a euphemism for "Elohim."

Revelation 20:13, "and the death and She'ol **gave (singular)** the dead ones": Oo.1.16, Alexandrinus, 82, 1773, etc. The Hebrew text uses a singular verb, which indicates that "death" and "She'ol" are synonymous, not two separate places from which the dead are raised for judgment.

---

[a] See e.g. Gen. 4:10-11; Ex. 22:1-2; 1 Sam. 25:26; 2 Sam. 16:7, etc.

[b] The Greek Septuagint commonly translated the singular form of "עדות" with a plural form of "μαρτυριον" – see Ex. 25:16, 25:21, 30:6, 40:20, Lev. 16:13; Ps. 119:88; 2 Chr. 23:11. Thus, the Alexandrinus' reading "μαρτυριων" is equivalent to the Hebrew reading "עדות" in terms of normal Greek translational techniques.

[c] According to NA28, this reading is also confirmed by Beatus of Liébana.

Revelation 21:3, "from the **throne**" (not "heaven"): Oo.1.16, Alexandrinus, Sinaiticus, Vulgate.

Revelation 21:21, "pearls/jewels" (not **twelve** pearls"): Oo.1.16, Sinaiticus, 2377.[a]

So firstly, it is clear that the text of the Hebrew Revelation traces back to the time of the earliest surviving Greek fragments and manuscripts.

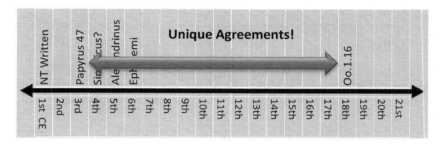

Unique agreements between the Hebrew Revelation and various ancient Greek manuscripts clearly show the antiquity of the Hebrew version.

Coincidence could perhaps account for one or two of the above agreements, but certainly not for all of them. The Hebrew version of Revelation cannot, in any way, derive from the medieval Greek manuscripts, neither from the printed Textus Receptus, nor from any translation which was based on the medieval or late Greek textual tradition.

Secondly, the Hebrew Revelation cannot derive from any particular ancient Greek manuscript, because it shares unique and exclusive agreements with P47, Sinaiticus, Alexandrinus, Ephraemi, etc. In other words, not all the agreements listed above can be found in one single manuscript. Rather, these agreements are scattered throughout various ancient copies. Each of these early Greek

---

[a] In both these Greek mss., "ιβ" was added above the main text as an apparent correction, to bring the text into harmony with other mss.

manuscripts contains a text which was in the process of being smoothed out, and various adjustments were made in different instances in the various manuscripts. Besides, these ancient Greek manuscripts were not available for study and translation in the Middle Ages.[a]

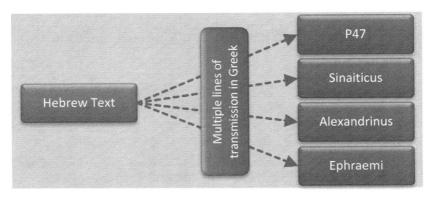

Each of these ancient Greek manuscripts preserved a certain subset of unique readings which are otherwise only found in the Hebrew version.

And finally, the Hebrew Revelation cannot be a translation from the Latin Vulgate nor from the Peshitta, as numerous of the above-discussed readings are not found in either of the two.

---

[a] Oo.1.16 was copied in the 1700's, when neither the Chester Beatty Papyri, nor the Oxyrhynchus Papyri, nor the oldest Greek Majuscule Manuscripts were publicly available for study.
See e.g. "It was not until the early 1930s that the scholarly public would welcome the first discovery of extensive biblical papyri… the now famous Chester Beatty biblical papyri" – Peter Malik, *P. Beatty III (P47): The Codex, its Scribe, and its Text*, Brill, 2017, pp. 2-3.
The first volume of the first facsimile edition of Codex Ephraemi was published in 1843 as: *Codex Ephraemi Syri Rescriptus*, ed. Constantin Tischendorf.
The first volume of the first facsimile edition of Codex Sinaiticus was published in 1862 as: *Bibliorum Codex Sinaiticus Petropolitanus*, ed. Constantin Tischendorf.
The first facsimile of the New Testament books of Codex Alexandrinus was published in 1879 as: *Facsimile of the Codex Alexandrinus, New Testament and Clementine Epistles*, ed. E. Maunde Thompson.

Thus, the origin of the Hebrew version of Revelation has to predate all known Greek manuscripts of Revelation, as even the most ancient Greek mss. all show different signs of diverging from the Hebrew.

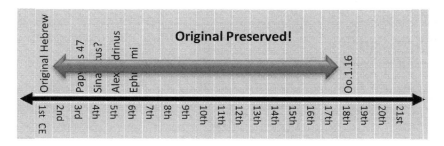

The Hebrew textual tradition had to precede the earliest Greek copies, which show many indications of partly preserving the Hebrew version, and partly diverging from the Hebrew. The Hebrew version cannot be a compilation of the earliest Greek manuscripts, because (i) these ancient Greek manuscripts were not available for study and translation until the 19th and 20th centuries; and (ii) the Hebrew version preserves multiple features of authenticity (pp. 21-83) which cannot be reclaimed from any known Greek manuscripts.

Agreements due to Hebrew influence in old Greek mss.

We will now turn our attention to agreements which show explicit Hebrew influence[a] in the ancient Greek manuscripts. This will confirm the above conclusion that the Greek version was translated from Hebrew.

Take note that Hebrew and Aramaic grammar are very similar, and therefore, many of the following readings will overlap with the Peshitta. However, a few of these grammatical examples do not overlap. Also keep in mind that in many of the examples discussed

---

[a] Although the Greek Revelation as a whole abounds with Hebrew influence (see footnotes on pp. 17-18), we will now discuss specific examples of Hebrew influence in the early Greek mss. which were lost in most medieval Greek mss.

in the previous section, the Hebrew Revelation differed from the Peshitta. Therefore, the Peshitta cannot possibly be the source for the following agreements.[a]

Although some of these Hebrew readings can also be reclaimed from the Greek simply by the rules of Hebrew grammar, these examples do show direct influence of the Hebrew language in the oldest Greek manuscripts.

Our first example is from Revelation 13:7a[6a]:

Oo.1.16: "ופתח את פיו לחרף"

= "So he opened his mouth **to blaspheme**"

P47: "και ηνοιξεν το στομα αυτου βλασφημησαι"

= "And he opened his mouth **to blaspheme**"

Other Greek mss.: "και ηνοιξεν το στομα αυτου εις βλασφημιας"

= "And he opened his mouth **in blasphemies**"

The Hebrew use of the infinitive has been reclaimed by e.g. Delitzsch,[b] but the point is that the Hebrew expression is preserved in the most ancient Greek copy of the verse, and smoothed out in all other known Greek copies later than P47. The infinitive form "βλασφημησαι" is used twice in this verse in P47, and it is possible

---

[a] The readings which do overlap with the Peshitta could be due to several possible reasons: 1. Requirements of Aramaic (Syriac) and Hebrew grammar overlap; 2. The Syriac version was influenced by the Hebrew Revelation; 3. The Syriac version was influenced by ancient Greek mss., which contained more Hebrew influence than the later medieval Greek mss.

[b] Also overlaps with the Peshitta for grammatical reasons. However, the Peshitta cannot be seen as the source for these agreements, because some of the grammatical examples and most of the general examples listed in this section do not overlap with the Peshitta.

that the standard Greek text had the first occurrence altered to avoid monotony.

Our next example is found in Revelation 12:13[8]:

Oo.1.16: "וגם לא נמצא... את מקומם בשמים"

= "neither was **their place** found in the heavens"[a]

P47: "ουδε τοπος αυτων ευρεθη εν τω ουρανω"

= "neither was **their place** found in the heaven"

Other Greek mss.: "ουδε τοπος ευρεθη αυτων... εν τω ουρανω"

= "neither was **a place** found **for them** in the heaven"

Most Greek manuscripts differ from the Hebrew Revelation in word order, by placing the verb "found" between "a place" and "their/for them." Although Hebrew translations from the Greek have reclaimed this difference based on Hebrew grammar,[b] and although the meaning could be the same in Greek regardless of word order, it is amazing to see that the Hebrew word order is preserved in the oldest surviving Greek copy[c] of Revelation 12:8!

Another good example is found in Revelation 18:22[23]:

Oo.1.16: "קול חתן וקול כלה"

---

[a] Note that 'heaven' is always plural in Hebrew, but usually rendered as singular in Greek. Compare e.g. Gen. 1:1, 1:8-9; Ex. 9:8,10; Is. 1:2, 13:5,10; Ps. 8:9, 11:4(10:4), etc. in the Hebrew Tanach vs. Greek LXX.

[b] See e.g. the translation of Franz Delitzsch.

[c] This reading is also found in e.g. mss. 1611, 2037, and some Syriac mss., but the point is that this reading traces back to the oldest surviving Greek copy.

= "*the* voice of a bridegroom and *the* **voice** of a bride"

Ephraemi: "φωνη νυμφιου και φονη νυμφης"

= "*the* voice of a bridegroom and *the* **voice** of a bride"

Other Greek mss.: "φωνη νυμφιου και νυμφης"

= "*the* voice of a bridegroom and of a bride"

This Hebrew-based reading is only found in a handful of Greek mss.,[a] while the greatest majority of Greek mss. omit the second occurrence of "voice."[b] Again, even the translations of Franz Delitzsch and others repeat the word "voice" before "bride," because that is standard in Hebrew grammar as also seen in the Tanach, e.g.:

Jeremiah 7:34:

Masoretic Text: "קוֹל חָתָן וְקוֹל כַּלָּה"

= "*the* voice of a bridegroom and *the* **voice** of a bride"

Thus, we have clear evidence that this reading in the Ephraemi Codex was influenced by Hebrew grammar, and consequently the text was smoothed out to match the style of Greek grammar, which prefers not to repeat the same word too often in close proximity.[c]

---

[a] E.g. Codex Ephraemi, 93, 1872, 2329.

[b] The Peshitta agrees with Oo.1.16 in this example, while the Latin Vulgate follows the standard Greek.

[c] The Greek language often shows gapping when the context is clear, and repeating a word would be redundant, yet Greek seeks to eliminate gapping when the meaning would be ambiguous. Conversely, the Hebrew Bible may repeat the same word over and over for emphasis and wordplay, but it may also regularly show gapping, even in ambiguous contexts. The basic difference is that Hebrew is very flexible with regards to gapping vs. repetition, while

A more complex agreement with P47 is found in Revelation 16:5:

Oo.1.16:

"הֹ הצדיק ההיה והוה וקדוש אתה שנתת זאת המשפט"

= "Yahweh the Righteous, who was and is **and qadosh**[a] are you that you gave this judgment!"[b]

The Hebrew Bible uses the 'Waw' conjunction[c] so often that it is often omitted in English translations for stylistic reasons,[d] and in some situations it is indeed close to impossible to translate.[e] There are even places where the Waw conjunction was deemed superfluous (or confusing), and was omitted in public reading of the Hebrew Bible![f] As in this example in Revelation 16, the text must at times be understood as if the Waw has no effect on the meaning of the sentence.

Amazingly, the unusual syntax of the Hebrew Revelation highlighted above, is again attested in P47 – the oldest known copy of Revelation 16:5![g]

Greek translations tend to smooth out or standardize anything extreme or unusual in the Hebrew Bible.

[a] Or "holy" – lit. "set-apart."

[b] This verse is rendered more literally here than in the main translation, to show the details of the Hebrew text.

[c] The 'Waw' conjunction means "and," "also," "but," "or," "so," "then," etc. For a discussion on the original pronunciation of the Hebrew letter Waw/Vav, see HebrewGospels.com/yhwh/video-15.

[d] For example, compare the Hebrew text with the ESV in Gen. 1:2, 1:10, 1:12, 2:9, 2:10, 2:13, 2:15, 3:1, 3:11, 3:14, 3:15, 3:18, 3:20, 3:24, etc.

[e] See e.g. Gen. 17:14; Ex. 12:44; 1 Sam. 25:27; 2 Sam. 14:10, 15:34; Jer. 6:19, 33:24. Compare *Gesenius' Hebrew Grammar: Second English Edition*, Clarendon Press, 1910, p. 458.

[f] See e.g. 2 Kin. 16:17, Jer. 4:5, 5:24; Neh. 9:17.

[g] This reading is found in roughly ten Greek mss. (out of hundreds), e.g. 911,

<u>P47</u>: "δικαιος ει ο ων και ος ην και οσιος οτι ταυτα εκρινας"

= "Just are you, who is and who was **and holy** that you judged thus"[a]

The structure of the sentence, as preserved by P47, is possible in Hebrew,[b] but unintelligible in Greek.[c] Most Greek manuscripts later than P47 contain a linguistically smoothed-out text, and there are even different ways in which the text was emended:

1. The conjunction "and" was omitted for easier understanding of the text:

<u>Acclaimed Greek manuscripts of Revelation</u>:[d] "δικαιος ει ο ων και ο ην οσιος οτι ταυτα εκρινας"

= "Just are you, who is and who was – **Holy One** – that you judged thus"[e]

2. The conjunction was omitted and a definite article added:

2028, 2057, etc., but the point is that this reading traces back to the oldest surviving copy.

[a] Lit. "these *things*."

[b] P47 is not too difficult to understand in terms of Hebrew grammar: "You – who was and is – are (i) just and (ii) holy, that you gave this judgment." It is not easy to understand P47 in terms of Greek grammar (see next footnote). See also discussion on Peshitta in footnote below.

[c] "...ὅσιος (anarthrous) cannot be taken as a predicate after ὁ ὢν καὶ ὁ ἦν, a procedure which the usage of the Apocalypse forbids, and to treat it as in apposition with δίκαιος creates an intolerable harshness." – Henry Barclay Swete, *The Apocalypse of St. John*, 2nd. ed., Macmillan, 1907, p. 199.

[d] Alexandrian Codex, Ephraemi Codex, etc. Similarly, the Latin Vulgate also omits the conjunction "and."

[e] Lit. "these *things*."

<u>NA 28 (and most Greek manuscripts)</u>:[a] "δίκαιος εἶ, ὁ ὢν καὶ ὁ ἦν, ὁ ὅσιος, ὅτι ταῦτα ἔκρινας"[b]

= "Just are you, who is and who was – **o Holy One** – that you judged thus"

3. In some Greek manuscripts the conjunction was retained, but they decided that the word for "holy" should at least be preceded by a definite article[c] (functioning as a relative particle):[d]

<u>Greek Textus Receptus</u>:[e] "δίκαιος, κύριε, εἶ, ὁ ὢν καὶ ὁ ἦν, καὶ ὁ ὅσιος, ὅτι ταῦτα ἔκρινας"

---

[a] Mss. 01, 051, 35, 254, 632, 1503, Byzantine Majority Text, etc.

[b] Lit. "these *things*."

[c] The Peshitta version should also be discussed at this point. The Peshitta reads "ܘܚܣܝܐ" (and the holy), literally the same as the Greek Textus Receptus (καὶ ὁ ὅσιος). On the other hand, if P47 were translated into Peshitta Aramaic (Syriac), it would also yield the same spelling for this word (ܘܚܣܝܐ), due to Syriac grammar requirements, regardless whether the Greek had a definite article or not. Some might suggest that the Peshitta thus also agrees with P47, but that cannot be proven, because in Syriac there would be no difference between "και ο οσιος" (TR) and "και οσιος" (P47), both would yield "ܘܚܣܝܐ" (determinate/definite). In Hebrew, unlike Syriac, the applicable word can be spelled without the definite article ("וקדוש" vs. "והקדוש"). Although part of the Hebrew reading of Oo.1.16 (וקדוש) can incidentally be reclaimed from the Peshitta, we have already seen multiple other examples where the Hebrew Revelation cannot possibly derive from the Peshitta. Finally, the Peshitta cannot be the basis for P47, because the Greek translator would obviously have retained the definite article found in the Peshitta for easier Greek grammar, rather than removing it to create an unintelligible Greek translation.

[d] Hebrew and Greek often use the definite article instead of a relative particle, as can be seen in this verse (Rev. 16:5): "ὁ ὢν" = "the one who is" or "who is."

[e] Stephanus' Textus Receptus (1550), Oxford Textus Receptus (1873), ms. 1773, etc.

= "Just are you, o Lord, who is and who was **and who is holy**, that you judged thus"[a]

Below is a diagram which shows the probable development of this reading in Revelation 16:5:

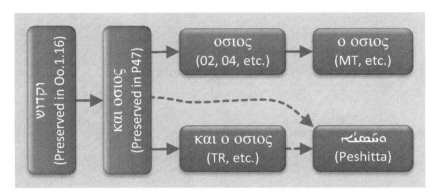

The evidence indicates that the Hebrew reading was literally translated into Greek, then smoothed out over time to accommodate easier understanding of the Greek text. Note that the arrows (lines of transmission) do not indicate that e.g. the Alexandrinus manuscript (02) was copied from P47, but rather that the **reading** found in 02 derived from the **reading** preserved by P47, etc.

Further examples where ancient Greek mss. agree with the Hebrew Revelation by following typical Hebrew grammar, are:[b]

Revelation 3:8, "your works" written with Hebrew word order ("τα εργα σου" not "σου τα εργα"): Oo.1.16, Sinaiticus, 2429, Vulgate.

Revelation 7:3, "**and** the sea" (not "**nor** the sea"; "και" not "μητε"): Oo.1.16, Alexandrinus, 2080, 2351.

---

[a] Lit. "these *things*."

[b] These examples have been reclaimed by Hebrew translations from Greek, and some are also found in the Peshitta Aramaic and/or some Latin mss. We have not listed all agreeing witnesses in each of the following examples, because the point is simply that the earliest Greek mss. show influence from Hebrew grammar. These readings are not shared with the Textus Receptus nor with the Byzantine Majority Text.

Revelation 9:4, "they/them" (masculine): Oo.1.16, Sinaiticus, 046, 424, 2329, Peshitta, etc. (Locusts are masculine in Hebrew, but feminine in Greek.)

Revelation 9:17[18], "was killed" (singular verb): Oo.1.16, P47, 254, 2845, etc.

Revelation 14:2b, "like the sound of" (vs. "like"): Oo.1.16, P47, 2053, some Latin mss.

Revelation 19:5, "a voice went out from the throne": Sinaiticus and 0229 [a] follow Hebrew word order by placing the verb "went out" before "from the throne."

We will now discuss the most exciting of all the grammar-based agreements. The following readings have not been reclaimed by Greek-to-Hebrew translations,[b] and show direct Hebrew influence in the oldest Greek manuscripts!

Revelation 8:2:

Oo.1.16: "ולהם נותן שבעה שופרות"

= "and seven shopharot **was given** to them" [c]

Alexandrinus: "και εδοθη αυτοις επτα σαλπιγγες"

= "and seven trumpets **was given** to them"

Other Greek mss.: "και εδοθησαν αυτοις επτα σαλπιγγες"

---

[a] Based on CNTTS apparatus.
[b] Checked against the translations of Franz Delitzsch; Salkinson Ginsburg; Bible Society in Israel. Note that some of these examples may be reclaimed by translations based on certain Syriac manuscripts, which preserved the Hebrew grammar better than the Greek.
[c] This phrase is rendered more literally here than in the main translation, to show the details of the Hebrew text.

= "and seven trumpets **were given** to them"

In Greek, a plural verb is required because the Greek word "σαλπιγγες" is feminine plural.[a] So, why does the oldest trusted Greek manuscript of this verse use a singular verb? The reason is obvious but startling: The Hebrew textual tradition of Revelation influenced the oldest highly-trusted Greek copy[b] of this verse.[c] As noted above, Hebrew can employ a singular passive verb, regardless of the gender of the subject.[d]

However, because Hebrew generally uses a plural passive verb with a plural subject, and only occasionally a singular verb, Greek-to-Hebrew translations did not reclaim the Hebrew reading of Oo.1.16.[e]

---

[a] In Greek, a **neuter plural** subject can take a **singular** verb, but a masculine plural or feminine plural subject cannot take a singular verb. "Greek often uses a singular verb when the subject is neuter plural." – William D. Mounce, *Basics of Biblical Greek Grammar,* 2nd ed., Zondervan, 2003 p. 68.

[b] "Codex Alexandrinus [was] recognized since the nineteenth century as the best witness to the Greek text of Revelation... Sinaiticus certainly preserved an "old text," but... it was a secondary witness relative to Alexandrinus and Ephraemi for the book of Revelation." – Juan Hernández Jr., *The Greek Text of Revelation,* in *The Oxford Handbook of the Book of Revelation*, Oxford University Press, 2020, p. 346.

[c] The Harklean Syriac version also uses a singular verb in this instance. However, we have already shown a number of unique agreements between the Hebrew Revelation and old Greek manuscripts which do not overlap with any known Syriac manuscripts. Therefore, the Syriac versions/manuscripts cannot be the source for these agreements between the Hebrew Revelation and ancient Greek mss.

[d] See e.g. Ex. 13:7; Num. 28:17; 2 Sam. 21:10; Jer. 6:7b, 46:15, 48:41 (x2); Ezek. 26:2, 32:25d, 45:21; Mic. 6:16; Ps. 87:3; Job 21:34, 22:9b, 42:15; Dan. 9:24, 9:26d; 1 Chr. 26:6.

[e] Compare readings below from Oo.1.16 vs. Greek-based translations:

A similar example is found in Revelation 12, where the Hebrew expression was literally translated and preserved in some Greek manuscripts and in the Peshitta:

Revelation 12:18[14]:

Oo.1.16: "ונותן להאשה שתי כנפים"

= "and two wings **was given** to the woman"[a]

P47, Sinaiticus Corrector:[b] "και εδοθη τη γυναικι δυο πτερυγας(ες)"[c]

= "and two wings... **was given** to the woman"

Other Greek mss.: "και εδοθησαν τη γυναικι αι δυο πτερυγες"

= "and the two wings... **were given** to the woman"

This reading with a singular verb was not reclaimed by Greek-to-Hebrew translations of Revelation, because Hebrew does not require a singular passive verb with a plural subject – it is optional in Hebrew. Again, we have clear evidence that Hebrew grammar, as

Oo.1.16	singular	נותן
Delitzsch	plural	וַיִּנָּתְנוּ
Ginsburg	plural	נתונים
Modern	plural	נִתְּנוּ

Note that some of these examples may be reclaimed by translations based on certain Syriac manuscripts, which preserved the Hebrew grammar better than the Greek. (The Syriac cannot be seen as the source of the Greek Revelation, because some of the grammatical examples and most of the general examples listed above do not overlap with any known Syriac manuscripts.)

[a] This phrase is rendered more literally here than in the main translation, to show the details of the Hebrew text.

[b] Noted as א² in NA28 and 01c in the CNTTS apparatus.

[c] "πτερυγας" (P47) and "πτερυγες" (Sinaiticus and most Greek mss.) are two

preserved in Oo.1.16, influenced the oldest surviving Greek manuscripts of Revelation. Over time, the Hebrew grammar was eliminated and the Greek text was standardized to conform to Greek grammar, which requires a plural verb with the feminine plural word "πτερυγες."

Thus, we have clear evidence that:

1. The oldest Greek manuscripts still preserve multiple examples of direct influence from Hebrew grammar, which were smoothed out later to conform to Greek grammar. This shows that the Book of Revelation was originally written in Hebrew, and that the Greek version was translated from Hebrew.[a]

2. Because some of these grammatical peculiarities cannot be reclaimed in Hebrew translations from other languages (being optional features of Hebrew grammar), we can know that the Hebrew Revelation contained in Oo.1.16 is not a translation into Hebrew, but rather preserves the original Hebrew text which was also the source for the Greek translation.

---

forms of the same word in Greek (both feminine plural): "πτερυγας" is in the accusative case while "πτερυγες" is in the nominative case.

[a] The Syriac cannot be seen as the source of the Greek Revelation, because some of the grammatical examples and most of the general examples listed above do not overlap with any known Syriac manuscripts.

This page is intentionally left blank.

אֵלֶּה הַסּוֹדוֹת פֶּרֶק א׳

1 (102r) [a] אֵלֶּה הַסּוֹדוֹת נָתַן יַהְוֶה [b] לְיֵשׁוּעַ [c] הַמָּשִׁיחַ לְהַרְאוֹת לַעֲבָדָיו מַה שֶׁיִּהְיֶה בְּקָרוֹב וְהוּא שָׁלַח אוֹתָם עַל יַד מַלְאָךְ שֶׁלּוֹ לְעַבְדּוֹ

---

[a] The number stated in brackets is the corresponding folio number of Oo.1.16 on which the Hebrew transcript is based.

[b] The Hebrew manuscript uses an abbreviation "הׄ" for "השם". It was common practice for many scribes to write 'Ha-Shem' or some abbreviation rather than writing the full name "יהוה". The fact that this abbreviation for 'Ha-Shem' really represents the name "יהוה" is evident when the Hebrew Revelation quotes from the Tanach, e.g.:

Isaiah 6:3:

Hebrew Masoretic Text: "קָדוֹשׁ | קָדוֹשׁ קָדוֹשׁ יהוה צְבָאוֹת"

Oo.1.16 (Revelation 4:8):   "קדוש קדוש קדוש הׄ צבאות"

Psalm 113:1:

Hebrew Masoretic Text: "הַלְלוּיָהּ הַלְלוּ עַבְדֵי יהוה הַלְלוּ אֶת־שֵׁם יהוה׃"

Oo.1.16 (Revelation 19:5):   "הללויה הללו עבדי הׄ הללו את שם הׄ"

Isaiah 60:19:

Hebrew Masoretic Text: "וְהָיָה־לָךְ יהוה לְאוֹר עוֹלָם"

Oo.1.16 (Revelation 22:5):   "והיה לך הׄ לאור עולם"

From the above examples it is very clear that this abbreviation "הׄ" used in the Hebrew Revelation actually represents the name "יהוה". For a full justification that the true pronunciation of the Name is "יַהְוֶה", based on the Masoretic Text, see HebrewGospels.com/yhwh.

[c] The short rabbinic spelling "ישו" used in the ms. was replaced with the full spelling "ישוע". See footnotes on p. 6 for more information.

Eleh Ha-Sodot [a]

1: 1 (102r) These are the confidential counsels [b] *which* Yahweh [c] gave to Yeshua [d] Ha-Mashiach, [e] to show his servants what will happen soon. [f] And he sent them by means of [g] his messenger [h] to his servant

---

[a] Or simply '*Sodot*' – the Hebrew title for the Book of 'Revelation.' See also next footnote.

[b] Hebrew "סודות" (*sodot*), plural of סוד (*sod*). Could also mean "secrets" or "mysteries." This Hebrew word is used both positively and negatively – compare e.g. Ps. 25:14; Pr. 3:32; Am. 3:7; Rev. 1:20 vs. Ps. 64:3(2), 83:4(3); Rev. 17:5.

[c] The manuscript uses the Hebrew abbreviation "ה׳" for '*Ha-Shem*,' which literally means "The Name." Today still, many Jews will read "*Ha-Shem*" when they see the Creator's Hebrew name יהוה. For further discussion on this abbreviation 'ה׳', see pp. 62-69. Our translations employ 'The Name' Yahweh in every instance indicated by the Hebrew manuscripts. The only grammatically possible pronunciation of יהוה, from which all other abbreviations/contractions of the Name can be formed, is "*Yah-weh*" – with emphasis on the second syllable. For more information, see HebrewGospels.com/yhwh.

[d] Hebrew name for 'Jesus' – meaning 'Yahweh is Salvation.'

[e] Or "The Messiah." The Hebrew word "משיח" (*mashiach*) was translated into the Greek '*christos*' but should be clearly distinguished from the Catholic symbolic 'Christ.' Literal meaning: "anointed one," usually referring to someone anointed as king of Israel, or as priest or prophet. However, when used as a name, it refers to the Son of Yahweh, whom he anointed as the ultimate King of Israel, the Everlasting High Priest, and the Prophet who would speak Yahweh's words to his people – and if anyone disobeys him, Yahweh himself will require it of him. See Deu. 18:18-19 and Acts 3:22-23.

[f] Lit. "at near" – the Biblical meaning of 'soon' or 'near' is not always what we expect. See e.g. Is. 13:22, stating that Babylon's destruction is near, yet Babylon was only destroyed generations later, and the ultimate fulfillment is still future! (Rev. 17-19.)

[g] Lit. "by the hand of" – a Hebrew idiom meaning "by," "through" or "by means of."

[h] Hebrew "מלאך" (*mal'ach*). Used for both human and heavenly messengers. The English word 'angel' is not really a translation – only a transliteration of the Greek '*aggelos*' (messenger). Besides, the average person reading 'angel'

יוֹחָנָן ‚ הָעֵד הַדִּיבּוּר [a] יַהְוֶה וְהָעֵדוּת מִיֵּשׁוּעַ הַמָּשִׁיחַ מִמַּה
שֶׁרָאָה ‚ קָדוֹשׁ הוּא הַקּוֹרֵא וְהַשּׁוֹמְעִים זֹאת הַנְּבִיאוּת
וּמְקַיְּימִים מַה שֶׁכָּתוּב ‚ יוֹחָנָן [לְ]הַשִּׁבְעָה זְקֵנִים בְּאַסְיָא
חֶסֶד וְשָׁלוֹם יִהְיֶה עִמָּכֶם מִזֶּה שֶׁהָיָה וְהֹוֶה וְיִהְיֶה וּמֵהַשִּׁבְעָה
רוּחוֹת שֶׁהֵמָּה מִכִּסְאוֹ ‚ וּמִיֵּשׁוּעַ הַמָּשִׁיחַ הָעֵד נֶאֱמָן וְרִאשׁוֹן
שֶׁקָם מֵהַמֵּתִים וְנָגִיד וּמְצַוֶּה עַל הָאָרֶץ הָאַהֲבָתֵנוּ וְרַחֲצָתֵנוּ [b]
מֵעֲווֹנוֹתֵינוּ עִם דָּמוֹ ‚ וְעָשָׂה אוֹתָנוּ לִמְלָכִים וּלְכֹהֲנִים לִפְנֵי
יַהְוֶה וְאָבִיו לוֹ תִּהְיֶה כָּבוֹד וְתִפְאֶרֶת מֵעוֹלָם וְעַד עוֹלָם אָמֵן

---

[a] Note that this word has the definite article and is still in construct state based on context. This phenomenon is very common in the Hebrew Revelation, James and Jude, and also occurs in the Tanach – see e.g. Judg. 16:14; 1 Kin. 14:24; 2 Kin. 16:14, 23:17; Jer. 25:26; 1 Chr. 9:26, etc.

[b] Or possibly "רָחֲצָתֵינוּ".

Yochanan[a] – 2 the witness of the word of Yahweh, and *of* the testimony of Yeshua Ha-Mashiach, of that which he saw.[b] 3 Blessed[c] is he who reads out loud, and those who hear this prophecy and establish[d] that which is written.

4 Yochanan, [to] the seven elders in Asia: Steadfast love[e] and shalom be with you, from him[f] who was and is and will be, and from the seven Ruchot[g] who are at[h] his throne. 5 And from Yeshua Ha-Mashiach the faithful witness, and *the* first who stood up from the dead ones, and *the* ruler and commander[i] over the earth – who is our love, and our washing from our iniquities with his blood, 6 and made us into kings and priests before Yahweh even his Father – to him be honor and glory, from everlasting and unto everlasting, amein.[j]

---

would probably envisage some female figure with wings. Heavenly 'mal'achim' or messengers are distinct from the cherubim; they do not have wings and appear as men. ('Angels' and 'men' are used interchangeably – see e.g. Gen. 18. Compare Mat. 28:2-5 and John 20:12 vs. Mark 16:5 and Luke 24:4, also see Heb. 13:2.) Ironically, the 'angels' depicted in many Christian books look more like the evil spirits described in Zec. 5:9.

[a] Hebrew name for 'John.'

[b] Yochanan repeatedly reminds us that he was an eyewitness of the things described in Revelation. See e.g. chapters 1:12, 1:19, 4:1, 4:2, 5:1, 6:1, etc.

[c] Hebrew "קדוש" (*qadosh*) – lit. "set-apart" but often used for "blessed."

[d] Or "perform."

[e] Hebrew "חסד" (*chesed*) – could also be translated as "faithful kindness" or "faithfulness."

[f] Lit. "this *one*," but often means 'he' or 'him.'

[g] Plural of "רוח" (*ruach*) – the Hebrew word for "spirit," "breath" or "wind." (See glossary for more information.)

[h] Or possibly 'from.'

[i] See Is. 55:4.

[j] When the Hebrew word "אמן" (*amein*) is used adverbially, it means "surely" or "truly."

7 רְאֵה הוּא יָבֹא בֶּעָנָן וְתִרְאוּ[a] אוֹתוֹ אֵלֶּה הַדֹּקְרִים אוֹתוֹ

וְיִבְכּוּ כָּל הַמִּשְׁפָּחוֹת הָאָרֶץ כֵּן אָמֵן 8 אֲנִי הוּא הָרִאשׁוֹן

וְהָאַחֲרוֹן תְּחִילַת[b] וְהַסּוֹף אָמַר הָאָדוֹן אַדִּיר הֶהָיָה וְהֹוֶה

וְיִהְיֶה 9 אֲנִי יוֹחָנָן הָיִיתִי בָּאִי הַנִּקְרָא פַּטְמֹס בִּשְׁבִיל הַדִּיבּוּר

יַהְוֶה וְהָעֵדוּת מֵיֵשׁוּעַ הַמָּשִׁיחַ 10 וְשׁוֹרָה עָלַי רוּחַ הַקּוֹדֶשׁ

וְשָׁמַעְתִּי מֵאַחֲרַי קוֹל גָּדוֹל 11 וְאָמְרָה אֲנִי הָרִאשׁוֹן וְהָאַחֲרוֹן

וְכָל מַה שֶּׁרָאִיתָ כְּתֹב בַּסֵּפֶר וּשְׁלַח אוֹתוֹ לְהַזְּקֵינִים[c] בְּאַסְיָא

וּלְעֶפֶהֵיזוֹם וְגַם לִסְמִירְנִין וּלְפֵירְגֵּימוֹם וְגַם לְטִיאָטִירָס

וּלְזַארְדֵּיס וְגַם לְפִילָדֶלְפִיַאן וְלָאֹדִיצֵאן 12 וְהָפַכְתִּי לִרְאוֹת

אֶת הַקּוֹל הַדּוֹבֶרֶת עִמִּי וּכְשֶׁהָפַכְתִּי רָאִיתִי שֶׁבַע מְנוֹרוֹת

שֶׁל זָהָב 13 וּבֵינֵיהֶם אֶחָד כִּדְמוּת אָדָם וְלָבוּשׁ בְּכֻתּוֹנוֹת[d] לָבָן

וְחָגוּר עַל הֶחָזֶה בַּחֲגֹר שֶׁל זָהָב

---

[a] The "ת" preformative is used several times instead of "י" with third person masculine 'imperfect' verbs. In these instances, the "ת" does not affect the person of the verb, it only seems to place extra emphasis on the subject. Compare chapter 2:20[2:22], 3:4, 3:5, 3:9, 7:15, 11:9, 18:5, 18:9, 22:11.

[b] Usually spelled "תחלה" or "תחילה". The Tanach also contains a number of feminine nouns which are construct in form, but not necessarily in meaning, e.g., "שִׁפְעַת" instead of "שִׁפְעָה" (2 Kin. 9:17b); "פוּגַת" instead of "פוּגָה" (Lam. 2:18); "חָכְמַת" instead of "חָכְמָה" (Is. 33:6); "נְגִינַת" instead of "נְגִינָה" (Ps. 61:1).

[c] Note that the definite article is often not merged with the inseparable prepositions in the Hebrew Revelation, James and Jude. This also happens occasionally in the Tanach, e.g. Gen. 39:11; Deu. 6:24; 1 Sam. 9:13, 13:21; Jer. 44:22; Ezek. 40:25, 47:22; Ps. 36:6; Eccl. 8:1; Ezra 9:7, 9:15; Neh. 5:11, 9:10, 9:19, 12:38; 2 Chr. 10:7, 25:10, 29:27, etc.

[d] Or possibly "בְּכֻתּוֹנוֹת" – compare e.g. "כֻּתֹּנֶת" (Gen. 37:31) vs. "כְּתֹנֶת" (Gen. 37:3). Although "כתונות" could possibly be a mistake for "כותנות", note that the 'construct' and 'absolute' pointings of this word may interchange, e.g., Ex. 39:27 reads "כָּתְנֹת" which looks like a 'construct,' but similar expressions in the context show that the word "כָּתְנֹת" in Ex. 39:27 is probably rather in the 'absolute' state. See also "הַכֻּתֹּנֶת" (Ex. 28:39) and "בְּכֻתֳּנֹתָם" (Lev. 10:5).

7 Look!^a – He will come with the clouds,^b and those who pierced him, **they** will see him, and all the families of the earth will weep,^c yes amein! 8 "I am the first and the last,^d *the* beginning and the end," says the mighty^e Adon,^{f, g} who was and is and will be.

9 I Yochanan was on the island called Patmos, because of the word of Yahweh and the testimony of Yeshua Ha-Mashiach. 10 As Ruach Ha-Qodesh^h was restingⁱ on me, I heard behind me a great voice. 11 And it said, "I am the first and the last, and everything that^j you see, write in a scroll, and send it to the elders in Asia, both to Ephesus and also to Smyrna, and to Pergamos and also to Thyatira, and to Sardis and also to Philadelphia and Laodicea."

12 So I turned about to see the voice which was speaking with me, and when I had turned about, I saw seven menorot^k of gold. 13 And among them, one like the appearance of a man, and *he* was clothed in white garments, and girded over the chest^l with a girdle of gold.

---

^a Or "behold."

^b Or "with a cloud" or "with a cloud mass."

^c Compare Zec. 12:10-14.

^d Compare Is. 44:6, 41:4. Yeshua is claiming to be Yahweh, see pp. 40-46 for more information.

^e Or "majestic."

^f The Hebrew word for 'lord' or 'master.'

^g Or "Ha-Adon *the* Mighty."

^h Meaning "the Set-Apart Spirit."

ⁱ Or "abode" or "was dwelling."

^j Or "whatever."

^k Plural of "מנורה" (*menorah*) – the Hebrew word for "lampstand."

^l The priestly ephod is worn over the shoulders and girded across the chest. See Ex. 28 for a detailed description of the ephod.

14 אֲבָל רֹאשׁוֹ וּשְׂעָרוֹ הָיָה לָבָן כְּצֶמֶר לָבָן וְעֵינָיו כְּלַהֶבֶת אֵשׁ
15 וְרַגְלָיו כִּנְחוֹשֶׁת וְקוֹלוֹ כְּרַעַשׁ מַיִם גְּדוֹלִים 16 וְשִׁבְעָה
כּוֹכָבִים בְּיַד יְמִינוֹ וּמִפִּיו הֹלֵךְ [a] חֶרֶב פִּיפִיּוֹת וּמַרְאֵהוּ זֹרֵחַ [b]
כַּשֶּׁמֶשׁ 17 וּכְשֶׁרָאִיתִי אוֹתוֹ נָפַלְתִּי לְרַגְלָיו כַּמֵּת וְהוּא מֵנִיחַ
אֶת יַד יְמִינוֹ עָלַי וְאָמַר לִי אַל תִּירָא אֲנִי הָרִאשׁוֹן וְהָאַחֲרוֹן
18 וְרֹאֶה אֲנִי הָיִיתִי מֵת וְעַכְשָׁיו חַי אֲנִי מֵעוֹלָם וְעַד עוֹלָם וְלִי
יֵשׁ הַמַּפְתְּחוֹת שֶׁל הַמָּוֶת וְהַגֵּיהִנֹּם [c] 19 כְּתוֹב מַה שֶׁרָאִיתָ וּמַה
שֶׁיִּהְיֶה אַחַר כָּךְ 20 וְהַסּוֹד מֵהַשִּׁבְעָה כּוֹכָבִים שֶׁרָאִיתָ בְּיַד
יְמִינִי וְשֶׁבַע מְנוֹרוֹת שֶׁל זָהָב כָּךְ הִיא הַשִּׁבְעָה כּוֹכָבִים אֵלֶּה
הֵמָּה שִׁבְעָה מַלְאָכִים וְהַשִּׁבְעָה מְנוֹרוֹת שִׁבְעָה זְקֵנִים

---

[a] Or possibly "הָלַךְ".

[b] Or possibly "זָרַח".

[c] Alternative spelling for "גֵּיא הִנֹּם". The full title found in the Tanach is
"גֵּי(א) בֶן הִנֹּם".

14 But his head, even his hair was white like white wool, and his eyes like a flame of fire. 15 And his feet were like copper, and his voice like the noise[a] of great waters. 16 And seven stars were in his right hand, and out of his mouth went a double-edged[b] sword, and his appearance[c] shone like the sun.

17 And when I saw him, I fell down at his feet like a dead one. But he laid his right hand on me, and said to me, "Do not fear, I am the first and the last. 18 And look![d] – I was dead, but now I am alive, from everlasting and unto everlasting.[e] And **I** have the keys of the death and Gei-Hinnom.[f] 19 Write what you have seen, and what will be after this. 20 Now the confidential counsel[g] of the seven stars which you saw in my right hand, and *the* seven menorot[h] of gold, so it is: The seven stars, they are seven messengers, and the seven menorot are seven elders."[i]

---

[a] Or "roaring" or "rumbling."

[b] Or "multi-edged."

[c] Or "face."

[d] Or "behold."

[e] A Hebrew idiom which often means "forever and ever" – see e.g. Jer. 7:7, 25:5; 1 Chr. 16:36; Neh. 9:5; Ps. 41:14(13), 103:17, 106:48.

[f] Lit. "The valley of Hinnom." This Hebrew word is transliterated into Greek as 'Gehenna,' and is inaccurately translated as 'Hell.' This is a literal valley right next to Jerusalem ordained for future punishment. See Mat. 25:41-46 in the HebrewGospels.com version: "And then he will say to those who are on the left side... go into the fire of Gei-Hinnom, which is prepared for Ha-Satan and his messengers... And these will go into the fire of Gei-Hinnom, but the righteous ones will go into everlasting light." To learn more about the Biblical definition of 'Gei-Hinnom,' see Jer. 7:30-33, Is. 30:33, 66:24, etc.

[g] Hebrew "סוד" (*sod*). Could also mean "secret" or "mystery." This Hebrew word is used both positively and negatively – compare e.g. Ps. 25:14, Pr. 3:32, Am. 3:7 vs. Ps. 64:3(2), 83:4(3).

[h] Plural of "מנורה" (*menorah*) – the Hebrew word for "lampstand."

[i] Probably means 'elders *of the assemblies*.'

פֶּרֶק ב'

1 וּלְהַמַּלְאָךְ מֵהָעֵדָה שֶׁל עֶפְהֶיזוֹם כְּתוֹב כֹּה אָמַר זֶה שֶׁיֵּשׁ בְּיַד יְמִינוֹ הַשִּׁבְעָה כּוֹכָבִים הַהוֹלֵךְ בְּתוֹךְ הַשִּׁבְעָה מְנוֹרוֹת שֶׁל זָהָב 2 אֲנִי יוֹדֵעַ אֶת מַעֲשֶׂיךָ וְתִקְוָתֶיךָ[a] וְאֶת לֹא תּוּכַל לִסְבּוֹל אֶת הָרְשָׁעִים וַתְּנַסֶּה לְאֵילוּ שֶׁאוֹמְרִים שֶׁהֵמָּה נְבִיאִים וְאֵינָם וַתִּמְצָא שֶׁהֵמָּה כַּזְּבָנִים 3 וְתִקְוָתֶיךָ וְטִרְחָתֶיךָ יֵשׁ הַכֹּל בִּשְׁבִיל שְׁמִי 4 אֲבָל תְּמִיהָ לִי מִפְּנֵי מַה תַּעֲזוֹב אַתָּה הָאַהֲבָה רִאשׁוֹנָה 5 זְכוֹר מִי אַתָּה וַעֲשִׂי[b] תְּשׁוּבָה וַעֲשִׂי מַעֲשֶׂיךָ רִאשׁוֹנִים וּבְאָם לָאוּ[c] בִּמְהֵרָה יְדָחֵף[d] מְנוֹרָתֶיךָ מִמְּקוֹמוֹ בְּאָם שֶׁלֹּא תַּעֲשֶׂה תְּשׁוּבָה

---

[a] Although such spellings are generally used with plural nouns, a "ָ " helping vowel is often inserted between a singular noun and a second person masculine singular suffix when the word is 'in pause,' e.g. "שְׁמֶךָ" (Gen. 12:2); "כַּסְפֶּךָ" (Gen. 17:13). Such 'pausal' pronunciations are often used throughout the Hebrew Revelation, James and Jude, even for words which are not in pause, and these spellings (e.g. "תִּקְוָתֶיךָ" instead of "תִּקְוָתְךָ") do not indicate a plural noun. This is also attested in the Dead Sea Scrolls (indicated by vowel letters), e.g. "רעיך" (Deu. 5:20, 4Q41); "שדיך" (Deu. 11:15, 4Q136); and rarely in the Masoretic Text: "מִשְׁנָאֶתֶיךָ" (Ezek. 35:11). Compare footnotes on chapter 2:12[13], 9:5.

[b] Alternative spelling for "וַעֲשֵׂה" (masculine singular imperative). Similar spellings are attested in the Dead Sea Scrolls and in the Mishnah, e.g. "צוי" for "צַוֵּה" (Is. 38:1, 1QIsa); "הוי" for "הֱוֵה" (Mishnah Avot 1:6, 4:2).

[c] Same meaning as "לֹא", also attested more than 140 times in the Mishnah.

[d] Note that masculine verbs are occasionally used with feminine subjects in Hebrew. See e.g. Judg. 21:21; 1 Sam. 25:27; 1 Kin. 22:36; Dan. 8:9; Neh. 6:9; 13:19; 2 Chr. 15:7, 20:37, etc.

2: ₁ "And to the messenger of the assembly of Ephesus write: Thus says he[a] who has the seven stars in his right hand, who walks amidst[b] the seven menorot of gold, ₂ 'I know your works and your hope;[c] and that you are not able to bear the wicked ones, so you tested those who say that they are prophets while they are not, and found that they are deceivers;[d] ₃ and your hope[e] and your trouble[f] – all of which is because of[g] my name.[h] ₄ However, I am amazed[i] because of what you yourself forsook – the first love.[j] ₅ Remember who you were,[k] and do repentance, and do your first[l] works. But if not, your menorah[m] will be thrust away **hastily** from its place – if you do not do repentance.

---

[a] Lit. "this *one*," but often means 'he' or 'him.'
[b] Or "among."
[c] Or "expectation" or by extension, possibly 'patience.'
[d] Or "liars."
[e] Or "expectation" or by extension, possibly 'patience.'
[f] Lit. "burden bearing." This phrase could also possibly mean 'and your hope during troubles/difficult times.'
[g] Or "for my name's sake."
[h] Or possibly "and *that* your hope and your trouble are all because of my name."
[i] Lit. "I have amazement."
[j] Or "that you yourself forsook the first love."
[k] Or possibly 'Consider who you are.'
[l] Or "former."
[m] Hebrew word for "lampstand."

6 [7] מִי שֶׁיֵּשׁ לוֹ אָזְנַיִם שׁוֹמֵעַ מַה שֶׁהָרוּחַ אוֹמֵר לְהָעֵדָה מִי
שֶׁמְּנַצֵּחַ יֹאכַל מֵעֵץ הַחַיִּים שֶׁיֵּשׁ בְּגַן עֵדֶן 7 [8] וּלְהַמַּלְאָךְ
מֵהָעֵדָה שֶׁל זְמִירְנִין כְּתוֹב כֹּה אָמַר הָרִאשׁוֹן וְהָאַחֲרוֹן הַמֵּת
וְקָם 8 [9] אֲנִי יוֹדֵעַ מַעֲשֶׂיךָ וְצָרוֹתֶיךָ וְהַחֵירוּף מֵאֵלּוּ
הָאוֹמְרִים שֶׁהֵם יְהוּדִים וְאֵינָם רַק הֵמָּה מִבְּנֵי הַשָּׂטָן 9 [10]
אַל תִּירָא מֵהֶם רְאֵה הַשָּׂטָן יִקַּח אֵיזֶה [מִכֶּם] בַּשִּׁבְיָה כְּדֵי
לְנַסּוֹת אֶתְכֶם וְהַצַּעַר יִהְיֶה לָכֶם עֲשָׂרָה יָמִים תְּהִי נֶאֱמָן עַד
יוֹם מוֹתְךָ כְּדֵי שֶׁאֶתֵּן לְךָ הַכֶּתֶר מֵהַחַיִּים

---

[a] Note that a participle is sometimes used with the same/similar meaning as
an imperative. Compare e.g. chapter 2:13[14], 2:14[15], 6:16; James 2:5. See
also Miguel Pérez Fernández, *An Introductory Grammar of Rabbinic Hebrew*,
Brill, 1997, pp. 138-139; M. H. Segal, *A Grammar of Mishnaic Hebrew*,
Clarendon Press, p. 159.

6 [7]^a Whosoever has ears must hear^b what the Ruach^c says to the assembly! Whosoever overcomes, will eat from the tree of life,^d which is in Gan 'Eden.'"^e

7 [8] "And to the messenger of the assembly of Smyrna write: Thus says the first and the last, who died and stood up, 8 [9] 'I know your works and your sufferings,^f and the reproach of those who say that they are Yehudim^g while they are not, but are of the sons^h of Ha-Satan.ⁱ 9 [10] Do not be afraid of them, look,^j Ha-Satan will take some of [you] in captivity in order to test you, and you will have suffering *for* ten days. Be faithful unto the day of your death, that I may give you the crown of life.

---

^a Verse numbers marked in manuscript mostly correspond to standard numbering in English translations. When the verse number in this manuscript differs from the standard numbering, the standard verse number is placed in brackets. E.g. verse 6 in this manuscript corresponds to verse [7] in standard Bibles. The verse numbered [6] in standard Bibles is absent in this ms.

^b Or "obey." The Hebrew word "שמע" (*shama'*) means both to "hear/listen" and to "obey."

^c The Hebrew word for "spirit," "breath" or "wind." (See glossary for more information.)

^d See pp. 35-40 for a discussion on the tree of life.

^e Hebrew name meaning "Garden of Joy/Delight." Usually translated as "the Garden of Eden" or "Paradise." Compare Gen. 2:8-15, 3:23-24, 4:16; Is. 51:3, Ezek. 28:13; 31:9-18; 36:35, Joel 2:3.

^f Or "pains."

^g Hebrew name for 'Jews.'

^h Or "children" – as a general rule, Hebrew masculine includes feminine.

ⁱ The Hebrew word "שטן" (*satan*) literally means "adversary" or "accuser." If it has the definite article (The Adversary) it is normally used as a title (e.g. Zech. 3:1; Job 1:6-11; Mat. 4:1; Mark 1:13, etc.), and is transliterated as '*Ha-Satan*'; however, '*satan*' (usually without the article, or plural) is used for 'enemy/adversary' (e.g. 1 Sam. 29:4; 2 Sam. 19:23(22); 1 Kin. 5:18(5:4), 11:14; Mat. 16:23, etc.) or as a synonym of 'demon' (e.g. Mat. 8:31; Mark 3:23; Rev. 18:2, etc.).

^j Or "behold."

10 [11] מִי שֶׁיֵּשׁ לוֹ אָזְנַיִם שׁוֹמֵעַ מַה שֶׁהָרוּחַ אוֹמֵר לְהָעֵדָה מִי שֶׁמְּנַצֵּחַ אַל תִּהְיֶה לוֹ צַעַר מִמָּוֶת אַחֶרֶת 11 [12] וּלְהַמַּלְאָךְ מֵהָעֵדָה שֶׁל פֵּירְגְּמוֹם כְּתוֹב כֹּה אָמַר זֶה שֶׁיֵּשׁ לוֹ חֶרֶב פִּיפִיּוֹת 12 [13] אֲנִי יוֹדֵעַ אֶת מַעֲשֶׂיךָ וּמָקוֹם שֶׁלְּךָ יֵשׁ בְּמָקוֹם שֶׁיֵּשׁ כִּסֵּא הַשָּׂטָן וְאַתָּה תַּאֲמִין בִּשְׁמִי וּבָאֱמוּנָתִי וּבִעֵיתֵי נֶהֱרַג^a אֶת חֲבֵירִי הַנֶּאֱמָן אַנְטִיפַס אֶצְלֵיכֶם^b בְּמָקוֹם שֶׁהַשָּׂטָן דָּר 13 [14] וְגַם אַתָּה שׂוֹנֵא מֵאֵילוּ שֶׁלּוֹמְדִים הַלִּימוּד שֶׁל בִּלְעָם הַלָּמֵד עַל יַד בָּלָק לַעֲשׂוֹת רַע לִבְנֵי יִשְׂרָאֵל לַחֲטוֹא אוֹתָם בִּזְנוּת 14 [15] וְגַם אַתָּה שׂוֹנֵא מִלִּימוּד נִיקָאלָטְצִיאַן וְאַף אֲנִי שׂוֹנֵא מֵאֵילוּ 15 [16] עֲשִׂי^c תְּשׁוּבָה וְאִם לָאוּ^d אָבֹא אֲנִי בִּמְהֵרָה לַעֲשׂוֹת עִמְּךָ מִלְחָמָה עַל יַד הַחֶרֶב שֶׁיֵּשׁ בְּפִי 16 [17] מִי שֶׁיֵּשׁ לוֹ אָזְנַיִם שׁוֹמֵעַ מַה שֶׁהָרוּחַ אוֹמֵר לְהָעֵדָה מִי שֶׁמְּנַצֵּחַ רוֹצֶה אֲנִי לִיתֵּן^e לוֹ לֶאֱכֹל מֵהַמָּן הַנִּסְתָּר

---

^a Or possibly "נֶהֱרַג".

^b In the Tanach, a number of prepositions take on a 'plural' form when a suffix is attached, e.g. "עֲלֵיכֶם" (Ex. 5:21); "אַחֲרֵיהֶם" (Gen. 41:23). In the Hebrew Revelation, James and Jude, the 'plural' form is used with a wider range of prepositions whenever a second person suffix is attached. Compare footnotes on chapter 2:2, 9:5.

^c Alternative spelling for "עֲשֵׂה" (masculine singular imperative). Similar spellings are attested in the Dead Sea Scrolls and the Misnnah, e.g. צוי for "צַוֵּה" (Is. 38:1, 1QIsa); "הוי" for "הֱוֵה" (Mishnah Avot 1:6, 4:2).

^d Same meaning as "לֹא".

^e This is an alternative form of the 'infinitive construct' with "ל" preposition (root: "נתן"). Normally spelled "לָתֵת" in the Tanach.

10 [11] Whosoever has ears must hear[a] what the Ruach[b] says to the assembly! Whosoever overcomes will not have suffering from the last[c] death.'"

11 [12] "And to the messenger of the assembly of Pergamos write: Thus says he[d] who has a double-edged[e] sword, 12 [13] 'I know your works – although your place is at the place where the throne[f] of Ha-Satan is, yet **you** believe in my name and in my faithfulness,[g] also in the times when my faithful joined-one Antipas was killed near you, at the place where Ha-Satan dwells. 13 [14] But you must also hate those who teach the teaching[h] of Bil'am,[i] who taught by means of Balaq[j] to do evil[k] to the children of Yisrael,[l] to cause[m] them to sin by fornication; 14 [15] and you must also hate the teaching of *the* Nicolaitans; for I also hate these. 15 [16] Do repentance! – And if not, I myself will come with haste to make war with **you** by the sword which is in my mouth. 16 [17] Whosoever has ears must hear what the Ruach says to the assembly! Whosoever overcomes, I will be pleased[n] to give him to eat of the hidden manna,

---

[a] Or "obey." The Hebrew word "שׁמע" (*shama'*) means both to "hear/listen" and to "obey."

[b] The Hebrew word for "spirit," "breath" or "wind." (See glossary for more information.)

[c] Or "latter" or "second."

[d] Lit. "this *one*," but often means 'he' or 'him.'

[e] Or "multi-edged."

[f] Or "seat."

[g] Could also mean "faith in me" or "faithfulness towards me."

[h] Or "doctrine."

[i] Hebrew name for 'Balaam.'

[j] Hebrew name for 'Balak.'

[k] Or "harm."

[l] Hebrew name for 'Israel.'

[m] Or "by causing."

[n] Or "I want."

וְגַם עֵדוּת טוֹבָה וּבָזֹה[a] הָעֵדוּת שֵׁם חָדָשׁ כָּתוּב שֶׁלֹּא יוּכַל
שׁוּם אֶחָד לִקְרוֹא רַק זֶה שֶׁקִּיבֵּל אוֹתוֹ 17 [18] וּלְהַמַּלְאָךְ
מֵהָעֵדָה שֶׁל טִיאָטִירָא כְּתוֹב כֹּה אָמַר בֶּן יַהְוֶה שֶׁעֵינָיו כַּמָּה
כְּמוֹ לַהֶבֶת אֵשׁ וְרַגְלָיו כִּנְחוֹשֶׁת [19] 18 אֲנִי יוֹדֵעַ אֶת מַעֲשֶׂיךָ
וְאַהֲבָתֶיךָ[b] וְשֵׁארוּתֶיךָ[c] וֶאֱמוּנָתֶיךָ וְתִקְוָתֶיךָ וּבְכָל עֵת תַּעֲשֶׂה
יוֹתֵר [20] 19 אֲבָל דָּבָר קָטוֹן יֵשׁ לִי עָלֶיךָ שֶׁתַּעֲזוֹב הָאִשָּׁה
יִזָאבֶל[d] הָאוֹמֶרֶת שֶׁהִיא נְבִיאָה וְלוֹמְדִים וּמַסִּיתִים[e] אֶת
עֲבָדַי לַעֲשׂוֹת זְנוּת [22] 20 רְאֵה אֲנִי מֵבִיא עָלֶיהָ וְעַל זֶה
שֶׁשָּׁכַב עִמָּהּ הַרְבֵּה צַעַר בְּאִם שֶׁלֹּא תַּעֲשׂוּ[f] תְּשׁוּבָה עַל
מַעֲשֵׂיהֶם 21 וַאֲנִי נָתַתִּי לָהּ עֵת לַעֲשׂוֹת תְּשׁוּבָה [23] 22 וְאֶת
בָּנֶיהָ יוֹמְתוּ וְכָל הָעֵדָה תַּכִּירוּ[g] שֶׁאֲנִי הוּא הַבּוֹחֵן כְּלָיוֹת
וָלֵב[h] וְכָל אֶחָד כְּפִי מִדוֹתָיו יְשׁוּלַם לוֹ

---

[a] Older spelling of "זוֹ" (feminine form of "זֶה"); also attested in the Tanach in Judg. 18:4; 2 Sam. 11:25; 1 Kin. 14:5; Eccl. 2:24, etc.

[b] See footnote on chapter 2:2.

[c] Alternative spelling for "וְשֵׁרוּתָךְ". The lexical form is normally spelled "שֵׁרוּת" or "שֵׁירוּת".

[d] Alternative spelling for "אִיזֶבֶל" – compare e.g. "יִשַׁי" (1 Sam. 16:1, etc.) vs. "אִישַׁי" (1 Chr. 2:13).

[e] Or possibly "וּמְסִיתִים".

[f] The "ת" preformative is used several times instead of "י" with third person masculine 'imperfect' verbs. In these instances, the "ת" does not affect the person of the verb, it only seems to place extra emphasis on the subject. Compare chapter 1:7, 3:4, 3:5, 3:9, 7:15, 11:9, 18:5, 18:9, 22:11.

[g] See above footnote.

[h] Phrase quoted from Jer. 11:20.

and also *to give him*[a] a good testimony[b] – and on this testimony, a new name will be written, which no one is able to read, except he[c] who received it.'"

17 [18] "And to the messenger of the assembly of Thyatira write: Thus says the Son of Yahweh, whose eyes are just like a flame of fire, and his feet like copper, 18 [19] 'I know your works and your love and your service and your faithfulness[d] and your hope, and *that* you always work more.[e] 19 [20] But I have a small[f] thing against you – that you allow the woman Izevel,[g] who says that she is a prophetess; and those who teach[h] and seduce my servants to commit fornication. 20 [22] Look, I am about to bring over her – and over him[i] who lies with her – great suffering, unless **they** do repentance concerning their works. 21 (And **I** did give her time to do repentance.) 22 [23] And her sons[j] will be put to death, and all the assembly will recognize that I am he who tests kidneys and heart.[k] And every one – according to his measures it will be rewarded[l] to him.

---

[a] Understood from preceding part of the verse. (Called 'gapping,' commonly found in the Hebrew Tanach. See pp. 52-59 and 250-255 for more information on gapping.)

[b] In context 'a written testimony.'

[c] Lit. "this *one*," but often means 'he' or 'him.'

[d] Or "faith." Hebrew "אמונה" (*emunah*) – refers to both believing and doing (being faithful). See e.g. James 2:19-25[20-26]; 2 Chr. 19:9; 2 Kin. 12:16(15); Is. 59:4; Hos. 2:22(20); Ps. 33:4, 143:1, etc.

[e] Or possibly "abundantly."

[f] Sarcastic.

[g] Hebrew name for 'Jezebel.'

[h] Or "and/so that they teach…"

[i] Lit. "this *one*," but often means 'he' or 'him.'

[j] Or "children" – as a general rule, Hebrew masculine includes feminine.

[k] Phrase quoted from Jer. 11:20.

[l] Or "repaid."

23 [24] אֲבָל לָכֶם וְלָאֲחֵרִים הָהֵמָּה בְּטִיאָטִירָא אוֹמֵר אֲנִי שֶׁלֹּא אָבִיא עֲלֵיכֶם עוֹד צַעַר כֵּיָן שֶׁלֹּא תַּלְמְדוּ מְלִימוּד הַשָּׂטָן 24 [25] אֲבָל תַּחֲזִקוּ[a] בָּזֶה שֶׁיֵּשׁ לָכֶם עַד שֶׁאָבֹא 25 [26] וּמִי שֶׁמְּנַצֵּחַ אֶתְּנָה גוֹיִם נַחֲלָתוֹ 26 [27] וְהוּא יְנַהֵג אוֹתָם בְּשֵׁבֶט בַּרְזֶל וְכִכְלִי יוֹצֵר תְּנַפְּצֵם[b] 27 וּכְמוֹ שֶׁקִּבַּלְתִּי מֵאָבִי [28] כָּךְ אֶתֵּן לוֹ הַשַּׁחַר 28 [29] מִי שֶׁיֵּשׁ לוֹ אָזְנַיִם שׁוֹמֵעַ מַה שֶׁהָרוּחַ אוֹמֵר לְהָעֵדָה

פֶּרֶק ג'

1 (102v) וּלְהַמַּלְאָךְ מֵהָעֵדָה שֶׁל זַארְדִּין כְּתוֹב כֹּה אָמַר זֶה שֶׁיֵּשׁ לוֹ הָרוּחוֹת יַהְוֶה וְהַשִּׁבְעָה כּוֹכָבִים אֲנִי יוֹדֵעַ אֶת מַעֲשֶׂיךָ כִּי שֶׁם יֵשׁ לְךָ שֶׁאַתָּה חַי וְאַתָּה מֵת 2 לָכֵן אַל תִּישַׁן וּתְחַזֵּק לָזֶה שֶׁרוֹצֶה לָמוּת כִּי לֹא מָצָאתִי אֶת מַעֲשֶׂיךָ שְׁלֵימָה לִפְנֵי יַהְוֶה 3 וְעַכְשָׁיו זְכוֹר הֵיאַךְ שֶׁקִּבַּלְתָּ וְשָׁמַעְתָּ וּמְקַיֵּים אוֹתָם וַעֲשֵׂי[c] תְּשׁוּבָה וְאִם לֹא אָבֹא אֲנִי עָלֶיךָ כַּגַּנָּב וְאַתָּה אֵינָה[d] יוֹדֵעַ בְּאֵיזֶה זְמַן שֶׁאָבֹא

---

[a] Or possibly "תֵּחֲזְקוּ".

[b] Similar to Ps. 2:8-9.

[c] See footnote on chapter 2:5.

[d] In the Hebrew Revelation and James, "אינו" or "אינה" is generally used instead of "אין". The "ו" or "ה" at the end does not always represent a third person singular pronominal suffix. Because these two spellings are used interchangeably, it is possible that "אינה" should actually be pointed as "אֵינָה". Compare e.g. the interchange of "שִׁלוֹ" (Jer 7:14; Judg. 21:19, 21:21, etc.) and "שִׁלֹה" (Josh. 18:1, 18:8, 18:9, 18:10, etc.); "אָהֳלוֹ" (Gen. 26:25, 31:25, 33:19, etc.) and "אָהֳלֹה" (Gen. 9:21, 12:8, 13:3, etc.); "זֹה" (2 Kin. 6:19; Ezek. 40:45, etc.) and "זוֹ" (Hos. 7:16; Ps. 132:10).

23 [24] But to you (that is, to the others who are in Thyatira) I say, that I will not bring more suffering ᵃ over you, because you did not learn ᵇ of the teaching ᶜ of Ha-Satan; 24 [25] but you must hold on ᵈ to this ᵉ which you have until I come. 25 [26] And whosoever overcomes, I will give nations as his inheritance, 26 [27] and **he** will lead them with a rod of iron, and you will shatter them like a **potter's vessel**.ᶠ 27 And like I received from my Father, [28] so I will give him the light.ᵍ 28 [29] Whosoever has ears must hear what the Ruach says to the assembly!'"

3: 1 (102v) "And to the messenger of the assembly of Sardis write: Thus says he ʰ who has the Ruchot ⁱ of Yahweh, and the seven stars, 'I know your works – that you have a name ʲ that you are alive, but you are dead. 2 Therefore, do not sleep but strengthen that which ᵏ wants to die – for I have not found your works complete before Yahweh. 3 And now, remember how you have received and heard; and establish ˡ them, and do repentance. But if not, I myself will come upon ᵐ you like a thief, and you will not know ⁿ at what time I will come.

ᵃ Or "distress" or "trouble."
ᵇ Or possibly "do not teach."
ᶜ Or "doctrine."
ᵈ Or possibly 'strengthen this.'
ᵉ Or "that."
ᶠ Similar to Ps. 2:8-9.
ᵍ Lit. "dawn" or "daybreak" – used as a synonym of "light," and in this context probably means "glory." Compare e.g. Is. 58:8, Is. 8:20, and John 17:22 in the HebrewGospels.com version.
ʰ Lit. "this *one*," but often means 'he' or 'him.'
ⁱ Plural of "רוח" (*ruach*) – the Hebrew word for "spirit," "breath" or "wind." (See glossary for more information.)
ʲ Or "reputation."
ᵏ Or possibly 'him who.'
ˡ Or "perform."
ᵐ Or "against."
ⁿ Or "while you do not know."

וְגַם שִׁמְךָ נִשְׁמַע בְּזַארְדִּין שֶׁלֹּא טִנְּפוּ אֶת בִּגְדֵיהֶם וְהֵמָּה ₄
תֵלְכוּ[a] עִמִּי בִּבְגָדִים לְבָנִים[b] כִּי הֵמָּה רְאוּיִים לְזֶה ₅ וּמִי
שֶׁמְנַצֵּחַ תֵּלֵךְ[c] בִּבְגָדִים לְבָנִים וַאֲנִי לֹא אֶמְחֶה אֶת שְׁמוֹ
מִסֵּפֶר הַחַיִּים וַאֲנִי מוֹדִיעַ אֶת שְׁמוֹ לִפְנֵי אָבִי וְלִפְנֵי מַלְאָכָיו
מִי שֶׁיֵּשׁ לוֹ אָזְנַיִם שׁוֹמֵעַ מַה שֶּׁהָרוּחַ אוֹמֵר לְהָעֵדָה ₆ ₇
וּלְהַמַּלְאָךְ מֵהָעֵדָה שֶׁל פִּילָאדֶעלְפִיָא כָּתוֹב כֹּה אָמַר הַקָּדוֹשׁ
וְהַנֶּאֱמָן זֶה שֶׁיֵּשׁ לוֹ הַמַּפְתֵּחַ שֶׁל דָּוִד הַפּוֹתֵחַ וְשׁוּם אֶחָד
יוּכַל לִסְגּוֹר הַמַּסְגּוֹר[d] וְשׁוּם אֶחָד יוּכַל לִפְתּוֹחַ ₈ אֲנִי יוֹדֵעַ
אֶת מַעֲשֶׂיךָ רְאֵה נָתַתִּי לְפָנֶיךָ פֶּתַח פָּתוּחַ וְשׁוּם אֶחָד יוּכַל
לִסְגּוֹר אוֹתָהּ[e] כִּי מְעַט כֹּחַ יֵשׁ לָךְ וְשָׁמַרְתָּ אֶת דְּבָרִי[f] וְאֵינָהּ[g]
כּוֹפֵר בִּשְׁמִי ₉ רְאֵה אֲנִי אֶתֵּן לְאֵילוּ שֶׁהֵמָּה מֵחַבְרוּתַת הַשָּׂטָן
הָאוֹמְרִים שֶׁהֵמָּה יְהוּדִים וְאֵינָם רַק כּוֹזְבִים

---

[a] In the ms., there is a "י" written above the "ת" as a proposed correction. However, see footnote on chapter 1:7.

[b] Or possibly "לְבָנִים" – see footnote on chapter 4:4.

[c] For the use of "ת" instead of "י", see footnote on chapter 1:7.

[d] Alternative form of masculine singular participle (with definite article).

[e] Or possibly "אוֹתה". Compare e.g. "אָהֳלֹה" (Gen. 9:21); "פְּרֻעֹה" (Ex. 32:25); "נִסְכֹּה" (Lev. 23:13); "כַּלֹּה" (Ezek. 36:10); "הֲוּמֹנֹה" (Ezek. 39:11), etc.

[f] Or possibly "דְּבָרַי".

[g] In the Hebrew Revelation and James, "אֵינוֹ" or "אֵינָה" is generally used instead of "אֵין". The "ו" or "ה" at the end does not always represent a third person singular pronominal suffix. Because these two spellings are used interchangeably, it is possible that "אֵינָה" should actually be pointed as "אֵינָה". Compare e.g. the interchange of "שִׁלוֹ" (Jer 7:14; Judg. 21:19, 21:21, etc.) and "שִׁלֹה" (Josh. 18:1, 18:8, 18:9, 18:10, etc.); "אָהֳלֹו" (Gen. 26:25, 31:25, 33:19, etc.) and "אָהֳלֹה" (Gen. 9:21, 12:8, 13:3, etc.); "זֹה" (2 Kin. 6:19; Ezek. 40:45, etc.) and "זֹו" (Hos. 7:16; Ps. 132:10).

₄ And also your name is heard in Sardis – *of those* who did not soil[a] their garments,[b] and they, **they** will walk with me in white garments, for they are worthy of this. ₅ And whosoever overcomes, **he** will walk in white garments, and **I** will not blot out his name from the scroll of life, but I will confess[c] his name before my Father and before his messengers. ₆ Whosoever has ears must hear what the Ruach says to the assembly!'"

₇ "And to the messenger of the assembly of Philadelphia write: Thus says the Qadosh[d] and the Faithful, he[e] who has the key of Dawid,[f] who opens and no one is able to shut, who shuts and no one is able to open – ₈ 'I know your works. Look, I have given[g] before you an open door and no one is able to shut it – for you have little strength, yet you have kept my word,[h] and have not denied my name. ₉ Look, **I** will give to those who are of the company of Ha-Satan, who say that they are Yehudim while they are not – only deceivers –

---

[a] Or "defile."
[b] Or "that *some* did not soil their garments."
[c] Or "acknowledge."
[d] Lit. "Set-Apart."
[e] Lit. "this *one*," but often means 'he' or 'him.'
[f] Hebrew name for 'David.'
[g] Or "I have set."
[h] Or possibly "my words."

רְאֵה שֶׁאֲנִי רוֹצֶה לַעֲשׂוֹת שֶׁהֵמָּה תָּבוֹאוּ [a]לְהִתְפַּלֵּל [b]לְרַגְלֶיךָ[c]
וּלְהַכִּיר שֶׁאָהַבְתִּי אוֹתְךָ 10 כֵּיוָן שֶׁשָּׁמַרְתָּ הַדִּבּוּר מִתִּקְוָתִי
כָּךְ אֲנִי אֶשְׁמוֹר אוֹתְךָ מֵהָעֵת שֶׁל הַנִּסָּיוֹן הַבָּא עַל הָאָרֶץ
לְנַסּוֹת לְאֵילוּ הַדָּרִים עַל הָאָרֶץ 11 רְאֵה אֲנִי אָבֹא בִּמְהֵרָה
שְׁמוֹר מַה שֶׁיֵּשׁ לְךָ כְּדֵי שֶׁלֹּא יִקַּח שׁוּם אֶחָד אֶת כִּתְרֶיךָ 12
מִי שֶׁמְּנַצֵּחַ אֶכְתּוֹב עָלָיו הַשֵּׁם מֵאֱלֹהַי וְהַשֵּׁם מִירוּשָׁלַיִם
הֶחָדָשׁ הָעִיר אֱלֹהַי שֶׁיָּבֹא מֵהַשָּׁמַיִם לְהָאָרֶץ מֵאֱלֹהַי וְגַם
שְׁמִי הֶחָדָשׁ 13 מִי שֶׁיֵּשׁ לוֹ אָזְנַיִם שׁוֹמֵעַ מַה שֶׁהָרוּחַ אוֹמֵר
לְהָעֵדָה 14 וּלְהַמַּלְאָךְ מֵהָעֵדָה לָאדִיצֵא כְּתוֹב כֹּה אָמַר אָמֵן
הָעֵד נֶאֱמָן הַתִּחְלָה מֵהַבְּרִיאוֹת 15 אֲנִי יוֹדֵעַ אֶת מַעֲשֶׂיךָ
שֶׁאַתָּה לֹא קַר וְלֹא חָם אוּלַי שֶׁתִּהְיֶה קַר אוֹ חָם 16 אֲבָל כֵּיוָן
שֶׁאַתָּה לֹא קַר וְלֹא חָם בִּשְׁבִיל זֶה יָרֵק אֲנִי אוֹתְךָ מִפִּי 17
וְאַתָּה תֹּאמַר אֲנִי עוֹשֵׁר וְיֵשׁ לִי דַּי וְאֵינָה צוֹרֶךָ[d] לְשׁוּם דָּבָר
אֲבָל אֵינָה יוֹדֵעַ שֶׁאַתָּה עָנִי וְאֶבְיוֹן 18 וַאֲנִי נוֹתֵן עֲצָתִי לְךָ
שֶׁתִּקְנֶה זָהָב מִמֶּנִּי וְתִלְבּוֹשׁ מַלְבּוּשִׁים לְבָנִים[e]

---

[a] For the use of "ת" instead of "ל", see footnote on chapter 1:7.

[b] Alternative spelling for "לְהִתְפַּלֵּל". Note that a preformative 'ה' is occasionally dropped in 'infinitive construct' verbs when an inseparable preposition is attached, even in the Tanach – see e.g. Pro. 24:17 ("וּבְכָשְׁלוֹ" for "וּבְהִכָּשְׁלוֹ"); Lam. 2:11 ("בֵּעָטֵף" for "בְּהֵעָטֵף"). See also Ex. 10:3, 34:24; Deu. 31:11; Is. 1:12; Job 33:30, etc.

[c] Compare Is. 45:14, 49:23, 60:14.

[d] Or possibly "צוֹרֵךָ".

[e] Or possibly "לְבָנִים" – see footnote on chapter 4:4.

look, I am pleased to make that **they** will come to do supplication [a] at your feet, and to acknowledge that I have loved you. 10 Because you have kept the word of my hope, so **I** will keep you from the time of testing, [b] which will come on the earth to test [c] those who dwell on the earth. 11 Look, **I** will come with haste! [d] – Guard what you have, that no one takes your crown. 12 Whosoever overcomes, I will write upon him the name of my Elohim, [e] and the name of the new Yerushalayim, [f] the city of my Elohim which will come from the heavens to the earth from my Elohim – and also my new name. 13 Whosoever has ears must hear what the Ruach says to the assembly!'"

14 "And to the messenger *of* the assembly of Laodicea write: Thus says Amein, [g] the faithful witness, the beginning of the creation, [h] 15 'I know your works, that you are neither cold nor warm – if only you could be cold or warm! [i] 16 But because you are neither cold nor warm, because of this I will spit you from my mouth. 17 Yet **you** say, 'I am rich and have sufficient and there is no need for anything,' [j] but *you* do not know that you are poor and needy. 18 Now, let me give [k] you my counsel: that you buy gold from me, and clothe yourself with white garments,

---

[a] Or "to pray" – see Is. 45:14, 49:23, 60:14.

[b] Or "trying" or "temptation."

[c] Or "try" or "tempt."

[d] Or "quickly."

[e] Usually translated as 'God.' In Hebrew however, the word 'luck' or 'fortune' is pronounced as "*gad*" and sometimes as "*god*" (medieval) – see e.g. Gen. 30:10-11, Josh. 11:17, Is. 65:11. Therefore we prefer not to use 'God.'

[f] Hebrew name for 'Jerusalem.'

[g] When the Hebrew word "אמן" (*amein*) is used as a title, it means "Sure," "Faithful" or "Truth."

[h] Or "created things."

[i] Or "perhaps you should be cold or warm!" – sarcastic.

[j] Or possibly "and *I* need nothing."

[k] Or "I am giving you."

וּמָשַׁחְתָּ אֶת עֵינֶיךָ בַּשֶּׁמֶן כְּדֵי שֶׁתּוּכַל לִרְאוֹת [a] ₁₉ וַאֲנִי מוֹסֵר לְאֵלּוּ שֶׁאָהַבְתִּי וְעַכְשָׁיו עֲשֵׂה תְּשׁוּבָה ₂₀ רְאֵה אֲנִי עוֹמֵד לִפְנֵי הַפֶּתַח וְדֹפֵק בָּהּ וּבָאם שֶׁאֶחָד יִשְׁמַע אֶת קוֹלִי וְיִפְתַּח הַפֶּתַח לָזֶה אֵלֵךְ ₂₁ מִי שֶׁמְּנַצֵּחַ לָזֶה אֶתֵּן לֵישֵׁב עִימִּי עַל כִּסְאִי כְּמוֹ שֶׁנִּצַּחְתִּי וְיָשַׁבְתִּי עִם אָבִי עַל כִּסְאוֹ ₂₂ מִי שֶׁיֵּשׁ לוֹ אָזְנַיִם שׁוֹמֵעַ מַה שֶׁהָרוּחַ אוֹמֵר

פֶּרֶק ד'

₁ וְאַחַר כָּךְ רָאִיתִי [ ] [b] שֶׁנִּפְתַּח פֶּתַח אֶחָד בַּשָּׁמַיִם וְהַקּוֹל הָרִאשׁוֹן שֶׁשָּׁמַעְתִּי הַמְדַבֶּרֶת עִימִּי כְּקוֹל שׁוֹפָר אָמַר לִי בֹּא לְכָאן וַאֲנִי רוֹצֶה לְהַרְאוֹת לְךָ מַה שֶׁיִּהְיֶה אַחַר כָּךְ ₂ וְתֵיכֶף וּמִיָּד שׁוֹרָה עָלַי רוּחַ הַקּוֹדֶשׁ וְרָאִיתִי כִּסֵּא אֶחָד יָשֵׁב בַּשָּׁמַיִם וְעַל הַכִּסֵּא יָשֵׁב אֶחָד ₃ וְהַיֹּשֵׁב עָלָיו הָיָה מַרְאֵיהוּ כְּמַרְאֵה אֶבֶן סַפִּיר וְיָשְׁפֵה וְסָבִיב לְהַכִּסֵּא הָיָה אֶחָד קֶשֶׁת כְּמוֹ נֹפֶךְ ₄ וְסָבִיב לְהַכִּסֵּא הָיָה אַרְבַּע וְעֶשְׂרִים כִּסְאִים

---

[a] This is a Hiphil participle from the root "יסר".

[b] Crossed-out letter.

and anoint your eyes with oil, that you may be able to see. 19 I[a] discipline[b] those whom I love, therefore do repentance. 20 Look! – I stand before the door and knock on it, and if one will hear my voice and will open the door, to this one I will come. 21 Whosoever overcomes, to him[c] I will give to sit down with me by my throne, like I overcame and sat down with my Father by his throne. 22 Whosoever has ears must hear what the Ruach says!'"

4: 1 And after this I saw that a door was opened in the heavens, and the first voice which I had heard – that spoke with me like the sound of a shophar[d] – said to me, "Come here and I want to show you what will happen after this."

2 And forthwith[e] and immediately Ruach Ha-Qodesh[f] rested[g] on me, and I saw a throne sitting in the heavens, and one sitting on the throne. 3 And he who sat on it, his appearance[h] was like the appearance of *the* stone sapphire[i] and jasper,[j] and around the throne was a bow[k] like turquoise.[l] 4 And around the throne were twenty-four thrones,[m]

---

[a] Lit. "And I."

[b] Or "chasten" or "rebuke."

[c] Lit. "this *one*," but often means 'he' or 'him.'

[d] Hebrew word for "ram's horn" or "trumpet."

[e] Or "instantly."

[f] Meaning "the Set-Apart Spirit."

[g] Or "abode" or "was dwelling."

[h] Or possibly 'face.'

[i] Or, a special kind of sapphire called 'lapis lazuli.'

[j] Or possibly 'jade.' The exact identification of many precious stones is debated.

[k] Meaning "a rainbow." Compare Ezek. 1:28.

[l] Or possibly 'malachite.'

[m] Or "seats."

וַעֲלֵיהֶם יוֹשְׁבִים אַרְבַּע וְעֶשְׂרִים זְקֵנִים לָבוּשׁ בְּמַלְבּוּשִׁים

לְבֵינִים[a] וְעַל רָאשֵׁיהֶם כֶּתֶר זָהָב , וּמֵהַכִּסֵּא יָצָא קוֹלוֹת

וּרְעָמִים וּבְרָקִים וְשִׁבְעָה נֵירוֹת לִפְנֵי הַכִּסֵּא וְאֵילוּ הֵמָּה

שִׁבְעָה רוּחוֹת יַהֲוֶה , וְלִפְנֵי הַכִּסֵּא הָיָה יָם אֶחָד שֶׁל צְלוֹחִית

כִּדְמוּת אַחְלָמָה וּבְתוֹךְ [ ][b] הַכִּסֵּא וְסָבִיב לְהַכִּסֵּא אַרְבַּע

חַיּוֹת מָלֵא עֵינַיִם מִלִּפְנֵיהֶם וּמֵאַחֲרֵיהֶם , וְהַחַיָּה הָרִאשׁוֹן

הָיָה כִּדְמוּת [ ][c] אַרְיֵה וְהַשְּׁנִיָּה כְּשׁוֹר וְהַשְּׁלִישִׁי כְּאָדָם

וְהָרְבִיעִי כְּנֶשֶׁר , וּלְכָל אֶחָד שִׁשָּׁה כְּנָפַיִם וּמִבִּפְנִים מְלוּאִים

עִם עֵינַיִם וְלֹא יֵשׁ לָהֶם מְנוּחָה יוֹם וָלַיְלָה וְאוֹמְרִים תָּמִיד

קָדוֹשׁ קָדוֹשׁ קָדוֹשׁ יַהֲוֶה צְבָאוֹת[d] הָאַדִּיר הֱהָיָה הֶהֹוֶה וְיִהְיֶה

---

[a] Alternative spelling for "לְבָנִים". Variation between an a-class and e/i-class vowel on the second root-letter of the adjective "לבן" can be seen in the Masoretic Text in Gen. 49:12 ("וּלְבֶן"); and in manuscripts of the Samaritan Torah (relevant vowels shown below – note that the Samaritan "ˉ" corresponds to the Tiberian "ַ" or "ָ"; while the "ˇ" corresponds to "ֵ" or "ִ"), e.g. Gen. 30:37 "לבנות" (New York Public Library ms. Heb. 228) vs. "לבֹנות" (British Library ms. Or. 6461); Lev. 13:43 "לבנה" (National Library of France, ms. Sam. 2) vs. "לבֹנה" (British Library ms. Or. 6461). See the respective passages in: S. Schorch, *The Samaritan Pentateuch, A Critical Edition Maior*, De Gruyter, vol. 3 (2018) and vol. 1 (2021). A similar spelling "לבינא" is also known in Mandaic Aramaic. See e.g. E. S. Drower and R. Macuch, *A Mandaic Dictionary*, Oxford University Press, 1963, p. 229.

[b] Crossed-out letters.

[c] Crossed-out letters.

[d] Quoted from Is. 6:3.

and twenty-four elders sat on them, clothed in white garments, and on their heads was a crown^a of gold. ₅ And from the throne there went out, voices and thunders and lightnings, and seven lamps were before the throne (and these are the seven Ruchot of Yahweh).

₆ And before the throne was a sea of glass, like the appearance of crystal.^b And in the midst^c of the throne and around the throne were four living creatures, full of eyes at their front and at their back. ₇ And the first living creature was like the appearance^d of a lion, and the second like a bull, and the third like a man, and the fourth like an eagle.^e ₈ And each one had six wings, also on the inside they were filled with eyes.^f And they do not have rest, day or night, but say continually, "Qadosh,^g qadosh, qadosh, is Yahweh Tseva'ot^{h, i} the Mighty,^j who was and is and will be."

---

[a] Or "on *each of* their heads was a crown of gold." Hebrew often uses a singular noun to imply plural (collective).

[b] Hebrew "אחלמה" (*achlamah*) – see chapter 22:1, which indicates that "אחלמה" is not a red or brown jasper as is commonly believed.

[c] Compare Ezek. 1:22-27. It seems that these cherubs are underneath and around Yahweh's throne, and here they are described as forming part of the throne structure (in the midst of the throne).

[d] Compare Ezek. 1:10: "the appearance of their faces..."

[e] Compare Ezek. 1:10, 10:14. They each have four different faces, and if they stand in / face four different directions, one set of the four different faces can be seen from every side.

[f] Probably means that their wings also had eyes underneath.

[g] Lit. "Set-apart."

[h] Hebrew word for "armies." The full name/title is "Yahweh Elohei Tseva'ot" (Yahweh, Elohim of Armies). See e.g. Jer. 5:14, Amos 4:13, Rev. 15:3.

[i] Quoted from Is. 6:3.

[j] Or "Majestic."

9 וּבְשָׁעָה שֶׁהַחַיּוֹת נוֹתְנִים שֶׁבַח וְהוֹדָאָה לְזֶה שֶׁיּשֵׁב עַל הַכִּסֵּא וְהַחַי מֵעוֹלָם וְעַד עוֹלָם 10 הָיוּ נוֹפְלִים הָאַרְבַּע וְעֶשְׂרִים זְקֵנִים לְפָנָיו וּמִתְפַּלְּלִים לְזֶה שֶׁחַי מֵעוֹלָם וְעַד עוֹלָם וְזוֹרְקִים כִּתְרֵיהֶם לְפָנָיו וְאוֹמְרִים 11 אָדוֹן אַתָּה רָאוּיָה לִיקַּח[a] כָּבוֹד וְתִפְאֶרֶת כִּי אַתָּה בָּרָא הַכֹּל וְעַל יַד רְצוֹנְךָ נַעֲשָׂה הַכֹּל

פֶּרֶק ה'

1 וְזֶה שֶׁיּשֵׁב עַל הַכִּסֵּא רָאִיתִי בְּיַד יְמִינוֹ סֵפֶר אֶחָד וְחָתוּם בַּחֲתִימוֹת מִבִּפְנִים וּמִבַּחוּץ בְּשִׁבְעָה חֲתִימוֹת 2 וְרָאִיתִי מַלְאָךְ אֶחָד צָעֵק בְּקוֹל גָּדוֹל מִי רָאוּיָה לִפְתוֹחַ אֶת הַסֵּפֶר וְלִשְׁבֹּר חֲתִימוֹתָיו 3 וְשׁוּם אֶחָד לֹא בַּשָּׁמַיִם וּבָאָרֶץ יוּכַל לִפְתוֹחַ הַסֵּפֶר וְלִרְאוֹת בּוֹ 4 וּבוֹכֶה אֲנִי מְאוֹד כֵּיוָן שֶׁלֹּא נִמְצָא אֶחָד שֶׁרָאוּיָה לְזֶה הַדָּבָר 5 וְאֶחָד מֵהַזְּקֵנִים אָמַר לִי אַל תִּבְכֶּה רְאֵה שֶׁנִּצַּח הָאַרְיֵה הַיֵּשׁ מִמִּשְׁפַּחַת [ ][b] יוּדָא מֵהַשׁוֹרֶשׁ דָּוִד לִפְתוֹחַ הַסֵּפֶר וְלִשְׁבֹּר הַשִּׁבְעָה חֲתִימוֹת 6 וְרָאִיתִי שֶׁבְּתוֹךְ הַכִּסֵּא וְהַחַיּוֹת וְהָאַרְבַּע וְעֶשְׂרִים זְקֵנִים עָמֵד[c] שֶׂה אֶחָד

---

[a] This is an alternative form of the 'infinitive construct' with "ל" preposition (root: "לקח"). Spelled "לָקַחַת" in the Tanach.

[b] Crossed-out letters.

[c] Or possibly "עָמַד".

₉ And when the living creatures give lauding^a and thanks^b to him^c who sits on the throne, and who lives^d from everlasting and unto everlasting, ₁₀ the twenty-four elders fall down before him and pray^e to him^f who lives from everlasting and unto everlasting, and *they* cast their crowns before him and say, ₁₁ "Adon,^g you are worthy to receive honor and glory, for you are the Creator^h of everything, and by your willⁱ everything was made."

5: ₁ And he^j who sat on the throne – I saw a scroll in his right hand, and *it* was sealed with seals on *the* inside and on the outside, with seven seals. ₂ And I saw a messenger crying out with a great voice, "Who is worthy to open the scroll and to break its seals?" ₃ But no one in the heavens or on the earth was able to open the scroll and to look in it.^k ₄ Now, I was weeping exceedingly because no one was found who was worthy of this matter. ₅ But one of the elders said to me, "Do not weep, look! – The Lion who is from the family of Yehudah,^l from the root of Dawid, has overcome to open the scroll and to break the seven seals."

₆ Then I saw that in the midst of the throne and the living creatures and the twenty-four elders, there stood a Lamb,

---

^a Or "praise."
^b Or "acknowledgment."
^c Lit. "this *one*," but often means 'he' or 'him.'
^d Or "even to him who lives."
^e Or "worship him."
^f Lit. "this *one*," but often means 'he' or 'him.'
^g The Hebrew word for 'lord' or 'master.'
^h Or "you created everything."
ⁱ Or "goodwill."
^j Lit. "this *one*," but often means 'he' or 'him.'
^k Or "or to look at it."
^l Hebrew name for 'Judah.'

כְּמוֹ שֶׁנֶּהֱרַג[a] וְלוֹ הָיָה שִׁבְעָה קְרָנַיִם וְשִׁבְעָה עֵינַיִם[b] וְאֵילוּ
הַשִּׁבְעָה רוּחוֹת יַהְוֶה נִשְׁלַח[c] בְּכָל הָאָרֶץ , וּבָא וְלָקַח הַסֵּפֶר
מִיַּד (103r) יְמִינוֹ מִזֶּה שֶׁיֵּשֵׁב עַל הַכִּסֵּא 8 וּבְשָׁעָה שֶׁלָּקַח הַסֵּפֶר
הָיוּ נוֹפְלִים הָאַרְבַּע חַיּוֹת וְאַרְבַּע וְעֶשְׂרִים זְקֵנִים לִפְנֵי הַשֶּׂה
וּבִידֵיהֶם כִּנּוֹר וּמַחְתּוֹת מְלֵאִים קְטוֹרֶת וְזֹאת הִיא תְּפִילַת
הַקְּדוֹשִׁים , וְזִמְּרוּ שִׁיר חָדָשׁ וְאָמְרוּ אַתָּה רָאוּיָה לִיקַח[d]
הַסֵּפֶר וְלִפְתּוֹחַ אֶת חֲתִימוֹתָיו כִּי אַתָּה נֶהֱרַג וְקָנִיתָ אוֹתָנוּ
בְּדָמֶיךָ 10 וְעָשִׂיתָ אוֹתָנוּ לְכֹהֲנִים וְלִמְלָכִים וַאֲנַחְנוּ נִהְיוּ[e]
מְלָכִים[f] עַל הָאָרֶץ 11 וְרָאִיתִי וְשָׁמַעְתִּי קוֹלוֹת הַרְבֵּה
מֵהַמַּלְאָכִים סָבִיב לְהַכִּסֵּא וּמִסְפָּרָם הָיָה אֲלָפִים רְבָבוֹת 12
וְאוֹמְרִים בְּקוֹל גָּדוֹל הַשֶּׂה הַנֶּהֱרַג רָאוּיָה לְכֹחַ וּלְכָבוֹד
וּלְתִפְאֶרֶת וְלִתְהִילֹת 13 וְכָל הַבְּרִיאוֹת הַיֵּשׁ בַּשָּׁמַיִם וְעַל
הָאָרֶץ וּמִתַּחַת הָאָרֶץ וּבַיָּם שָׁמַעְתִּי שֶׁאוֹמְרִים לְזֶה הַיּוֹשֵׁב
עַל הַכִּסֵּא וּלְהַשֶּׂה כָּבוֹד וּתְהִילוֹת וְשֶׁבַח מֵעוֹלָם וְעַד עוֹלָם

---

[a] Or possibly "שֶׁנֶּהֱרָג".

[b] Compare Zech. 3:9, 4:10.

[c] Or possibly "נִשְׁלַח".

[d] This is an alternative form of the 'infinitive construct' with "ל" preposition (root: "לקח"). Spelled "לָקַחַת" in the Tanach.

[e] Based on the context, this verb cannot be a Niphal 'perfect' third person plural. The unusual spelling "נהיו" instead of "נהיה" indicates the plural aspect of the verb twice – it looks like "נהיה" with a "ו" added as a plural ending (compare e.g. "יהיה" vs. "יהיו"). Similar spellings (with double indication of the plural) were sometimes used by medieval Jewish scribes. E.g., in Luke 20:14, Vat. Ebr. 100 and JTS Breslau 233 read "ונהרגהו", but St. Petersburg A 207 spells the same word as "ונהרגוהו". Compare chapter 19:7.

[f] Or possibly "מְלָכִים".

like[a] he had been slain. And he had seven horns and seven eyes[b] (and these are the seven Ruchot of Yahweh, sent into all the earth). 7 So he came and took the scroll from the right hand (103r) of him[c] who sat on the throne. 8 And when he took the scroll, the four living creatures and twenty-four elders fell down before the Lamb, and in their hands were lyres and fire pans full of incense (and this is the prayer of the set-apart ones). 9 And they sang[d] a new song and said, "You are worthy to take[e] the scroll and to open its seals, for you were slain and bought us with your blood, 10 and you made us priests and kings, that we may be kings[f] over the earth."

11 Then I saw and I heard many voices of the messengers around the throne – and their number was twenty million.[g] 12 And they said with a great voice, "The Lamb who was slain is worthy of power and honor and glory and praises!" 13 And all the creations[h] which are in the heavens and on the earth and under the earth and in the sea, I heard saying, "To him[i] who sits on the throne, and to the Lamb, be honor and praises and lauding, from everlasting and unto everlasting."

---

[a] Or "as if."
[b] Compare Zech. 3:9, 4:10.
[c] Lit. "this *one*," but often means 'he' or 'him.'
[d] Hebrew uses root "זמר" (*zamar*) which can refer to singing while playing instruments.
[e] Or "receive."
[f] Or possibly 'that we may reign over the earth.'
[g] Lit. "two thousand ten-thousands."
[h] Or "created things." Could also possibly mean 'persons.' Compare e.g. Mark 16:15 in the HebrewGospels.com version, where a similar Hebrew word is used.
[i] Lit. "this *one*," but often means 'he' or 'him.'

14 וְאַרְבַּע הַחַיּוֹת עוֹנִים אָמֵן וְאַרְבַּע וְעֶשְׂרִים זְקֵנִים נוֹפְלִים וּמִתְפַּלְּלִים לָזֶה שָׁחַי מֵעוֹלָם וְעַד עוֹלָם

פֶּרֶק ו'

1 וְרָאִיתִי שֶׁהַשֶּׂה פֹּתֵחַ[a] אֶחָד מֵחֲתִימוֹת וְשָׁמַעְתִּי שֶׁהָאַרְבַּע חַיּוֹת אוֹמְרִים כְּקוֹל אֶחָד בֹּא וּרְאֵה 2 וְרָאִיתִי סוּס אֶחָד לָבָן וְהַיּוֹשֵׁב עָלָיו הָיָה בְּיָדוֹ קֶשֶׁת אֶחָד וְלוֹ נוּתַּן כֶּתֶר אֶחָד וְהוּא הָלַךְ לְנַצֵּחַ וְנִצַּח 3 וְכֵיוָן שֶׁנִּפְתַּח חֲתִימוֹת הַשֵּׁנִי שָׁמַעְתִּי שֶׁחַיָּה הַשְּׁנִיָּה אָמַר[b] בֹּא וּרְאֵה 4 וְהָלַךְ לַחוּץ סוּס אַחֵר[c] אָדֹם וְהַיּוֹשֵׁב עָלָיו נוּתַּן לִיקַּח הַשָּׁלוֹם מֵהָאָרֶץ וְלוֹ נוּתַּן חֶרֶב גָּדוֹל 5 וּבְשָׁעָה שֶׁפָּתַח חֲתִימַת הַשְּׁלִישִׁי אָמַר[d] הַחַיָּה הַשְּׁלִישִׁי בֹּא וּרְאֵה וְרָאִיתִי סוּס אֶחָד שָׁחֹר וְהַיּוֹשֵׁב עָלָיו הָיָה בְּיָדוֹ מֹאזְנַיִם אֶחָד 6 וְשָׁמַעְתִּי קוֹל אֶחָד בְּתוֹךְ הָאַרְבַּע חַיּוֹת אָמַר מִדָּה אַחַת חִיטִים בִּשְׁנֵי פָנִים וּשְׁלוֹשָׁה מִדּוֹת שְׂעוֹרִים בִּשְׁנֵי פָנִים וּלְהַשֶּׁמֶן וְהַיַּיִן אַל תַּעֲשֶׂה רַע

---

[a] Or possibly "פָּתַח".

[b] Or possibly "אָמַר".

[c] Or possibly "אֶחָד" – "ד" and "ר" were sometimes confused when copying the Hebrew Bible.

[d] Or possibly "אָמֵר".

14 So the four living creatures answered "Amein," and *the* twenty-four elders fell down and prayed to him[a] who lives from everlasting and unto everlasting.

6: 1 Then I saw that the Lamb opened one of *the* seals, and I heard the four living creatures say – like one voice – "Come and see!" 2 Then I saw a white horse, and he who sat on it had a bow in his hand, and a crown was given to him, and he went to overcome, and he overcame.[b]

3 And when the second seal[c] was opened, I heard the second living creature say, "Come and see!" 4 Then another horse went out – a red one[d] – and he who sat on it was given to take away the shalom from the earth, and a great sword was given to him.

5 And when he opened the third seal, the third living creature said, "Come and see!" Then I saw a black horse, and he who sat on it had a pair of balances[e] in his hand. 6 And I heard a voice in the midst of the four living creatures, saying, "One measure of wheat for a coin,[f] and three measures of barley for a coin,[g] and to the oil and the wine, do not do damage!"

---

[a] Lit. "this *one*," but often means 'he' or 'him.'
[b] Or "to conquer, and he conquered."
[c] Or possibly 'the second of the seals.'
[d] Or possibly 'Then a red horse went out.'
[e] Or "scales."
[f] Lit. "two faces," possibly referring to a specific coin or specific value of coin. Various ancient Roman coins were issued with two rulers depicted on one coin. This was either done with one portrait on each side, or with both portraits on the obverse (front) of the coin, in various typical orientations (face-to-face, back-to-back, side-by-side). Specifically during Yeshua's time, a coin is believed to have depicted Tiberius on the obverse and Augustus on the reverse. However, the Roman Denarius also often depicted the two-faced pagan god, from which this term possibly could have derived.
[g] See above note.

7 וְכֵיוָן שֶׁפָּתַח חֲתִימַת הָרְבִיעִת שָׁמַעְתִּי הַחַיָּה הָרְבִיעִי אוֹמֵר
בֹּא וּרְאֵה 8 וְרָאִיתִי סוּס אֶחָד בָּרֹד וְאַמֵּץ[a] וְזֶה שֶׁיָּשֵׁב עָלָיו
הָיָה שְׁמוֹ מַלְאַךְ הַמָּוֶת וְהַגֵּיהִנֹּם הָלֵךְ[b] אַחֲרָיו וְלוֹ נוּתַּן
רְשׁוּת לְהָמִית חֵלֶק רְבִיעִי עַל הָאָרֶץ בַּחֶרֶב וּבָרָעָב וּבַמָּוֶת
וְעַל יַד חַיּוֹת הָאָרֶץ 9 וְכֵיוָן שֶׁפָּתַח הַחֲמִישִׁי רָאִיתִי תַּחַת
הַהֵיכָל הַנְּשָׁמוֹת שֶׁנֶּהֶרְגוּ עַל קְדֻשַּׁת יַהְוֶה וּבִשְׁבִיל הָעֵדוּת
שֶׁהָיָה לָהֶם 10 וְצוֹעֲקִים בְּקוֹל גָּדוֹל וְאוֹמְרִים אָדוֹן הַקָּדוֹשׁ
וְהַנֶּאֱמָן עַד מָתַי תִּשְׁפּוֹט וְאֵינְךָ תִּנְקַם דָּמֵינוּ מֵאֵילוּ הַדָּרִים
עַל הָאָרֶץ 11 וּלְכָל אֶחָד מֵהֶם נוּתַּן מַלְבּוּשֵׁי לָבָן וְנֶאֱמַר לָהֶם
שֶׁתִּשְׁקְטוּ עוֹד זְמָן מוּעָט

---

[a] Compare Zech. 6:3.
[b] Or possibly "הָלַךְ".

7 And when he opened the fourth seal, I heard the fourth living creature say, "Come and see!" 8 Then I saw a speckled and strong[a] horse, and he[b] who sat on it, his name was The Messenger of Death, and Gei-Hinnom[c] followed after him. And authority was given to him to put to death a fourth part on the earth, with the sword and with famine and with death, and by the animals of the earth.[d]

9 And when he opened the fifth, I saw under the temple the neshamot[e] who were killed because of the set-apartness of Yahweh, and because of the testimony[f] which they had. 10 And they cried out with a great voice and said, "Set-apart and faithful Adon, until when will you judge without avenging our blood from those who dwell on the earth?!" 11 And to every one of them were given white garments,[g] and it was said to them that, "You must rest[h] yet a little time."

---

[a] Compare Zech. 6:3.

[b] Lit. "this *one*," but often means 'he' or 'him.'

[c] Lit. "The valley of Hinnom." This Hebrew word is transliterated into Greek as 'Gehenna,' and is inaccurately translated as 'Hell.' This is a literal valley right next to Jerusalem ordained for future punishment. See Mat. 25:41-46 in the HebrewGospels.com version: "And then he will say to those who are on the left side... go into the fire of Gei-Hinnom, which is prepared for Ha-Satan and his messengers... And these will go into the fire of Gei-Hinnom, but the righteous ones will go into everlasting light." To learn more about the Biblical definition of 'Gei-Hinnom,' see Jer. 7:30-33, Is. 30:33, 66:24, etc.

[d] Hebrew expression meaning "by the wild animals."

[e] Plural of "נשמה" (*neshamah*) – the Hebrew word for "blowing/breath," "soul" or "spirit." Neshamah is also specifically used to refer to a person's "spirit/soul" which continues to exist after a person dies (as in this verse). (See glossary for more information.)

[f] Hebrew "עדות" (*'edut*) – one of the names for the Torah.

[g] Lit. "garments of white."

[h] Or "be quiet."

‫12 וְרָאִיתִי שֶׁפָּתַח הַשִּׁשִּׁי וְהָיָה רַעֲדוֹת הָאָרֶץ וְהַשֶּׁמֶשׁ הָיָה‬
‫שָׁחוֹר וְהַיָּרֵחַ הָיָה אָדֹם כַּדָּם 13 וְכָל צְבָאָם יִבּוֹל כִּנְבֹל עָלֶה‬
‫מִגֶּפֶן וּכְנֹבֶלֶת מִתְּאֵנָה a 14 וְכָל הֶהָרִים וּגְבָעוֹת נָדָעֲזוּ b‬
‫מִמְּקוֹמָם 15 וּמַלְכֵי אֶרֶץ וְרוֹזְנִים c וְהָעֲשִׁירִים וְהַשּׁוֹטְרִים‬
‫וְהָעֲבָדִים וְהַחוֹפְשִׁים סוֹתְרִים בַּמְּעָרוֹת צֵרִים וּבִמְחִלּוֹת‬
‫עָפָר d 16 וְאוֹמְרִים לֶהָרִים וְלַסְּלָעִים נְפֹל עָלֵינוּ וְסוֹתֵר‬
‫אוֹתָנוּ מִפְּנֵי הַמַּרְאֶה שֶׁל זֶה הַיּוֹשֵׁב עַל הַכִּסֵּא וּמִפְּנֵי חֲרוֹן‬
‫הַשֶּׂה 17 כִּי הַיּוֹם מֵחֲרוֹן אַפּוֹ בָּא וּמִי יוּכַל לַעֲמוֹד לְפָנָיו‬

פֶּרֶק ז'

‫1 וְאַחַר כָּךְ רָאִיתִי אַרְבַּע מַלְאָכִים עוֹמְדִים אֶל אַרְבַּע פִּינוֹת‬
‫הָאָרֶץ וּמִתְאַפְּקִים e הָאַרְבַּע רוּחוֹת הָאָרֶץ‬

---

a Quoted from Is. 34:4.

b Or "‫נָדָעֲזוּ‬", or possibly "‫נִדָּעֲזוּ‬" (if pointed as a Nitpael rather than a Nitpalpel). This word "‫נדעזו‬" is an alternative spelling for "‫נִזְדַּעְזְעוּ‬" (Nitpalpel 'perfect' third person plural, from the root "‫זוע‬"). In Hebrew and Aramaic, if the first root-letter is a "‫ז‬", the preformative 'dental' can be merged with this "‫ז‬" in the Hitpael and similar conjugations. Usually the "‫ז‬" would be retained and the "‫ד‬" dropped, e.g. "‫הִזַּכּוּ‬" for "‫הִזְדַּכּוּ‬" (Is. 1:16); "‫הזמנתון‬" vs. "‫הזדמנתון‬" (Dan. 2:9, Ketiv vs. Qere). But the Dead Sea Scrolls also show a good example where the "‫ד‬" was retained and the "‫ז‬" dropped (as also attested in this word "‫נדעזו‬"): "‫תדהרון‬" (5/6Hev50 1:6) vs. "‫תזדהרון‬" (4Q542 f1ii:12). For the use of "‫זו‬" vs. "‫זעו‬" at the end of the word, compare e.g. Gen. 42:27 (vowel points added for clarity): "‫טוּנֵיהּ‬" (Targum Pseudo Jonathan) vs. "‫טָעוּנֵהּ‬" (Targum Neofiti), both from the root "‫טען‬". See also "‫שאפרך‬" for "‫שאפרעך‬" (XHev/Se49 f1R:8).

c Phrase quoted from Ps. 2:2.

d Phrase quoted from Is. 2:19.

e Crossed out and replaced with "‫ואחזים בידם‬" – in similar script to main text.

₁₂ And I saw that he opened the sixth, and there was an earthquake and the sun was ᵃ black and the moon was ᵇ red like blood, ₁₃ and all their host withered ᶜ like a leaf withers from a vine, and like that which withers ᵈ from a fig tree.ᵉ ₁₄ And all the mountains and hills were shaken away from their place. ₁₅ And *the* kings of *the* earth and *the* rulers ᶠ and the rich ones and the officers and the slaves and the free ones, hid in caves in *the* rocks and holes in *the* ground.ᵍ ₁₆ And they said to the mountains and to the rocks, "Fall on us, and hide us because of the appearance ʰ of him ⁱ who sits on the throne, and because of the fury of the Lamb! ₁₇ For the day of his burning anger has come, and who is able to stand before him?!"

7: ₁ And after this I saw four messengers standing at the four corners ʲ of the earth, and holding back ᵏ the four winds of the earth,

---

ᵃ Or "became."

ᵇ Or "became."

ᶜ Or "will wither." The Hebrew word "נבל" (*navel*) "to wither/fall" is used three times in this verse, and can mean to "wither and fall."

ᵈ Or possibly 'the withering of a fig tree.'

ᵉ Quoted from Is. 34:4.

ᶠ Phrase quoted from Ps. 2:2.

ᵍ Phrase quoted from Is. 2:19.

ʰ Or possibly 'hide us from the face.'

ⁱ Lit. "this *one*," but often means 'he' or 'him.'

ʲ An expression which means something like 'ends' or 'quarters' of the earth. Compare chapter 20:8, which indicates that these are not literal corners (the nations do not dwell on the corners of the earth, they dwell all over the earth). See also Is. 11:12 and Ezek. 7:2.

ᵏ Crossed out and replaced with "holding in their hand" – in similar script to main text.

כְּדֵי שֶׁלֹּא תִּהְיֶה רוּחַ עַל הָאָרֶץ וְעַל הַמַּיִם וְעַל שׁוּם עֵץ 2 וְרָאִיתִי מַלְאָךְ אַחֵר שֶׁבָּא מִמִּזְרַח הַשֶּׁמֶשׁ וְלוֹ הָיָה הַחוֹתָם מֵהָאֵל חַי וְקִיָּם וְצָעַק בְּקוֹל גָּדוֹל לְהָאַרְבַּע מַלְאָכִים הַנּוּתָן לָהֶם לְהַזִּיק הָאָרֶץ וְהַיָּם 3 וְאָמַר אַל תַּזִּיקוּ לְהָאָרֶץ וְלַהַיָּם אוֹ לָעֵץ עַד שֶׁאִתֶּן תָּו עַל מִצְחוֹת עַבְדֵי יַהְוֶה 4 וְשָׁמַעְתִּי הַמִּסְפָּר מֵאֵילוּ שֶׁנֶּחְתְּמוּ הָיָה מֵאָה וְאַרְבַּע וְאַרְבָּעִים אֲלָפִים שֶׁנֶּחְתְּמוּ מִמִּשְׁפָּחוֹת בְּנֵי יִשְׂרָאֵל 5 מִשֵּׁבֶט יְהוּדָא שְׁנֵים עָשָׂר אֶלֶף מִשֵּׁבֶט רְאוּבֵן שְׁנֵים עָשָׂר אֶלֶף וּמִשֵּׁבֶט גָּד שְׁנֵים עָשָׂר אֶלֶף 6 מִשֵּׁבֶט אָשֵׁר שְׁנֵים עָשָׂר אֶלֶף מִשֵּׁבֶט נַפְתָּלִי שְׁנֵים עָשָׂר אֶלֶף מִשֵּׁבֶט מְנַשֶּׁה שְׁנֵים עָשָׂר אֶלֶף 7 מִשֵּׁבֶט שִׁמְעוֹן שְׁנֵים עָשָׂר אֶלֶף מִשֵּׁבֶט לֵוִי שְׁנֵים עָשָׂר אֶלֶף וּמִשֵּׁבֶט יִשָּׂשכָר[a] שְׁנֵים עָשָׂר אֶלֶף 8 מִשֵּׁבֶט זְבוּלוּן שְׁנֵים עָשָׂר אֶלֶף וּמִשֵּׁבֶט יוֹסֵף שְׁנֵים עָשָׂר אֶלֶף וּמִשֵּׁבֶט בִּנְיָמִין שְׁנֵים עָשָׂר אֶלֶף 9 וְאַחַר כָּךְ רָאִיתִי חַבְרוּתָה גְּדוֹלָה שֶׁלֹּא יוּכַל לִסְפּוֹר מִכָּל הָעַמִּים עוֹמְדִים לִפְנֵי הַכִּסֵּא וְלִפְנֵי הַשֶּׂה וְלוּבְשִׁים בְּמַלְבּוּשִׁים לְבֵינִים[b] וּבִידֵיהֶם עֲנָפִים 10 וְצוֹעֲקִים בְּקוֹל גָּדוֹל וְאוֹמְרִים לַיַהְוֶה הַיְשׁוּעָה[c] וּלְהַשֶּׂה 11 וְכָל הַמַּלְאָכִים עוֹמְדִים סָבִיב לְהַכִּסֵּא וְהַזְּקֵנִים וְהַחַיּוֹת

---

[a] The original pronunciation of this name was most probably "יִשְׂשָׂכָר", however, it is traditionally pronounced as "יִשָּׂכָר" (the "שְׂשָׂ" merged to "שָּׂ" with doubling Dagesh). The hybrid spelling "יִשָּׂשכָר" is commonly employed in the Tanach and other Jewish writings as a 'ketiv qere' perpetuum, and is meant to be read as "Yissachar" and not as "Yisaskar." For more information on 'ketiv qere' perpetuum, see www.hebrewgospels.com/yhwh/video-3.

[b] See footnote on chapter 4:4.

[c] Compare Ps. 3:9, Jonah 2:10.

so that there would not be wind on the earth or on the waters or on any tree. ₂ Then I saw another messenger who came from the rising of the sun,ᵃ and he had the seal of the living El, and he imposedᵇ and cried out with a great voice to the four messengers to whom it was given to damage the earth and the sea, ₃ and he said, "Do not damage the earth or the sea or the trees, until I placeᶜ a mark on the foreheads of the servants of Yahweh!"

₄ And I heard the number of those who were sealed: it was a hundred and forty-four thousand – who were sealed, of the families of the children of Yisrael. ₅ From the tribe of Yehudah, twelve thousand; from the tribe of Re'uven, twelve thousand; and from the tribe of Gad, twelve thousand. ₆ From the tribe of Asher, twelve thousand; from the tribe of Naphtali, twelve thousand; from the tribe of Menasheh, twelve thousand. ₇ From the tribe of Shim'on, twelve thousand; from the tribe of Lewi,ᵈ twelve thousand; and from the tribe of Yisachar, twelve thousand. ₈ From the tribe of Zevulun, twelve thousand; and from the tribe of Yoseph, twelve thousand; and from the tribe of Binyamin, twelve thousand.

₉ And after this I saw a great crowd which one is not able to number, from all the peoples,ᵉ standing before the throne and before the Lamb, and *they* were clothed in white garments, and in their hands were branches, ₁₀ and they cried out with a great voice and said, "The salvation belongs **to Yahweh**,ᶠ and to the Lamb!" ₁₁ And all the messengers were standing around the throne and the elders and the living creatures,

---

ᵃ Hebrew way of saying "east."
ᵇ Or "charged."
ᶜ Or "set" or "give."
ᵈ For a discussion on the original pronunciation of the Hebrew letter Waw/Vav, see HebrewGospels.com/yhwh/video-15.
ᵉ Does not refer to "people" but "nations."
ᶠ Compare Ps. 3:9(8), Jonah 2:10(9).

12 וְנוֹפְלִים עַל פְּנֵיהֶם לִפְנֵי הַכִּסֵּא וּמִתְפַּלְלִים לַיהֹוָה
וְאוֹמְרִים שֶׁבַח וְהוֹדָאָה וּתְהִלּוֹת וְכָבוֹד וְתִפְאֶרֶת וְכֹחַ
וּגְבוּרָה תִּהְיֶה לֵאלֹהֵינוּ [מֵעוֹלָם] וְעַד עוֹלָם אָמֵן 13 וַיַּעַן
אֶחָד מֵהַזְּקֵנִים וְאָמַר לִי מִי אֵילּוּ (103v) הַלּוּבְשִׁים
בַּמַּלְבּוּשִׁים לְבָנִים וּמֵאֵיזֶה מָקוֹם בָּאִים הֵמָּה 14 וְאָמַרְתִּי לוֹ
אֲדוֹן אַתָּה יוֹדֵעַ וְהוּא אָמַר לִי אֵילּוּ הֵמָּה הַבָּאִים מִתּוֹךְ
הַרְבֵּה צַעַר וְרָחֲצוּ בִּגְדֵיהֶם וְזִקְּקוּ בִּגְדֵיהֶם בְּדַם הַשֶּׂה 15
וּבִשְׁבִיל זֶה הֵמָּה לִפְנֵי הַכִּסֵּא יַהֹוָה וְשֵׁרְתוּ אוֹתוֹ יוֹם וָלַיְלָה
וְזֶה שֶׁיֵּשֵׁב עַל הַכִּסֵּא תָּדוּר[a] עֲלֵיהֶם 16 וְהִיא[b] לֹא יִרְעָבוּ וְלֹא
יִצְמָאוּ וְלֹא יַכֵּם שָׁרָב וָשָׁמֶשׁ[c] 17 כִּי הַשֶּׂה יְנַהֲגֵם אוֹתָם לִבְאֵר
מַיִם[d] וּמָחָה יַהֹוָה אֱלֹהִים[e] דִּמְעָה מֵעַל כָּל פָּנִים[f]

פֶּרֶק ח׳

1 וְכֵיוָן שֶׁפָּתַח הַשְּׁבִיעִי שׁוֹתְקִים כּוּלָם בַּשָּׁמַיִם כְּשָׁעָה חֲדָא[g]
2 וְרָאִיתִי שִׁבְעָה מַלְאָכִים בָּאִים לִפְנֵי יַהֹוָה

---

[a] For the use of "ת" instead of "י", see footnote on chapter 1:7. Margin reads "יגן" – in different script than main text.

[b] Probably means "And this is:" – used to introduce the following quote from the Tanach.

[c] Quoted from Is. 49:10.

[d] Compare Is. 49:10.

[e] The Masoretic Text reads "אדני יהוה". Note that "אדני יהוה" can interchange with "יהוה אלהים", as both phrases are traditionally pronounced as 'Adonai Elohim.' Compare e.g. the Dead Sea Scrolls against the Masoretic Text in Is. 61:1 (1Q8 "]יה[וה אלהים" vs. MT "אדני יהוה") and Is. 61:11 (1QIsa "אדני יהוה" vs. MT "יהוה אלהים").

[f] Quoted from Is. 25:8.

[g] Aramaic expression quoted from Dan. 4:16.

and *they* fell on their faces before the throne and prayed[a] to Yahweh, ₁₂ and said, "Lauding and thanks[b] and praises and honor and glory and power and might[c] be to our Elohim, from [everlasting] and unto everlasting, amein!"

₁₃ Then one of the elders answered and said to me, "Who are these (103v) that are clothed in white garments, and from what place do they come?" ₁₄ So I said to him, "Adon, you know." And he said to me, "These are they who come from the midst of much[d] suffering, and they have washed their garments and purified their garments with the blood of the Lamb. ₁₅ And because of this they are before the throne of Yahweh, and they will serve him day and night, and he[e] who sits on the throne, **he** will dwell[f] by them. ₁₆ And this is: 'They will not be hungry nor thirsty, and burning heat and the sun will not smite them,'[g] ₁₇ for the Lamb will lead **them** to a well of waters,[h] 'and Yahweh Elohim will wipe off *the* tears from all faces.'"[i]

8: ₁ And when he opened the seventh, all of them in the heavens were silent for a moment, ₂ and I saw seven messengers coming before Yahweh,

---

[a] Or "worshiped Yahweh."
[b] Or "acknowledgment."
[c] Or "strength" or possibly 'victory.'
[d] Or "great."
[e] Lit. "this *one*," but often means 'he' or 'him.'
[f] Margin reads "will protect them" – in different script than main text.
[g] Quoted from Is. 49:10.
[h] Compare Is. 49:10.
[i] Quoted from Is. 25:8.

וְלָהֶם נוּתַּן שִׁבְעָה שׁוֹפָרוֹת , וּמַלְאָךְ אַחֵר בָּא וְדָרַךְ אֵצֶל
הַהֵיכָל וּבְיָדוֹ מַחְתּוֹת שֶׁל זָהָב וְלוֹ נוּתַּן הַרְבֵּה קְטוֹרֶת לִיתֵּן [a]
לִתְפִילַת הַקְּדוֹשִׁים לִפְנֵי הַהֵיכָל וְלִפְנֵי הַכִּסֵּא , וְהֶעָשָׁן
מֵהַקְּטוֹרֶת הַקְּדוֹשִׁים הָלַךְ מִיַּד הַמַּלְאָךְ לִפְנֵי יַהְוֶה ,
וְהַמַּלְאָךְ לָקַח הַמַּחְתָּה וּמִלֵּא אוֹתוֹ בָּאֵשׁ וְיָצַק עַל הָאָרֶץ
וּבָא קוֹלוֹת וּרְעָמִים וּבְרָקִים , וְהַשִּׁבְעָה מַלְאָכִים עִם
הַשִּׁבְעָה שׁוֹפָרוֹת הָיוּ מוּכָנִים לִתְקוֹעַ , וְהַמַּלְאָךְ הָרִאשׁוֹן
תּוֹקֵעַ וְהָיָה בָּרָד וְאֵשׁ בָּלֵל בַּדָּם וְנָפַל עַל הָאָרֶץ וְשָׁלִישׁ
מֵהָעֵצִים נִשְׂרָף [b] וְכָל יֶרֶק הַשָּׂדֶה נִשְׂרָף [c] , וְהַשֵּׁנִי תּוֹקֵעַ וְהָיָה
כְּהַר גָּדוֹל שֹׂרֵף בָּאֵשׁ וְהָלַךְ בַּיָּם וּשְׁלִישׁ הַיָּם הָיָה דָם ,
וְשָׁלִישׁ מִבְּרִיאוֹת הַיָּם מֵתִים וְשָׁלִישׁ מִסְּפִינוֹת נִיטְבָּעִים

---

[a] This is an alternative form of the 'infinitive construct' with "ל" preposition
(root: "נתן"). Normally spelled "לתת" in the Tanach.

[b] Or possibly "נִשְׂרַף", but compare verse 9.

[c] Or possibly "נִשְׂרַף", but compare verse 9.

and seven shopharot[a] were[b] given to them. ₃ And another messenger came and stepped[c] next to the temple, and golden fire pans were in his hand. And much incense was given to him, to give *it* as[d] the prayer of the set-apart ones, before the temple, even[e] before the throne. ₄ And the smoke of the incense of the set-apart ones went *up* from the hand of the messenger, before Yahweh. ₅ Then the messenger took the fire pan, and filled it with fire and poured *it* out on the earth, and there came voices and thunders and lightnings.

₆ And the seven messengers with the seven shopharot[f] were ready[g] to blow. ₇ Then the first messenger blew,[h] and there was[i] hail and fire mixed with blood, and it fell on the earth, and a third of the trees were burned up, and all the green plants of the field were burned up.

₈ Then the second blew,[j] and there was[k] *something* like a great mountain burning with fire, and it went into the sea, and a third of the sea was[l] blood. ₉ And a third of the creatures of the sea died, and a third of *the* ships sank.

---

[a] Plural of "שופר" (*shophar*) – the Hebrew word for "ram's horn" or "trumpet."

[b] Singular in Hebrew, see pp. 111-112 for more information.

[c] Or "stood."

[d] Or "for."

[e] Or "that is."

[f] Plural of "שופר" (*shophar*) – the Hebrew word for "ram's horn" or "trumpet."

[g] Or "made ready" or "prepared."

[h] Or "And as the first messenger was blowing, there came…"

[i] Or "there came."

[j] Or "And as the second was blowing, there came…" The same also applies for 8:10, 8:12, 9:1, 9:12[13], 12:1[11:15].

[k] Or "there came."

[l] Or "became."

10 וְהַשְּׁלִישִׁי תּוֹקֵעַ וְנָפַל כּוֹכָב אֶחָד מִשָּׁמַיִם וְשָׂרֵף וְנָפַל עַל
שְׁלִישׁ הַבְּאֵרוֹת[a] מַיִם 11 וְשֵׁם הַכּוֹכָב הָיָה תּוֹלַעַת וּשְׁלִישׁ
הַמַּיִם הָיָה מַר וְהַרְבֵּה בְּנֵי אָדָם מֵתִים עַל יַד הַמַּיִם מִפְּנֵי
מוֹרְרֵיהֶם[b] 12 וְהָרְבִיעִי תּוֹקֵעַ וְנִלְקָה [ ][c] הַשְּׁלִישׁ מֵהַשֶּׁמֶשׁ
וְהַיָּרֵחַ וְכוֹכָבִים וּשְׁלִישׁ מֵהַיּוֹם לֹא זֹרַח[d] וְגַם הַלַּיְלָה 13
וְרָאִיתִי וְשָׁמַעְתִּי מַלְאָךְ אֶחָד רֹחֵף בַּשָּׁמַיִם וְצָעַק[e] בְּקוֹל גָּדוֹל
אוֹי אוֹי אוֹי לְאֵילוּ הַדָּרִים עַל הָאָרֶץ מִפְּנֵי הַקּוֹל הַשּׁוֹפָרֹת
שֶׁצְּרִיכִים עוֹד לִתְקוֹעַ הַשְּׁלוֹשָׁה מַלְאָכִים

פֶּרֶק ט'

1 וְהַמַּלְאָךְ הַחֲמִישִׁי תּוֹקֵעַ וְרָאִיתִי כּוֹכָב אֶחָד נֹפֵל[f] עַל הָאָרֶץ
מִשָּׁמַיִם וְלוֹ נוּתַּן הַמַּפְתֵּחַ [ ][g] מִתְּהוֹם 2 וּפָתַח הַתְּהוֹם
וַיֵּצֵא עָשָׁן מִתְּהוֹם כְּמוֹ עָשָׁן מִתַּנּוּר גָּדוֹל וְהֶחֱשַׁךְ[h] הַשֶּׁמֶשׁ
וְהָאֲוִיר מֵעֲשַׁן הַתְּהוֹם

---

[a] Ms. reads "הבערות", altered to "הבארות" by proofreader/scribe. Compare also the use of "כעב" for "כאב" in chapter 9:11[12].

[b] Alternative spelling for "מָרְרֵיהֶם" (with added vowel letter), from "מֹר" (root מרר). (For the plural-like ending, see footnote on 9:5.) Compare e.g. "שָׁרֶךְ" in Song. 7:3, from "שֹׁר" (root שרר). Margin reads "מרירותם" – in different script than main text.

[c] Crossed-out letters.

[d] Or possibly "זָרַח", but compare verse 9.

[e] Or possibly "וְצָעֵק".

[f] Or possibly "נָפַל".

[g] Crossed-out letters.

[h] Or possibly "הֶחֱשַׁךְ".

10 Then the third blew, and a star fell from *the* heavens, and it was burning, and it fell on a third of the wells[a] of water. 11 And the name of the star was Tola'at;[b] and a third of the waters were[c] bitter, and many sons of man[d] died by means of[e] the waters, because of their bitterness.

12 Then the fourth blew, and there was stricken[f] – a third of the sun[g] and the moon and stars; and a third of the day did not shine, and also the night.[h] 13 Then I saw and heard a messenger flying in the heavens, and he cried out with a great voice, "Woe, woe, woe to those who dwell on the earth, because of the sound of the shopharot which the three messengers still have to blow!"

9: 1 Then the fifth messenger blew, and I saw a star[i] falling onto[j] the earth from the heavens, and to him the key of *the* Deep[k] was given. 2 So he opened the Deep, and there went out smoke from *the* Deep, like smoke from a great furnace, and the sun and the air were darkened by the smoke of the Deep.

---

[a] Or possibly 'cisterns.'

[b] Or "Crimson Worm" or "Crimson-Red," probably named so because the water was changed to red, bitter blood (compare verse 8, and Ex. 7:15-25).

[c] Or "became."

[d] Or "descendants of Adam," meaning "people" or "humans."

[e] Or "through" or "by."

[f] Or "smitten" or possibly 'eclipsed.'

[g] Or "and a third of the sun was stricken, and *of* the moon and stars."

[h] Meaning 'also *a third of* the night' – the phrase 'a third' is implied in the second half of this sentence. (Called gapping, commonly found in the Hebrew Tanach.)

[i] Meaning "a messenger (angel)." Compare chapter 1:20.

[j] Or possibly 'to.'

[k] Hebrew "תהום" (*tehom*) – used synonymously with She'ol in the Dead Sea Scrolls, see e.g. 1QHa 18:35-36; 4Q200 f6:6. Compare also Ps. 71:20 vs. Ps. 30:4(3).

3 וּמֵהֶעָשָׁן בָּאִים [אַרְבָּהִים]ᵃ עַל הָאָרֶץ וְלָהֶם נוּתַּן רְשׁוּת

[ ]ᵇ לְהַשְׁחִית 4 וְנֶאֱמַר לָהֶם שֶׁלֹא תַזִּיקוּ לְיֶרֶק וּלְעֵשֶׂב

הַשָּׂדֶה אוֹ לְעֵץ רַק לְבַד לִבְנֵיᶜ אָדָם שֶׁלֹא יֵשׁ לָהֶם הַחֲתִימֹת

בְּמִצְחֵיהֶם מִיַּהֲוֶה 5 וְלָהֶם נוּתַּן לֹא לְהָמִית אוֹתָם רַק לְצַעֵר

אוֹתָם חֲמִשָּׁה חֳדָשִׁים וְצַעֲרֵיהֶםᵈ הָיָה כְּצַעַר עַקְרַבִּים בְּאם

שֶׁנּוֹשֵׁךְ 6 וּבַיָּמִים הָהֵמָּה תַּחְכִּימוּ לָמוּת וְלֹא תִמְצָאֻנוּ 7

וְאַרְבָּהִים הֵמָּה כְּמוֹ הַסּוּסִים הַמּוּכָנִים לַמִּלְחָמָה וְעַל

רָאשֵׁיהֶם כִּדְמוּת כִּתְרֵי זְהָבִים וּמַרְאֵיהֶם כַּמַּרְאוֹת הָאָדָם 8

וְשַׂעֲרוֹתֵיהֶם כְּשַׂעֲרוֹת הַנָּשִׁים וְשִׁנָּיו כְּשִׁנֵּי אַרְיֵה 9 [10]

וְזַנְבֵיהֶם הָיָה כְּזַנְבֵי אַרְבֶּה וְלָהֶם נוּתַּן רְשׁוּת לְצַעֵר הַבְּנֵי

אָדָם חֲמִשָּׁה חֳדָשִׁים 10 [11] וּמֶלֶךְ שֶׁלָּהֶם הָיָה מַלְאָךְ אֶחָד

מִתְּהוֹם

ᵃ Main text reads "צפרדעים", but this word was crossed out and replaced with "ארבהים" – in same script as main text.

ᵇ Scribe wrote "לכלות", then crossed it out immediately and continued with the correct word in the main text.

ᶜ Ms. had "ובני", corrected to "לבני" – by proofreader/scribe.

ᵈ In the Tanach, 'light' and 'heavy' third person plural suffixes (e.g. "־ם" vs. "־הֶם") are used interchangeably on plural nouns, e.g. "מִשְׁפְּחֹתֵיהֶם" (Gen. 8:19) vs. "מִשְׁפְּחֹתָם" (Gen 10:5). In the Hebrew Revelation, James and Jude, the use of such 'heavy' suffixes (with a preceding helping vowel) has been extended to masculine and feminine singular nouns (and thus do not indicate a plural noun). This is also standard in the Tanach for singular nouns ending in "־ֶה", e.g. "מִקְנֶה" > "מִקְנֵיהֶם" (Gen. 36:7); "מַרְאֶה" > "מַרְאֵיהֶן" (Gen 41:21); "מַחֲנֶה" > "מַחֲנֵיהֶם" (Num. 5:3). See also Zeph. 3:20 ("שְׁבוּתֵיכֶם"). Compare footnotes on chapter 2:2, 2:12[13].

₃ And from the smoke there came [locusts]ᵃ over the earth, and authority was given to them to destroy.

₄ And it was said to them that, "You must not damage the green plants or the plants of the field or the trees, but only the sons of manᵇ who do not have the seal from Yahweh on their foreheads."ᶜ ₅ And to them it was given, not to kill them, but to inflict them with pain *for* five months. And their pain was like *the* pain of scorpions when they sting. ₆ And in those days youᵈ will try cleverlyᵉ to die, but you will not find it.

₇ And *the* locusts were like horses that are prepared for war – and on their heads were *something* likeᶠ crowns of gold, and their appearanceᵍ was like the appearanceʰ of man. ₈ And their hair was like the hair of women, and theirⁱ teeth were like the teeth of a lion, ₉ [10] ʲ and their tails were like the tails of locusts. And authority was given to them to inflict the sons of man with pain, *for* five months. ₁₀ [11] And their king was a messenger of *the* Deep,

---

ᵃ Scribe first wrote "frogs," then crossed it out and replaced it with "locusts" – in same script as main text.

ᵇ Or "descendants of Adam," meaning "people" or "humans."

ᶜ Could also mean: 'who were not sealed on their foreheads by Yahweh.'

ᵈ Plural throughout verse.

ᵉ Or "try skillfully."

ᶠ Or "with the appearance of."

ᵍ Or "face."

ʰ Or 'faces' – plural in Hebrew.

ⁱ Lit. "its" – collective use.

ʲ Verse numbers marked in manuscript mostly correspond to standard numbering in English translations. When the verse number in this manuscript differs from the standard numbering, the standard verse number is placed in brackets. E.g. verse 9 in this manuscript corresponds to verse [10] in standard Bibles. The verse numbered [9] in standard Bibles is absent in this ms.

וּשְׁמוֹ בִּלְשׁוֹן עִבְרִי אֲבַדּוֹן וּבִלְשׁוֹן יָוָן אֲפֹלְלִיאֹן[ᵃ] 11 [12] אֶחָד
כְּעָב[ᵇ] הָלַךְ רָאֵה עוֹד שְׁנֵי כְּעָבִים[ᶜ] בָּאִים 12 [13] וְהַמַּלְאָךְ
הַשִּׁשִּׁי תָּקַע וְשָׁמַעְתִּי קוֹל אֶחָד מֵאַרְבַּע פִּינוֹת הַהֵיכָל לִפְנֵי
יְהוָֹה 13 [14] וְאוֹמֶרֶת לְהַמַּלְאָךְ הַשִּׁשִּׁי שֶׁתָּקַע לֵךְ וְחַפֵּשׂ
לְהָאַרְבַּע מַלְאָכִים הָאֲסוּרִים אֵצֶל הַיָּם הַגָּדוֹל הַנִּקְרָא פְּרָת
14 [15] וְהָאַרְבַּע מַלְאָכִים הָיוּ מוּכָנִים לְהָמִית הַשְּׁלִישׁ מִבְּנֵי
אָדָם בְּשָׁעָה וּבְיוֹם וּבְחוֹדֶשׁ וּבְשָׁנָה אֶחָד 15 [16] וְרִכְבֵּיהֶם[ᵈ]
הָיָה מִסְפָּרָם רִבְּתַיִם אַלְפֵי וְשָׁמַעְתִּי מִסְפָּרָם 16 [17] וְאַחַר כָּךְ
רָאִיתִי בְּצוּרַת הַסּוּסִים וְהַיּוֹשְׁבִים עֲלֵיהֶם שֶׁהָיָה לָהֶם
מַלְבּוּשִׁים שֶׁל זֶפֶת וְגָפְרִת וָאֵשׁ

[ᵃ] Or possibly "אֲפֹלְלִיאֹן".

[ᵇ] Alternative spelling for "כאב". See also footnote chapter 8:10.

[ᶜ] Alternative spelling for "כאבים". See also footnote chapter 8:10.

[ᵈ] Or possibly "רֹכְבֵיהֶם".

and his name in the Hebrew tongue is Avadon,[a] and in the Greek[b] tongue, Apollyon.[c] **11 [12]** One[d] suffering[e] has gone by, look, two more sufferings[f] are coming!

12 [13] Then the sixth messenger blew, and I heard a voice from the four corners of the temple, before[g] Yahweh, **13 [14]** and it said to the sixth messenger who blew, "Go and set free the four messengers who are bound at the great river[h] which is called Perat."[i] **14 [15]** And these[j] four messengers were made ready[k] to kill a third[l] of *the* sons of man in an hour and in a day and in a month and in a year.[m]

15 [16] And the number of their chariots[n] was twenty million,[o] and I heard their number. **16 [17]** And after this I saw the shape[p] of the horses and those who sat on them, that they had garments of pitch and sulphur and fire.

---

[a] Meaning "Destruction."
[b] Hebrew "יון" (*yawan*) – see e.g. Gen. 10:2-4; Zech. 9:13; Dan. 8:21.
[c] Meaning "Destroyer."
[d] Or "The first."
[e] Or "pain."
[f] Or "pains."
[g] Or "in the presence of."
[h] Lit. "sea," but could also mean 'river,' compare chapter 16:11[12], see also 12:18[15] and Is. 19:5.
[i] Hebrew name for 'Euphrates.'
[j] Lit. "the."
[k] Or "prepared."
[l] Or "the third part."
[m] Meaning "at a certain hour of a certain day of a certain month of a certain year."
[n] Or possibly 'riders' or 'charioteers.' But note the factor 10 difference between the Hebrew 20 000 000 and Greek rendering of 200 000 000. Compare the difference between 2 Sam. 10:18 and 1 Chron. 19:18. "Chariots/chariot teams" vs. "charioteers/riders" gives the 10-fold difference.
[o] Lit. "twenty thousand thousands of."
[p] Or "appearance."

וְרָאשֵׁי הַסּוּסִים כְּרָאשֵׁי הָאֲרָיֵה [ ]ᵃ וּמִפִּיהֶם הֹלֵךְᵇ אֵשׁ
וְעָשָׁן וְגָפְרִית ₁₇ [18] וּמֵאֵילוּ הַשְּׁלוֹשָׁה נֶהֱרַג הַשְּׁלִישׁ מִבְּנֵי
אָדָם ₁₈ [19] כִּי כוֹחָם הָיָה בְּפִיהֶם וְזַנְבֵיהֶם הָיָה כַּנְּחָשִׁים
וְרָאשִׁים הָיָה לָהֶם וּבְאֵילוּ הוֹרְגִים אוֹתָם ₁₉ [20] אֲבָל הָיָה
עוֹד הַרְבֵּה בְּנֵי אָדָם שֶׁלֹּא יוּמְתוּ עַל יַד אֵילוּ הַנְּגָעִים בִּשְׁבִיל
שֶׁעָשׂוּ תְּשׁוּבָה עַל מַעֲשֵׂיהֶם הָרָעִים וְלֹא מִתְפַּלְּלִים לְהַשָּׂטָן
וְלֹא לַעֲבוֹדָה זָרָה הַנַּעֲשָׂה מֵחֶרֶס וּמֵאֶבֶן אוֹ מֵעֵץ וְכֶסֶף וְזָהָב
שֶׁלֹּא יֵשׁ בָּהֶם יְכוֹלֶת לֵילֵךְᶜ אוֹ לְדַבֵּר אוֹ לִשְׁמוֹעַ ₂₀ [21] וְשֶׁלֹּא
עָשׂוּ תְּשׁוּבָה עַל כִּשְׁפֵיהֶם וְעַל [ ]ᵈ זְנוּתֵיהֶםᵉ אוֹ עַל
גְּנֵבוֹתֵיהֶם

פֶּרֶק י'

₁ וְרָאִיתִי מַלְאָךְ אַחֵר יֵרֵד מִשָּׁמַיִם וְלָבוּשׁ בֶּעָנָן אֶחָד וְקֶשֶׁת
עַל רֹאשׁוֹ וּמַרְאֵיהוּ כַּשֶּׁמֶשׁ וְרַגְלָיו כְּלַהֲבַת אֵשׁ ₂ (104r) וּבְיָדוֹ
סֵפֶר אֶחָד פָּתוּחַ וְדָרַךְ עִם רֶגֶל יְמִינוֹ עַל הַיָּם וְעִם שְׂמֹאלוֹ
עַל הַיַּבָּשָׁה ₃ וְצָעַק בְּקוֹל גָּדוֹל כִּצְעֹק הָאֲרָיֵה וּבְשָׁעָה שֶׁצָּעַק
מְדַבְּרִים שִׁבְעָה קוֹלוֹת בְּקוֹלֵיהֶם

ᵃ Crossed-out letters.
ᵇ Or possibly "הָלַךְ".
ᶜ This is an alternative form of the 'infinitive construct' with "ל" preposition (root: "הלך"). Spelled "ללכת" in the Tanach.
ᵈ Crossed-out letters.
ᵉ See footnote on chapter 9:5.

And the heads of the horses were like the heads of the lion, and from their mouth there went out fire and smoke and sulphur. 17 [18] And by these three, a third[a] of *the* sons of man were[b] killed, 18 [19] for their power was in their mouth, and their tails were like serpents, and they had heads, and with these they killed them. 19 [20] But there were still many sons of man who were not put to death by these plagues – because they did[c] repentance concerning their evil deeds, by not praying to Ha-Satan, neither to idols which are made of pottery and of stone, or of wood and silver and gold, which do not have in them the ability to walk or to speak or to hear – 20 [21] but who did not do repentance concerning their sorceries or concerning their fornication or concerning their thefts.

10: 1 Then I saw another messenger descending from *the* heavens, and *he* was clothed with a cloud,[d] and a bow[e] was over[f] his head, and his appearance[g] was like the sun, and his feet like a flame of fire. 2 (104r) And in his hand was an open scroll, and he stepped[h] on the sea with his right foot, and on the dry land with his left. 3 And he cried out with a great voice, like the lion roars.[i] And when he had cried out, seven voices[j] spoke with their voices.[k]

---

[a] Or "the third part."
[b] Singular in Hebrew, see p. 111 for more information.
[c] Or possibly (but not very likely) 'in order that they should do.'
[d] Or "a cloud mass."
[e] Meaning "a rainbow." Compare Ezek. 1:28.
[f] Or "above" or "on."
[g] Or "face."
[h] Or "stood."
[i] Lit. "cries out."
[j] Hebrew often uses "voices" for "thunders."
[k] Or "spoke out loud." Compare e.g. Ps. 142:2(1).

4 וְאַחַר שֶׁדִּבְּרוּ בְּקוֹלֵיהֶם רָצִיתִי לִכְתּוֹב אוֹתָם שָׁמַעְתִּי בַּת קוֹל מִשָּׁמַיִם הָאוֹמֶרֶת לִי סְתֹם[a] אוֹתָם וְאַל תִּכְתּוֹב , 5 וְהַמַּלְאָךְ הָעוֹמֵד עַל הַיָּם וְעַל הַיַּבָּשָׁה [ ][b] שֶׁרָאִיתִי יָרֵם[c] יְמִינוֹ וּשְׂמֹאלוֹ אֶל הַשָּׁמַיִם , 6 וַיִּשָּׁבַע בְּחֵי הָעוֹלָם[d] הַבֹּרֵא הַשָּׁמַיִם וּמַה שֶּׁיֵּשׁ בָּהּ וְהָאָרֶץ וְהַיָּם וְכָל מַה שֶּׁיֵּשׁ בָּהֶם שֶׁלֹּא יֵשׁ עוֹד עֵת[e] , 7 רַק בְּאִם שֶׁהַשִּׁבְעָה מַלְאָכִים תּוֹקְעִים בַּשּׁוֹפָרוֹת תִּכְלֶינָה כָּל אֵלֶּה[f] הַסּוֹדוֹת יַהֲוֶה כְּמוֹ שֶׁמוֹדִיעַ לַעֲבָדָיו וְלִנְבִיאָיו , 8 וְשָׁמַעְתִּי עוֹד פַּעַם בַּת קוֹל אָמַר לִי לֵךְ וְקַח הַסֵּפֶר [ ][g] הַפָּתוּחַ מִיַּד הַמַּלְאָךְ הָעוֹמֵד עַל הַיָּם וְעַל הַיַּבָּשָׁה , 9 וְהָלַכְתִּי לְהַמַּלְאָךְ וְאָמַרְתִּי לוֹ תְּנוּ[h] לִי הַסֵּפֶר וְהוּא אָמַר לִי קַח וּבוֹלֵעַ אוֹתָהּ[i] וְיִהְיֶה לְךָ כִּדְבַשׁ בְּפִיךָ אֲבָל בְּמֵעֶיךָ יַעֲשֶׂה לְךָ צַעַר

---

[a] Altered to "סגור" – in similar/same script as main text.

[b] Crossed-out letter.

[c] This word begins a quote from Daniel 12:7. We have therefore pointed this word as a Waw-consecutive (based on the Tanach), even though the verb is here quoted without the accompanying "ו".

[d] Phrase quoted from Dan. 12:7.

[e] Margin reads "יהיה עוד כך" – in different script than main text.

[f] Phrase quoted from Dan. 12:7.

[g] Crossed-out letters.

[h] Or possibly "תְּנֵנִ" – but compare e.g. 1 Kin. 3:26 and Ex. 17:2 where a similar expression is used.

[i] Or possibly "אוֹתָהּ". Compare e.g. "אָהֳלֹה" (Gen. 9:21); "פַּרְעֹה" (Ex. 32:25); "כֵּלָּה" (Lev. 23:13); "הֲוֻמְנָה" (Ezek. 36:10); "נִסְכֹּה" (Ezek. 39:11), etc.

₄ And after they had spoken with their voices, I wanted to write them,[a] *but* I heard a voice[b] from *the* heavens which said to me, "Seal[c] them up, and do not write."

₅ And the messenger who was standing on the sea and on the dry land, whom I had seen, lifted up his right hand and his left hand unto the heavens. ₆ And he swore by the Ever-Living[d] – who created the heavens and what is in them, and the earth and the sea and whatever is in them – that, "There is[e] no more time, ₇ but, when the seven messengers blow with the shopharot, all these confidential counsels[f] of Yahweh will be completed, just like he made *it* known to his servants and[g] to his prophets."

₈ Then I again heard a voice[h] saying to me, "Go, and take the open scroll from the hand of the messenger who is standing on the sea and on the dry land." ₉ So I went to the messenger and said to him, "Give me the scroll." And he said to me, "Take and swallow it, and it will be for you like honey in your mouth, but in your stomach it will cause you pain."[i]

---

[a] Refers to the "seven voices."

[b] Hebrew "בת קול‎" (*bat qol*) – an idiom meaning 'a voice from heaven.'

[c] Altered to "Shut" in same/similar script as main text.

[d] Phrase quoted from Dan. 12:7.

[e] Or possibly 'will be.'

[f] Hebrew "סודות‎" (*sodot*) – see footnote on chapter 1:1.

[g] Could mean "even."

[h] Hebrew "בת קול‎" (*bat qol*) – an idiom meaning 'a voice from heaven.'

[i] Or "suffering."

₁₀ וְלָקַחְתִּי הַסֵּפֶר מִיַּד הַמַּלְאָךְ וּבוֹלֵעַ אוֹתוֹ[a] וְהָיָה כִדְבַשׁ בְּפִי וְאַחַר שֶׁאֲכַלְתִּי עָשָׂה לִי צַעַר בְּמֵעַי ₁₁ וְהוּא אָמַר לִי אַתָּה צָרִיךְ לְנִיבָּא[b] עוֹד פַּעַם לְאוּמִּים וּלְעַמִּים וְלִמְלָכִים

פֶּרֶק י"א

₁ וְנוּתַּן לִי קָנֶה אֶחָד כִּדְמוּת מַטֶּה וְאָמַר קוּם לִמְדוֹד הַהֵיכָל יַהְוֶה וּמִזְבְּחוֹ וְאֵילוּ הַמִּתְפַּלְלִים בּוֹ ₂ אֲבָל הַהֵיכָל הַפְּנִימִי זְרוֹק לַחוּץ וְלֹא תִמְדֹד כִּי הוּא נוּתַּן לָהָעַמִּים וְדָרְסוּ הָעִיר הַקּוֹדֶשׁ אַרְבָּעִים וּשְׁנַיִם חֳדָשִׁים ₃ וַאֲנִי נוֹתֵן אֶת שְׁנֵי עֵדִים שֶׁלִּי וְהֵם מִנַּבְּאִים[c] אֶלֶף וּשְׁנֵי מֵאוֹת וְשִׁשִּׁים יוֹם וְלָבוּשׁ בַּשַּׂקִּים ₄ וְאֵלֶּה הֵמָּה שְׁנֵי זֵיתִים וּשְׁנֵי אֲבוּקוֹת עוֹמְדִים לִפְנֵי אֱלֹהֵי הָאָרֶץ ₅ וְאִם שֶׁאֶחָד רוֹצֶה לַעֲשׂוֹת לָהֶם רָעָה תָּבוֹא אֵשׁ וְשָׂרַף[d] אוֹתָם ₆ וְלָהֶם יֵשׁ רְשׁוּת לִסְגּוֹר הַשָּׁמַיִם

---

[a] The letters "תי" were added to the end of this word – in different script than main text.

[b] This seems to be a Niphal 'infinitive' with the same form as the 'perfect' third person masculine singular (3ms). Compare e.g. "נָמוֹג" used as a Niphal 'perfect' 3ms in Nah. 2:7; but as a Niphal 'infinitive absolute' in Is. 14:31. Alternatively, this word could also be pointed as "לְנִיבֵּא" (if it is a Piel verb and not a Niphal).

[c] Alternative spelling for "מִתְנַבְּאִים". Compare e.g. "הַנַּבְּאוּ" for "הִתְנַבְּאוּ" (Jer. 23:13) and "וְהַנַּבֵּתִי" for "וְהִתְנַבֵּתִי" (Ezek. 37:10). Alternatively, this word could also be pointed as "מְנַבְּאִים" (if it is a Piel verb and not a Hitpael).

[d] Or possibly "וְשָׂרַף".

10 So I took the scroll from the hand of the messenger and swallowed it, and it was like honey in my mouth; but after I ate *it*, it caused me pain[a] in my stomach. **11** Then he said to me, "You must prophesy again to[b] nations and to peoples and to kings."

11: 1 Then a reed like[c] a rod was given to me, and he said, "Stand up, measure the temple of Yahweh, and its[d] altar, and those who pray[e] in it, **2** but cast out the inner temple, and do not measure *it*, for it is given to the nations, and they will tread down the set-apart city, forty-two months. **3** And I will give my two witnesses; and they will prophesy, a thousand two hundred and sixty days, clothed in sackcloth."

4 And these are *the* two olive trees and *the* two torches, standing before the Elohim of the earth. **5** And if one wants to do them evil,[f] fire comes and burns them up.[g] **6** And they have authority to shut the heavens,

---

[a] Or "suffering."
[b] Or "about nations and peoples and kings."
[c] Or "with the appearance of."
[d] Or possibly "his."
[e] Or "worship."
[f] Or "harm."
[g] Or "consumes them."

שֶׁלֹּא יָבֹא גֶּשֶׁם עַל הָאָרֶץ בִּימֵי נִבָּאֵיהֶם [a] וְעַל הַמַּיִם לַהֲפֹךְ
בְּדָם וּלְהַכּוֹת הָאָרֶץ בִּנְגָעִים בְּכָל עֵת שֶׁיִּרְצוּ , וְאַחַר שֶׁכָּלָא [b]
עֵדוּתָם יַעֲשֶׂה הַחַיָּה שֶׁהָלַךְ [c] מִתְּהוֹם מִלְחָמָה עִמָּם וִינַצַּח
אוֹתָם וְיַהֲרֹג אוֹתָם 8 , וְנִבְלָתֵיהֶם [d] תִּזָּרְקוּ עַל הָרְחוֹבוֹת
מֵהָעִיר הַקְּדוֹשָׁה הַנִּקְרָא סְדוֹם וּמִצְרַיִם כֵּיוָן שֶׁשָּׁם [e] נִצְלַב
אֲדוֹנֵינוּ , וְאֵיזֶה מֵהָעַמִּים וּמֵהַשְּׁבָטִים יִרְאוּ אֶת נִבְלָתֵיהֶם [f]
שְׁלוֹשָׁה יָמִים וָחֵצִי וְלֹא תִּקְבְּרוּ [g] אוֹתָם 10 וְאֵילוּ הַדָּרִים עַל
הָאָרֶץ יִשְׂמְחוּ עֲלֵיהֶם וְיִשְׁלְחוּ מַתָּנוֹת אִישׁ לְרֵעֵיהוּ כִּי [   ] [h]
הַנְּבִיאִים הַלָּלוּ עָשׂוּ הַרְבֵּה צַעַר לְאֵילוּ הַדָּרִים עַל הָאָרֶץ 11
וְאַחַר שְׁלוֹשָׁה יָמִים וָחֵצִי קָמִים [i] הֵמָּה וְדוֹרְסִים עַל רַגְלֵיהֶם
וּפַחַד וְאֵימָה גְּדוֹלָה נָפַל עַל אֵילוּ הָרוֹאִים אוֹתָם

---

[a] Compare chapter 10:11, where "ניבא" is used for the 'infinitive construct.' Here it seems that the same form is used, but with a suffix. (For the plural-like ending, see footnote on 9:5). Alternatively, this word could also be pointed as "נַבָּאֵיהֶם" (if formed from the Piel 'infinitive') or "נְבָאֵיהֶם" (if formed from the Qal passive participle).

[b] Alternative spelling for "שכלה". Compare e.g. "לְכַלֵּא" (Dan. 9:24) vs. "לְכַלֵּה" (2 Chr. 24:10). See also Mishnah Shevi'it 9:5, "שכלא" (ms. Kaufmann) vs. "שכלה" (ms. Parma/De Rossi 138).

[c] Or possibly "שֶׁהֹלֵךְ".

[d] Or possibly "וּנְבָלָתֵיהֶם" – compare e.g. "נְבָלָתוֹ" (Jer. 26:23) vs. "נְבֵלָתִי" (Is. 26:19).

[e] Crossed out and margin reads "וגם המקום ששם" – in different script than main text.

[f] Or possibly "נְבָלָתֵיהֶם" – compare e.g. "נְבָלָתוֹ" (Jer. 26:23) vs. "נְבֵלָתִי" (Is. 26:19).

[g] For the use of "ת" instead of "י", see footnote on chapter 1:7.

[h] Crossed-out letters.

[i] Altered to "יקומו" – in similar/same script as main text.

so that rain will not come on the earth in the days of their prophesying; and over the waters, to turn *them* into blood; and to smite the earth with plagues at any time that they want.

7 And after their testimony is completed, the animal[a] which came[b] from *the* Deep will make war with them, and will overcome them and kill them. 8 And their corpses will be thrown on the plains[c] of the set-apart city; which is called Sedom[d] and Mitsrayim[e] because our Adon was crucified there. 9 And some of the peoples[f] and of the tribes will see their corpses, three and a half days, and **they** will not bury them. 10 And those who dwell on the earth will rejoice over them, and will send one another gifts, for these prophets had caused much suffering to those who dwell on the earth.

11 And after three and a half days they stood up and stepped[g] on their feet! And fear and great terror fell on those who saw them.

_____

[a] Or "beast." Compare Daniel chapters 7 and 8. — The Bible often uses the term 'animal' or 'beast' to refer to a kingdom and/or its leader or king.
[b] Or possibly "comes."
[c] Or "open places," or possibly "streets."
[d] Hebrew name for 'Sodom.'
[e] Hebrew name for 'Egypt.'
[f] Does not refer to "people" but "nations."
[g] Or "were standing – stepping on their feet!"

12 וְשׁוֹמְעִים קוֹל אֶחָד אֹמֵר לָהֶם עֲלוּ וַיַּעֲלוּ לְמַעְלָה בַּשָּׁמַיִם בֶּעָנָן אֶחָד וְרָאוּ אוֹתָם שׂוֹנְאֵיהֶם 13 וּבַשָּׁעָה הַזֹּאת הָיָה רַעֲדוֹת הָאָרֶץ וְחֵלֶק עֲשִׂירֵי מֵהָעִיר נָפַל וַיָּמָת שִׁבְעָה אֲלָפִים מִבְּנֵי אָדָם וַאֲחֵרִים נִבְהֲלוּ וְנָתְנוּ שֶׁבַח לֵאלֹהֵי הַשָּׁמַיִם 14 רָאֵה הַצַּעַר הַשֵּׁנִי הָלַךְ וְהַשְּׁלִישִׁי בָּא

פֶּרֶק י"ב

1 [11:15] וְהַמַּלְאָךְ הַשְּׁבִיעִי תָּקַע וְהָיוּ קוֹלוֹת הַרְבֵּה בַּשָּׁמַיִם הָאוֹמְרִים הָעֲשִׁירִים[a] מֵהָעוֹלָם הַזֶּה הוֹלְכִים כּוּלָם אַחַר אֲדוֹנֵינוּ יֵשׁוּעַ וְהוּא יִמְשֹׁל מֵעוֹלָם וְעַד עוֹלָם 2 [11:16] וְאַרְבַּע וְעֶשְׂרִים זְקֵנִים הַיּוֹשְׁבִים עַל כִּסְאֵיהֶם לִפְנֵי יַהֲוֶה נוֹפְלִים עַל פְּנֵיהֶם וּמִתְפַּלְלִים לְיַהֲוֶה 3 [11:17] וְאוֹמְרִים אָנוּ נוֹתְנִים שֶׁבַח לְךָ אָדוֹן[b] צְבָאוֹת הֶהָיָה וְהֹוֶה וְיִהְיֶה 4 [11:18] וְהָעַמִּים נִתְמַלְאוּ אַף וְחֵימָה וּבָא אַפְּךָ וְהָעֵת לִשְׁפּוֹט הַמֵּתִים וְלִיתֵּן הַשָּׂכָר לַעֲבָדֶיךָ הַנְּבִיאִים וְלַקְּדוֹשִׁים וּלְאֵילוּ הַיְרֵאִים מִפָּנֶיךָ לַקְּטַנִּים וְלַגְּדוֹלִים וּלְהַשְׁחִית לְאֵילוּ שֶׁהִשְׁחִיתוּ הָאָרֶץ

---

[a] Altered to "הכשרים" – in different script than main text.
[b] Or possibly "אָדוֹן". Compare "אלהים צבאות" (e.g. Ps. 80:5, 80:8, 80:15, 80:20) vs. "אלהי צבאות"(e.g. Amos 4:13, 6:8).

12 And they heard a voice saying to them, "Come up!" Then they went up into the heavens in^a a cloud, and their haters^b saw them. 13 And in that hour there was an earthquake, and a tenth part of the city fell, and seven thousand of *the* sons of man died, and *the* others were terrified and gave praise^c to the Elohim of the heavens. 14 Look, the second suffering^d has gone by, and the third is coming!

12: 1 [11:15] Then the seventh messenger blew, and there were many voices in the heavens, which said, "The rich^e ones of this world – all of them are coming^f after our Adon Yeshua, and **he** will reign from everlasting and unto everlasting!"^g 2 [11:16] And *the* twenty-four elders who sat on their thrones^h before Yahweh, fell on their faces and prayed to Yahweh, 3 [11:17] and said, "We give praiseⁱ to you Adon Tseva'ot,^j who was and is and will be! 4 [11:18] When the peoples^k were filled with anger and wrath, your anger came; also the time to judge the dead ones; and to give the reward^l to your servants the prophets, and to the set-apart ones, and to those who fear you,^m to the small ones and to the great ones;ⁿ and to destroy those who destroyed the earth."

---

^a Or "with."
^b Synonym of "enemies."
^c Or "lauding."
^d Or "pain."
^e Altered to "right/worthy/lawful ones" – in different script than main text.
^f Or "came."
^g A Hebrew idiom which often means "forever and ever" – see e.g. Jer. 7:7, 25:5; 1 Chr. 16:36; Neh. 9:5; Ps. Ps. 41:14(13), 103:17, 106:48.
^h Or "seats."
ⁱ Or "lauding."
^j Meaning "Lord of Armies."
^k Does not refer to "people" but "nations."
^l Or "wages."
^m Lit. "before you." Could also mean "because of you."
ⁿ Could mean 'young and old ones' or 'unimportant and important ones.'

5 ‏[19:11] וּבֵית תְּפִילַת יַהְוֶה נִפְתַּח ᵃ בַּשָּׁמַיִם וְנִתְרָאָה אֲרוֹן
לוּחוֹת הַבְּרִית בְּבֵית תְּפִילָתוֹ וְהָיָה קוֹלוֹת וּרְעָמִים וּבְרָקִים
וְרַעֲדוֹת הָאָרֶץ וּבָרָד גָּדוֹל 6 ‏[1:12] וְנִתְרָאָה נֵס גָּדוֹל בַּשָּׁמַיִם
אֶחָד אִשָּׁה לָבֵשׁ בַּשֶּׁמֶשׁ וְהַיָּרֵחַ תַּחַת רַגְלֶיהָ וְעַל רֹאשָׁהּ כֶּתֶר
אֶחָד מִן שְׁנֵים עָשָׂר כּוֹכָבִים 7 ‏[2] וְהִיא הָיָה מְעוּבֶּרֶת וְצוֹעֶקֶת
וְהִיא [ ]ᵇ יוֹשֶׁבֶת עַל הַמַּשְׁבֵּר וְהָיָה לָהּ הַרְבֵּה צַעַר בִּשְׁבִיל
הַלֵּידָה 8 ‏[3] וְנֵס אַחֵר הָיָה בַּשָּׁמַיִם וְרָאִיתִי אֶחָד תַּנִּין וְלוֹ
הָיָה שִׁבְעָה רָאשִׁים וַעֲשָׂרָה קְרָנַיִם וְעַל רָאשָׁיו שִׁבְעָה
כְּתָרִים 9 ‏[4] וּזְנָבוֹ לָקַח שָׁלִישׁ מֵהַכּוֹכָבִים וְזָרַק אוֹתָם עַל
הָאָרֶץ וְהַתַּנִּין דָּרַךְ לִפְנֵי הָאִשָּׁה שֶׁתֵּילֵד כְּדֵי לֶאֱכוֹל הַיֶּלֶד
בְּאִם שֶׁנּוֹלַד ᶜ 10 ‏[5] וְיָלְדָה בֵּן אֶחָד הַמְנַהֵג הָעַמִּים בְּשֵׁבֶט
בַּרְזֶל ᵈ וְהַיֶּלֶד מוּבָא לִפְנֵי יַהְוֶה וְכִסְאוֹ 11 ‏[6] וְהָאִשָּׁה הָלְכָה
בַּמִּדְבָּר כֵּיוָן שֶׁהָיָה מוּכָן לָהּ שָׁם מָקוֹם אֶחָד מִיַּהְוֶה לְפַרְנֵס
אוֹתָהּ שָׁם אֶלֶף וּשְׁנֵי מֵאוֹת וְשִׁשִּׁים יוֹם 12 ‏[7] וְנַעֲשָׂה מִלְחָמָה
בַּשָּׁמַיִם הַמַּלְאָךְ מִיכָאֵל עִם מַלְאָכָיו נִלְחֲמוּ עִם הַתַּנִּין

ᵃ Or possibly "נִפְתַּח".

ᵇ Crossed-out word.

ᶜ Or possibly "שֶׁנּוֹלַד".

ᵈ Compare Ps. 2:9.

5 [11:19] And Yahweh's house of prayer was opened in the heavens, and the ark of the tables of the covenant was seen in his house of prayer, and there were voices and thunders and lightnings and an earthquake, and great hail.

6 [12:1] And a great sign appeared in the heavens: a woman clothed with the sun, and the moon was under her feet, and on her head was a crown of twelve stars. 7 [2] And she was pregnant and cried out, and she was at the point to give birth, and she had much pain because of the birth.

8 [3] And there was another sign in the heavens, and I saw a dragon, and he had seven heads and ten horns, and on his heads were seven crowns. 9 [4] And his tail took a third of the stars,[a] and cast them on the earth. And the dragon stepped[b] before the woman who would give birth, in order to devour the Child[c] when he was born. 10 [5] Then she gave birth to a Son,[d] who would lead[e] the peoples[f] with a rod of iron,[g] and the Child[h] was brought before Yahweh and his throne. 11 [6] Then[i] the woman went into the wilderness, for there a place was prepared for her by Yahweh, to sustain her there a thousand two hundred and sixty days.

12 [7] And there was[j] war in the heavens: the messenger Micha'el[k] with his messengers made war with the dragon,

---

[a] Meaning "messengers (angels)." Compare chapter 1:20; Dan. 8:10.
[b] Or "stood."
[c] Hebrew "ילד" (yeled) – could also translate as "Son." Compare Is. 9:5(6).
[d] Hebrew "בן" (ben).
[e] Or possibly 'rule.'
[f] Does not refer to "people" but "nations."
[g] Compare Ps. 2:9.
[h] Hebrew "ילד" (yeled) – could also translate as "Son." Compare Is. 9:5(6).
[i] Meaning next in the vision.
[j] Lit. "was made."
[k] Pronounced "Mi-cha-el" in Hebrew.

13 [8] וּמַלְאָכָיו לָחֲמוּ עִימָם [a] וְלֹא נָצְחוּ וְגַם לֹא נִמְצָא עוֹד אֶת

14 [9] מְקוֹמָם בַּשָּׁמַיִם וַיֻּשְׁלַךְ [b] לַחוּץ הַתַּנִּין הַגָּדוֹל הַנִּקְרָא

הַשָּׂטָן הַמַּשְׁחִית וְהַמַּסִּית [c] אֶת כָּל הָעוֹלָם וְהוּא עִם מַלְאָכָיו

15 [10] (104v) נִשְׁלָכִים עַל הָאָרֶץ לָדוּר שָׁם וְשָׁמַעְתִּי קוֹל גָּדוֹל

בַּשָּׁמַיִם שֶׁאָמַר עַכְשָׁיו נִתְרָאֶה גְּבוּרוֹת אֱלֹהֵינוּ וּמְשִׁיחוֹ כֵּיוָן

15 [11] [e] שֶׁנֻּשְׁלַךְ [d] לַחוּץ זֶה שֶׁהָיָה כָּל עֵת לַשָּׂטָן עֲלֵיהֶם וַיְנַצְחוּ

אוֹתוֹ עַל יַד דַּם הַשֶּׂה וְעַל יַד הַדִּיבּוּר מֵעֵדוּתֵיהֶם [f] וְחָשְׁבוּ

16 [12] אֶת חַיֵּיהֶם לִכְלוּם וּבִשְׁבִיל זֶה תִּשְׂמְחוּ הַשָּׁמַיִם וְכָל

אֲשֶׁר בָּהּ וְאוֹי לְאֵילוּ הַדָּרִים עַל הָאָרֶץ וְעַל הַיָּם כִּי הַשָּׂטָן

17 [13] יָרַד לָכֶם בַּחֲרוֹן אַף גָּדוֹל וְיוֹדֵעַ שֶׁיֵּשׁ לוֹ זְמָן מוּעָט

וְכֵיוָן שֶׁרָאָה הַתַּנִּין שֶׁנֻּשְׁלַךְ עַל הָאָרֶץ רָדַף אַחַר הָאִשָּׁה

18 [14] שֶׁיָּלְדָה וְנוּתַן לְהָאִשָּׁה שְׁתֵּי כְּנָפַיִם כְּנֶשֶׁר גָּדוֹל כְּדֵי

לֵילֵךְ [g] בַּמִּדְבָּר בַּמָּקוֹם שֶׁנָּתַן לָהּ יַהֲוֶה לְפַרְנֵס אוֹתָהּ שָׁם עֵת

אֶחָד וּשְׁנֵי עִיתִּים וָחֲצִי מִפְּנֵי הַתַּנִּין

---

[a] Word was added above the line in same script as main text.

[b] Or possibly "וַנֻּשְׁלַךְ".

[c] Or possibly "וְהַמֵּסִית".

[d] Or possibly "שֶׁנֻּשְׁלַךְ".

[e] Take note that the scribe numbered two verses in a row as verse 15, and never noted his mistake (see also verses 18[14]-18[15]). This is one of several indications (see e.g. verse numbers added in margin of ms. in 21:22, 22:15) which show that the previous Hebrew manuscript being copied by the scribe did not contains verse numbers, although it possibly did contain verse divisions (e.g. the Hebrew Tanach was divided into verses many centuries before verse numbers were added to the Bible). If the scribe was copying/translating from a modern Bible with verse numbers, he would have noted his mistake with each of the following verses until the end of the chapter.

[f] See footnote on chapter 9:5.

[g] This is an alternative form of the 'infinitive construct' with "ל" preposition (root: "הלך"). Spelled "ללכת" in the Tanach.

also his messengers fought^a with them. **13** **[8]** But they did not overcome, neither was their place in the heavens found^b anymore. **14 [9]** So the great dragon was cast out, who is called Ha-Satan,^c who destroys and seduces the whole world. And he with his messengers were cast onto the earth to dwell there.

15 [10] (104v) Then I heard a great voice in the heavens which said, "Now the might^d of our Elohim and his Mashiach has appeared,^e for he^f who was as an adversary^g against them **all the time**, is cast out. **15**^h **[11]** And they overcame him by the blood of the Lamb and by the word of their testimony, and they consideredⁱ their lives as nothing. **16 [12]** And because of this you must rejoice o heavens and all who are in them, but woe to those who dwell on the earth and on the sea^j – for Ha-Satan went down to you with great burning anger, and^k he knows that he has little time."

17 [13] And when the dragon saw that he was cast onto the earth, he pursued after^l the woman who gave birth. **18 [14]** But there was^m given to the woman, two wings like a great eagle – to go into the wilderness, into the place that Yahweh gave her, to sustain her there a time, and two and a half times, away fromⁿ the dragon.

---

^a Or possibly 'made war.' Same root-word as in first part of verse, but different conjugation/stem.

^b Or possibly "neither was their place found in the heavens anymore."

^c Lit "The Adversary."

^d Or "mighty deeds" or possibly 'victory.'

^e Lit. "has become visible."

^f Lit. "this *one*."

^g Hebrew "שטן" (*satan*) – means "adversary" or "accuser."

^h See footnote in Hebrew transcript regarding verse 15[11].

ⁱ Or "regarded."

^j Or possibly "by the sea."

^k Or "for."

^l Or "persecuted."

^m Singular in Hebrew, see pp. 113-114 for more information.

ⁿ Or "because of."

18 ‏[15]‏ וְהִשְׁלִיךְ הַתַּנִּין אַחַר הָאִשָּׁה מַיִם [מִפִּיו]‏^a כְּיָם גָּדוֹל כְּדֵי לְהַשְׁקִיט^b אוֹתָהּ 19 ‏[16]‏ אֲבָל הָיָה לְהָאִשָּׁה יְשׁוּעָה מֵהָאֲדָמָה כֵּיוָן שֶׁפָּתְחָה אֶת פִּיהָ וּבָלַע^c הַמַּיִם שֶׁהִשְׁלִיךְ הַתַּנִּין אַחֲרֶיהָ 20 ‏[17]‏ וְהַתַּנִּין נִתְמַלֵּא בְּאַף עַל אוֹדוֹת הָאִשָּׁה וְהָלַךְ לִלְחוֹם עִם הַנּוֹתָרִים מִזַּרְעָהּ הָעוֹשִׂים אֶת מִצְוֹת יַהְוֶה וְהַמַּאֲמִינִים בָּעֵדוּת שֶׁל מְשִׁיחוֹ

פֶּרֶק י"ג

1 וְדָרַכְתִּי עַל חוֹל הַיָּם 2 ‏[1]‏ וְרָאִיתִי חַיָּה אֶחָד יָצֵא מֵהַיָּם וְלוֹ הָיָה שִׁבְעָה רָאשִׁים וַעֲשָׂרָה קְרָנַיִם וְעַל קַרְנָיו עֲשָׂרָה כְּתָרִים וְעַל רָאשֶׁיהָ שֵׁמוֹת שֶׁל חֵירוּפִים וְגִדּוּפִים 3 ‏[2]‏ וְהַחַיָּה שֶׁרָאִיתִי הָיָה כִּדְמוּת סוּס וְרַגְלָיו כְּרַגְלֵי דוּבִּים וּפִיו כְּפִי הָאַרְיֵה וְהַתַּנִּין נָתַן לוֹ אֶת כֹּחוֹ וְכִסְאוֹ וּגְבוּרַת^d גְּדוֹלָה ‏[3]‏ 4 וְרָאִיתִי אֶחָד מֵרָאשָׁיו דּוֹמֶה לְחַבּוּרָה שֶׁל מָוֶת וְחַבּוּרָה נִתְרַפְּאָה וְכָל הָעוֹלָם מִשְׁתּוֹמֵם בִּשְׁבִיל הַחַיָּה הַזֹּאת 5 ‏[4]‏ וּמִתְפַּלְלִים לְהַתַּנִּין הַנּוֹתֵן לְהַחַיָּה כֹּחַ וּמֶמְשָׁלָה וּמִתְפַּלְלִים לְהַחַיָּה וְאוֹמְרִים מִי דּוֹמֶה לָזֹאת הַחַיָּה וּמִי יוּכַל לִלְחוֹם עִימוֹ

---

^a See footnote on verse 15[11].

^b Compare e.g. "דמם", "דמה" and "צמת" – to "silence" often means to "destroy/annihilate/corrupt."

^c Or possibly "וּבְלַע".

^d Usually spelled "גְּבוּרָה". The Tanach also contains a number of feminine nouns which are construct in form, but not necessarily in meaning, e.g., "שִׁפְעַת" instead of "שִׁפְעָה" (2 Kin. 9:17b); "פּוּגַת" instead of "פּוּגָה" (Lam. 2:18); "חָכְמַת" instead of "חָכְמָה" (Is. 33:6); "נְגִינַת" instead of "נְגִינָה" (Ps. 61:1).

18 [a] [15] Then the dragon cast waters from [his] mouth after the woman, like a great sea,[b] to annihilate[c] her. 19 [16] But the woman had deliverance from the earth,[d] for it opened its mouth and swallowed the waters which the dragon cast after her. 20 [17] Then the dragon was filled with anger because of the woman, and he went to make war with the remaining ones of her seed, who perform the commandments of Yahweh and believe[e] in the testimony of his Mashiach.

13: 1 And I stepped[f] on the sand of the sea, 2 [1 cont.] and I saw an animal[g] coming out of the sea, and he had seven heads and ten horns, and on his horns were ten crowns, and on his heads were names of reproach and blasphemy.[h] 3 [2] And the animal which I saw was like[i] a horse, and his feet like the feet of bears, and his mouth like the mouth of the lion. And the dragon gave him his power and his throne, and great might.[j]

4 [3] Then I saw *that* one of his heads was like a deadly wound -- but *the* wound was healed, and all the world was astonished because of this animal. 5 [4] Then they prayed to the dragon who gave the animal power and dominion, and they prayed to the animal and said, "Who is like **this** animal, and who is able to make war with him?"

---

[a] See footnote in Hebrew transcript regarding verse number 15[11].
[b] Lit. "sea," but could also mean 'river,' compare chapter 9:13[14] vs. 16:11[12], see also Is. 19:5.
[c] Or "destroy" – lit. "silence."
[d] Or "ground."
[e] Or "and those who believe."
[f] Or "stood."
[g] Or "beast." Compare Daniel chapters 7 and 8. – The Bible often uses the term 'animal' or 'beast' to refer to a kingdom and/or its leader or king.
[h] Lit. "reproaches and blasphemies."
[i] Lit. "like the appearance of."
[j] Or "strength."

6 [5] וְנוּתַּן לְהַחַיָּה לִפְתּוֹחַ אֶת פִּיו לְדַבֵּר דִּבְרֵי נִפְלָאוֹת

7 [6] וְחֵירוּף עַד שֶׁכָּלָא הַזְּמָן שֶׁל הָאַרְבָּעִים וּשְׁנַיִם חֳדָשִׁים

8 [7] וּפָתַח אֶת פִּיו לְחָרֵף כְּנֶגֶד יַהְוֶה וּכְנֶגֶד הַדָּרִים בַּשָּׁמַיִם

וְנוּתַּן לוֹ לִלְחוּם עִם הַקְּדוֹשִׁים וּלְנַצֵּחַ אוֹתָם וְכָל הָעַמִּים

וְאוֹמִים , [8] וְכוּלָם הַדָּרִים עַל הָאָרֶץ מִתְפַּלְלִים לוֹ אִילוּ

שֶׁלֹא נִכְתַּב אֶת שְׁמָם בְּסֵפֶר הַחַיִּים שֶׁל הַשֶּׂה הַנֶּהֱרָג

מִכִּתְחִילַתᵃ בְּרִיאַת הָעוֹלָם 10 [9] מִי שֶׁיֵּשׁ לוֹ אָזְנַיִם שׁוֹמֵעַ 11

[10] בְּאָם שֶׁאֶחָד יָנֵהַג בַּמִּשְׁמָר יֵלֵךְ בַּמִּשְׁמָר וּבְאָם שֶׁאֶחָד

הָרֵג נֶפֶשׁ אַחֵר בַּחֶרֶב יֵהָרֵג בַּחֶרֶב וּבְכָאן יֵשׁ תִּקְוָה וֶאֱמוּנַת

הַקְּדוֹשִׁים 12 [11] וְרָאִיתִי חַיָּה אַחֵר יָצֵא מֵהָאֲדָמָה וְלוֹ הָיָה

שְׁתֵּי קַרְנַיִם כְּמוֹ לְהַשֶּׂה וּמְדַבֵּר כַּתַּנִּיןᵇ 13 [12] וְעָשָׂה נִפְלָאוֹת

גְּדוֹלוֹת לִפְנֵי הַחַיָּה הָרִאשׁוֹנָה וְעָשָׂה שֶׁהָאֲדָמָה וְהַדָּרִים

עָלֶיהָ מִתְפַּלְלִים לְהַחַיָּה הָרִאשׁוֹנָה שֶׁנִּתְרַפְּאָה [ ]ᶜ

חַבּוּרָתֶיהָ 14 [13] וְעָשָׂה שֶׁנָּפַל אֵשׁ מִשָּׁמַיִם לִפְנֵי הָאָדָם

ᵃ Altered to "מתחילת" – in different script than main text.

ᵇ Or possibly "כְּתַנִּין".

ᶜ Crossed-out letters.

6 [5] And it was given to the animal to open his mouth to speak astonishing things [a] and reproach [b] until the time of the forty-two months was completed. 7 [6] So he opened his mouth to blaspheme against Yahweh, and against those who dwell in the heavens. 8 [7] And it was given to him to make war with the set-apart ones; and to overcome them, and all the peoples and nations. 9 [8] And all those who dwell on earth prayed to him – those whose name was [c] not written in the scroll of life of the Lamb who was slain, from the beginning of the creation of the world.

10 [9] Whosoever has ears must hear! 11 [10] – If one drives *another* into prison, he will go into prison, and if one kills another nephesh [d] with the sword he will be killed by the sword; and here is hope, and the faithfulness [e] of the set-apart ones.

12 [11] Then I saw another animal coming out of the earth, and he had two horns like the Lamb but spoke like the dragon. [f] 13 [12] And he did great wonders before the first animal, and made that the earth and those who dwell on it pray to the first animal, who was healed of his wounds. [g] 14 [13] And he made fire fall from the heavens before man.

---

[a] Or "incredible things" or "wondrous words" – compare Dan. 11:36.

[b] Or "blasphemy."

[c] Hebrew collective use, meaning, "whose names were not written."

[d] Lit. "breath" (e.g. Job 11:20, 41:13), can mean 'person' (e.g. Gen. 12:5, 14:21, 46:18-27; Ex. 16:16; Lev. 17:15), 'life' (e.g. Gen. 19:17; Lev. 17:11), 'soul' (e.g. Ps. 49:16-20(15-19); Gen. 35:18; Ex. 30:16; Is. 10:18; Ezek. 18:4), etc. But take note that nephesh rarely (if ever) refers to the spirit of a human [which continues to exist after a person dies] (contrast ruach and neshamah). Biblically speaking, a nephesh can die (e.g. Num. 6:6, 9:6; Lev. 22:4; Ezek. 13:19). (See glossary for more information.)

[e] Or "faith." Hebrew "אמונה" (*emunah*) – refers to both believing and doing (being faithful). See e.g. James 2:19-25[20-26]; 2 Chr. 19:9; 2 Kin. 12:16(15); Is. 59:4; Hos. 2:22(20); Ps. 33:4, 143:1, etc.

[f] Or possibly "like a lamb... like a dragon."

[g] Or possibly 'whose wounds were healed.'

15 [14] וְהִסִּית^a הַבְּנֵי אָדָם עִם אוֹתוֹת וּמוֹפְתִים שֶׁלוֹ וְאָמַר
לְאֵילוּ הַדָּרִים עַל הָאָרֶץ שֶׁיַּעֲשׂוּ פֶּסֶל לְהַחַיָּה שֶׁיֵּשׁ לָהּ
חַבּוּרוֹת חֶרֶב וְנִתְרַפְּאָה 16 [15] וְלוֹ נוּתַּן לִיתֵּן לְפֶסֶל הַחַיָּה
רוּחַ וְנֶפֶשׁ כְּדֵי שֶׁיּוּכַל לְדַבֵּר וְלַעֲשׂוֹת מִי שֶׁלֹּא יִרְצֶה לְתַפַּלֵּל
לַפֶּסֶל מֵהַחַיָּה שֶׁיֵּהָרֵג 17 [16] וְעָשָׂה לְכוּלָּם הַגְּדוֹלִים
וְהַקְּטַנִּים הָעֲשִׁירִים וְהָעֲנִיִּים הָעֲבָדִים וְהַמְּשׁוּחְרָרִים סִימָן
אֶחָד בְּיַד יְמִינוֹ אוֹ בְּמִצְחֵיהֶם 18 [17] כְּדֵי שֶׁלֹּא יוּכַל שׁוּם
אֶחָד לִקְנוֹת אוֹ לִמְכּוֹר רַק בְּאָם שֶׁיֵּשׁ לוֹ זֶה הַסִּימָן בְּיָדוֹ אוֹ
בְּמִצְחוֹ אוֹ הַשֵּׁם שֶׁל הַחַיָּה אוֹ הַמִּסְפָּר שֶׁל שְׁמוֹ 19 [18] בְּכָאן
יֵשׁ חָכְמָה וּתְבוּנָה מִי שֶׁיֵּשׁ בַּעַל שֶׂכֶל צָרִיךְ לַחֲשֵׁב הַמִּשְׁפָּר
מֵהַחַיָּה כִּי הִיא מִסְפָּר שֶׁל אָדָם אֶחָד וְתִמָּצֵא^b הַסַּךְ הִיא
שֵׁשׁ מֵאוֹת וְשִׁשִּׁים וְשִׁשָּׁה^c

---

^a Or possibly "וְהֵסִית".

^b Or possibly "וְתִמְצָא".

^c Margin has the number written as "תרסו" – in different script than main text.

15 [14] And he seduced the sons of man with his signs and wonders, and said to those who dwell on the earth that they should make a carved image[a] for[b] the animal that had the wounds of a sword,[c] but was healed. 16 [15] And to him it was given, to give the carved image of the animal a ruach and nephesh[d] (so that it[e] was able to speak); and to make *that* whosoever does not want[f] to pray to the carved image of the animal, that he be killed.

17 [16] And he made for them all – the great ones and the small ones, the rich ones and the poor ones, the slaves and the freed ones – a sign on his right hand or on their[g] forehead; 18 [17] so that no one is able to buy or to sell, unless he has this sign on his hand or on his forehead, or the name of the animal, or the number of his name. 19 [18] Here is wisdom and understanding: whosoever has insight needs to reckon the number of the animal (for it is the number of a man),[h] and the amount[i] will be found – it is[j] six hundred and sixty and six.[k]

---

[a] Or simply "an image."

[b] Or "to."

[c] Or "sword wounds."

[d] Lit. "breath" (e.g. Job 11:20, 41:13), can mean 'person' (e.g. Gen. 12:5, 14:21, 46:18-27; Ex. 16:16; Lev. 17:15), 'life' (e.g. Gen. 19:17; Lev. 17:11), 'soul' (e.g. Ps. 49:16-20(15-19); Gen. 35:18; Ex. 30:16; Is. 10:18; Ezek. 18:4), etc. (See glossary for more information.)

[e] I.e. "the image."

[f] Or "is not willing."

[g] The Hebrew Bible often interchanges "his" and "their" synonymously. Compare e.g. Ps. 5:10(9); Ps. 62:5(4); Is. 57:2.

[h] This explanation shows clearly that the 'animal' is not a literal animal, but a human leader. Compare Daniel chapters 7 and 8.

[i] Or "sum."

[j] Or possibly "he will find *that* the amount is."

[k] This number is written with spelled-out words in the main text. The margin has this number written with letters employed as numerals (in different script than main text): "תרסו" – lit. "400, 200, 60, 6." This is the standard way to indicate 666 with Hebrew letters (as numerals) instead of words.

פֶּרֶק י"ד

1 וְרָאִיתִי שֶׂה אֶחָד עֹמֵד עַל הַר צִיוֹן וְעִמּוֹ מֵאָה וְאַרְבַּע וְאַרְבָּעִים אֲלָפִים וַעֲלֵיהֶם נִכְתַּב הַשֵּׁם שֶׁל אָבִיו 2 וְשָׁמַעְתִּי קוֹל אֶחָד מִשָּׁמַיִם כְּרַעַשׁ מַיִם גְּדוֹלִים וּכְקוֹל קוֹלוֹת גְּדוֹלִים וְהַקּוֹל שֶׁשָּׁמַעְתִּי הָיָה כְּקוֹל[a] כִּנּוֹר 3 וּמְזַמְּרִים כְּשִׁיר חָדָשׁ לִפְנֵי הַכִּסֵּא וְלִפְנֵי הָאַרְבַּע חַיּוֹת וְהַזְּקֵנִים וְשׁוּם אֶחָד יוּכַל לִלְמֹד הַשִּׁיר הַזֹּאת רַק אֵילוּ הַמֵּאָה וְאַרְבַּע וְאַרְבָּעִים אֲלָפִים שֶׁקָּנָה מֵהָאֲדָמָה 4 וְאֵילוּ הֵמָּה שֶׁלֹּא חָטְאוּ בַּנָּשִׁים [וְהֵם][b] כִּבְתוּלוֹת וְהוֹלְכִים אַחַר הַשֶּׂה וְהֵמָּה נִקְנִים לִבְכּוּרֹת יַהְוֶה וְהַשֶּׂה 5 וְאֵין בְּרוּחָם רְמִיָּה[c] וְהֵם נְקִיִּים לִפְנֵי הַכִּסֵּא יַהְוֶה 6 וְרָאִיתִי מַלְאָךְ אֶחָד רֹחֵף בְּאֶמְצַע הַשָּׁמַיִם וְלוֹ הָיָה אֶחָד אָוֶן גִּלָּיוֹן[d] לְהוֹדִיעַ לְאֵילוּ הַדָּרִים עַל הָאָרֶץ וּלְכָל הָעַמִּים וּלְאוּמִּים 7 וְאָמַר בְּקוֹל גָּדוֹל יִרְאוּ יַהְוֶה וַעֲשׂוּ תְּפִילַּתְכֶם לוֹ כִּי הַיּוֹם הַדִּין בָּא וַעֲשׂוּ תְּפִילָּה לָזֶה שֶׁבָּרָא הַשָּׁמַיִם וְהָאָרֶץ וְהַיָּם וְהַבְּאֵרוֹת

---

[a] Or possibly "בקול" – "ב" and "כ" can look similar.

[b] Correction from margin. The main text had "והמם בתולות" which is clearly a mistake and should read "והם כבתולות" (as crossed out and corrected by proofreader/scribe). "כ" and "ם" can look very similar in the script used in manuscript.

[c] Compare Ps. 32:2.

[d] Alternative phrase for "בְּשׂוֹרָה". The Peshitta New Testament also uses "אונגליון" (as one word) in e.g. Mark 1:1; Rom. 1:1; 1 Cor. 9:18; 2 Cor. 4:3; Gal. 2:14; Eph. 3:6; Phil. 1:5, etc. Note that "און גיליון" has been used to refer to the gospel(s) **since the Talmudic era**, see Shabbat 116a:10-116b:2, where both "און גליון" and "עוון גליון" are used (though sarcastically).

14: ₁ And I saw a Lamb standing on mount Tsiyon,ª and with him a hundred and forty-four thousand, and on them the name of his Father was written. ₂ Then I heard a voice from *the* heavens like the noise ᵇ of great waters, and like the sound of great voices,ᶜ and the voice which I heard was like the sound of a lyre.

₃ And they were singing like a new song before the throne and before the four living creatures and the elders, and no one was able to learn this song except these hundred and forty-four thousand whom he bought from the earth. ₄ (And these are they who did not sin with women,ᵈ and they are like virgins ᵉ and follow ᶠ after the Lamb, and they are bought as first fruits of Yahweh and the Lamb. ₅ And there is no deceit in their ruach,ᵍ and they are blameless ʰ before the throne of Yahweh.)

₆ Then I saw a messenger flying in the midst of the heavens, and he had one good news ⁱ to make known to those who dwell on the earth, and to all the peoples and nations. ₇ And he said with a great voice, "Fear Yahweh and do your prayer to him, for the day of judgment has come, and do prayer to him ʲ who created the heavens and the earth, and the sea and the fountains!"

ª Hebrew name for 'Zion.'

ᵇ Or "roaring" or "rumbling."

ᶜ Or "thunders."

ᵈ Proper, life-long, biblical marriage (between one man and one woman) is never defined as sin by Yahweh.

ᵉ The Hebrew word for "virgins" "בתולות" (*betulot*) is feminine plural in this verse, showing clearly that this is a comparison only. These men are not female virgins; but they go after the lamb like virgins go after the bride and groom. Compare Matthew 25 in the HebrewGospels.com version.

ᶠ Lit. "walk."

ᵍ Compare Ps. 32:2.

ʰ Or "pure."

ⁱ Or "one gospel." Compare e.g. Is. 61:1, 52:7; Nah. 2:1(1:15).

ʲ Lit. "this *one*," but often means 'he' or 'him.'

8 וְאַחַר זֶה הַקּוֹל בָּא מַלְאָךְ אַחֵר וְצָעַק נָפְלָה נָפְלָה בָּבֶל[a] הָעִיר הַגְּדוֹלָה כִּי הִיא הִשְׁקִיט[b] עִם הַיַּיִן שֶׁל זְנוּתָהּ[c] כָּל[d] הָעַמִּים , 9 וְאַחַר זֶה בָּא מַלְאָךְ הַשְּׁלִישִׁי וְאָמַר בְּקוֹל גָּדוֹל בְּאִם שֶׁאֶחָד יַעֲשֶׂה תְּפִילָתוֹ לְהַפֶּסֶל וּלְהַחַיָּה וְיִקַּח הַסִּימָן עַל יָדוֹ אוֹ עַל מִצְחוֹ 10 זֶה יִשְׁתֶּה מֵהַיַּיִן שֶׁל חֲרוֹן יַהְוֶה הַיֵּשׁ בְּכוֹס הֶחָרוֹן וְיֵעָנֵשׁ בָּאֵשׁ וְגָפְרִית לִפְנֵי מַלְאָכָיו הַקְּדוֹשִׁים וְהַשֶּׂה 11 וְהֶעָשָׁן מֵעוֹנֶשׁ שֶׁלָהֶם יֵלֵךְ לְמַעְלָה מֵעוֹלָם וְעַד עוֹלָם וְלֹא יִהְיֶה לָהֶם מְנוּחָה יוֹם וָלַיְלָה אֵילוּ שֶׁלָּקְחוּ הַסִּימָן וּמִתְפַּלְּלִים לַפֶּסֶל 12 בְּכָאן יֵשׁ תִּקְוָה מִקְּדוֹשִׁים וּבְכָאן יֵשׁ הָעוֹשִׂים מִצְוֹת יַהְוֶה וּמַאֲמִינִים בְּיֵשׁוּעַ 13 וְשָׁמַעְתִּי בַּת קוֹל מִשָּׁמַיִם אָמֵר לִי כְּתוֹב קְדוֹשִׁים הֵמָה הַמֵּתִים עַל קִידּוּשׁ יַהְוֶה מֵעַכְשָׁיו וֶאֱמֶת הִיא שֶׁהָרוּחַ אָמֵר שֶׁהֵמָּה שׁוֹכְנִים מִמַּעֲשֵׂיהֶם כִּי מַעֲשֵׂיהֶם הוֹלְכִים אַחֲרֵיהֶם

---

[a] Phrase quoted from Is. 21:9.

[b] Compare e.g. "דמם", "דמה" and "צמת" – to "silence" often means to "destroy/annihilate/corrupt."

[c] Altered to "זנותם" – in different script than main text.

[d] Altered to "לכל" – in different script than main text.

₈ And after this voice another messenger came and cried out, "Fallen, fallen has Bavel[a, b] the great city! – For she corrupted[c] all the peoples[d] with the wine of her fornication."[e]

₉ And after this, the third messenger came and said with a great voice, "If one will do his prayer to the carved image[f] and to the animal, and will take the sign on his hand or on his forehead – ₁₀ this one will drink of the wine of the fury of Yahweh, which is in the cup of fury, and he will be punished with fire and brimstone before his set-apart messengers and the Lamb. ₁₁ And the smoke of their punishment will go up from everlasting and unto everlasting,[g] and they will not have rest, day or night – those who took the sign and prayed to the carved image."

₁₂ Here is *the* hope of *the* set-apart ones, and here are those who do the commandments of Yahweh, and believe in Yeshua. ₁₃ And I heard a voice[h] from *the* heavens saying to me, "Write: Blessed[i] are they who die on account of the set-apartness[j] of Yahweh from now on! And what the Ruach says is true: that they rest from their works, for their works follow after them."

---

[a] Hebrew name for 'Babylon.'
[b] Phrase quoted from Is. 21:9.
[c] Or "destroyed" – lit. "silenced" – compare chapter 12:18[15].
[d] Does not refer to "people" but "nations."
[e] Hebrew word order emphasizes "with the wine of her fornication."
[f] Or simply "the image."
[g] A Hebrew idiom which often means "forever and ever" – see e.g. Jer. 7:7, 25:5; 1 Chr. 16:36; Neh. 9:5; Ps. 41:14(13), 103:17, 106:48.
[h] Hebrew "בת קול" (*bat qol*) – an idiom meaning 'a voice from heaven.'
[i] Hebrew "קדושים" (*qedoshim*) – lit. "set-apart" but often means "blessed."
[j] Or "sanctification."

14 וְרָאִיתִי עָנָן אֶחָד לָבָן וְעָלָיו יֹשֵׁב אֶחָד כִּדְמוּת אָדָם וְעַל
רֹאשׁוֹ כֶּתֶר זָהָב וּבְיָדוֹ חֶרְמֵשׁ אֶחָד 15 וּמַלְאָךְ אַחֵר הָלַךְ
מִבֵּית הַתְּפִילָה וְצָעַק בְּקוֹל גָּדוֹל לָזֶה שֶׁיֹּשֵׁב עַל הֶעָנָן הַךְ
בַּחֶרְמֵשׁ שֶׁלְּךָ וּקְצֹר כִּי הָעֵת הַקְּצִירָה בָּא 16 וְזֶה שֶׁיֹּשֵׁב עַל
הֶעָנָן הִכָּה בַּחֶרְמֵשׁ שֶׁלּוֹ וְקָצַר 17 וּמַלְאָךְ אַחֵר הָלַךְ לַשָּׁמַיִם
וּבְיָדוֹ הָיָה מַעְגָּל^a אֶחָד 18 וּמַלְאָךְ אַחֵר יָצָא מֵהַמִּזְבֵּחַ וְלוֹ
הָיָה מֶמְשָׁלָה עַל הָאֵשׁ וְצָעַק בְּקוֹל גָּדוֹל לָזֶה שֶׁהָיָה לוֹ
הַמַּגָּל וְאָמַר הַךְ בַּמַּגָּל שֶׁלְּךָ וּקְצֹר אֶת עִנְבֵי אֶרֶץ כִּי פֵּירוֹתֶיהָ
[נִתְבַּשֵּׁל]^b [19] וַיַּךְ הַמַּלְאָךְ בַּמַּגָּל שֶׁלּוֹ וְקָצַר אֶת עִנְבֵי אֶרֶץ
וְזָרַק בְּיֶקֶב גָּדוֹל הֶחָרוֹן יַהְוֶה 19 [20] וְהַיֶּקֶב הָיָה מִחוּץ לָעִיר^c

---

^a Here used as an alternative spelling for "מגל".

^b Manuscript has "תֹּנֻבשל" with correction dots indicating "נתבשל".

^c Margin reads "וזרק יקב של דם חוץ לעיר" – in different script than main text.

₁₄ Then I saw a bright[a] cloud, and on it there sat one with the appearance[b] of a man, and on his head was a crown of gold, and in his hand was a sickle. ₁₅ And another messenger came from the house of prayer, and cried with a great voice to him[c] who sat on the cloud, "Thrust with your sickle and harvest, for the time of the harvest has come!" ₁₆ Then he[d] who sat on the cloud thrust with his sickle and harvested.

₁₇ And another messenger came to the heavens, and in his hand was a sickle.[e] ₁₈ Then another messenger went out from the altar (and he had control[f] over the fire), and he cried out with a great voice to him[g] who had the sickle and said, "Thrust with your sickle and harvest *the* grapes of *the* earth, for its fruits have ripened." [19] So the messenger thrust with his sickle and harvested *the* grapes of *the* earth, and cast *them* into the great winepress *of* the fury of Yahweh.[h] ₁₉ [20] And the winepress was outside the city,[i]

---

[a] Or "white."
[b] Lit. "like the appearance."
[c] Lit. "this *one*," but often means 'he' or 'him.'
[d] Lit. "this *one*," but often means 'he' or 'him.'
[e] Verses 17-[19] use the Hebrew word "מגל/מעגל" (*magal*) for "sickle," but verses 14 - 16 use "חרמש" (*chermesh*).
[f] Or "charge" or "authority."
[g] Lit. "this *one*," but often means 'he' or 'him.'
[h] Or "a great winepress – the fury of Yahweh."
[i] Margin reads "And he cast the winepress of blood outside the city" – in different script than main text.

וְהַדָּם מִיֶּקֶב הָלַךְ עַד הָרֶסֶן שֶׁל הַסּוּסִים דֶּרֶךְ אֶלֶף וְשֵׁשׁ
מֵאוֹת קִבְרוֹת הַשָּׂדֶה[a]

פֶּרֶק ט"ו

(105r) 1 וְרָאִיתִי נִיסִים וְנִפְלָאוֹת גְּדוֹלִים בַּשָּׁמַיִם כִּי שִׁבְעָה
מַלְאָכִים בָּאִים וְלָהֶם הָיָה הַשִּׁבְעָה [ ][b] נְגָעִים אַחֲרוֹנִים כִּי
בָּהֶם כָּלָא הַחָרוֹן אַף מֵיַּהֲוֶה [ ][c] וְרָאִיתִי כְּמוֹ 2 יַם צְלוֹחִית
בָּלַל עִם אֵשׁ וְאֵילוּ שֶׁנִּצְּחוּ עִם[d] הַחַיָּה וּפֶסֶל שֶׁלּוֹ עוֹמְדִים
אֵצֶל הַיַּם צְלוֹחִית וְלָהֶם הָיָה כִּינּוֹרוֹת יַהֲוֶה 3 וּמְזַמְּרִים
הַשִּׁירָה שֶׁל מֹשֶׁה וְהַשִּׁיר הַשֶּׂה וְאוֹמְרִים גְּדוֹלָה מַעֲשֵׂי יַהֲוֶה
אֱלֹהֵי הַצְּבָאוֹת צֶדֶק וֶאֱמֶת דְּרָכֶיךָ מֶלֶךְ הַמְּלָכִים 4 וּמִי לֹא
יִרְאֶה[e] לְפָנֶיךָ וְלִיתֵּן שֶׁבַח לְשִׁמְךָ כִּי אַתָּה לְבַדּוֹ קָדוֹשׁ

---

[a] Altered to "כברת ארץ" – in different script than main text.

[b] Crossed-out letters.

[c] Crossed-out letter.

[d] The preposition "עם" is clearly used here to introduce the object(s), and it may even imply "against" (e.g. 'fight/make war with' means to 'fight against,' not to 'fight for' the enemy) – compare e.g. Rev. 12:12[7], 12:20[17]; 13:8[7]; Ex. 17:8; Josh 9:2; 1 Sam 17:19, 17:32, 17:33, etc.

[e] Note that "יראה" stands parallel to "ליתן" in this verse, showing clearly that it is an 'infinitive' verb and not a noun or a 'perfect.' Compare e.g. Deu. 28:58; Ps. 86:11.

and the blood of the winepress went *up* to the bridle of the horses, a way[a] of one thousand six hundred graves[b] of the field.[c]

15: 1 (105r) And[d] I saw great signs and wonders[e] in the heavens, for seven messengers came, and they had the seven last plagues, for by these the burning anger of Yahweh is completed.

2 And I saw *something* like a sea of glass mixed with fire, and those who overcame[f] the animal and his carved image[g] stood next to the sea of glass, and they had the lyres of Yahweh. 3 And they sang[h] the song of Mosheh[i] and the song of the Lamb, and said, "Great are the works of Yahweh Elohei Ha-Tseva'ot![j] Righteousness and truth[k] are your ways, o King of kings! 4 And who will not fear before your face,[l] and give praise to your name? – For you alone are qadosh![m]

---

[a] Meaning "a distance."

[b] Altered to "distances of land" – in different script than main text.

[c] Or "field graves" or "graveyards." This probably indicates a traditional measure of distance based on Jewish customs and laws (compare e.g. "a Sabbath day's journey"). The Mishnah records various customs about the spacing of graves (4 to 8 cubits), as well as the distance of land which becomes 'unclean' when a grave is plowed in a field (100 cubits). See Mishnah Nazir 9:3; Mishnah Bava Batra 6:8; Mishnah Oholot 17:1. Compare also Rev. 21:16.

[d] Or "Then."

[e] Hebrew word order and gender of adjective indicate "great signs and great wonders."

[f] Or possibly "overcame against the animal."

[g] Or simply "his image."

[h] Hebrew uses root "זמר" (*zamar*) which can refer to singing while playing instruments.

[i] Hebrew name for 'Moses.'

[j] Meaning, "Yahweh the Elohim of the Armies."

[k] Or "faithfulness."

[l] Could also mean "in your presence."

[m] Lit. "set-apart."

כִּי כָל הָעַמִּים יָבוֹאוּ וְיִשְׁתַּחֲוּ[a] לְפָנֶיךָ כִּי מִשְׁפָּטֶיךָ נִתְגַּלָּה ‪5‬ וְאַחַר כָּךְ רָאִיתִי שֶׁנִּפְתַּח אֲרוֹן הַבְּרִית בַּשָּׁמַיִם ‪6‬ וְיָצָא[b] לַחוּץ הַשִּׁבְעָה מַלְאָכִים שֶׁהָיָה לָהֶם הַשִּׁבְעָה נְגָעִים וְלָבוּשׁ בְּמַלְבּוּשֵׁי לְבֵינִים וַחֲגוֹר שֶׁל זָהָב עַל מָתְנֵיהֶם ‪7‬ וְאֶחָד מֵהָאַרְבַּע חַיּוֹת נָתַן לְהַשִּׁבְעָה מַלְאָכִים שֶׁבַע קְעָרוֹת שֶׁל זָהָב מְלֵאִים בַּחֲרוֹן יַהְוֶה הַחַי מֵעוֹלָם וְעַד עוֹלָם ‪8‬ וּבֵית הַתְּפִלָּה נִתְמַלְאָה בֶּעָשָׁן וּכְבוֹד יַהְוֶה מָלֵא אֶת הַמִּשְׁכָּן וְשׁוּם אֶחָד יוּכַל לֵילֵךְ לְתוֹכָהּ עַד שֶׁכָּלָא הַשִּׁבְעָה נְגָעִים מֵהַשִּׁבְעָה מַלְאָכִים

פֶּרֶק ט"ז

‪1‬ וְשָׁמַעְתִּי קוֹל אֶחָד מִבֵּית הַתְּפִלָּה וְאָמַר[c] לְהַשִּׁבְעָה מַלְאָכִים לְכוּ וְצַאקוּ[d] מֵהַקְּעָרוֹת עַל הָאֲדָמָה הַחֲרוֹן יַהְוֶה ‪2‬ וְהָרִאשׁוֹן הָלַךְ וַיָּצַק[e] אֶת קַעֲרוֹ[f] עַל הָאֲדָמָה וְהָיָה לִשְׁחִין פֶּרַח עַל הָאָדָם שֶׁהָיָה לָהֶם הַסִּימָן מֵהַחַיָּה וְהַמִּתְפַּלְלִים לַפֶּסֶל שֶׁלּוֹ ‪3‬ וַיָּצַק[g] הַמַּלְאָךְ הַשֵּׁנִי אֶת קַעֲרוֹ[h] בַּיָּם וְהָיָה דָם כְּמוֹ מֵמֵת וְכֹל אֲשֶׁר בַּהַיָּם תָּמוּת

---

[a] Or possibly "וְיִשְׁתַּחוּ". Compare e.g. Gen. 27:29, 43:28; 1 Kin. 9:9.

[b] Or possibly "וַיֵּצֵא".

[c] Or possibly "וְאֹמֶר".

[d] The Aleph is a vowel letter, thus "וצאקו" = "וְצָקוּ" (root "יצק"). Compare e.g. "הָבוּ" (Gen. 47:16; Deu. 1:13, etc.) from root "יהב". This word was later altered to "ותשפכו" – in different script than main text.

[e] Or possibly "וַיִּצֹק".

[f] Or possibly "קְעָרוֹ".

[g] Or possibly "וַיִּצֹק".

[h] Or possibly "קְעָרוֹ".

Indeed, all the peoples[a] will come and bow down before you, for your judgments are[b] revealed!"[c, d]

5 And after this I saw *that* the ark of the covenant was opened in the heavens. 6 Then the seven messengers who had the seven plagues went out, clothed in white garments, and a girdle of gold was on their loins. 7 Then one of the four living creatures gave the seven messengers seven bowls of gold, full of the fury of Yahweh who lives from everlasting and unto everlasting. 8 And the house of prayer was filled with smoke, and the glory of Yahweh filled the tabernacle, and no one was able to go into it until the seven plagues of the seven messengers were completed.

16: 1 Then I heard a voice from the house of prayer, and it[e] said to the seven messengers, "Go and pour out the fury of Yahweh from the bowls onto the earth."

2 So the first went and poured out his bowl on the earth, and it became boils, breaking out on the men[f] who had the sign of the animal and prayed[g] to his carved image.[h]

3 Then the second messenger poured out his bowl on the sea, and it was[i] blood like *that* of a dead one, and all that was in the sea died.[j]

---

[a] Does not refer to "people" but "nations."
[b] Singular in Hebrew, see pp. 94-96 for more information.
[c] Or possibly 'For all the nations will come and bow down before you when your judgments are revealed.'
[d] Compare Jer. 10:7; Ps. 86:9-10.
[e] Or possibly "he."
[f] Or "people."
[g] Or "and those who prayed."
[h] Or simply "his image."
[i] Or 'became.'
[j] Or "and all that is in the sea will die."

4 וְהַשְּׁלִישִׁי יָצַק אֶת קַעֲרוֹ בִּבְאֵרוֹת מַיִם וְהָיָה דָם 5 וְשָׁמַעְתִּי
שֶׁהַמַּלְאָךְ אֹמֵר[a] יַהְוֶה הַצַּדִּיק הֶהָיָה וְהֹוֶה וְקָדוֹשׁ[b] אַתָּה
שֶׁנָּתַתָּ זֹאת הַמִּשְׁפָּט 6 כִּי הֵמָּה שָׁפְכוּ דְּמֵי הַקְּדוֹשִׁים
וְהַנְּבִיאִים כַּמַּיִם וְאַתָּה נָתַתָּ לָהֶם דָּם לִשְׁתּוֹת כִּי הֵמָּה
רְאוּיִם לָזֶה 7 וְשָׁמַעְתִּי מַלְאָךְ אַחֵר שֶׁדִּיבֵּר מִתּוֹךְ הַהֵיכָל כֵּן
אֱלֹהֵי הַצְּבָאוֹת מִשְׁפָּטֶיךָ צֶדֶק הֵמָּה 8 וְהָרְבִיעִי יָצַק אֶת
קַעֲרוֹ בַּשֶּׁמֶשׁ וְלוֹ נוּתַּן לַעֲשׂוֹת חֹם לָאָדָם 9 וְהָיָה הַרְבֵּה חֹם
לָאָדָם וּמְקַלְּלוּ[c] לְיַהְוֶה בִּשְׁבִיל הַנְּגָעִים הַלָּלוּ וְלֹא עָשׂוּ
תְּשׁוּבָה לִיתֵּן לוֹ כָּבוֹד 10 וְהַחֲמִישִׁי יָצַק אֶת קַעֲרוֹ עַל הַכִּסֵּא
שֶׁל הַחַיָּה וְהֶחָשֵׁךְ[d] אוֹתוֹ וְהֵמָּה נוֹשְׁכִים לְשׁוֹנֵיהֶם מִפְּנֵי צַעַר
11 [12] וְהַשִּׁשִּׁי יָצַק אֶת קַעֲרוֹ עַל הַנָּהָר פְּרָת וַיֵּבַשׁ[e] אֶת הַנָּהָר
כְּדֵי לִהְיוֹת מְסִלָּה לְהַמְּלָכִים שֶׁהֵמָּה מִמִּזְרַח הַשֶּׁמֶשׁ

---

[a] Or possibly "אָמַר".

[b] See pp. 107-110 for a discussion on this verse.

[c] Or possibly "מְקַלְּלוּ" (see Jer. 15:10). This is either a participle with a 'perfect' ending (such mixed forms do occasionally occur in the Tanach, e.g. "משתחויתם" in Ezek. 8:16; see also "תבאתי" in 1 Sam. 25:34 (Ketiv), which looks like a combination of the perfect "באת" and imperfect "תבאי"); or else this could be a mistake for "מקללים" = "מקללי". Compare James 4:5 and Jude v. 21.

[d] Or possibly "הֶחְשַׁךְ". Note that passive verbs are sometimes used with the direct object marker "את", even in the Tanach. The 'subject' of a genuinely passive verb is in fact the object (to whom/which the action described by the verb is done). See e.g. Gen. 21:8; Lev. 6:13, 14:48; Num. 7:10, 7:84, 26:55; Deu. 12:22; 2 Kin. 18:30; Jer. 50:20.

[e] See footnote on verse 10.

₄ Then the third poured out his bowl on the fountains of waters and it was ᵃ blood. ₅ Then I heard that the messenger said, "Yahweh the Righteous, who was and is and ᵇ – you are qadosh that you gave this judgment, ₆ for **they** have shed the blood of the set-apart ones and the prophets like waters, and **you** gave them blood to drink, for they are worthy of ᶜ this!" ₇ Then I heard another messenger who spoke from inside the temple, "Yes, Elohei Ha-Tseva'ot, ᵈ your judgments are righteousness."

₈ Then the fourth poured out his bowl on the sun, and to it was given to make heat for man. ₉ Then man had much heat, and they cursed Yahweh because of these plagues, but they did not do repentance to give him glory.

₁₀ Then the fifth poured out his bowl on the throne of the animal, and it was darkened, and they bit their tongues because of *the* pain. ᵉ

₁₁ ₍₁₂₎ Then the sixth poured out his bowl on the river Perat, ᶠ and the river was dried up, to be ᵍ a path ʰ for the kings who are at ⁱ the rising of the sun. ʲ

ᵃ Or 'became.'

ᵇ The "ו" (*waw*) conjunction is used so often in Hebrew that it is sometimes difficult or impossible to translate. Thus, the translation could simply read "...who was and is – you are qadosh." See pp. 107-110 for a discussion on this verse.

ᶜ Or "they deserve this!"

ᵈ Meaning "Elohim of the Armies." Hebrew "אלהי הצבאת".

ᵉ Or "suffering."

ᶠ Hebrew name for 'Euphrates.'

ᵍ Or possibly 'that there could be.'

ʰ Or "road."

ⁱ Or "from."

ʲ Hebrew way of saying "east."

12 [13] וְרָאִיתִי שֶׁהָלַךְ מִפִּי הַתַּנִּין וּמִפִּי הַחַיָּה וּמִפִּי הַנָּבִיא שֶׁקֶר שְׁלֹשָׁה שְׁרָצִים טְמֵאִים כִּדְמוּת צְפַרְדְּעִים 13 [14] וְאֵלּוּ הֵמָּה רוּחוֹת הַשָּׂטָן וְעוֹשִׂים נִסִּים וְאוֹתוֹת וְהוֹלְכִים לַמַּלְכֵי אֶרֶץ וּלְכָל הָעוֹלָם לְקַבֵּץ[a] אוֹתָם לַמִּלְחָמָה עַל הַיּוֹם יַהְוֶה הָאַדִּיר 14 [15] רְאֵה אֲנִי אָבֹא כַּגַּנָּב וְקָדוֹשׁ[b] אֵילוּ שֶׁלֹּא יְשַׁנִים וְשָׁמוּר אֶת עַצְמוֹ שֶׁלֹּא יֵלֵךְ עָרֹם בְּלִי מַלְבּוּשִׁים כְּדֵי שֶׁלֹּא יְגַלֶּה[c] אֶת עֶרְוָתוֹ 15 [16] וְהוּא קָבֵץ[d] אוֹתָם בְּמָקוֹם אֶחָד הַנִּקְרָא בִּלְשׁוֹן עִבְרִי הַרְמָגִדּוֹן 16 [17] וְהַשְּׁבִיעִי יָצַק אֶת קַעֲרוֹ בָּאֲוִיר וְהָלַךְ קוֹל אֶחָד מֵהַכִּסֵּא וְאָמַר זֹאת עָבַר 17 [16] וְהָיָה קוֹלוֹת וּרְעָמִים וּבְרָקִים וְרַעֲדוֹת הָאָרֶץ שֶׁלֹּא הָיָה מֵעוֹלָם 18 [19] וּמֵהָעִיר הַגְּדוֹלָה נַעֲשָׂה שְׁלֹשָׁה חֲלָקִים וְהֶעָרִים מֵהָעַמִּים נוֹפְלִים וְנִזְכַּר[e] הָעִיר הַגְּדוֹלָה בָּבֶל לִפְנֵי יַהְוֶה לִיתֵּן לָהּ הַכּוֹס עִם הַיַּיִן שֶׁל חֲרוֹן אַפּוֹ 19 [20] וְכָל הֶהָרִים וּגְבָעוֹת נָסוּ וְלֹא נִרְאוּ עוֹד 20 [21] וּבָרָד גָּדוֹל נָפַל עַל הָאָדָם מִשָּׁמַיִם וְהֵמָּה מְחָרְפִים לְיַהְוֶה בִּשְׁבִיל הַנֶּגַע שֶׁל הַבָּרָד

פֶּרֶק י"ז

1 וּבָא אֶחָד מֵהַשִּׁבְעָה מַלְאָכִים שֶׁהָיָה לָהֶם הַשִּׁבְעָה קְעָרוֹת וְדִבֶּר לִי וְאָמַר בֹּא וְהִרְאָה לְךָ הַמִּשְׁפָּט שֶׁל הַזּוֹנָה הַגְּדוֹלָה הַיּוֹשֶׁבֶת עַל מַיִם הַרְבֵּה

---

[a] Or possibly "לְקַבֵּץ".

[b] Could possibly be a truncated form of "קדושים", but note the singular words further on in the sentence.

[c] See footnote on verse 10.

[d] Or possibly "קֹבֵץ" or "קֹבֵץ".

[e] Or possibly "וְנִזְכָּר".

12 [13] And I saw that there came forth from the mouth of the dragon and from the mouth of the animal and from the mouth of the false prophet, three unclean creeping things like ᵃ frogs. 13 [14] And these are the ruchot of Ha-Satan, and *they* do signs and wonders, and go to *the* kings of *the* earth and to all the world, to gather them to war for the day of Yahweh the Mighty.ᵇ 14 [15] ("Look! – **I** will come like a thief, and blessed are those who do not sleep, but keeps himself that he does not walk naked without clothes, that his nakedness will not be uncovered.") 15 [16] And he gathered them to a place which is called in the Hebrew tongue, Har-Megidon.ᶜ

16 [17] Then the seventh poured out his bowl in the air, and there came a voice from the throne, and said, "This is over!" 17 [18] And there were voices and thunders and lightnings, and an earthquake which had never happened before – 18 [19] and of the great city was made three parts, and the cities of the peoples ᵈ fell. And the great city Bavel ᵉ was remembered before Yahweh, to give her the cup with the wine of his burning anger. 19 [20] And all the mountains and hills fled, and were seen no more. 20 [21] And great hail fell on man from *the* heavens, and they blasphemed Yahweh because of the plague of the hail.

17: 1 Then one of the seven messengers who had the seven bowls came and spoke with me and said, "Come, and you will be shown ᶠ the judgment of the great harlot who sits over ᵍ much waters,

---

ᵃ Lit. "like the appearance of."

ᵇ Or "Majestic."

ᶜ Or "Mount Megiddo." Compare Zech. 12:11; Josh. 12:21; Judg. 1:27, 5:19; 1 Kings 4:12; 2 Chron. 35:22; etc.

ᵈ Does not refer to "people" but "nations."

ᵉ Hebrew name for 'Babylon.'

ᶠ Or "and there will appear to you."

ᵍ Hebrew idiom meaning 'rules over' or 'reigns over.'

2 וְעִמָּהּ עוֹשִׂים זְנוּת מַלְכֵי אֶרֶץ וְאֵילוּ הַמְשַׁכֶּרֶת מִיֵּינָהּ 3 וְהֵבִיא אוֹתִי בַּמִּדְבָּר וְרָאִיתִי הָאִשָּׁה שֶׁיָּשְׁבָה עַל הַחַיָּה שֶׁמַּרְאֵיהוּ הָיָה כְּמַרְאֵה שׁוֹשַׁנִּים וּמָלֵא הָיָה בְּשֵׁמוֹת שֶׁל חֵירוּפִים וְלוֹ הָיָה שֶׁבַע רָאשִׁים וַעֲשָׂרָה קְרָנַיִם 4 וְהָאִשָּׁה הָיָה לָבוּשׁ בְּמַלְבּוּשֵׁי אָדוֹם כְּמַרְאֵה שׁוֹשַׁנִּים וְעָלֶיהָ הָיָה הַרְבֵּה זָהָב וַאֲבָנִים טוֹבוֹת וּמַרְגָּלִיּוֹת וְכוֹס שֶׁל זָהָב[a] בְּיָדָהּ מָלֵא טֻמְאוֹת 5 וּבְמִצְחָהּ הָיָה כָּתוּב הַשֵּׁם שֶׁל הַסּוֹד מֵהָעִיר הַגְּדוֹלָה בָּבֶל הָאֵם מֵהַזּוֹנוֹת וּמְטֻמְאוֹת הָאָרֶץ 6 וְרָאִיתִי שֶׁהָאִשָּׁה שָׁתָה מִדַּם הַקְּדוֹשִׁים וּמִדַּם הָעֵדוּת שֶׁל יֵשׁוּעַ וּתְמִיָּה גְּדוֹלָה הָיָה לִי כְּשֶׁרָאֵה אוֹתָהּ 7 וְהַמַּלְאָךְ אָמַר לִי מִפְּנֵי מַה יֵּשׁ לְךָ תְּמִיָּה אֲנִי רוֹצֶה לֵאמֹר לְךָ הַסּוֹד מֵהָאִשָּׁה וּמֵהַחַיָּה שֶׁיָּשְׁבָה עָלֶיהָ וּמִפְּנֵי מַה שֶּׁיֵּשׁ לוֹ שֶׁבַע רָאשִׁים וַעֲשָׂרָה קְרָנַיִם

---

[a] Compare Jer. 51:7.

₂ with whom[a] *the* kings of *the* earth commit adultery, and[b] those whom she makes drunk with her wine."

₃ So he brought me into the wilderness, and I saw the woman who sat on the animal whose appearance was like the appearance of lilies, and was full of names of reproach,[c] and he had seven heads and ten horns. ₄ And the woman was clothed in red garments[d] with the appearance of lilies, and upon her there was much gold and goodly[e] stones and gems,[f] and there was a golden cup[g] in her hand, full of uncleanness.[h] ₅ And on her forehead was written the name of the secret[i] of the great city Bavel, the mother of the harlots and uncleanness[j] of the earth. ₆ And I saw that the woman drank[k] of the blood of the set-apart ones, and of the blood of the testimony of Yeshua. And I had a great amazement[l] when *I* saw her.[m]

₇ But the messenger said to me, "Because of what do you have amazement? I want to tell you the secret of the woman and of the animal which she sits upon, and because of what[n] he has seven heads and ten horns.

---

[a] Lit. "and with her."
[b] Or "even."
[c] Or "blasphemy." Lit. "reproaches."
[d] Lit. "garments of red."
[e] Or "precious." Lit. "good."
[f] Or "jewels" or "pearls."
[g] Compare Jer. 51:7.
[h] Plural in Hebrew.
[i] Or "mystery."
[j] Plural in Hebrew.
[k] Or "was drinking."
[l] Meaning "I was greatly amazed."
[m] Lit. "when seeing her."
[n] Or "for what *reason*."

8 הַחַיָּה שֶׁרָאִיתָ הָיָה וְלֹא הֹוֶה וְיָבֹא עוֹד פַּעַם מִתְּהוֹם וְיֵלֶךְ לִשְׁאוֹל וְיִשְׁתּוֹמֵם עָלֶיהָ אַנְשֵׁי הָאֲדָמָה בְּאִם שֶׁיִּרְאוּ הַחַיָּה שֶׁהָיָה וְלֹא יֵשׁ אַף עַל פִּי שֶׁיֵּשׁ , וּבְכָאן יֵשׁ דָּבָר שֶׁצָּרִיךְ שֵׂכֶל וְחָכְמָה וּתְבוּנָה הַשִּׁבְעָה רָאשִׁים הֵמָּה שִׁבְעָה הָרִים שֶׁהָאִשָּׁה יוֹשֵׁב עָלֶיהָ [10] וְאֵילוּ הֵמָּה שִׁבְעָה [מְלָכִים][a] 10 וּמֵהֶם נָפַל חֲמִשָּׁה וְאֶחָד יֵשׁ וְהַשֵּׁנִי עֲדַיִין לֹא יֵשׁ וּבְאִם שֶׁיָּבֹא צָרִיךְ הוּא לִהְיוֹת זְמָן מוּעָט 11 וְהַחַיָּה שֶׁהָיָה וְלֹא יֵשׁ זֶה הַשְּׁמִינִי וְהוּא יֵשׁ מֵהַשִּׁבְעָה וְהֹלֵךְ לִשְׁאוֹל 12 וְהָעֲשָׂרָה קְרָנַיִם שֶׁרָאִיתָ הֵם עֲשָׂרָה [מְלָכִים][b] שֶׁעֲדַיִין לֹא קִבְּלוּ הַמַּלְכוּת אֲבָל הֵמָּה תִּמְשְׁלוּ כִּמְלָכִים עִם הַחַיָּה עַל זְמָן מוּעָט 13 וְלָהֶם יֵשׁ מַחְשָׁבָה אֶחָד וְהֵם יִתְּנוּ אֶת כּוֹחָם וּגְבוּרָתָם לְהַחַיָּה 14 וְהֵם יַעֲשׂוּ מִלְחָמָה עִם הַשֶּׂה וְהַשֶּׂה יְנַצַּח אוֹתָם

---

[a] See footnote on verse 14.
[b] See footnote on verse 14.

₈ The animal which you saw, was, but is not, and will come again from *the* Deep, (but he will go to She'ol).[a] Then the men[b] of the earth will be amazed about him, when they see the animal who was, but is not, although he is.[c]

₉ And here is a word[d] which needs insight and wisdom and understanding: the seven heads are seven mountains which the woman sits upon,[e] [10] and these are seven [kings]. ₁₀ And of them, five are fallen and one is, but the second[f] is not yet, and when he comes, he must be for a little time. ₁₁ And the animal which was, but is not, this is the eighth, and he is of[g] the seven, and goes to She'ol. ₁₂ And the ten horns which you saw are ten [kings] who have not yet received the kingdom, but **they** will rule as[h] kings with the animal for[i] a little time. ₁₃ And they have one plan,[j] and they will give their power and their might[k] to the animal. ₁₄ And they will make war with the Lamb, but the Lamb will overcome them,

---

[a] The place of the dead. To learn more about the Biblical definition of She'ol, see: Gen. 37:35; Num. 16:30-33; 1 Sam. 2:6; Is. 14:9-15; Ezek. 31:15-18; Jonah 2:3(2), etc.

[b] Or "people."

[c] In the Hebrew Bible, an animal not only represents a specific kingdom, but also its leader/king (see Daniel chapters 7 and 8). Thus the animal "who was, but is not although he is," can be easily understood: The leader of this kingdom was (had existed/lived), and then he died (is not), but yet he is in "*the* Deep" and will "come again from *the* Deep" and assume leadership. This will amaze just about everyone in the world.

[d] Or "matter."

[e] Hebrew idiom meaning 'rules over' or 'reigns over' – could also mean "dwells on."

[f] I.e. 'the second' of the last two of the seven kings.

[g] Or "from." Could mean that he is part of this succession of kings, or that he originates from them.

[h] Or "like."

[i] Lit. "over."

[j] Or possibly 'they are of one mind.'

[k] Or "strength."

כִּי הוּא אָדוֹן מֵהָאֲדוֹנִים וּמֶלֶךְ הַמְּלָכִים [a] וְעִימּוֹ הַבְּחִירִים
וְהַמַּאֲמִינִים 15 וְהוּא אָמַר לִי הַמַּיִם שֶׁרָאִיתָ שֶׁיֹּשֵׁב הַזּוֹנָה
הֵם עַמִּים וַחֲבָרוּתוֹת וְאוּמִּים 16 וְהָעֲשָׂרָה קְרָנַיִם שֶׁרָאִיתָ עַל
הַחַיָּה הֵם יִהְיוּ שׂוֹנְאִים לְהַזּוֹנָה וְיַעֲשׂוּ שְׁמָמָה מִמֶּנָּה וְיֹאכְלוּ
אֶת בְּשָׂרָהּ וְעִם אֵשׁ תִּשְׂרְפוּ אוֹתָהּ 17 כִּי יַהֲוֶה נָתַן
בְּלִבְבֵיהֶם [b] לַעֲשׂוֹת רְצוֹנוֹ לִיתֵּן עֲשָׂרוּתֵיהָ [c] לְהַחַיָּה עַד
שֶׁתִּכְלֵא [d] דִּיבּוּרַת יַהֲוֶה 18 וְהָאִשָּׁה שֶׁרָאִיתָ הִיא הָעִיר
הַגְּדוֹלָה הַמֹּלֵךְ עַל כָּל מַלְכֵי אֶרֶץ

פֶּרֶק י"ח

1 (105v) וְאַחַר כָּךְ רָאִיתִי מַלְאָךְ אַחֵר יָרֵד מִשָּׁמַיִם וְלוֹ הָיָה כֹּחַ
וּגְבוּרָה גְּדוֹלָה וְהָאֲדָמָה הֵאִיר מֵאוֹרוֹ 2 וְצָעַק בְּכָל כֹּחוֹ
וְאָמַר נָפְלָה נָפְלָה הָעִיר הַגְּדוֹלָה בָּבֶל [e] וְהָיְיתָה לְדִירַת
הַשְּׂטָנִים וּלְהַסְתִּיר כָּל הַטְּמֵאִים מֵעוֹפוֹת וּשְׁרָצִים

---

[a] Manuscript has "המלאכים" – altered by original scribe to read "המלכים".
We have made the same correction in verses 9 and 12, based on this
correction and the context.

[b] Or possibly "בִּלְבָבֵיהֶם" (if singular with plural-like ending. Compare footnote
on 9:5).

[c] Or possibly "עֲשִׁירוֹתֶיהָ" – but compare footnotes on chapter 2:2, 9:5.

[d] Alternative spelling for "שתכלה". Compare e.g. "לְכַלֵּא" (Dan. 9:24) vs.
"לְכַלֵּה" (2 Chr. 24:10). See also Mishnah Shevi'it 9:5, "שכלא" (ms. Kaufmann)
vs. "שכלה" (ms. Parma/De Rossi 138).

[e] Compare Is. 21:9.

for he is *the* Adon of the adonim,[a] and the King of the kings, and with him are the chosen ones and the believing[b] ones."

15 And he said to me, "The waters which you saw, which the harlot sits *over*, are peoples and crowds and nations. 16 And the ten horns which you saw on the animal, they will be haters[c] of the harlot, and they will make a desolation of her, and will eat her flesh, and with fire **they** will burn her. 17 For Yahweh gave it in their hearts to do his will by giving her riches to the animal until the word of Yahweh is completed.[d] 18 And the woman which you saw is the great city, which reigns over all *the* kings of *the* earth."

18: 1 (105v) And after this I saw another messenger descending from *the* heavens, and he had power and great might,[e] and the earth shone with[f] his light.[g] 2 And he cried out with all his power and said, "Fallen, fallen has the great city Bavel![h] And it became the dwelling of the satans,[i] and to hide all the unclean ones of the birds and creeping things!

---

[a] Or "*the* Lord of lords."
[b] Refers to both believing and doing (being faithful). See e.g. James 2:19-23[20-24].
[c] Synonym of "enemies."
[d] Or "fulfilled."
[e] Or "strength."
[f] Or "because of."
[g] Or possibly 'and he illuminated the earth with his light.'
[h] Compare Is. 21:9.
[i] The Hebrew word "שׂטן" (*satan*) literally means "adversary" or "accuser." If it has the definite article (The Adversary) it is normally used as a title (e.g. Zech. 3:1; Job 1:6-11; Mat. 4:1; Mark 1:13, etc.), and is transliterated as '*Ha-Satan*'; however, '*satan*' (usually without the article, or plural) is used for 'enemy/adversary' (e.g. 1 Sam. 29:4; 2 Sam. 19:23(22); 1 Kin. 5:18(5:4), 11:14; Mat. 16:23, etc.) or as a synonym of 'demon' (e.g. Mat. 8:31; Mark 3:23; Rev. 18:2, etc.).

‫3 כִּי כֻלָּם שָׁתוּ מִיֵּינָהּ וּמַלְכֵי אֶרֶץ עָשׂוּ זְנוּת עִימָהּ וְכָל‬
‫הַסּוֹחֲרִים נִתְעַשְּׁרוּ מִתַּאֲוָתֵיהֶם[a] הַגְּדוֹלָה 4 וְשָׁמַעְתִּי קוֹל‬
‫אַחֵר מִשָּׁמַיִם וְאָמַר[b] צְאוּ מִמֶּנָּה עַמִּי כְּדֵי שֶׁלֹּא [תִּ]תְעַנְּשׁוּ[c]‬
‫עִימָהּ בִּשְׁבִיל עֲווֹנוֹתֶיהָ[d] 5 כִּי עֲווֹנוֹתֶיהָ נָגַע[e] אֶל הַשָּׁמַיִם‬
‫וַיַהֲוֶה תִּזְכּוֹר[f] אוֹתָהּ 6 וְכַאֲשֶׁר עָשְׂתָה עָשׂוּ לָהּ וְשַׁלֵּם לָהּ‬
‫כֶּפֶל[g] כִּפְלַיִם כְּפִי מַעֲשֶׂיהָ 7 וְכַאֲשֶׁר הִתְגָּאָה וְהָלְכָה אַחַר‬
‫תַּאֲווֹתֶיהָ כְּצַד זֶה עֲשׂוּ לָהּ עִינּוּיִם כִּי הִיא מְחַשֵּׁב בְּלִיבָּהּ אֲנִי‬
‫מַלְכָּה וְלֹא אֶהְיֶה אַלְמָנָה[h] וְשׁוּם צַעַר לֹא אֶרְאֶה 8 וּבִשְׁבִיל‬
‫זֶה יָבֹא צָרוֹתֵיהֶם בְּיוֹם אֶחָד[i] הַמָּוֶת וְהַצַּעַר וְהָרָעָב וְעִם‬
‫אֵשׁ תִּשָּׂרֵף כִּי עָצוּם הָאָדוֹן יַהֲוֶה שֶׁיִּשְׁפּוֹט אוֹתָהּ 9 וְשָׁמְמוּ‬
‫עָלֶיהָ מַלְכֵי אֶרֶץ שֶׁעָשׂוּ זְנוּת עִימָהּ בְּאָם שֶׁתִּרְאוּ[j] הֶעָשָׁן‬
‫מֵהָאֵשׁ‬

---

[a] Or possibly "מִתַּאֲוֹתֵיהֶם" (but note the singular adjective "גדולה"). See also footnote on chapter 9:5.

[b] Or possibly "וַיֹּאמֶר".

[c] Ms. has "נתענשו" – but note that "כדי" in all other instances is followed by an 'imperfect' or 'infinitive' verb in the Hebrew Revelation and James, never by a 'perfect.' The letters "ת" and "נ" were occasionally confused in this manuscript (compare 14:18).

[d] Compare Jer. 51:6.

[e] Possibly truncated from "נָגְעוּ".

[f] For the use of "ת" instead of "י", see footnote on chapter 1:7.

[g] Or possibly "כִּפֹל".

[h] Compare Is. 47:7-8.

[i] Compare Is. 47:9.

[j] For the use of "ת" instead of "י", see footnote on chapter 1:7.

₃ For all of them [a] have drunk of her wine, and *the* kings of *the* earth have committed fornication with her, and all the merchants have become rich by [her][b] great desires!" [c]

₄ Then I heard another voice from *the* heavens, and it [d] said, "Go out of her my people, that [you] be not punished with her because of her iniquities! [e] ₅ For her iniquities have reached unto the heavens, and Yahweh, **he** will remember her! ₆ And as she did, do [f] to her! And repay [g] her double, two-double, according to her works! [h] ₇ And as she exalted herself and walked after her desires [i] – according to this make torments [j] for her, for she thinks in her heart, 'I am a queen, and I will not be a widow, and I will not see any suffering.' [k, l] ₈ But because of this [her] [m] sufferings will come in one day [n] – the death and the suffering and the hunger, and she will be burned **with fire**, for mighty is Ha-Adon Yahweh who will judge her.

₉ And the kings of the earth who committed fornication with her will be astonished over her, when **they** see the smoke of the fire.

---

[a] I.e. the "peoples" (chapter 14:8). See pp. 53-57 for a discussion about this verse and 'gapping.'
[b] Lit. "their," but in context this most likely refers to the inhabitants of the city Bavel. Compare verse 8.
[c] Lit. "desire" (singular) – collective use. Or "lusts."
[d] Or possibly "he."
[e] Compare Jer. 51:6.
[f] Plural imperative.
[g] Singular imperative.
[h] Or "And repay her – double *it* two-double according to her works!"
[i] Or "lusts."
[j] Or "sufferings."
[k] Or "pain."
[l] Compare Is. 47:7-8.
[m] Lit. "their," but in context this most likely refers to the inhabitants of the city Bavel. Compare verse 3.
[n] Compare Is. 47:9.

₁₀ וְהֵמָּה יַעַמְדוּ מֵרָחוֹק מִפְּנֵי אֵימָה וְיֹאמְרוּ אוֹיי וַאֲהָהּ
הָעִיר הַגְּדוֹלָה בָּבֶל פִּתְאוֹם יָבֹא שְׁבוּרָתַיִךְ[a] ₁₁ וְהַסּוֹחֲרִים
יִבְכּוּ[b] וְשָׁרְקוּ[c] עָלַיִךְ בִּשְׁבִיל שֶׁלֹּא יִקְנֶה שׁוּם אֶחָד עוֹד
סְחוֹרָה מֵהֶם ₁₂ הַסְּחוֹרָה מִזָּהָב וְכֶסֶף וַאֲבָנִים טוֹבִים
וּמַרְגָּלִיּוֹת וּמֶשִׁי וְכָל מִינֵי עֵצִים וּמִינֵי כֵּלִים שֶׁל כֶּסֶף וּבַרְזֶל
וּבְדִיל וְעוֹפֶרֶת ₁₃ וְיַיִן וְשֶׁמֶן וְלֶחֶם לָבָן וְחִיטִים וּבְקָרִים
וּכְשָׂבִים וְסוּסִים וַעֲגָלִים וְנִשְׁמוֹת אָדָם ₁₄ וְהַפֵּירוֹת שֶׁהָיָה
לְנַחַת רוּחַ לָךְ הָלַךְ מִמֵּךְ וְכָל הַחֲשׁוּבִים הָלַךְ וְלֹא תִּמְצָא
עוֹד ₁₅ וְהַסּוֹחֲרִים שֶׁמָּכְרוּ לָהּ אֵילוּ הַדְּבָרִים יַעַמְדוּ מֵרָחוֹק
וְיִבְכּוּ עָלֶיהָ ₁₆ וְיֹאמְרוּ אוֹי וַאֲהָהּ עִיר[d] הַגְּדוֹלָה בָּבֶל

---

[a] Or possibly "שְׁבוּרָתֵיךְ"– but compare footnotes on chapter 2:2, 9:5. See also Is. 47:13 for a similar example in the Tanach.

[b] Margin reads "ישבו" – in different script than main text.

[c] Margin reads "ויבכו" – in different script than main text.

[d] "ואהה עיר" could possibly be a mistake for "ואהה העיר".

10 And they will stand far away because of terror and will say, 'Woe! And alas! – O great city Bavel! Your destruction came **suddenly**!'ᵃ

11 And the merchants will weep and hissᵇ over you, for no one will buy merchandise from them anymore. **12** The merchandise of gold and silver and goodlyᶜ stones and gemsᵈ and fine linen and all kinds of wood and *all*ᵉ kinds of vesselsᶠ of silver and iron and tin and lead. **13** And wine and oil and white breadᵍ and wheat and bulls and sheep and horses and calves and neshamotʰ of man. **14** And the fruits which were to satisfyⁱ your ruach,ʲ went away from you, and all the esteemed thingsᵏ went away *from you*ˡ and you will not find *them*ᵐ anymore.ⁿ

15 And the merchants who sold these things to her will stand far away and weep over her, **16** and say, 'Woe! And alas! – The great city Bavel,

---

ᵃ Or possibly 'How suddenly did your destruction come!'
ᵇ Or "whistle." Margin reads "will sit and weep" – in different script than main text.
ᶜ Or "precious." Lit. "good."
ᵈ Or "jewels" or "pearls."
ᵉ Understood from preceding part of the verse. (Called gapping, commonly found in the Hebrew Tanach.)
ᶠ Or "objects."
ᵍ Could also mean "fine flour."
ʰ Plural of "נשמה" (*neshamah*) – the Hebrew word for "blowing/breath," "soul" or "spirit." (See glossary for more information.)
ⁱ Or "to calm."
ʲ Lit. "to give rest of spirit to you." Could mean "to give you satisfaction/ pleasure."
ᵏ Or possibly 'important ones.'
ˡ Understood from first part of the verse. (Called gapping, commonly found in the Hebrew Tanach.)
ᵐ Gapped, see above note.
ⁿ Or "again."

שֶׁהָיָה לָבוּשׁ בַּמֶּשִׁי וּבַזָּהָב וּבָאֲבָנִים טוֹבִים וּמַרְגָּלִיּוֹת 17, כִּי בְּשָׁעָה אֶחָד נֶחֱרַב הַכֹּל מַעֲרָבֵךְ[a] מַלָּחַיִךְ וְחֹבְלָיִךְ מַחֲזִיקֵי בִדְקֵךְ וְעֹרְבֵי מַעֲרָבֵךְ וְכָל אַנְשֵׁי מִלְחַמְתֵּךְ[b] יַעַמְדוּ מֵרָחוֹק 18 [c] [ ] וְצוֹעֲקִים בְּשָׁעַת[d] שֶׁרָאוּ הֶעָשָׁן וְאוֹמְרִים מִי נִדְמָה[e] לָעִיר הַגְּדוֹלָה, 19 וַיִּזְרְקוּ עָפָר עַל רָאשֵׁיהֶם[f] וְצוֹעֲקִים וּבוֹכִים וּמִתְאַבְּלִים וְאוֹמְרִים אוֹי אוֹי לָעִיר הַגְּדוֹלָה בָּבֶל כִּי מִמֶּנָּה נִתְעַשְּׁרוּ כָּל הַסּוֹחֲרִים שֶׁהָיָה לָהֶם סְפִינוֹת בַּיָּם מִסְחוֹרָתֵיהָ[g] וְעַכְשָׁיו בְּשָׁעָה אֶחָד נֶחֱרַב הַכֹּל 20 תִּשְׂמְחוּ הַשָּׁמַיִם וּקְדוֹשָׁיו וּנְבִיאָיו כִּי יַהְוֶה נָקַם אֶת נִקְמָתֵיהֶם[h] בָּהּ 21 וּמַלְאָךְ אֶחָד לָקַח אֶבֶן אֶחָד גָּדוֹל כְּמוֹ אֶבֶן רֵחַיִם וְזָרַק אוֹתוֹ בַּיָּם וְאָמַר כָּכָה תִּשָּׁקַע בָּבֶל וְלֹא תָקוּם[i] עוֹד 22 וְלֹא נִשְׁמַע עוֹד בָּהּ קוֹל שָׂשׂוֹן וְקוֹל שִׂמְחָה

---

[a] Margin reads "מעירך" – in different script than main text.

[b] Quoted from Ezek. 27:27.

[c] Crossed-out word.

[d] Compare e.g. "רָעַת" > "רָעָה" in the Tanach. Could also be pointed as "בִּשְׁעַת" (later pronunciation on analogy with e.g. "שְׁנַת" > "שָׁנָה"). Older sources (e.g. vocalized manuscripts of the Mishnah) use "שָׁעַת" (as well as "שַׁעַת", "שַׁעְת" and "שָׁעְת" by interchange of Patach and Qamets). See also Ben Yehudah's dictionary entry on the noun "שָׁעָה".

[e] Or possibly "נִדְמֶה".

[f] Compare Ezek. 27:30.

[g] Or possibly "מִסְחוֹרָתֵיהָ", but compare footnotes on chapter 2:2, 9:5.

[h] See footnote on chapter 9:5.

[i] Quoted from Jer. 51:64.

which was clothed with fine linen and with gold and with goodly[a] stones and gems[b] 17 – for in one hour[c] everything is laid waste!'

Your merchandise, your mariners and your rope-men,[d] those who repair your breaches[e] and those who trade your merchandise, and all the men of your war[f,g] will stand far away 18 and *they* will cry out when they see the smoke, and say, 'Who was like this[h] great city!' 19 And they will cast dust over their heads,[i] crying out and weeping and mourning, saying, 'Woe! Woe to the great city Bavel! For by her all the merchants who had ships in the sea[j] were made rich – by her merchandise – and now in one hour[k] everything is laid waste!'

20 Rejoice o heavens, and his set-apart ones and his[l] prophets! – For Yahweh has avenged their vengeance against her!"

21 Then one messenger took a great stone like a millstone, and cast it into the sea[m] and said, "So will Bavel sink, and will rise up no more![n] 22 And there will no more be heard in her, *the* voice of joy and *the* voice of gladness,

---

[a] Or "precious." Lit. "good."
[b] Or "jewels" or "pearls."
[c] Could also mean "moment."
[d] Or "pilots" or "sailors."
[e] Or "ship seams."
[f] Meaning "all your soldiers."
[g] Verse 17b up to this point is quoted from Ezek. 27:27.
[h] Lit. "the."
[i] Compare Ezek. 27:30.
[j] Lit. "sea," but could also refer to rivers, compare e.g. chapter 16:11[12] vs. 9:13[14]. See also Is. 19:5.
[k] Could also mean "moment."
[l] Meaning "Yahweh's set-apart ones and Yahweh's prophets." 'The Name' Yahweh is found in the second half of the verse and gapped in the first half. Compare e.g. Hos. 12:15; Zech. 9:17; Ps. 20:8(7) for examples of backward 'gapping.'
[m] See footnote on "sea" in verse 19.
[n] Quoted from Jer. 51:64.

קוֹל חָתָן וְקוֹל כַּלָּה וְלֹא שׁוּם כְּלִי מְלָאכָה מִבַּעֲלֵי מְלָאכוֹת וְהַקּוֹל מֵרֵחַיִים לֹא נִשְׁמָע עוֹד בָּךְ [a] 23 וְלֹא זָרַח עוֹד אוֹר הַמְּאוֹרֹת כִּי הַסּוֹחֲרִים שֶׁלָּךְ הָיוּ שָׂרִים עַל הָאֲדָמָה כִּי עַל יַד כְּשׁוּפַיִךְ הֵסִיתוּ [b] כָּל הָעַמִּים 24 וּבָהּ נִמְצָא דַם הַקְּדוֹשִׁים וּנְבִיאִים וּמִכָּל אֵילוּ שֶׁנֶּהֶרְגוּ עַל הָאֲדָמָה

פֶּרֶק י"ט

1 וְאַחַר כָּךְ שָׁמַעְתִּי קוֹל אֶחָד מֵחַבְרוּתָה גְּדוֹלָה הָאוֹמְרִים הַלְלוּיָה וְכָבוֹד וּגְבוּרָה וְתִפְאֶרֶת תִּהְיֶה לַיהוֶה אֲדוֹנֵינוּ 2 כִּי צֶדֶק וֶאֱמֶת מִשְׁפָּטוֹ שֶׁשָּׁפַט אֶת הַזּוֹנָה הַגְּדוֹלָה הַמַּשְׁחִית הָאָרֶץ עִם זְנוּתָהּ וְנִקַּם אֶת דְּמֵי עֲבָדוֹ [c] מִמֶּנָּה 3 וְאוֹמְרִים פַּעַם שֵׁנִית הַלְלוּיָה וְהֶעָשָׁן הֹלֵךְ מָדוֹר לְדוֹר 4 וְהָאַרְבַּע וְעֶשְׂרִים זְקֵינִים וְהָאַרְבַּע חַיּוֹת נוֹפְלִים וּמִתְפַּלְלִים לַיהוֶה הַיּוֹשֵׁב עַל הַכִּסֵּא וְאוֹמְרִים אָמֵן הַלְלוּיָה

---

[a] Compare Jer. 25:10.

[b] Or possibly "הֵסִיתוּ".

[c] Or possibly "עֲבָדוֹ".

the voice of a bridegroom and *the* voice of a bride, nor any equipment[a] of the skilled workers[b] – also the sound of millstones will no more be heard in you,[c] 23 neither will the light of light-sources[d] shine *in you*[e] anymore! – For your merchants were princes over the earth, for by your sorceries they deceived all the peoples.[f] 24 And in her was found the blood of the set-apart ones and prophets, and of all those who were killed on the earth."

19: 1 And after this I heard a voice of a great crowd, who said, "Hallelu-Yah![g] Both honor and might[h] and glory be to Yahweh our Adon! 2 For righteousness and truth[i] is his judgment – for[j] he judged the great harlot who corrupted[k] the earth with her fornication, and he avenged the blood of his servant[l] from her!"

3 Then they said a second time,[m] "Hallelu-Yah! And the[n] smoke goes *up* from generation to generation!" 4 So the twenty-four elders and the four living creatures fell down and prayed to Yahweh who sits on the throne, and *they* said, "Amein! Hallelu-Yah!"

---

[a] Or "tools" – lit. "utensils of work."

[b] Or "skillful tradesmen."

[c] Compare Jer. 25:10.

[d] Lit. "the light sources."

[e] Understood from preceding verse. (Called gapping, commonly found in the Hebrew Tanach.)

[f] Could also mean "all the nations were deceived."

[g] Lit. "Praise Yah!" – Yah is a shortened form of Yahweh.

[h] Or "strength."

[i] Or "faithfulness."

[j] Lit. "that."

[k] Or "destroyed."

[l] The term "servant" is often used for Yahweh's people. See e.g. Is. 41:9, 44:1, 44:2, 44:21, 45:4, 49:3; Jer. 30:10, 46:27-28; Ezek. 28:25, 37:25, etc. The Hebrew word "עבדו" could also possibly be read as "his servants" (plural).

[m] Or "again."

[n] Or "her" – referring to the smoke of Babylon (18:17-18).

5 וְקוֹל אֶחָד יָצָא מֵהַכִּסֵּא הַלְלוּיָהּ הַלְלוּ עַבְדֵי יַהְוֶה הַלְלוּ
אֶת שֵׁם יַהְוֶה[a] וְהַמִּתְיָרְאִים לְפָנָיו שְׁנֵיהֶם קְטַנִּים וּגְדוֹלִים[b] 6
וְשָׁמַעְתִּי קוֹל אֶחָד כְּקוֹל מֵחַבְרוּתָה גָּדוֹל וּכְקוֹל מַיִם
גְּדוֹלִים וּכְמוֹ קוֹלוֹת גְּדוֹלִים הָאוֹמְרִים הַלְלוּיָהּ כִּי יַהְוֶה גָּבַר
7 נִהְיִנוּ[c] שְׂמֵחִים וְלִיתֵּן לוֹ כָּבוֹד כִּי הַזְּמַן הַחֲתֻנָּה מֵהַשֶּׂה בָּא
וְאִשְׁתּוֹ מוּכֶנֶת 8 וְנוּתַּן לָהּ לִלְבּוֹשׁ בַּמֶּשִׁי[d] נָקִי וְטוֹב וְיָפֶה 9
וְהוּא אָמַר לִי קְדוֹשִׁים הֵם שֶׁקְּרָא לֶאֱכוֹל אֲכִילַת עֶרֶב עִם
הַשֶּׂה וְהוּא אָמַר לִי אֵלֶּה דִּבְרֵי יַהְוֶה בֶּאֱמֶת 10 וְנָפַלְתִּי
לְרַגְלָיו לְהִתְפַּלֵּל לוֹ וְהוּא אָמַר לִי רְאֵה אַל תַּעֲשֶׂה אֲנִי
חֲבֵרֶיךָ[e] וּמֵאַחֶיךָ וּמֵאִילוּ שֶׁיֵּשׁ לָהֶם הָעֵידוּת מִיֵּשׁוּעַ עֲשִׂי[f]
תְּפִילָּתְךָ לַיַהְוֶה 11 וְרָאִיתִי שֶׁהַשָּׁמַיִם נִפְתָּחִים וְרָאִיתִי סוּס
אֶחָד לָבָן וְזֶה שֶׁיֵּשֵׁב עָלָיו שְׁמוֹ הָיָה נֶאֱמָן וֶאֱמֶת וְהוּא
יִשְׁפּוֹט בְּצֶדֶק 12 וְעֵינָיו הָיָה כְּלַהֶבֶת אֵשׁ וְעַל רֹאשׁוֹ הַרְבֵּה
כְּתָרִים

---

[a] Quoted from Ps. 113:1.

[b] This phrase was altered to read "הכל כקטנים וגדולים" – in different script than main text.

[c] Margin substitutes "נהיה" for "נהיינו" – in different script than main text. The unusual spelling "נהיינו" indicates the plural aspect of the verb twice – it looks like a combination of "נהיה" and "הינו". Similar spellings (with double indication of the plural) were sometimes used by medieval Jewish scribes. E.g., in Luke 20:14, Vat. Ebr. 100 and JTS Breslau 233 read "ונהרגהו", but St. Petersburg A 207 spells the same word as "ונהרגוהו". Compare chapter 5:10.

[d] Or possibly "בְּמֶשִׁי".

[e] See footnote on chapter 2:2.

[f] See footnote on chapter 2:5.

5 Then a voice went out from the throne: "Hallelu-Yah! Praise o servants of Yahweh, praise the name of Yahweh,[a] even those who fear before him, both small ones and great ones!"[b] 6 And I heard a voice like the voice of a great crowd, and like the sound of great waters, and like great voices,[c] who said, "Hallelu-Yah! – For Yahweh overcame![d] 7 Let us be glad and give him honor, for the time of the wedding of the Lamb has come, and his wife is prepared!"[e] 8 And it was given to her to be clothed[f] in fine linen, pure and good and beautiful.

9 Then he said to me, "Blessed are those whom he called[g] to eat *the* feast[h] with the Lamb." And he said to me, "These are the words of Yahweh in truth."[i] 10 So I fell down at his feet to pray to him, but he said to me, "Look! Do not do *this*![j] – I am your fellow, and of your brothers, even[k] of those who have the testimony of Yeshua. Do your prayer to Yahweh!"

11 Then I saw that the heavens were opened, and I saw a white horse. And he[l] who sat on it, his name was Faithful[m] and Truth, and he judges with righteousness. 12 And his eyes were like a flame of fire, and on his head were many crowns,[n]

---

[a] Quoted from Ps. 113:1.
[b] Could mean 'young and old ones' or 'unimportant and important ones.'
[c] Or "thunders."
[d] Or "For Yahweh is mighty!"
[e] Or "made ready."
[f] Lit. "to clothe herself with."
[g] Or "invited."
[h] Lit. "evening meal" but implies 'festive meal.'
[i] Meaning "These are truly the words of Yahweh."
[j] Meaning 'Be sure not to do this!'
[k] Or "and."
[l] Lit. "this *one*," but often means 'he' or 'him.'
[m] Or "Faithful One."
[n] Take note that the Hebrew concept of 'crown' is not the same as in English. See Lev. 8:9.

וְשֵׁם אֶחָד כָּתוּב עָלָיו וְשׁוּם אֶחָד יוֹדֵעַ אוֹתוֹ רַק הוּא לְבַדּוֹ

₁₃ וְלָבוּשׁ בְּמַלְבּוּשׁ אֶחָד שֶׁהָיָה זֹרֵק עָלָיו דָּם וּשְׁמוֹ הָיָה דִּיבּוּר יַהְוֶה ₁₄ וְכָל צִבְאוֹת הַשָּׁמַיִם הוֹלְכִים אַחֲרָיו עַל סוּסֵי לְבֵינָה[a] וְכוּלָּם לוֹבְשִׁים מַלְבּוּשֵׁי שֶׁל מֶשִׁי לְבֵינָה ₁₅ וּמִפִּיו הֹלֵךְ[b] חֶרֶב פִּיפִיּוֹת כְּדֵי לְהַכּוֹת בּוֹ הָעַמִּים וְהוּא יְנַהֵג אוֹתָם בְּשֵׁבֶט בַּרְזֶל[c] וְהוֹכִיחַ בְּמִישׁוֹר לְעִנְבֵי אֶרֶץ בַּחֲרוֹן אַף יַהְוֶה ₁₆ וְשֵׁם אֶחָד כָּתוּב עַל בִּגְדוֹ כָּךְ מֶלֶךְ הַמְּלָכִים וַאֲדוֹן הָאֲדוֹנִים ₁₇ וְרָאִיתִי מַלְאָךְ אֶחָד עָמֵד בַּשֶּׁמֶשׁ וְצָעַק בְּקוֹל גָּדוֹל וְאָמַר לְכָל הָעוֹפוֹת שֶׁהֵם מִתַּחַת הַשָּׁמַיִם לְכוּ אִסְפוּ כּוּלְכֶם לַאֲכִילַת עֶרֶב מֵאֱלֹהֵי הַגָּדוֹל ₁₈ כְּדֵי שֶׁתֹּאכְלוּ הַבָּשָׂר מֵהַמְּלָכִים וְהַשָּׂרִים וְהַבָּשָׂר מִגְּבּוֹרִים וּבְשַׂר הַסּוּסִים וּמֵאִילוּ הָרוֹכְבִים עָלֶיהָ

---

[a] Alternative spelling for "לְבָנָה". Variation between an a-class and e/i-class vowel on the second root-letter of the adjective "לבן" can be seen in the Masoretic Text in Gen. 49:12 ("וּלְבֶן"); and in manuscripts of the Samaritan Torah (relevant vowels shown below – note that the Samaritan "ˉ" corresponds to the Tiberian " ַ" or " ֲ"; while the "ˇ" corresponds to " ֵ" or " ִ"), e.g. Gen. 30:37 "לבנות" (New York Public Library ms. Heb. 228) vs. "לבנות" (British Library ms. Or. 6461); Lev. 13:43 "לבנה" (National Library of France, ms. Sam. 2) vs. "לבנה" (British Library ms. Or. 6461). See the respective passages in: S. Schorch, *The Samaritan Pentateuch, A Critical Edition Maior*, De Gruyter, vol. 3 (2018) and vol. 1 (2021). A similar spelling "לבינא" is also known in Mandaic Aramaic. See e.g. E. S. Drower and R. Macuch, *A Mandaic Dictionary*, Oxford University Press, 1963, p. 229.
[b] Or possibly "הָלַךְ".
[c] Compare Ps. 2:9.

and a name was written on him,[a] but no one knew it except he himself. 13 And he was clothed in a garment on which blood was sprinkled,[b] and his name was the Word[c] of Yahweh.

14 And all the armies[d] of the heavens went after him, on white horses,[e] and they all wore garments of fine white linen. 15 And a double-edged[f] sword went out of his mouth, to smite the peoples[g] with it; and he will lead them with a rod of iron[h] and will punish *the* grapes[i] of *the* earth in equity with the burning anger of Yahweh. 16 And a name was written on his garment, thus: "The King of the kings and the Adon of the adonim."[j]

17 Then I saw a messenger standing by[k] the sun, and he cried out with a great voice and said to all the birds which are under the heavens, "Come, gather all of you[l] to the feast[m] of my great Elohim! 18 That you may eat the flesh of the kings and the princes, and the flesh of mighty warriors, and the flesh of the horses and of those who ride on them,

---

[a] Or "on it." Compare verse 16.

[b] Or "spattered."

[c] Hebrew "דיבור" (*dibur*).

[d] Hebrew "צבאות" (the Tseva'ot of) – same word as used in the name 'Yahweh Tseva'ot.' See e.g. chapter 4:8, 12:3[11:17], 15:3, 16:7, 21:22, 22:6.

[e] Lit. "horses of white."

[f] Or "multi-edged."

[g] Does not refer to "people" but "nations."

[h] Compare Ps. 2:9.

[i] Compare 14:18-19[20]. It seems the grapes are Yahweh's enemies who gather together against him for war. (Chapter 16:11-15[12-16] mentions the gathering of the armies, and here in chapter 19:19-21 we read of Yeshua's victory over his enemies).

[j] Or "the Lord of the lords."

[k] Or "at."

[l] Or "Come assemble yourselves."

[m] Lit. "evening meal" but implies 'festive meal.'

וְהַבָּשָׂר הַקְּטַנִּים וּגְדוֹלִים וּמֶעֱבָדִים וּמְשׁוּחְרָרִים 19, וְרָאִיתִי
הַחַיָּה וּמַלְכֵי אֶרֶץ אָסְפוּ אֶת מַחֲנֵיהֶם לַעֲשׂוֹת מִלְחָמָה עִם
זֶה שֶׁיֹּשֵׁב עַל [ ]ᵃ 20 הַסּוּס וְעִם מַחֲנָיוᵇ וְנִשְׁבָּה הַחַיָּה עִם
נְבִיא הַשֶּׁקֶר הָעוֹשֶׂה הָאוֹתוֹת לְפָנֶיהָ כְּדֵי לְהַסִּיתᶜ לְאֵילוּ
שֶׁלָּקְחוּ הַסִּימָן מֵהַחַיָּה [ ]ᵈ וּמִתְפַּלְלִים לוֹ וְנִשְׁלְכוּ בִּשְׁאוֹל
הַבּוֹעֵר בְּגָפְרִית 21 וְהָאֲחֵרִים נֶהֶרְגוּ עַל יַד הַחֶרֶב מִזֶּה שֶׁיֹּשֵׁב
עַל הַסּוּס שֶׁיָּצָאᵉ מִפִּיו (106r) וְכָל חַיּוֹת הַשָּׂדֶה נִשְׂבְּעוּ מִבְּשָׂרָם

פֶּרֶק כ'

1 וְרָאִיתִי מַלְאָךְ אֶחָד יָרֵד מִשָּׁמַיִם וְלוֹ הָיָה הַמַּפְתֵּחַ מִתְּהוֹם
וּבְיָדוֹ שַׁלְשֶׁלֶת גְּדוֹלָה 2 וְלָקַח הַתַּנִּין שֶׁהִיא הַשָּׂטָן וְאָסַר
אוֹתוֹ אֶלֶף שָׁנִים 3 וְהִשְׁלִיךְ אוֹתוֹ לַתְּהוֹם וְסָגוֹרᶠ אוֹתוֹ
וְחָתוֹםᵍ מִלְמַעְלָה כְּדֵי שֶׁלֹּא יוּכַל לְהַסִּיתʰ הָעַמִּים עַד שֶׁכָּלָא
אֶלֶף שָׁנִים וְאַחַר כָּךְ יִהְיֶה חֵפֶשׁ זְמָן מוּעָט 4 וְרָאִיתִי כִּסְאוֹת
וְהֵם יוֹשְׁבִים עֲלֵיהֶם וְלָהֶם נוּתַּן לִשְׁפּוֹט אֵילוּ הַמַּאֲמִינִים
וּמְעִידִים עַל יֵשׁוּעַ

ᵃ Crossed-out word.

ᵇ Crossed out and replaced with "חייליו" – in different script than main text.

ᶜ Or possibly "לְהֵסִית".

ᵈ Crossed-out letters.

ᵉ Or possibly "שֶׁיָּצָא".

ᶠ Altered to "וסגר" – in different script than main text. See also next footnote.

ᵍ The Tanach also uses 'infinitive absolute' verbs in this way. For examples of the 'infinitive absolute' used with a consecutive or simultaneous sense, compare e.g. Hag. 1:6; Dan. 9:5, 9:11; 1 Sam. 2:28; Is. 37:19; Zech. 12:10; Jer. 32:44.

ʰ Or possibly "לְהֵסִית".

and the flesh of the small ones and great ones[a] and of slaves and freed ones!"

19 And I saw *that* the animal and *the* kings of *the* earth gathered their camps to make war with him[b] who sits on the horse, and with his camps.[c] 20 Then the animal was captured, with the false prophet – who did the signs before him in order to deceive those who took the sign of the animal and prayed to him – and they were cast into She'ol, which burns with sulfur. 21 And the others were killed by the sword of him[d] who sits on the horse, which went out of his mouth, (106r) and all the animals of the field[e] were satisfied with their flesh.

20: 1 And I saw a messenger descending from *the* heavens, and he had the key of *the* Deep, and in his hand was a great chain. 2 And he took the dragon, which is Ha-Satan, and bound him *for* a thousand years. 3 And[f] he cast him into the Deep, and shut him in, and sealed *him* from above, that he would not be able to seduce[g] the peoples[h] until *the* thousand years were completed. And after this he will be freed *for* a little time.

4 Then I saw thrones,[i] and they sat on them, and it was given to them to judge[j] those who believe and bear witness of[k] Yeshua,

---

[a] Could mean 'young and old ones' or 'unimportant and important ones.'
[b] Lit. "this *one*," but often means 'he' or 'him.'
[c] Crossed out and replaced with "armies" – in different script than main text.
[d] Lit. "this *one*," but often means 'he' or 'him.'
[e] Hebrew idiom meaning 'wild animals.'
[f] Or "So."
[g] Or "deceive."
[h] Does not refer to "people" but "nations."
[i] Or "seats."
[j] Or "do justice to" – This does not mean that believers will be condemned but that justice will be done to them, and that they will be rewarded according to their works. See e.g. Dan. 7:9 and 7:22; Mat. 19:28; Luke 22:30; 1 Cor. 4:5.
[k] Or "about."

וְאִילוּ שֶׁלֹּא לָקְחוּ עַל מִצְחֵיהֶם הַסִּימָן מֵהַחַיָּה וְלֹא הִתְפַּלְלוּ

לוֹ אוֹ לַפֶּסֶל שֶׁלּוֹ וְאִילוּ חַיִּים וּמוֹשְׁלִים עִם יֵשׁוּעַ אֶלֶף שָׁנִים

5 אֲבָל הַמֵּתִים אֲחֵרִים לֹא קָמִים עַד שֶׁכָּלָא הָאֶלֶף שָׁנִים

וְזֶה[a] הִיא תְּקוּמַת[b] הָרִאשׁוֹנָה 6 קָדוֹשׁ הוּא מִי שֶׁיֵּשׁ לוֹ חֵלֶק

בַּתְּקוּמָה הָרִאשׁוֹנָה כִּי עֲלֵיהֶם לֹא יֵשׁ כֹּחַ מִמָּוֶת אַחֶרֶת רַק

הֵמָּה יִהְיוּ כֹּהֲנִים לְיַהְוֶה וּמְשִׁיחוֹ וּמוֹשְׁלִים עִימּוֹ אֶלֶף שָׁנִים

7 וְאַחַר אֶלֶף שָׁנִים יִגָּאֵל הַשָּׂטָן מִשְׁבְיוֹ[c] 8 וַיֵּלֶךְ[d] לְהָסִית[e]

הָעַמִּים עַל אַרְבַּע פִּינוֹת הָאָרֶץ וְגוֹג וּמָגוֹג[f] לֶאֱסֹף אֶת חֵילוֹ[g]

לָבוֹא לַמִּלְחָמָה וּמִסְפָּרָם יֵשׁ כְּחוֹל הַיָּם 9 וְהֵם דָּרְסוּ עַל

רֹחַב הָאֲדָמָה וְסָבְבוּ הַחֵילוֹת הַקְּדוֹשִׁים וְהָעִיר הָאֲהוּבָה

וְנָפַל אֵשׁ מִשָּׁמַיִם וְשָׂרַף אוֹתָם 10 וְהַשָּׂטָן הַמַּסִּית[h] אוֹתָם

הוּשְׁלַךְ בָּאֵשׁ שֶׁל הַשְּׁאוֹל שֶׁהָיָה שָׁם הַחַיָּה וּנְבִיא הַשֶּׁקֶר

וְיִתְעַנּוּ אוֹתָם יוֹם וָלַיְלָה מֵעוֹלָם וְעַד עוֹלָם

---

[a] Older spelling of "זוֹ" (feminine form of "זֶה"); also attested in the Tanach in Judg. 18:4; 2 Sam. 11:25; 1 Kin. 14:5; Eccl. 2:24, etc.

[b] Usually spelled "תקומה". The Tanach also contains a number of feminine nouns which are construct in form, but not necessarily in meaning, e.g., "שִׁפְעַת" instead of "שִׁפְעָה" (2 Kin. 9:17b); "פוּגַת" instead of "פוּגָה" (Lam. 2:18); "חָכְמַת" instead of "חָכְמָה" (Is. 33:6); "נְגִינַת" instead of "נְגִינָה" (Ps. 61:1).

[c] Margin reads "מאסוריו" – in different script than main text.

[d] Or possibly "וַיֵּלֶךְ".

[e] Or possibly "לְהַסִּית".

[f] See Ezek. chapters 38-39.

[g] Or possibly "חֲיָלָו".

[h] Or possibly "הַמֵּסִית".

and those who did not take the sign of the animal on their foreheads, and did not pray to him or to his image. And these lived, and ruled with Yeshua *for* a thousand years, ₅ (but the other dead ones did not rise until the thousand years were completed), and this is the first resurrection.

₆ Blessed is he who has ᵃ a part in the first resurrection, for over them there is no power of the last ᵇ death, but they will be priests to Yahweh and his Mashiach, and will rule with him, a thousand years.

₇ But after a thousand years, Ha-Satan will be delivered from his captivity.ᶜ ₈ Then he will go ᵈ to deceive the peoples ᵉ on the four corners ᶠ of the earth, and Gog and Magog,ᵍ to gather his army ʰ to come to war. (And their number is like the sand of the sea.)

₉ And they trampled ⁱ over the breadth of the earth,ʲ and surrounded the armies of the set-apart ones, and the beloved city. Then fire fell from the heavens and burned them up. ₁₀ And Ha-Satan who seduced them was cast into the fire of She'ol, where the animal and the false prophet are, and **they** will be afflicted ᵏ day and night from everlasting and unto everlasting.ˡ

ᵃ Lit. "whosoever has."

ᵇ Or "latter" or "second."

ᶜ Margin reads "fetters" – in different script than main text.

ᵈ Or "he went."

ᵉ Does not refer to "people" but "nations."

ᶠ An expression which means something like 'ends' or 'quarters' of the earth. This verse indicates that these are not literal corners (the nations do not dwell on the corners of the earth, they dwell all over the earth). See also Is. 11:12 and Ezek. 7:2.

ᵍ See Ezek. chapters 38-39.

ʰ Or possibly "their armies."

ⁱ Or possibly 'ran' or 'marched.'

ʲ Or "land."

ᵏ Or "tormented."

ˡ A Hebrew idiom which often means "forever and ever" – see e.g. Jer. 7:7, 25:5; 1 Chr. 16:36; Neh. 9:5; Ps. Ps. 41:14(13), 103:17, 106:48.

11 וְרָאִיתִי [ ]ᵃ אֶחָד כִּסֵּא גָּדוֹל וְלָבָן הָיָה וְזֶה שֶׁיָּשַׁב עָלָיו וּמִפָּנָיו נָס הַשָּׁמַיִם וְהָאֲדָמָה וְלֹא נִמְצָא לוֹ מָקוֹם 12 וְרָאִיתִי הַמֵּתִים שֶׁבָּהֶם הַקְּטַנִּים וְהַגְּדוֹלִים עוֹמְדִים לִפְנֵי יַהְוֶה וְנִפְתְּחוּ הַסְּפָרִים וְסֵפֶר אַחֵר נִפְתַּחᵇ וְזֶה סֵפֶר הַחַיִּים לִשְׁפֹּט הַמֵּתִים כְּפִי שֶׁכָּתוּב בַּסְּפָרִים וּכְפִי מַעֲשֵׂיהֶם 13 וַיָּרֶק הַיָּם אֶת הַמֵּתִים שֶׁהָיוּ בָּהּ לַחוּץ וְהַמָּוֶת וְהַשְּׁאוֹל נָתַן אֶת הַמֵּתִים וַיִּשָּׁפְטוּ כָּל אֶחָד כְּפִי מַעֲשָׂיו 14 וְהַמָּוֶת וְהַגֵּיהִנֹּם נִשְׁלַךְᶜ בָּאֵשׁ וְזֹאת מָוֶת אַחֶרֶת 15 וְאִם לֹא נִמְצָא אֶחָד כָּתוּב בְּסֵפֶר הַחַיִּים הוּשְׁלַךְ בָּאֵשׁ

פֶּרֶק כ"אᵈ

1 וְרָאִיתִי שָׁמַיִם חֲדָשִׁים וַאֲדָמָה חֲדָשָׁה כִּי הַשָּׁמַיִם וְהָאָרֶץ הָרִאשׁוֹנִים יָגְוֹעַ וְהַיָּם לֹא יֵשׁ עוֹד 2 וַאֲנִי יוֹחָנָן רָאִיתִי הָעִיר הַקְּדוֹשָׁה יְרוּשָׁלַיִם הַחֲדָשָׁה יֵרֵד מִשָּׁמַיִם לָאָרֶץ וּמְקֻשָּׁט הָיָה כְּאִשָּׁה הַמְקֻשָּׁט לִפְנֵי בַּעְלָהּ 3 וְשָׁמַעְתִּי קוֹל גָּדוֹל מֵהַכִּסֵּא שֶׁאָמַר רְאֵה מִשְׁכַּן יַהְוֶה אֵצֶל הָאָדָם וְהָיָה לָהֶם לֵאלֹהִים

ᵃ Crossed-out letters.

ᵇ Or possibly "נִפְתָּח".

ᶜ Or possibly "נִשְׁלַךְ".

ᵈ A reader commented "זֶה פֶּרֶק טוֹב מְאֹד" "טוֹב" "טוֹב" – in different script than main text.

₁₁ Then I saw a great throne which was white, and him who sat on it. And from before him the heavens and the earth fled away, but no place was found for them. ₁₂ And I saw the dead ones, that the small ones and the great ones ᵃ of them stood before Yahweh. And the scrolls were opened – also another scroll was opened and this is the scroll of life – to judge the dead ones according to what is written in the scrolls, even ᵇ according to their works.

₁₃ And the sea emptied out the dead ones who were in it, and the death ᶜ and ᵈ She'ol gave ᵉ the dead ones – and they were judged, every one according to his deeds. ₁₄ Then the death and Gei-Hinnom were cast into the fire, and this is *the* last ᶠ death. ₁₅ And if one was not found written in the scroll of life, he was cast into the fire.

21: ₁ Then I saw new heavens and a new earth, for the first heavens and earth had perished, also the *first* ᵍ sea was no more. ₂ And I Yochanan, I saw the set-apart city, the new Yerushalayim, ʰ descending from *the* heavens to the earth, and it was adorned ⁱ like a wife who is adorned before her husband.

₃ And I heard a great voice from the throne which said, "Look! – The tabernacle of Yahweh is with man, and he will be Elohim to them,

---

ᵃ Could mean 'young and old ones' or 'unimportant and important ones.'
ᵇ Or "and."
ᶜ Crossed out and replaced with "and also" – in different script than main text.
ᵈ Or "even" or "that is."
ᵉ Singular in Hebrew, see p. 100 for more information.
ᶠ Or "latter" or "second."
ᵍ Probably gapped (implied by context). John is not necessarily saying that the new earth has no sea, but rather that the first heaven and earth passed away, even the [first] sea was no more.
ʰ Hebrew name for 'Jerusalem.'
ⁱ Or "decorated."

וְהֵם יִהְיוּ לוֹ לְעָם [a] 4 וּמָחָה יַהְוֶה אֱלֹהִים [b] דִּמְעָה מֵעַל כָּל
פָּנִים [c] וְהַמָּוֶת לֹא יִמְשֹׁל עוֹד וְלֹא שׁוּם צַעַר וּצְעָקוֹת וְעִנּוּיִם
כִּי הָרִאשׁוֹן עָבַר 5 וְזֶה שֶׁיֹּשֵׁב עַל הַכִּסֵּא אָמַר רְאֵה אֲנִי
עָשִׂיתִי הַכֹּל חָדָשׁ וְהוּא אָמַר לִי כְּתוֹב כִּי אֵלֶּה הַדְּבָרִים
אֱמֶת הִיא 6 וְאָמַר לִי עָבַר הַכֹּל אֲנִי הָרִאשׁוֹן וְהָאַחֲרוֹן
תְּחִילַת [d] וְהַסּוֹף וַאֲנִי אֶתֵּן לְהַצָּמֵא מַיִם חַיִּים בְּחִנָּם 7 מִי
שֶׁמְּנַצֵּחַ יִהְיֶה יוֹרֵשׁ מֵהַכֹּל וַאֲנִי [אֶ]הְיֶה [e] לוֹ לֵאלֹהִים וְהוּא
יִהְיֶה לִי לְבֵן 8 אֲבָל לְהָאֵינוּ [f] מַאֲמִינִים וְלָרְצְחָנִים וְלַזּוֹנִים
וְלַמְכַשְּׁפִים וְלַכַּזְבָנִים אֶתֵּן אֶת שְׂכָרָם מֵאֵשׁ הַשְּׁאוֹל הַשּׂוֹרֵף
בָּאֵשׁ וְגָפְרִית וְזֹאת הִיא הַמִּיתָה הַשְּׁנִיָּה 9 וּבָא לִי אֶחָד
מֵהַשִּׁבְעָה מַלְאָכִים שֶׁהָיָה בְּיָדָם הַקְּעָרוֹת מְלֵאִים בְּשִׁבְעָה
נְגָעִים אַחֲרוֹנִים וְאָמַר לִי בֹּא וְרְאֶה הָאִשָּׁה הַכַּלָּה מֵהַשֶּׂה 10
וְנָהַג [g] אוֹתִי עַל הַר אֶחָד שֶׁהָיָה גָּדוֹל וְגָבוֹהַּ

---

[a] Compare Ezek. 37:26-27.

[b] The Masoretic Text reads "אדני יהוה". Note that "אדני יהוה" can interchange with "יהוה אלהים", as both phrases are traditionally pronounced as 'Adonai Elohim.' Compare e.g. the Dead Sea Scrolls against the Masoretic Text in Is. 61:1 (1Q8 "יה[ו]ה אלהים" vs. MT "אדני יהוה") and Is. 61:11 (1QIsa "אדני יהוה" vs. MT "יהוה אלהים").

[c] Quoted from Is. 25:8.

[d] See footnote on chapter 1:8.

[e] Ms. reads "אני יהיה" (contraction of "אני אהיה"). Compare chapter 22:7 and 22:12.

[f] Or possibly "לְהָאֵינוּ" (alternative pronunciation). Also note that in the Hebrew Revelation and James, "אינו" or "אינה" is generally used instead of "אין". The "ו" or "ה" at the end does not always represent a third person singular pronominal suffix.

[g] Or possibly "וְנָהֵג".

and they will be a people to him!^a 4 And Yahweh Elohim will wipe off *the* tears from all faces,^b and the death will no longer rule, neither any suffering^c or outcries or afflictions,^d for the former has passed by!"

5 And he^e who sat on the throne said, "Look! – **I** made everything new!" Then he said to me, "Write, for these words are truth!" 6 And he said to me, "It is all over,^f I am the first and the last, *the* beginning and the end, and **I** will give the thirsty living waters, for free! 7 Whosoever overcomes will be an heir^g of everything,^h and I will be Elohim to him, and he will be a son to me. 8 However, to those who do not believe, and to the murderers and to the fornicators and to the sorcerers and to the liars, I will give their reward from the fire of She'ol which burns with fire and sulfur, and this is the second death."

9 Then there came to me one of the seven messengers, who had in their hand the bowls full of *the* seven last plagues, and he said to me, "Come and see the wife, the bride of the Lamb!" 10 So he led me onto a mountain which was great and high,

---

^a Compare Ezek. 37:26-27.
^b Quoted from Is. 25:8.
^c Or "pain."
^d Or "suffering" or "oppression."
^e Lit. "this *one*," but often means 'he' or 'him.'
^f Lit. "everything is over."
^g Or "possessor."
^h Compare Heb. 1:2; Rom. 8:17.

וְהֶרְאָה [a] לִי הָעִיר הַגְּדוֹלָה הָעִיר הַקְּדוֹשָׁה יְרוּשָׁלַיִם יֵרֶד
מִשָּׁמַיִם לָאָרֶץ 11 וְתִפְאֶרֶת יַהְוֶה עָלֶיהָ וּמְאוֹרָהּ הָיָה כָּאוֹר
שֶׁל הָאֶבֶן טוֹבָה הַנִּקְרָא יָשְׁפֶּה 12 וְלָהּ הָיָה חוֹמָה גְּדוֹלִים
וּשְׁנַיִם [b] עָשָׂר שְׁעָרִים וְעַל הַשְּׁעָרִים שְׁנֵים עָשָׂר מַלְאָכִים
וּשְׁנַיִם עָשָׂר שֵׁמוֹת מִשְׁנֵים עָשָׂר שְׁבָטִים שֶׁל יִשְׂרָאֵל 13
מִמִּזְרָח שְׁלֹשָׁה שְׁעָרִים וּמִמַּעֲרָב שְׁלֹשָׁה וּמִצָּפוֹן שְׁלֹשָׁה
וּמִדָּרוֹם שְׁלֹשָׁה 14 וּלְחוֹמַת הָעִיר הָיָה שְׁנֵים עָשָׂר יְסוֹדוֹת
וּבָהֶם הָיָה כָּתוּב הַשֵּׁמוֹת מִשְׁנֵים עָשָׂר שְׁלוּחִים שֶׁל הַשֶּׂה 15
וְזֶה שֶׁדִּבֵּר עִימִּי הָיָה בְּיָדוֹ קָנֶה אֶחָד שֶׁל זָהָב כְּדֵי לִמְדּוֹת [c]
בּוֹ הָעִיר וְהַחוֹמָה וְהַשְּׁעָרִים 16 וְהָעִיר מוּנָּח [מְרוּבַּעַת] [d]
וְאָרְכָּהּ כְּרָחְבָּהּ וּמָדַד הָעִיר עִם הַקָּנֶה שְׁנֵים עָשָׂר אֶלֶף
קִבְרוֹת הַשָּׂדֶה וְאָרְכָּהּ וְרָחְבָּהּ וְגָבוֹהַּ מֵהָעִיר הֵמָּה שָׁוִים

---

[a] Or possibly "וְהֶרְאָה".

[b] The "יְ" vowel was sometimes indicated by "יי" in unpointed Hebrew.
Compare e.g. Mishnah Bava Kama 5:5 in the Kaufmann ms., where the initial
scribe wrote "כדייי"; but the Naqdan (scribe adding vowels to ms.) marked the
second "י" as redundant when adding the vowel points: "כְּדֵיי". The phrase
"שניים עשר" (with this spelling) is also attested in a fragment from the Cairo
Genizah (NLI ms. 577.4.28).

[c] Alternative spelling for "למדוד".

[d] Original scribe wrote "ברובעת" (most likely a copyist mistake). This word
was altered to "מרבעת" in different script than main text, and the margin
reads "מרובע" – in different script than main text.

and showed[a] me the great city, the set-apart city Yerushalayim, descending from the heavens to the earth. 11 And the glory of Yahweh was upon[b] it, and its light-source was like the radiance of the goodly[c] stone which is called jasper.[d]

12 And it had a great wall and twelve gates; and at the gates were twelve messengers, and *the* twelve names[e] of *the* twelve tribes of Yisrael. 13 At the east were three gates, and at the west three, and at the north three, and at the south three. 14 And the wall of the city had twelve foundations,[f] and on them were written the names of the twelve sent ones of the Lamb.

15 And he[g] who spoke with me had a reed of gold in his hand, to measure with it the city and the wall and the gates. 16 And the city lay as a square,[h] and its length was the same as its width, and he measured the city with the reed, twelve thousand graves of the field,[i] and its length and its width and the height of the city[j] are equal.

---

[a] Or possibly "and there appeared to me."
[b] Or "over."
[c] Or "precious." Lit. "good."
[d] Or possibly 'jade.'
[e] Prepositional phrase understood from preceding part of the verse. (Called gapping, see pp. 52-59 and 250-255 for more information). Implied meaning: 'and *upon/above the gates, were the* twelve names…'
[f] Or "foundation walls."
[g] Lit. "this *one*," but often means 'he' or 'him.'
[h] Or "lay square" or "lay squared."
[i] Or "field graves" or "graveyards." This probably indicates a traditional measure of distance based on Jewish customs and laws (compare e.g. "a Sabbath day's journey"). The Mishnah records various customs about the spacing of graves (4 to 8 cubits), as well as the distance of land which becomes 'unclean' when a grave is plowed in a field (100 cubits). See Mishnah Nazir 9:3; Mishnah Bava Batra 6:8; Mishnah Oholot 17:1. Compare also Rev. 14:19[20].
[j] Or "the length and width and height of the city."

17 וְחוֹמוֹתֶיהָ הָיוּ מֵאָה וְאַרְבַּע וְאַרְבָּעִים אַמּוֹת כְּמִדַּת אָדָם
שֶׁהָיָה לַמַּלְאָךְ (106v) 18 וְהַחוֹמָה הָיְתָה מִיָּשְׁפֵה וְהָעִיר מִזָּהָב
טָהוֹר 19 וְהַיְסוֹד מֵהַחוֹמָה וּמֵהָעִיר הָיוּ מְקֻשָּׁט בָּאֲבָנִים
טוֹבִים הַיְסוֹד הָרִאשׁוֹן הָיָה יָשְׁפֵה אַחַת הַשֵּׁנִי סַפִּיר
וְהַשְּׁלִישִׁי קַאלְקֶידְנִיר בְּלַעַז וְהָרְבִיעִי נֹפֶךְ 20 וְהַחֲמִישִׁי אֹדֶם
וְהַשִּׁשִּׁי שֹׁהַם וְהַשְּׁבִיעִי אַחְלָמָה וְהַשְּׁמִינִי תַּרְשִׁישׁ וְהַתְּשִׁיעִי
פִּטְדָה וְהָעֲשִׂירִי שְׁבוֹ וְהָאַחַד עָשָׂר לֶשֶׁם וְהַשְּׁנַייםª עָשָׂר
נִקְרָא בְּלַעַז אָמֶטִיסְט 21 וְהַשְּׁנַיִם עָשָׂר שְׁעָרִים הָיוּ מִן
מַרְגָּלִיּוֹת וְכָל שַׁעַר אֶחָד הָיָה מִמַּרְגָּלִיּוֹתᵇ אֶחָד וּרְחוֹבוֹת
הָעִיר הָיוּ מִזָּהָב טָהוֹר כִּצְלוֹחִיתᶜ זַךְ

ª The " יִ " vowel was sometimes indicated by "יי" in unpointed Hebrew.
Compare e.g. Mishnah Bava Kama 5:5 in the Kaufmann ms., where the initial
scribe wrote "כדיי"; but the Naqdan (scribe adding vowels to ms.) marked the
second "י" as redundant when adding the vowel points: "כְּדֵיֵי". The phrase
"שניים עשר" (with this spelling) is also attested in a fragment from the Cairo
Geniza (NLI ms. 577.4.28).

ᵇ Although this could possibly be a spelling mistake for "מְמַּרְגָּלִית", the plural
form may rather indicate that each gate is made of multiple gems/precious
stones of one particular type.

ᶜ Ms. has "כצלוח" – probably truncated to make line fit in manuscript. Margin
reads "עששית" – in different script than main text.

17 And its walls were a hundred and forty-four cubits, according to the measure of man[a] which the messenger had. 18 (106v) And the wall was of jasper,[b] and the city of pure gold. 19 And the foundations of the wall – even[c] of the city – were decorated with goodly[d] stones: the first foundation was a jasper,[e] the second sapphire,[f] and the third [chalcedony],[g] and the fourth turquoise,[h] 20 and the fifth ruby,[i] and the sixth carnelian,[j] and the seventh crystal,[k] and the eighth topaz,[l] and the ninth chrysolite,[m] and the tenth agate, and the eleventh jacinth, and the twelfth [amethyst].[n]

21 And the twelve gates were of gems,[o] and every gate[p] was of one gem.[q] And the plains[r] of the city were of pure gold, like clear[s] glass.

---

[a] Or "human measure."

[b] Or possibly 'jade.'

[c] Or "and."

[d] Or "precious." Lit. "good."

[e] Or possibly 'jade.' The exact identification of many precious stones is debated.

[f] Or, a special kind of sapphire called 'lapis lazuli.'

[g] Or possibly 'agate' – Ms. reads 'qalqedonir in a foreign language.'

[h] Or possibly 'malachite.'

[i] Or possibly 'sardius.'

[j] Or possibly 'onyx.'

[k] Hebrew "אחלמה" (achlamah) – see chapter 22:1, which indicates that "אחלמה" is not a red or brown jasper as is commonly believed.

[l] Or possibly 'beryl' or 'chrysolite.'

[m] Or possibly 'topaz.'

[n] Ms. reads 'is called ametist in a foreign language.'

[o] Or "jewels" or "pearls."

[p] The Hebrew word "שער" (sha'ar) generally refers to the gateway (built structure or entrance), but can also refer to a hinged gate (door).

[q] Lit. "gems/jewels/pearls" (plural). The plural noun possibly indicates that each gate is made of multiple gems/precious stones of one particular type.

[r] Or "open places," or possibly "streets."

[s] Or "pure."

22 וְלֹא רָאִיתִי בָהּ בֵּית הַתְּפִילָה כִּי יַהְוֶה צְבָאוֹת הָיָה בֵּית הַמִּקְדָּשׁ שֶׁלָּהֶם וְהַשֶּׂה 23 וְלֹא צָרִיךְ הָעִיר אוֹר מִשֶּׁמֶשׁ אוֹ מֵהַיָּרֵחַ[a] כִּי תִּפְאֶרֶת יַהְוֶה מָאוֹר לָהֶם וְאוֹרָהּ יֵשׁ הַשֶּׂה 24 וְהָעַמִּים הַקְּדוֹשִׁים הוֹלְכִים בָּאוֹר הַזֶּה וּמַלְכֵי אֶרֶץ יָבֹאוּ אֶת חֵילָם בָהּ 25 וּפִתְּחוּ שְׁעָרַיִךְ תָּמִיד יוֹמָם וָלַיְלָה לֹא יִסָּגֵרוּ[b] כִּי לֹא יִהְיֶה לַיְלָה 26 וְהֵמָּה יָבֹאוּ בָהּ תִּפְאֶרֶת וְכָבוֹד מֵהָעַמִּים[c] 27 וְזָר לֹא יִקְרַב אֵלָיו רַק אֵילוּ שֶׁכָּתוּב שְׁמָם בְּסֵפֶר הַחַיִּים

פֶּרֶק כ"ב

1 וְהֶרְאָה[d] לִי נַחַל אֶחָד שֶׁהָיָה מָלֵא מִמַּיִם חַיִּים וְזַךְ כְּאַחְלָמָה יָצֵא מִכִּסֵּא יַהְוֶה וְהַשֶּׂה 2 בְּאֶמְצַע הָרְחוֹבוֹת וְעַל הַנַּחַל יַעֲלֶה עַל שְׂפָתוֹ מִזֶּה וּמִזֶּה

---

[a] Compare Is. 60:19-20.

[b] Quoted from Is. 60:11.

[c] Compare Is. 60:5 and 60:11.

[d] Or possibly "וְהַרְאָה".

22 And I did not see the house of prayer in it, for Yahweh Tseva'ot was the house of their sanctuary,[a] and the Lamb.

23 And the city does not need light from *the* sun or the moon,[b] for the glory of Yahweh is a light-source for them, and its light is the Lamb. 24 And the set-apart peoples[c] will walk in this light, and *the* kings of *the* earth will bring their wealth into it.[d] 25 And your[e] gates will be open continually, day and night they will not be shut,[f] for there will not be night.[g] 26 And they will bring into it, glory and honor from the peoples.[h] 27 But no stranger will come near[i] to him,[j] only those whose name is written in the scroll of life.

22: 1 Then he showed[k] me a stream which was full of living waters, and it was clear[l] like crystal,[m] coming out of the throne of Yahweh and the Lamb. 2 In the midst[n] of the plains,[o] even[p] beside the stream, there grew up[q] on its bank – on this side and on that side –

---

[a] The presence of Yahweh will sanctify the whole city, so that the whole city will be Yahweh's tabernacle/temple with man (see verses 1-3).

[b] Compare Is. 60:19-20.

[c] Does not refer to "people" but "nations."

[d] Compare Is. 60:5 and 60:11.

[e] Feminine singular in Hebrew, referring to the city.

[f] Quoted from Is. 60:11.

[g] Meaning, there will be no 'darkness' in the city, even at night time. See pp. 29-35 for more information.

[h] Does not refer to "people" but "nations."

[i] Or "approach him."

[j] Probably refers to Yahweh, could also possibly refer to the city. ('City' is occasionally referred to as masculine in Hebrew).

[k] Or possibly "Then there appeared to me."

[l] Or "pure."

[m] Hebrew "אחלמה" (*achlamah*) – this verse clearly indicates that "אחלמה" is not a red or brown jasper as is commonly believed.

[n] Or possibly 'among.'

[o] Or "open places," or possibly "streets."

[p] Or possibly 'and.'

[q] Or "will grow up."

כָּל עֵץ מַאֲכָל וְעֵץ הַחַיִּים וְעָלָיו הָיָה שְׁנֵים עָשָׂר מִינֵי פֵּירוֹת
וְהָיָה פִּרְיוֹ לְמַאֲכָל וְעָלֵהוּ לִתְרוּפָה[a] וְחֵרֶם לֹא יִהְיֶה עוֹד[b]
וְכִסֵּא יַהְוֶה וְהַשֶּׂה יִשְׁכּוֹן בָּהּ וַעֲבָדָיו יְשָׁרְתוּהוּ 4 וְיִרְאוּ אֶת
פָּנָיו וּשְׁמוֹ יִהְיֶה כָּתוּב בְּמִצְחֵיהֶם 5 וְלֹא יִהְיֶה עוֹד בָּהּ
הַשֶּׁמֶשׁ לְאוֹר יוֹמָם

---

[a] Quoted from Ezek. 47:12.
[b] Phrase quoted from Zech. 14:11.

every tree of food,[a] even[b] the tree of life.[c] And on it were twelve kinds[d] of fruit, and its fruit was[e] for food, and its[f] foliage for healing.

3 And there will be no more destruction,[g] but the throne of Yahweh and the Lamb will dwell in it,[h] and his servants will serve him.[i] 4 And they will see his face, and his name will be written on their foreheads.[j] 5 And in it[k] the sun will no more be for light by day,

---

[a] An idiom meaning "all kinds of fruit trees."

[b] Or "that is."

[c] This verse is largely quoted from Ezek. 47:12. The Hebrew Bible usually uses the singular "עץ" (*'ets*) for plural 'trees' (collective), so there is no indication that there will be only one tree of life. See pp. 35-40 for more information. (See also Ezek. 47:7).

[d] This does not indicate that one tree bears twelve kinds of fruit, but that the "tree of life" collectively refers to "every tree of food." Among the many different kinds of trees, fresh fruit will be produced every month (Ezek. 47:12). Trees bear fruit after their kind! One tree does not bear more than one kind of fruit (Gen. 1:11-12).

[e] Or "will be."

[f] For easier understanding in English, the Hebrew collective use can be translated as plural (most English translations do that with Ezek. 47:12). "And among the plains, even beside the stream, there grew up on both sides of its banks, all kinds of fruit trees, namely, the trees of life. And on them were twelve kinds of fruit, and their fruit was for food, and their foliage for healing."

[g] Hebrew "חרם" (*cherem*). Could also be translated as "ban" or "something dedicated for destruction." Phrase quoted from Zech. 14:11.

[h] Lit. "her," referring to the city, which is feminine in Hebrew. Compare Ezek. 43:7. Yahweh's throne in the city will cause it to be the 'Temple' (Yahweh's tabernacle with men). See chapter 21:3, which indicates that the New Jerusalem and the Tabernacle of Yahweh are synonyms. See also Ezek. 47:1-12 – the river of life flows from underneath the Temple.

[i] Or "will attend to him" or "will minister to him."

[j] Compare Ex. 28:36-38, where the Name Yahweh is written on a plate of gold and placed on Aaron's forehead.

[k] Lit. "her," referring to the city, which is feminine in Hebrew.

וּלְנֹגַהּ וְהַיָּרֵחַ[a] לֹא יָאִיר לָךְ וְהָיָה לָךְ יְהוָה לְאוֹר עוֹלָם
וֵאלֹהַיִךְ לְתִפְאַרְתֵּךְ[b] ‚6‚ וְאָמַר לִי אֵלֶּה הַדְּבָרִים הֵן אֱמֶת
וַיהוָה צְבָאוֹת שָׁלַח אֶת מַלְאָכָיו לְהַרְאוֹת לַעֲבָדָיו מַה
שֶּׁיִּהְיֶה בְּקָרוֹב ‚7‚ רְאֵה אֲנִי [אָ]בָא[c] בִּמְהֵרָה וְקָדוֹשׁ הוּא מִי
שֶׁמַּאֲמִין בְּדִבְרֵי הַנְּבִיאוֹת מַה שֶּׁכָּתוּב בַּסֵּפֶר הַזֶּה ‚8‚ וַאֲנִי
יוֹחָנָן שָׁמַעְתִּי וְרָאִיתִי כָּל אֵלֶּה וְכֵיוָן שֶׁשָּׁמַעְתִּי וְרָאִיתִי זֹאת
נָפַלְתִּי לָאָרֶץ וְהִתְפַּלַּלְתִּי לְהַמַּלְאָךְ שֶׁהֶרְאָה לִי זֹאת ‚9‚ וְהוּא
אָמַר לִי רְאֵה אַל תַּעֲשֶׂה זֹאת כִּי גַם אֲנִי מֵחַבְרוּתְךָ וּמֵאַחִים
הַנְּבִיאִים וּמֵאֵילוּ הַמְקַיְּימִים הַדְּבָרִים מִסֵּפֶר הַזֶּה עֲשֵׂי[d]
תְּפִלָּתְךָ לַיהוָה ‚10‚ וְאָמַר לִי אַל תִּסְתֹּם הֶחָזוֹן מִסֵּפֶר הַזֶּה כִּי
הָעֵת קָרוֹב ‚11‚ מִי שֶׁיֵּשׁ רַע תִּהְיֶה[e] כָּל עֵת כָּךְ

---

[a] Masoretic text omits the "ו".

[b] Quoted from Is. 60:19.

[c] Ms. reads "אני יבא" (contraction of "אני אבא"). Compare chapter 21:7 and 22:12.

[d] See footnote on chapter 2:5.

[e] For the use of "ת" instead of "י", see footnote on chapter 1:7.

neither for brightness will the moon[a] shine for you,[b] but Yahweh will be an eternal light for you, and your Elohim will be your[c] glory.[d]

6 Then he said to me, "These words are truth, and Yahweh Tseva'ot sent his messengers to show his servants what will happen soon."[e]

7 "Look, I will come with haste!" – So, blessed is he who believes[f] the words of the prophecy which is written in this scroll. 8 And I Yochanan heard and saw all these *things*, and when I had heard and seen this I fell down to the earth and prayed to the messenger who showed me this. 9 But he said to me, "Look! Do not do this![g] – For I am also of your company and of *your*[h] brothers the prophets, and of those who establish the words of this scroll. Do your prayer to Yahweh."

10 Then he said to me, "Do not seal up the vision of this scroll, for the time is near.[i] 11 Whosoever is evil, **he** will be so all the time;

---

[a] Could also be translated: "And in it the sun will no more be for light by day, and for brightness; neither will the moon shine for you..."
[b] Feminine singular throughout this verse, referring to the city.
[c] Lit. "as your glory" or "for your glory."
[d] Verse 5 is mostly quoted from Is. 60:19.
[e] Lit. "at near" – the Biblical meaning of 'soon' or 'near' is not always what we expect. See e.g. Is. 13:22, stating that Babylon's destruction is near, yet Babylon was only destroyed generations later, and the ultimate fulfillment is still future! (Rev. 17-19.)
[f] Lit. "believes in."
[g] Meaning 'Be sure not to do this!'
[h] Understood from preceding part of the verse. (Called gapping, commonly found in the Hebrew Tanach.)
[i] Compare footnote on verse 6.

מִי שֶׁיֵּשׁ טָמֵא יִהְיֶה גַּם כֵּן כָּךְ אֲבָל מִי שֶׁיֵּשׁ חָסִיד יִהְיֶה כָּל
עֵת כָּךְ וּמִי שֶׁיֵּשׁ קָדוֹשׁ גַּם כֵּן כְּמוֹ זֶה ₁₂ וּרְאֵה אֲנִי [אָ]בָא ᵃ
בִּמְהֵרָה לְשַׁלֵּם לְכָל אִישׁ כְּמַעֲשֵׂהוּ ₁₃ אֲנִי הָרִאשׁוֹן וְהָאַחֲרוֹן
תְּחִלַּת וְהַסּוֹף ₁₄ קְדוֹשִׁים הֵם שֶׁעוֹשִׂים מִצְוֹתָיו כְּדֵי שֶׁיִּהְיֶה
לָהֶם חֵלֶק בְּעֵץ הַחַיִּים וְיִזְכֶּה לֵילֵךְ מֵהָעִיר ᵇ ₁₅ כִּי מִבַּחוּץ
עוֹמְדִים הַכְּלָבִים וְהַמְּכַשְּׁפִים וְהַזּוֹנוֹת וְהָרַצְחָנִים וְהַכַּזְבָנִים
₁₆ אֲנִי יֵשׁוּעַ שָׁלַחְתִּי מַלְאָכִי לְהַרְאוֹת לָעֵדָה וַאֲנִי שֹׁרֶשׁ
מִמִּשְׁפְּחוֹת דָּוִד ₁₇ וְהָרוּחַ וְהַכַּלָּה אָמְרוּ ᶜ בֹּא וּמִי שֶׁיִּשְׁמַע
יֹאמַר בֹּא וּמִי שֶׁצָּמֵא לְכוּ לְמַיִם חַיִּים וּשְׁתוּ בְּלוֹא כֶסֶף
וּבְלוֹא מְחִיר ᵈ

ᵃ Ms. reads "אני יבא" (contraction of "אני אבא"). Compare chapter 21:7 and
22:7.

ᵇ The preposition "מן" can mean "in," "into," "toward," etc. See e.g. Lev. 4:17,
14:16; Pro. 5:18; Lam. 1:20; Gen. 13:11.

ᶜ Or possibly "אָמְרוּ".

ᵈ Phrase quoted from Is. 55:1.

whosoever is unclean will also be so; but whosoever is faithful [a] will be so all the time; and whosoever is set-apart, also just like this."

12 "And look! – I will come with haste, to reward [b] every man according to his work! 13 I am the first and the last, *the* beginning and the end! 14 Blessed are they who do his commandments, that they may have part [c] in the tree of life, and be pure to walk in the city. 15 For the dogs and the sorcerers and the harlots and the murderers and the liars stay **outside**. 16 I Yeshua sent my messengers [d] to show *this* to the assembly. Even I am *the* root of the families of Dawid!

17 Both the Ruach and the bride – say 'Come'! [e] And whosoever hears, let him say, 'Come!' And whosoever thirsts, 'Come to *the* living waters! And drink without money [f] and without price!' [g]

---

[a] Or "loyal" (usually towards Yahweh). Hebrew "חסיד" (*chasid*) – from the same root-word as "חסד" (*chesed*) "faithful kindness/love." See e.g. Deu. 33:8; 2 Sam. 22:26; Mic. 7:2; Ps. 145:17, 149:1, 149:5, 149:9; Pro. 2:8.

[b] Or "repay."

[c] Or "a share."

[d] Compare verse 6.

[e] Or "And the Ruach and the bride say, 'Come!'" The word for "say" (אמרו) could either have an imperative or indicative meaning in unpointed Hebrew.

[f] Lit. "silver," in Biblical times money was mostly made of silver.

[g] Phrase quoted from Is. 55:1.

18 אֲבָל אֲנִי מֵעִיד לְכָל הַשּׁוֹמְעִים הַנְּבִיאוֹת מֵהַסֵּפֶר הַזֶּה
וּבְאָם[a] שֶׁאֶחָד יוֹסִיף לוֹ אֵיזֶה דְּבָרִים יוֹסִיף עָלָיו יַהְוֶה
הַנְּגָעִים שֶׁכְּתוּבִים בַּסֵּפֶר הַזֶּה 19 וּבְאִם שֶׁאֶחָד יִגְרַע אֵיזֶה
דְּבָרִים מִזֶּה הַסֵּפֶר יִמְחֶה יַהְוֶה אֶת שְׁמוֹ מִסֵּפֶר הַחַיִּים 20
וְכֹה אָמַר הַמֵּעִיד זֹאת כֵּן אֲנִי אָבֹא בִּמְהֵרָה אָמֵן כֵּן בֹּא
אָדוֹן יֵשׁוּעַ 21 הַחֶסֶד מֵאֲדוֹנֵינוּ יֵשׁוּעַ הַמָּשִׁיחַ יִהְיֶה עִם
כּוּלְכֶם אָמֵן

---

[a] Ms. has "ובא" – probably truncated to make line fit in manuscript. Compare
"ובאם" in verse 19 (spelled out in manuscript).

18 But I testify to all who hear the prophecy of this scroll, that if one will add any^a words to it, Yahweh will add to him the plagues which are written in this scroll, 19 and if one will diminish any^b words from this scroll, Yahweh will blot out his name from the scroll of life." 20 And thus says he who testifies this, "Yes, I will come with haste!" Amein! Yes, come Adon Yeshua!

21 The steadfast love of our Adon Yeshua Ha-Mashiach be with you all, amein!

---

^a Or "some."
^b Or "some."

The Hebrew Epistle of James

אגרת יעקב

Based on Ms. Oo.1.32 from the Cambridge
University Library. Also supported by Ms. Gaster
1616 from the Manchester University Library.

Version 2.2 © April 2024

Introduction

The Epistle of James (Ya'aqov) was specifically addressed to the twelve dispersed tribes of Israel – not to the Gentiles!

> "Ya'aqov[a] a servant of Yahweh[b] and Adon[c] Yeshua[d] Ha-Mashiach,[e] **to *the* twelve tribes** who are scattered into all the places: firstly, joy!"[f, g]

Did these dispersed Israelites only read Greek, or did they also read Hebrew?

The Hebrew Bible was kept in use throughout the world wherever the Jews were dispersed.[h] Even if some people did not understand Hebrew, at synagogue they would still read from the Hebrew Bible first. After a verse of Hebrew scripture was read, a translation of the applicable verse was also read to help those who were not familiar

---

[a] The Hebrew name for 'James' or 'Jacob.'

[b] The manuscript uses the Hebrew abbreviation 'ה׳' (*he*) for "*Ha-Shem,*" which literally means 'The Name.' For further discussion on this abbreviation 'ה׳', see pp. 62-69. Our translations employ 'The Name' Yahweh in every instance indicated by the Hebrew manuscripts. The only grammatically possible pronunciation of יהוה, from which all other abbreviations/contractions of the Name can be formed, is "*Yah-weh*" – with emphasis on the second syllable. For more information, see HebrewGospels.com/yhwh.

[c] The Hebrew word for 'lord' or 'master.'

[d] The Hebrew name for 'Jesus.'

[e] Or "the Messiah."

[f] Jas. 1:1, translated from Oo.1.32.

[g] All emphasis throughout introductory sections was added for clarity. However, in the transcript/translation section, emphasis in the English translation reflects emphasis in the Hebrew text.

[h] E.g. "...until its 20th-century revitalization... Hebrew survived as a language spoken and written... in most diaspora communities in synagogue worship and religious texts." – J. F. Elwolde, *Hebrew, Biblical and Jewish*, in *Encyclopedia of Language and Linguistics*, ed. K. Brown, Elsevier, 2006, vol. 5, p. 260.

with the Hebrew language.[a] The official Bible in the Jewish synagogues remained the Hebrew Bible.

Could it be that the Epistle of James was also originally written in Hebrew? If James spoke Hebrew,[b] and Hebrew was used as the official language in synagogues throughout the diaspora, why would he have written the original copy in Greek? Would it not make more sense to expect that the Epistle of James would originally have been written in Hebrew?

Are there any Hebrew manuscripts of the Epistle of James? If so, could such a Hebrew manuscript shed more light on the original meaning of this epistle? The amazing answer is 'Yes!'

We are excited to share with you a translation of a Hebrew manuscript of Ya'aqov which has proven to be authentic. In other words, from a linguistic perspective, this Hebrew copy of Ya'aqov is not a translation from the Greek, Aramaic, or Latin versions; but rather proves to derive from the original Hebrew copy which Ya'aqov wrote.[c]

If the Greek version of James is indeed a translation of the original Hebrew epistle, then Greek-based English translations are third-hand translations at best. Being a direct translation from Hebrew to English, we hope that this translation of Ya'aqov will be a blessing to all who read it.

---

[a] Mishnah Megillah 4:4-10 gives detailed instructions regarding the reading and translating of the Tanach in synagogue.

[b] E.g. "...what was the language of ordinary life of educated native Jews in Jerusalem and Judea in the period from 400 B.C.E. to 150 C.E.? The evidence presented by MH [Mishnaic Hebrew] and its literature leaves no doubt that that language was MH [Mishnaic Hebrew]. Of course, those educated Judeans also understood Aramaic, and used it even in writing, but only occasionally, and not habitually..." – M. H. Segal, *A Grammar of Mishnaic Hebrew*, Clarendon Press, 1980, p. 13.

[c] Evidence will be presented below in the 'Evidence of Authenticity' section.

Evidence of Authenticity and Interesting Readings

Below we will discuss a few of the many intriguing differences between the Hebrew and Greek versions of James. These unique differences will also show that the Hebrew version is authentic, and not merely a translation which derives from Greek, Aramaic or Latin.

Quotes from the Book of Job

The Hebrew version of James contains three direct quotes from the Book of Job in instances where the Greek version does not quote from the Old Testament at all!

This is significant, as all standard Bible translations clearly mention Job in James 5:11:

> "you have heard of the endurance of Job"[a]

In the Greek-based versions, this is nothing more than a once-off reference to Job and his troubles. But not so in the Hebrew version. The Hebrew version of James quotes from the Book of Job in chapter 1:11, 1:12 and again in chapter 5:5! Below are the applicable verses:

> James 1:11 (quoted from Job 14:2): "And 'like a flower he comes out, then withers – and he runs away[b] like a shadow and does not remain standing.'"[c]

---

[a] James 5:11, NASB.
[b] Or "flees."
[c] Translated from Oo.1.32.

James 1:12 (quoted from Job 5:17): "And 'blessed is the man whom Eloah[a] chastens,[b] so do not refuse the discipline of Shaddai...'"[c, d]

James 5:5 (quoted from Job 21:12): "'and they rejoiced at *the* sound of a flute'"[e]

Job is then mentioned by name in James 5:11, only after the theme of Job is well established:

"for you have heard of the endurance of **'Iyov**"[f, g]

These quotes from Job in the Hebrew Epistle of James create a theme throughout the book by linking the first chapter to the last chapter. This theme is totally absent from the Greek version, and also from the Latin and Aramaic translations.

If the Hebrew version is the original, it is understandable that this theme could have vanished in a paraphrased and interpreted second-hand Greek translation. But if the Greek version were the original, why would this theme exist so clearly in the Hebrew version?

This theme, supported by three direct quotes from the Book of Job, is clear evidence that this Hebrew version of James is authentic.[h]

---

[a] One of the Hebrew words for 'God.'

[b] Or possibly "rebukes."

[c] Or "the Almighty."

[d] Translated from Oo.1.32.

[e] Translated from Oo.1.32.

[f] The Hebrew name for 'Job.'

[g] Jas. 5:11, translated from Oo.1.32.

[h] Especially in James 5:5 it is entirely impossible for any Greek-based translation to reclaim the applicable quote from the Book of Job. Even the quotes in James 1:11 and 1:12 were not reclaimed in Hebrew translations from Greek. (See e.g. the translation by Hebrew scholar Franz Delitzsch, and that of Salkinson/Ginsburg.)

Hebrew keyword repetition

Another theme in the Hebrew version of Ya'aqov is "joy." The Hebrew word for "joy" is "שמחה" (*simchah*), and occurs **four times** in the first two chapters, starting with chapter one, verse one!

James 1:1 "...firstly, **joy**!"[a]

James 1:2 "...consider it as **joy** when you fall into a trial."[b, c]

James 1:24[25] "the law of **joy**"[d]

James 2:12 "...you must speak and do as those who will be judged by the law **with joy**."[e, f]

At least half of this theme of "joy" was lost in the Greek tradition and subsequent translations. The Greek version seems to have interpreted the Hebrew word '*simchah*' as having a different meaning in various passages. In James 1:1 the Greek version interprets "joy" as "greeting" (although using a Greek word related to "joy");[g] but in chapter 1:25 and 2:12, "joy" is interpreted as "liberty" (using a totally different and unrelated Greek word).[h]

It is known that the Greek translators of the Hebrew Old Testament often rendered the same re-occurring Hebrew word with different synonyms, to break what they viewed as monotony.[i] This technique

---

[a] Translated from Oo.1.32.
[b] Or "temptation."
[c] Translated from Oo.1.32.
[d] Translated from Oo.1.32.
[e] Could also possibly mean 'law of joy.'
[f] Translated from Oo.1.32.
[g] The Greek word for "greeting" in James 1:1 is "χαιρειν" (lexical form: χαιρω), and "joy" in 1:2 is "χαραν" (lexical form: χαρα), both from the root "χαρ."
[h] The Greek word for "liberty" in James 1:25 and 2:12 is "ελευθεριας" (lexical form: ελευθερια), whereas the Greek word for "joy" would be "χαρα."
[i] E.g. "...the influence of Graeco-Roman rhetoric on the Septuagint... The most readily noticeable and widespread is μεταβολή, *variatio*, "elegant variation,"

unfortunately reduces the number and extent of such keyword-based themes, which also aided in scripture memorization.

It is very interesting that Ya'aqov refers to the "law of **joy**" rather than "the law of **liberty**." Scholars and Bible teachers alike have often misinterpreted the Greek word for "**liberty**" (ἐλευθερία), claiming that we are **liberated**[a] from keeping the Torah,[b] but the context in the Epistle of James does not support this view at all.[c] So, what does "the law of **joy**" in the Hebrew version of James refer to? Compare below, some verses from the Hebrew Tanach:

---

that is, the avoidance of repeating, within a short space, a noticeable word. This is a standard stylistic device likely to crop up in any classical or later [Graeco-Roman] writer." – J. A. L. Lee, *Translations of the Old Testament, Greek*, in *Handbook of Classical Rhetoric in the Hellenistic Period, 330 B.C.-A.D. 400*, ed. S. E. Porter, Brill, 2001, pp. 776-777. See ibid. pp. 776-778 for examples and further references.

[a] E.g. "ἐλευθερία; **liberty... from the yoke of the Mosaic law**" – Joseph H. Thayer, *Greek-English Lexicon of the New Testament*, American Book Company, 1889, p. 204.

"ἐλευθερία, ... **liberty**... Esp[ecially] of **freedom** which stands **in contrast to** constraint of **the Mosaic law**" – W. Arndt, F. W. Danker, and W. Bauer, *A Greek-English Lexicon of the New Testament and Other Early Christian Literature*, University of Chicago Press, 2000, p. 316.

"...the "law of liberty"... the modifier "**liberty**"... implies the Mosaic Law really binds and brings guilt and condemnation... Here we have **liberty** from... the **Mosaic Law**... It [the law of liberty] is a law which brings freedom as opposed to the condemnation and bondage that were inherent in the Mosaic Law." – Matthew A. Postiff and Dr. R. Bruce Compton, *The Identification of The Law in James 2:8–12*, Detroit Baptist Theological Seminary, 2008, pp. 25-30.

[b] The Hebrew word '*torah*' means "instruction" or "law." The Creator established his perfect and everlasting Torah (instruction/law) as the basis of his covenant with his people. These instructions/laws were recorded by Mosheh in written form, and thus the Torah is also known as the 'Law of Moses,' although in reality it is Yahweh's law/instructions for his people.

[c] In James 2:8-13, this "law" is clearly equated with obedience to Yahweh's commandments as spelled out in the Torah; and in James 1:21-24[22-25] this "law" is equated with the "word" – take note that there was no "New Testament" Bible when James wrote this epistle, only the Tanach (O.T.).

Jeremiah 15:16: "...**your word** has been to me, for **joy** and for **gladness** of my heart..." [a]

Psalm 19:8-9[7-8]: "The Torah of Yahweh is complete... the **statutes of Yahweh** are right, they **rejoice** the heart." [b]

Psalm 112:1: "Blessed is the man who fears Yahweh, who **delights** exceedingly in **his commandments**." [c]

Psalm 119:77: "Let your mercies come upon me that I may live, for your **Torah** is my **delight**." [d]

Psalm 119:111: "I have inherited **your testimonies** for ever, for they are the **joy** of my heart." [e]

Psalm 119:162: "I **rejoice** about **your word** like one who finds a great spoil." [f]

It should be clear from the above examples that the "law of joy" referred to by Ya'aqov is Yahweh's Torah, his word and his statutes. Ya'aqov did not teach any liberation from the Torah, on the contrary – he taught that we should obey Yahweh's Torah, with joy!

This is not only an interesting difference between the Hebrew and Greek versions, but again shows that the Hebrew version preserves a keyword-based theme which was partly lost in the Greek translation. [g]

---

[a] Translated from Hebrew Masoretic Text.
[b] Translated from Hebrew Masoretic Text.
[c] Translated from Hebrew Masoretic Text.
[d] Translated from Hebrew Masoretic Text.
[e] Translated from Hebrew Masoretic Text.
[f] Translated from Hebrew Masoretic Text.
[g] Not only is half of this keyword theme invisible in the Greek version, but it can also not be reclaimed by translating the Greek text back to Hebrew. (See e.g. the translation by Hebrew scholar Franz Delitzsch, and that of Salkinson/Ginsburg.)

Inversed word order

Changed word order is one of the frequent differences when comparing the original Hebrew vs. the second-hand Greek Septuagint translation of the Old Testament. Often two or more words are placed in a different order, but at times two phrases are also found in the opposite order in Greek. Below is an example:[a]

Genesis 8:18:

Hebrew Masoretic Text: "וַיֵּצֵא־נֹחַ וּבָנָיו וְאִשְׁתּוֹ"

= "Then Noach went out, **and his sons**, and his wife..."

Septuagint Greek: "καὶ ἐξῆλθεν νωε καὶ ἡ γυνὴ αὐτοῦ καὶ οἱ υἱοὶ αὐτοῦ"

= "Then Noah went out, and his wife, **and his sons**..."

In the Hebrew version, Noah's sons are mentioned first, but in the Greek version his wife is mentioned first. This was probably done for **stylistic**[b] **reasons**, as there is **no grammatical reason** for the difference.

There are similar differences between the Hebrew and Greek versions of James. Below we will look at two examples where the Greek version has phrases in a different order than the Hebrew version while there is **no grammatical requirement** for the difference:

---

[a] For further examples, see pp. 46-52.
[b] Could also be for reasons of harmonization or cultural preference, but there is no grammatical requirement for this change.

James 4:12:

Oo.1.32:

"ויש לבד אחד שנותן הדת שיוכל לענוש ולמחול"

= "And there is only one who gives the law, who is able **to punish**[a] and to forgive..."

Byzantine Greek: "εἷς ἐστιν ὁ νομοθέτης, ὁ δυνάμενος σῶσαι καὶ ἀπολέσαι"

= "There is one lawgiver, who is able to save and **to destroy**..."

James 1:13:

Oo.1.32:

"כי ה׳ לא מנסה את האדם לרע והוא אינה מנסה לשום אחד"

"...for Yahweh does not tempt man with evil,[b] and he **is not tempted** by anyone."[c]

Byzantine Greek: "ὁ γὰρ θεὸς ἀπείραστός ἐστιν κακῶν, πειράζει δὲ αὐτὸς οὐδένα"

= "...for God **is not tempted** with evil, and he tempts no one."

Take note that these differences in order are **not required** by grammar and thus do not occur in the Greek-to-Hebrew

---

[a] Or "condemn."
[b] Or "to *do* evil."
[c] For easier comparison, this verse is rendered more literally here than in the main translation.

translations by e.g. Franz Delitzsch and by Salkinson/Ginsburg. The Aramaic and Latin versions also follow the Greek tradition, while this Hebrew version is unique. Thus, the Hebrew version of James contained in Oo.1.32 does not seem to derive from the Greek or Greek-based versions.

Rather, the fact that the Greek version uses a different order is perfectly in line with the frequent differences in word order between the Hebrew and the Greek versions of the Old Testament. This difference in word order shows that the Greek version of James could be a translation from the Hebrew version, but the Hebrew **cannot** be a translation from the Greek version.

Verb gapping

'Gapping'[a] is a typical feature found in the Hebrew Old Testament as well as in other authentic Hebrew documents. Gapped words are **understood** in the Hebrew text without being explicitly written out. Greek translators often inserted these gapped words into their translations. Below we will focus on examples of gapping in the Hebrew James of Oo.1.32 that **cannot** be obtained from the Greek, Aramaic, or Latin versions, and are thus evidence of linguistic authenticity.[b] In these examples, Hebrew grammar and syntax **do not require** gapping and thus the Greek-to-Hebrew translations by Franz Delitzsch and by Salkinson/Ginsburg, etc. do not have these words gapped.

---

[a] 'Gapping' is also known by the term 'ellipsis.'

[b] Some Greek verbs (e.g. "εχω," and in some contexts "ειμι") are regularly written in Greek but gapped in Hebrew, and thus any Hebrew translation from Greek may/will have these verbs gapped, depending on the context. However, in this section we will focus on examples of verb gapping which were not reclaimed by Hebrew translations from the Greek (and/or Latin and Aramaic), and therefore show authenticity.

We will now focus on verb gapping which is relatively common in the Hebrew Old Testament. A sentence which contains two or more phrases may use a verb only once, whereafter it is understood in the second phrase without being repeated. Here is an example from Genesis 7:2:

> "Of all the clean animals, **take** for you seven-seven,[a] a male and its female; and of the animals which are not clean, [*take*] two, a male and its female."[b]

The verb "take" is only written once in Genesis 7:2, but it is understood a second time and supplied in square brackets in the above translation – to indicate to the reader that it is not part of the original text. Some modern translations (e.g. the New Living Translation) repeat the verb "take" in Genesis 7:2 but do not indicate that the second occurrence of this verb was added to the text.

Likewise, in some cases the Greek translators of the original Hebrew Bible also added such gapped words in their Greek translations. Let's consider two O.T. examples from the Septuagint Greek translation vs. Hebrew Masoretic Text:

1 Kings 5:11(4:31):

Hebrew Masoretic Text:

"וַיֶּחְכַּם֙ מִכָּל־הָ֣אָדָ֔ם מֵאֵיתָ֥ן הָאֶזְרָחִ֖י"

= "And **he was wiser** than all men, [*he was wiser*] than Eitan the Ezrachi..."

---

[a] Though the exact meaning is debated, this probably implies seven each of male and female – seven pairs.
[b] Gen. 7:2, translated from the Masoretic Text.

The words in square brackets in the above verse are **not** actually written in the Hebrew Bible, they are only **understood by context**. The Hebrew verb "יֶחְכַּם" (he was wiser) is **gapped** in the second part of this verse. For easier reading and to remove any ambiguity, the Septuagint translators **supplied** (inserted) the gapped word in their Greek translation:

1 Kings 5:11(4:31):

<u>Greek Septuagint</u>: "καὶ ἐσοφίσατο ὑπὲρ πάντας τοὺς ἀνθρώπους καὶ ἐσοφίσατο ὑπὲρ γαιθαν τὸν εζραΐτην"

= "And **he was wiser** than all men, and **he was wiser** than Ethan the Ezrahite..."

In the Septuagint Greek translation, the verb for "he was wiser" is inserted where it is understood from the Hebrew text. The fact that the Hebrew version has this verb gapped while the Greek Septuagint has it written, clearly shows that the Hebrew is the original version whereas the Greek is a second-hand interpreted translation.

1 Kings 2:30:

<u>Hebrew Masoretic Text</u>: "כֹּה־אָמַר הַמֶּלֶךְ צֵא וַיֹּאמֶר l לֹא"

= "...thus says the king, 'Come out!' Then he said, '**No**!'"

Based on the context of the above verse, "**No**" obviously means '**I will not come out**.' This is also how the Septuagint translators interpreted this in their Greek translation!

1 Kings 2:30:

<u>Greek Septuagint</u>: "τάδε λέγει ὁ βασιλεύς ἔξελθε. καὶ εἶπεν ιωαβ οὐκ ἐκπορεύομαι"

= "Thus says the king, 'Come out!' And Joab[a] said, **'I will not come out**...'"

The Septuagint translators inserted the implied verb "**come out**" in Joab's reply, though it originally only occurred in the first half of the verse.

The fact that the verb "**come out**" is gapped in the Hebrew version, and supplied in the Greek version, clearly shows that the Hebrew is the original version, while the Greek is an interpreted second-hand translation.

Now, here is a similar example when comparing the Hebrew and Greek versions of James:

James 2:2:

<u>Oo.1.32</u>:

"כי באם שבא אחד... במלבושים נעים וגם אחד עני במלבושים רעים"

= "For when[b] one **enters**... with lovely clothes, and also a poor one [*enters*] with worthless[c] clothes..."[d]

---

[a] Apart from adding the verb "come out," the LXX translators also supplied the explicit subject "Joab" (gapped in Hebrew) to remove any possible ambiguity. See pp. 53-57 and 307-312 for more information about explicit subject gapping.
[b] Or "if."
[c] Lit. "bad."
[d] For easier comparison, this verse is rendered more literally here than in the main translation.

The Hebrew version of James 2:2 **does not** repeat the word for "enter" in the second phrase. It is only **implied** in the second half of the verse and is supplied in square brackets in the above English translation.

The Greek translation of James repeats the word for "enters" in the second phrase for simpler reading and less ambiguity:

James 2:2:

<u>Byzantine Greek</u>: "ἐὰν γὰρ εἰσέλθῃ... ἀνὴρ... ἐν ἐσθῆτι λαμπρᾷ, εἰσέλθῃ δὲ καὶ πτωχὸς ἐν ῥυπαρᾷ ἐσθῆτι"

= "For if there **comes in**... a man... in bright clothing; and there also **comes in** a poor man, in filthy clothes..."

The fact that the Hebrew version has this verb **gapped** while the Greek version has it **supplied**, clearly indicates that the Hebrew version preserved the original reading, while the Greek reading is an interpreted, second-hand translation.

Another example is found in James 5:18:

<u>Oo.1.32</u>: "ונתן השמים את מימם והארץ את פריה"

= "... so the heavens **gave** their waters and the earth [*gave*] its fruit."

<u>Byzantine Greek</u>: "ὁ οὐρανὸς ὑετὸν ἔδωκεν καὶ ἡ γῆ ἐβλάστησεν τὸν καρπὸν αὐτῆς."

= "...the heaven **gave** rain and the earth **produced** its fruit."

The second occurrence of the verb "gave" is gapped in the Hebrew version but supplied in the Greek version together with a slight interpretation. The implied Hebrew verb for "gave" is rendered as "produced." Note that the verb for 'produced' is also supplied (added) in the Latin and Aramaic versions, as well as in the Greek-to-Hebrew translations by Franz Delitzsch and by Salkinson/Ginsburg.

These repeated examples[a] of gapping in the Hebrew version of James, and subsequent interpretation in the Greek and Greek-based versions again show the Hebrew version to be the original, and the Greek version to be an interpreted, second-hand translation.

---

[a] Apart from these examples of verb gapping, further examples of gapping of explicit subjects/objects in the Hebrew Epistle of James (which were not reclaimed by Hebrew translations from Greek) may be found in e.g. James 1:24[25] ("does it" vs. "a doer of the work"); James 4:16 ("this" vs. "all such boasting"); James 5:3 ("it" vs. "their rust"); James 5:4 ("their" vs. "of the reapers"); James 5:20 ("him" vs. "a sinner").

אִיגֶּרֶת יַעֲקֹב פֶּרֶק א'

1 (158a) ^a יַעֲקֹב עֶבֶד יַהְוֶה ^b וְאָדוֹן יֵשׁוּעַ ^c הַמָּשִׁיחַ לִשְׁנֵים עָשָׂר שְׁבָטִים הַמְּפוּזָּרִים בְּכָל הַמְּקוֹמוֹת שִׂמְחָה מִקוֹדֶם ^d אַחַי 2 אֲהוּבִים תַּחְשְׁבוּ זֹאת לְשִׂמְחָה בְּאִם שֶׁאַתֶּם נוֹפְלִים בְּנִסָּיוֹן

---

^a The number stated in brackets is the corresponding folio number of Oo.1.32 on which this Hebrew transcript is based.

^b The Hebrew manuscript uses an abbreviation "הֿ" for "השם". It was common practice for many scribes to write 'Ha-Shem' or some abbreviation rather than writing the full name "יהוה". The fact that this abbreviation for 'Ha-Shem' really represents the name "יהוה" is evident when the Hebrew Epistle of James quotes from the Tanach, e.g.:

Ps. 145:18:

<u>Hebrew Masoretic Text</u>: "קָרוֹב יְהוה לְכָל־קֹרְאָיו לְכֹל אֲשֶׁר יִקְרָאֻהוּ בֶאֱמֶת׃"

<u>Oo.1.32</u> (James 5:16):   "קרוב הֿ לכל קראיו לכל אשר יקראהו באמת"

Gen. 15:6:

<u>Hebrew Masoretic Text</u>:   "הֶאֱמִן בַּיהוה וַיַּחְשְׁבֶהָ לּוֹ צְדָקָה׃"

<u>Oo.1.32</u> (James 2:22[23]):   "האמין בהֿ ויחשבה לו צדקה"

From the above examples it is very clear that this abbreviation "הֿ" used in the Hebrew James actually represents the name "יהוה". For a full justification that the true pronunciation of the Name is "יַהְוֶה", based on the Masoretic Text, see HebrewGospels.com/yhwh.

^c The short rabbinic spelling "ישו" used in the ms. was replaced with the full spelling "ישוע". See footnotes on p. 6 for more information.

^d "אחי" could also possibly be a truncated form of "אחים".

The Letter of Ya'aqov

1:1 (158a) Ya'aqov,[a] the servant of Yahweh[b] and Adon[c] Yeshua[d] Ha-Mashiach,[e] to *the* twelve tribes who are scattered into[f] all the places: firstly, joy![g] 2 My beloved brothers, consider it[h] as joy when you fall into a trial.[i]

---

[a] The Hebrew name for 'James' or 'Jacob.'

[b] The manuscript uses the Hebrew abbreviation "הֿ" for '*Ha-Shem,*' which literally means "The Name." Today still, many Jews will read "*Ha-Shem*" when they see the Creator's Hebrew name יהוה. For further discussion on this abbreviation 'הֿ', see pp. 62-69. Our translations employ 'The Name' Yahweh in every instance indicated by the Hebrew manuscripts. The only grammatically possible pronunciation of יהוה, from which all other abbreviations/contractions of the Name can be formed, is "*Yah-weh*" – with emphasis on the second syllable. For more information, see HebrewGospels.com/yhwh.

[c] The Hebrew word for 'lord' or 'master.'

[d] The Hebrew name for 'Jesus' – meaning 'Yahweh is Salvation.'

[e] Or "The Messiah." The Hebrew word "משיח" (*mashiach*) was translated into the Greek '*christos*' but should be clearly distinguished from the Catholic symbolic 'Christ.' Literal meaning: "anointed one," usually referring to someone anointed as king of Israel, or as priest or prophet. However, when used as a name, it refers to the Son of Yahweh, whom he anointed as the ultimate King of Israel, the Everlasting High Priest, and the Prophet who would speak Yahweh's words to his people – and if anyone disobeys him, Yahweh himself will require it of him. See Deu. 18:18-19 and Acts 3:22-23.

[f] Or "in."

[g] Could mean 'rejoice' or 'joy *to you.*'

[h] Lit. "this."

[i] Or "temptation." Lit. "testing."

3 וּדְעוּ שֶׁאֱמוּנָתֵיכֶם [a] בְּאָם שֶׁהִיא שְׁלֵימָה גּוֹרֵם [b] הִיא סַבְלָנוּת

4 אֲבָל הַסַבְלָנוּת צָרִיךְ לִהְיוֹת עַד הַסּוֹף כְּדֵי שֶׁתִּהְיוּ בִּמְלוּאָה

וְלֹא תֶחְסַר [c] שׁוּם דָּבָר מִמְּכֶם 5 אֲבָל בְּאָם שֶׁיֵּשׁ אֶחָד בָּכֶם

שֶׁחָסֵר לוֹ חָכְמָה זֶה צָרִיךְ לְהִתְפַּלֵל [d] מֵיַהְוֶה שֶׁנּוֹתֵן לְכָל אָדָם

וְגַם הוּא יִתֵּן [e] לוֹ 6 אֲבָל הוּא צָרִיךְ לְהִתְפַּלֵל [f] בֶּאֱמוּנָה וְלֹא

בְּסָפֵק כִּי מִי שֶׁמְסוּפָּק זֶה הוּא דּוֹמֶה לְמֵאזְנַיִם עַל הַיָּם

---

[a] In the Tanach, second person plural suffixes are normally attached to feminine plural nouns with a " יֵ " helping vowel, e.g. "בְּנֹתֵיכֶם" (Ex. 3:22); "חַטֹאתֵיכֶם" (Amos 5:12). In the Hebrew Revelation, James and Jude, the use of such helping vowels between the noun and suffix has been extended to singular nouns as well (the " יֵ " does not make the noun plural). This is also rarely attested in the Tanach, e.g. "שְׁבוּתֵיכֶם" (Zeph. 3:20) and similarly (with plural-like form) "מִשְׂנְאָתֶיךָ" (Ezek. 35:11). Compare also footnote on chapter 2:8 and 4:1.

[b] Note that masculine verbs are occasionally used with feminine subjects in Hebrew. See e.g. Judg. 21:21; 1 Sam. 25:27; 1 Kin. 22:36; Dan. 8:9; Neh. 6:9, 13:19; 2 Chr. 15:7, 20:37, etc.

[c] The "ת" preformative is used several times instead of "י" with third person masculine 'imperfect' verbs. In these instances, the "ת" does not affect the person of the verb, it only seems to place extra emphasis on the subject. Compare chapter 1:13, 4:7, 5:14.

[d] Alternative spelling for "לְהִתְפַּלֵל". A preformative 'ה' is occasionally dropped in the 'infinitive construct,' even in the Tanach – see e.g. Pro. 24:17 ("בֶּעָטֵף" for "בְּהֵעָטֵף"); Lam. 2:11 ("וּבְהִכָּשְׁלוֹ" for "וּבְכָּשְׁלוֹ"). See also Ex. 10:3, 34:24; Deu. 31:11; Is. 1:12; Job 33:30, etc.

[e] Or possibly "יֻתַּן" – compare the use of "נוּתַּן" in the Hebrew Revelation, e.g. Rev. 6:2, 6:4, 6:8, etc.

[f] Alternative spelling for "להתפלל" – see footnote on verse 5.

₃ And know that your faith,ᵃ when it is complete, brings aboutᵇ longsuffering.ᶜ ₄ But the longsuffering must be unto the end, so that you may be completeᵈ and nothing be lacking from you.

₅ But if there is one among you who lacks wisdom, heᵉ must pray *for it* from Yahweh, who gives to every man,ᶠ and he himself will also give *it* to him.ᵍ ₆ But he must pray with faithʰ and not with doubt;ⁱ for whosoever is doubtful, heʲ is likeᵏ a pair of balancesˡ on the sea.

ᵃ Lit. "faithfulness." Hebrew "אמונה" (*emunah*) – refers to both believing and doing (being faithful). See e.g. James 2:19-25[20-26]; 2 Chr. 19:9; 2 Kin. 12:16(15); Is. 59:4; Hos. 2:22(20); Ps. 33:4, 143:1, etc.

ᵇ Or "causes" or 'produces.'

ᶜ Or "patience" or "endurance."

ᵈ Lit. "with fullness/abundance."

ᵉ Lit. "this *one*," but often means 'he' or 'him.'

ᶠ Compare Proverbs 2:6.

ᵍ Or possibly 'and it will also be given to him.'

ʰ Or "while being faithful" – the Hebrew word "אמונה" (*emunah*) refers to both believing and doing (being faithful). Compare Pro. 2:1-7: "If you accept my words and treasure up my commandments... then you will... find the knowledge of Elohim. For Yahweh gives wisdom... he stores up wisdom for the upright ones..."

ⁱ Or "with faithfulness and not with uncertainty."

ʲ Lit. "this *one*," but often means 'he' or 'him.'

ᵏ Or "he resembles."

ˡ Or "scales."

7 וְזֶה הָאָדָם אֵינָה[a] צָרִיךְ לַחְשֹׁב שֶׁיְּקַבֵּל אֵיזֶה דָּבָר מֵהָאָדוֹן
8 וּבַעַל מְסוּפָּק הוּא בְּלִי יְדִיעַת[b] בְּכָל דְּרָכָיו 9 אֲבָל אָח אֶחָד
שֶׁשָּׁפָל[c] יוּכַל לְהִתְפָּאֵר אֶת גָּבְהוֹ 10 וְהָעוֹשֵׁר צָרִיךְ לִתְפָּאֵר[d]
אֶת שִׁפְלֻתוֹ[e] כִּי כְּצִיץ הַשָּׂדֶה יִבַשׁ[f] 11 וּכְצִיץ יָצָא וַיִּמָּל וַיִּבְרַח
כַּצֵּל וְלֹא יַעֲמוֹד[g] 12 וְאַשְׁרֵי הָאֱנוֹשׁ יוֹכִיחֶנּוּ אֱלוֹהַּ וּמוּסַר
שַׁדַּי אַל תִּמְאָס[h]

[a] In the Hebrew Revelation and James, "אינו" or "אינה" is generally used instead of "אין". The "ו" or "ה" at the end does not always represent a third person singular pronominal suffix. Because these two spellings are used interchangeably, it is possible that "אינה" should actually be pointed as "אֵינֹה". Compare e.g. the interchange of "שִׁלוֹ" (Jer 7:14; Judg. 21:19, 21:21, etc.) and "שִׁלֹה" (Josh. 18:1, 18:8, 18:9, 18:10, etc.); " אָהֳלוֹ" (Gen. 26:25, 31:25, 33:19, etc.) and "אָהֳלֹה" (Gen. 9:21, 12:8, 13:3, etc.); " זֹה" (2 Kin. 6:19; Ezek. 40:45, etc.) and "זוֹ" (Hos. 7:16; Ps. 132:10).

[b] Usually spelled "ידיעה". The Tanach also contains a number of feminine nouns which are construct in form, but not necessarily in meaning, e.g., "שִׁפְעַת" instead of "שִׁפְעָה" (2 Kin. 9:17b); "פוּגַת" instead of "פוּגָה" (Lam. 2:18); "חָכְמַת" instead of "חָכְמָה" (Is. 33:6); "נְגִינַת" instead of "נְגִינָה" (Ps. 61:1). Alternatively, this word "ידיעת" might be some type of 'infinitive construct' used as a noun.

[c] Or possibly "שֶׁשָּׁפֵל".

[d] Alternative spelling for "לְהִתְפָּאֵר" – see footnote on verse 5.

[e] Or possibly "שִׁפְלָתוֹ".

[f] Or possibly "יָבֵשׁ".

[g] Quoted from Job 14:2.

[h] Quoted from Job 5:17.

₇ And this man must not think that he will receive anything from Ha-Adon. ₈ And[a] he who is doubtful[b] is without knowledge[c] in all his ways.

₉ But a brother who is low,[d] is able to[e] boast in[f] his exaltation,[g] ₁₀ while the rich one must boast in[h] his lowness, for like the flower of the field he will dry up:[i] ₁₁ And "like a flower he comes out, then withers – and he runs away[j] like a shadow and does not remain standing."[k] ₁₂ And "blessed is the man whom Eloah[l] chastens,[m] so do not refuse the **discipline of Shaddai**,"[n,o]

---

[a] Or "For."

[b] Lit. "an owner of doubting" – Hebrew expression most likely refers to someone who doubts habitually and not occasionally.

[c] Or "understanding."

[d] Or "humble."

[e] Or "can."

[f] Lit. "with."

[g] Lit. "height."

[h] Lit. "with."

[i] Or "wither."

[j] Or "flees."

[k] Quoted from Job 14:2.

[l] Singular of "אלהים" (*Elohim*), and usually translated as 'God.' In Hebrew however, the word 'luck' or 'fortune' is pronounced as "*gad*" and sometimes as "*god*" (medieval) – see e.g. Gen. 30:10-11; Josh. 11:17; Isa. 65:11. Therefore we prefer not to use 'God.'

[m] Or possibly "rebukes."

[n] Or "*the* Almighty."

[o] Quoted from Job 5:17.

כִּי אַחַר הַיִּסּוּרִים תְּקַבֵּל הַכֶּתֶר[a] הַחַיִּים שֶׁמַּבְטִיחַ יַהְוֶה לְאֵלֶּה שֶׁאָהוֹב[b] אוֹתוֹ 13 וְאַל תֹּאמַר[c] אֶחָד בְּאִם שֶׁנִּיסָּיוֹן בָּא עָלָיו זֶה בָּא מִיַהְוֶה כִּי יַהְוֶה לֹא מְנַסֶּה אֶת הָאָדָם לְרַע[d] וְהוּא אֵינָה[e] מְנַסֶּה לְשׁוּם אֶחָד 14 רַק כָּל אֶחָד יְנַסֶּה בְּאִם שֶׁתַּאֲוָתוֹ מְנַצֵּחַ אוֹתוֹ 15 וְאַחַר כָּךְ[f] בְּאִם שֶׁקַּבֵּל הַתַּאֲוָה גּוֹרֵם הִיא הַחֵטְא אֲבָל הַחֵטְא בְּאִם שֶׁכָּלָא גּוֹרֵם הִיא הַמָּוֶת 16 אַל תִּתְעוּ אַחִים אֲהוּבִים 17 כָּל מַתָּנָה טוֹבָה בָּא מִלְמַעְלָה מֵאוֹר הָאָב וְאֶצְלוֹ לֹא יֵשׁ חִילּוּף וְשִׁינּוּי מֵאוֹר וּמֵהַחֹשֶׁךְ 18 וְהוּא הֶרְאָה[g] לָנוּ כְּפִי רְצוֹנוֹ עַל יַד דִּיבּוּר הָאֱמֶת שֶׁאָנוּ בִּכּוּרִים מִבְּרִיאָתוֹ

---

[a] Note that this word has the definite article and is still in construct state based on context. This phenomenon is very common in the Hebrew Revelation, James and Jude, and also occurs in the Tanach – see e.g. Judg. 16:14; 1 Kin. 14:24; 2 Kin. 16:14, 23:17; Jer. 25:26; 1 Chr. 9:26, etc.

[b] Or possibly "שֶׁאֲהוֹב". The Tanach also sometimes uses the 'infinitive absolute' in this way (similar to a participle or 'finite' verb). See e.g. Is. 5:5, 22:13, 59:13; 2 Chr. 31:10; Jer. 9:23; Hab. 3:13; Hag. 1:6; Ps. 35:16; Ezek. 1:14, etc. See also "עָשׁוֹק" for "עוֹשֵׁק" (Jer. 22:3); "חָמוֹץ" for "חוֹמֵץ" (Is. 1:17).

[c] The "ת" preformative is used several times instead of "י" with third person masculine 'imperfect' verbs. In these instances, the "ת" does not affect the person of the verb, it only seems to place extra emphasis on the subject. Compare chapter 1:4, 4:7, 5:14.

[d] Or possibly "לָרַע".

[e] In the Hebrew Revelation and James, "אינו" or "אינה" is generally used instead of "אין". The "ו" or "ה" at the end does not always represent a third person singular pronominal suffix. See footnote on verse 7 for more information.

[f] Ms. uses abbreviation "ואח"כ", which could also be read as "ואחרי כן" (same meaning).

[g] Or possibly "הֶרְאָה".

for after the chastisements[a] you[b] will receive the crown of life, which Y: ve promises to those who love him.[c]

13 But let **no one** say – when a temptation[d] comes on him – "This comes from Y: for Y: does not tempt man with evil,[e] neither is he tempted by anyone. 14 Only, everyone is tempted when his desire[f] overcomes him. 15 And afterwards, if he accepts the desire, it causes the sin;[g] but the sin – when it is completed – causes the death.[h] 16 Do not go astray[i] beloved brothers. 17 Every good gift comes from above, from the light of the Father; and with him there is no change, nor alteration of light and darkness. 18 And **he** has shown us, according to his will, by the word of truth, that we are first fruits of his creation.[j]

---

[a] Or "disciplines."

[b] Singular in Hebrew, thus speaking to each person individually.

[c] Compare Deu. 30:6 and 30:16.

[d] Or "trial." Same Hebrew word as in verse 2.

[e] Or "to *do* evil."

[f] Or "covetousness" or "lust."

[g] Or "brings about sin."

[h] Or "brings about death."

[i] Or "err."

[j] Or possibly "And he was shown to us according to his will, by the word of truth, so that we can be first fruits of his creation."

19 בִּשְׁבִיל זֶה אַחִים אֲהוּבִים כָּל בְּנֵי אָדָם[a] צָרִיךְ לִהְיוֹת מָהִיר לִשְׁמוֹעַ אֲבָל לֹא לְדַבֵּר וְלֹא לְאַף 20 (158b) כִּי הָאַף מִבְּנֵי אָדָם אֵינוּ[b] עוֹשֶׂה מַה שֶּׁטּוֹב לִפְנֵי יַהְוֶה 21 [22] אֲבָל תִּהְיוּ מֵאֵלוּ שֶׁעוֹשִׂים הַדִּיבּוּר וְלֹא מֵהַשּׁוֹמְעִים לְבַד שֶׁבְּעַצְמוֹ מְרַמְּאִים אֶתְכֶם 22 [23] כִּי בְּאִם שֶׁאֶחָד יֵשׁ הַשּׁוֹמֵעַ הַדִּיבּוּר וְאֵינוּ[c] עוֹשֶׂה זֶה הוּא דּוֹמֶה לְאִישׁ שֶׁרוֹאֶה אֶת עַצְמוֹ בְּמַרְאוֹת הַצּוֹבְאוֹת[d] 23 [24] כֵּיוָן שֶׁאַחַר שֶׁרָאָה אֶת עַצְמוֹ הוֹלֵךְ הוּא מִמֶּנּוּ וְשׁוֹכֵחַ אֶת מַה שֶׁרָאָה 24 [25] אֲבָל מִי שֶׁרוֹאֶה בִּמְלוֹאָה בְּדַת הַשִּׂמְחָה וּמְקַיֵּים אוֹתוֹ וְאֵינוּ שׁוֹכֵחַ מַה שֶּׁשָׁמַע רַק עוֹשֶׂה זֶה יִהְיֶה קָדוֹשׁ בְּכָל מַעֲשָׂיו 25 [26] אֲבָל בְּאִם שֶׁאֶחָד בָּכֶם מְחַשֵּׁב לוֹ שֶׁהוּא עוֹבֵד יַהְוֶה

---

[a] Possibly a scribal mistake. Should possibly read "בֶּן".

[b] Or possibly "אֵינוֹ" (alternative pronunciation).

[c] Or possibly "וְאֵינוֹ" (alternative pronunciation).

[d] Phrase quoted from Ex. 38:8.

19 Because of this, beloved brothers, all the sons[a] of man must be quick to listen;[b] but not to speak and not to anger. 20 **(158b)** For the anger of the sons of man does not do that which is good before Yahweh.

21 [22][c] But you must be of those who do the word and not of those who hear only – by which you are deceived.[d] 22 [23] For if one is he who hears[e] the word, but does not do *it*; he[f] is like a man who sees himself in the "mirrors of the serving *women*."[g,h] 23 [24] For after he saw himself, he goes away from it, and forgets what he saw. 24 [25] But whosoever sees with fullness[i] into the law of joy, and establishes[j] it, and does not forget what he heard, but does[k] *it*, this one will be blessed[l] in all his deeds.

25 [26] However, if one among you thinks by himself that he serves Yahweh,

---

[a] Or possibly 'every son of man.'

[b] Or "obey." The Hebrew word "שמע" (*shama'*) means both to "hear/listen" and to "obey."

[c] Verse numbers marked in manuscript mostly correspond to standard numbering in English translations. When the verse number in this manuscript differs from the standard numbering, the standard verse number is placed in brackets. E.g. verse 21 in this manuscript corresponds to verse [22] in standard Bibles. The verse numbered [21] in standard Bibles is absent in this ms.

[d] Or possibly "the very thing by which they deceive you."

[e] Or possibly "For if one does hear."

[f] Lit. "this *one*," but means 'he' or 'him.'

[g] Lit. "serving ones" (feminine plural).

[h] Hebrew "מראות הצובאות" – phrase quoted from Ex. 38:8. Because "מראה" (*mar'ah*) (plural "מראות") would usually mean 'vision,' an expression from the Tanach is used to ensure the correct meaning of 'mirror.'

[i] Or "completeness."

[j] Or "performs."

[k] Or "performs."

[l] Hebrew "קדוש" (*qadosh*) – lit. "set-apart" but often used for "blessed."

וְאֵינוֹ מְשַׁמֵּר אֶת לְשׁוֹנוֹ בְּרֶסֶן רַק הִסִּית[a] לְבָבוֹ זֶה הַשֵּׁאֵירוּת[b] יַהְוֶה אֵינוֹ טוֹב 26 [27] וְהַשֵּׁאֵירוּת הַטָּהוֹר מִבְּלִי חֶסְרוֹן לִפְנֵי יַהְוֶה הָאָב זֶה הוּא הַהוֹלֵךְ לְבַקֵּר הַיְתוֹמִים וְהָאַלְמָנוֹת בְּצַעֲרוֹתֵיהֶם

פֶּרֶק ב'

אַחִים אֲהוּבִים אַל תַּחְשְׁבוּ שֶׁהָאֱמוּנָה בְּיֵשׁוּעַ הַמָּשִׁיחַ אֲדוֹנֵינוּ שְׁנוּשָׂא פָּנִים 2 כִּי בְּאִם שֶׁבָּא אֶחָד אֵצֶל הַבֵּית דִּין בְּטַבַּעַת זָהָב וּבְמַלְבּוּשִׁים נָעִים וְגַם עָנִי בְּמַלְבּוּשִׁים רָעִים 3 וְאַתֶּם רוֹאִים עַל זֶה שֶׁנּוּשָׂה[c] הַמַּלְבּוּשִׁים נָעִים וְאוֹמְרִים לוֹ שֵׁב לָנוּ עַל הַטּוֹב וְאוֹמְרִים לֶעָנִי עֲמוֹד שָׁם אוֹ שֵׁב לְרַגְלֵינוּ 4 וְאֵינָם מַשְׁגִּיחִים בְּטוֹב עַל זֶה רַק אַתֶּם שׁוֹפְטִים וְתַעֲשׂוּ חִילוּק רַע 5 שׁוֹמְעִים[d] לִי אַחִים אֲהוּבִים הֲלֹא יַהְוֶה בָּחַר בָּעֲנִיִּים בָּעוֹלָם הַזֶּה הָעוֹשְׁרִים בֶּאֱמוּנָה

---

[a] Or possibly "הֵסִית".

[b] Alternative spelling for "הַשֵּׁירוּת". The lexical form is normally spelled "שֵׁירוּת" or "שֵׁרוּת".

[c] Alternative spelling for "שֶׁנּוּשָׂא" (and could also be pointed with the exact same vowels, "שֶׁנּוּשָׂה"). Take note that "נשה" is also used as an alternative spelling for "נשא" in the Dead Sea Scrolls, e.g. "ונשה" for "ונשא" (1QIsa, Is. 11:12); "יאשה" for "יאשא" (XHev/Se49 f1R:9); "נושה" for "נושא" (4Q398 f1_3:1 and 4Q266 f7i:4); "תשה" for "תשא" (4Q417 f2i:23).

[d] Note that a participle is sometimes used with the same/similar meaning as an imperative. Compare e.g. Revelation 2:6[7], 2:13[14], 2:14[15], 6:16. See also Miguel Pérez Fernández, *An Introductory Grammar of Rabbinic Hebrew*, Brill, 1997, pp. 138-139; M. H. Segal, *A Grammar of Mishnaic Hebrew*, Clarendon Press, p. 159.

but does not keep his tongue with a bridle,[a] but deceives[b] his heart,[c] this service to[d] Yahweh is not good. 26 [27] But the pure service, without lack before Yahweh the Father, is he[e] who goes to visit the fatherless ones and the widows in their distresses.[f]

2:1 Beloved brothers, do not think that the faith in Yeshua Ha-Mashiach our Adon shows partiality.[g] 2 For when[h] one arrives at the house of judgment,[i] with a golden ring and with lovely clothes, and also a poor one with worthless[j] clothes; 3 and you show partiality[k] to him[l] who wears the lovely clothes, and say to him, "Sit on this good *seat*[m] for us;"[n] and say to the poor, "Stand there" or "Sit at our feet." 4 – Then they will not look justly[o] on this *poor* one, but you will be judges[p] who make a bad division.[q]

5 Listen to me beloved brothers, did not Yahweh choose the poor ones in this world, who are rich in faith,

---

[a] Compare chapter 3:2-3.

[b] Or possibly "he only deceives."

[c] Meaning "himself."

[d] Lit. "of."

[e] Or possibly "is this: he who."

[f] Or "sufferings."

[g] Lit. "lifts up faces" – i.e. to respect/favor a particular individual more than others. Compare e.g. Lev. 19:15; Deu. 10:17; Pro. 18:5.

[h] Or "if."

[i] Hebrew "בית דין" (*beit din*) – the standard term used for a "court of law."

[j] Lit. "bad."

[k] Lit. "look upon him."

[l] Lit. "this *one*," but often means 'he' or 'him.'

[m] Or 'in this good *place*."

[n] Probably an expression (as in Ex. 24:14). Or possibly "by us."

[o] Or "well" or "favorably."

[p] Or "you will make a bad decision/division when you judge."

[q] Or "decision."

וְיוֹרְשִׁים מֵהַבְטָחָה שֶׁהִבְטִיחַ לְאֵילֶּה שֶׁאָהוֹב[a] אוֹתוֹ ‚ אֲבָל 6
אַתֶּם תַּעֲשׂוּ בִּיוּשׁ לֶעָנִי וְהָעֲשִׁירִים הֲלֹא הֵמָּה שֶׁעוֹשִׂים הַכֹּל
בְּחוֹזֶק עִמָּכֶם וּמוֹצִיאָם[b] אֶתְכֶם לַמִּשְׁפָּט ‚ 7 וַהֲלֹא הֵמָּה
מְחָרְפִים וּמְגַדְּפִים הַשֵּׁם הַטּוֹב מִזֶּה שֶׁאַתֶּם תִּקְרָאוּ ‚ 8 בְּאִם
שֶׁאַתֶּם תַּעֲשׂוּ הַדָּת כְּפִי שֶׁכָּתוּב בַּתּוֹרָה וְאָהַבְתָּ לְרֵעֶיךָ[c] כָּמוֹךָ
תַּעֲשׂוּ טוֹב ‚ 9 אֲבָל בְּאִם שֶׁאַתֶּם רוֹאִים עַל הָאָדָם תַּעֲשׂוּ חֵטְא
[וְתֵעָנְשׁוּ][d] מִדַּת כְּמוֹ הָעוֹבְרִים ‚ 10 כִּי בְּאִם שֶׁאֶחָד מְקַיֵּים כָּל
הַתּוֹרָה כּוּלָהּ וְחוֹטֵא בְּאֶחָד הוּא חַיָּיב בַּכֹּל ‚ 11 כִּי זֶה שֶׁאָמַר
לֹא תִּנְאָף גַּם הוּא אָמַר לֹא תִּרְצָח וּבְאִם שֶׁאַתָּה אֵינוֹ[e] מְנָאֵף

---

[a] Or possibly "שֶׁאָהוֹב". The Tanach also sometimes uses the 'infinitive absolute' in this way (similar to a participle or 'finite' verb). See e.g. Is. 5:5, 22:13, 59:13; 2 Chr. 31:10; Jer. 9:23; Hab. 3:13; Hag. 1:6; Ps. 35:16; Ezek. 1:14, etc. See also "עָשׁוֹק" for "עוֹשֵׁק" (Jer. 22:3); "חָמוֹץ" for "חוֹמֵץ" (Is. 1:17).

[b] Alternative spelling for "ומוציאים". Such 'defective' spellings of masculine plural nouns/participles are commonly found in the Tanach. See e.g. Gen. 1:21 (תנינם), 25:24 (תומם); Ex. 8:10 (חמרם); Lev. 10:16 (הנותרם). Compare also chapter 4:15 and Jude v. 12.

[c] Although such spellings are generally used with plural nouns, a " ֶ " helping vowel is often inserted between a singular noun and a second person masculine singular suffix when the word is 'in pause,' e.g. "שְׁמֶךָ" (Gen. 12:2); "כַּסְפֶּךָ" (Gen. 17:13). Such 'pausal' pronunciations are often used throughout the Hebrew Revelation, James and Jude, even for words which are not in pause, and these spellings (e.g. "לרעיך" instead of "לרעך") do not indicate a plural noun. This is also attested in the Dead Sea Scrolls (indicated by vowel letters), e.g. "רעיך" (Deu. 5:20, 4Q41); "שדיך" (Deu. 11:15, 4Q136); and rarely in the Masoretic Text: "מִשְׁנְאָתֶיךָ" (Ezek. 35:11). Compare footnotes on chapter 1:3 and 4:1.

[d] Ms. reads "ותענוש" which is very likely a mistake for "ותענשו".

[e] In the Hebrew Revelation and James, "אינו" or "אינה" is generally used instead of "אין". The "ו" or "ה" at the end does not always represent a third person singular pronominal suffix.

and possessors^a of *the* promise which he promised to those who love him? ₆ But you, you put the poor one to shame.^b As for the rich ones, is it not they who do everything to you with force, and bring you out to the judgment? ₇ And do they not reproach and blaspheme the good name of him whom **you** call *upon*?

₈ If **you**^c perform the law as it is written in the Torah,^d "but you must love your fellow as yourself," you do good. ₉ But if you show partiality^e to man, you do sin and are convicted^f by the law as transgressors.^g ₁₀ For if one establishes^h the whole Torah – all of it – but sins in one *matter*,ⁱ he is guilty of the whole.^j ₁₁ For he^k who said, "You must not commit adultery," **he** also said, "You must not murder." So, if you do not commit adultery,

---

^a Or "heirs."

^b Lit. "you made shame/disgrace for the poor one."

^c Plural throughout verse, except for quote from the Torah which is singular.

^d The Hebrew word '*torah*' means "instruction" or "law." The Creator established his perfect and everlasting Torah (instruction/law) as the basis of his covenant with his people. These instructions/laws were recorded by Mosheh in written form, and thus the Torah is also known as the 'Law of Moses,' although in reality it is Yahweh's law/instructions (as covenant stipulations) for his people.

^e Lit. "look upon man."

^f Or "punished" or "condemned."

^g Or possibly "just like the *other* transgressors."

^h Or "performs."

ⁱ Or "against one *command*."

^j Meaning that someone who breaks one command (applicable to him/her) is not innocent when measured against the whole Torah, but guilty. This does not mean that such a person is guilty of breaking every command in the whole Torah.

^k Lit. "this *one*," but often means 'he' or 'him.'

אֲבָל תַּעֲשֶׂה רְצִיחָה אַתָּה עוֹבֵר עַל הַדָּת 12 בִּשְׁבִיל זֶה זֶה תְּדַבְּרוּ
וְתַעֲשׂוּ כְּמוֹ אֵלּוּ שֶׁנִּשְׁפְּטוּ עַל יַד הַדָּת בְּשִׂמְחָה 13 אֲבָל יָבָא
מִשְׁפָּט רַע עַל זֶה שֶׁלֹּא עָשָׂה רַחֲמִים וְהָרַחֲמִים מִתְפָּאֵר כְּנֶגֶד
הַמִּשְׁפָּט 14 וּמַה תּוֹעֶלֶת יֵשׁ אַחִים אֲהוּבִים בְּאִם שֶׁאֶחָד אֹמֵר
שֶׁיֵּשׁ לוֹ הָאֱמוּנָה וְלֹא יֵשׁ לוֹ הַמַּעֲשִׂים וּלְהָאֱמוּנָה[a] לֹא יֵשׁ
יְכוֹלֶת לְקַדֵּשׁ אוֹתוֹ 15 וּבְאִם שֶׁיֵּשׁ אֶחָד אָח אוֹ אָחוֹת שֶׁחָסֵר
לָהֶם לְפַרְנֵס כָּל יוֹם וָיוֹם [16] וְאֶחָד מִכֶּם תֹּאמַר לָהֶם דִּבְרֵי
נֶחָמָה יַהֲוֶה יִתֵּן לָכֶם לָשׂוֹבַע וְהוּא לֹא יִתֵּן לָהֶם שׁוּם דָּבָר
לְתוֹעֶלֶת הַגּוּף מַה תּוֹעֶלֶת יֵשׁ לָהֶם בָּזֶה הַדְּבָרִים 16 [17] כָּךְ
הָאֱמוּנָה בְּאִם שֶׁלֹּא יֵשׁ לוֹ הַמַּעֲשִׂים מֵת הוּא בְּעַצְמוֹ 17 [18]
אֲבָל יוּכַל אֶחָד לֵאמֹר לְךָ יֵשׁ הָאֱמוּנָה וְלִי הַמַּעֲשִׂים הַעִיד לִי
אֱמוּנָתְךָ עִם מַעֲשֶׂיךָ גַּם אֲנִי מֵעִיד לְךָ אֱמוּנָתִי וּמַעֲשִׂים שֶׁלִּי

---

[a] Note that the definite article is often not merged with the inseparable
prepositions in the Hebrew Revelation, James and Jude. This also happens
occasionally in the Tanach, e.g. Gen. 39:11; Deu. 6:24; 1 Sam. 9:13, 13:21; Jer.
44:22; Ezek. 40:25, 47:22; Ps. 36:6; Eccl. 8:1; Ezra 9:7, 9:15; Neh. 5:11, 9:10,
9:19, 12:38; 2 Chr. 10:7, 25:10, 29:27, etc.

but you do commit murder,[a] you transgress[b] the law. 12 Because of this, you must speak and do as those who will be judged by the law with joy.[c] 13 But severe judgment will come on him who did not perform mercy;[d] for the mercy boasts against the judgment.

14 And what profit is there, beloved brothers, if one says that he has the faith, but he does not have the works? – For this faith does not have the ability to set him apart![e] 15 For if there is a brother or sister who lacks to sustain themselves every day,[f] [16] and one of you speak words of comfort to them: "May Yahweh give you to gratification,"[g] – but he does not give them anything to profit the body, what profit will they have by these words? 16 [17] So the faith, if it does not have the works, is dead by[h] itself.

17 [18] Truly, one is able to say, "**You** have the faith; but **I** have the works. Bear witness to me of your faith with[i] your works; I am also bearing witness to you of my faith, for I have works."[j]

---

[a] Lit. "if you are not committing adultery, but you do commit a murder."
[b] Lit. "passing over the law."
[c] Could also possibly mean 'law of joy.'
[d] Or "compassion."
[e] Or "to sanctify him."
[f] Or "day by day." Lit. "every day and day."
[g] Probably refers to both food and clothing, etc.
[h] Or "in."
[i] Or "by."
[j] Or "also I, even by my works, bear witness to you of my faith."

18 [19] אַתָּה תַּאֲמִין שֶׁיַּהְוֶה אֶחָד אַתָּה עוֹשֶׂה טוֹב הַשָּׂטָנִים גַּם
כֵּן מַאֲמִינִים וְרֹעֲדִים 19 [20] אֲבָל רוֹצֶה אַתָּה לֵידַע שֶׁהָאֱמוּנָה
בְּלִי מַעֲשִׂים מֵת הוּא 20 [21] הֲלֹא [אָבִינוּ]ᵃ אַבְרָהָם נִצְטַדֵּק עַל
יַד מַעֲשָׂיו שֶׁהֵבִיא אֶת בְּנוֹ לְקָרְבָּן עַל הַמִּזְבֵּחַ 21 [22] וּבְזֶה
תּוּכַל אַתָּה לִרְאוֹת שֶׁהָאֱמוּנָה פָּעַל בְּמַעֲשָׂיו וְעַל יַד הַמַּעֲשִׂים
נַעֲשָׂה הָאֱמוּנָה בִּמְלוּאָה 22 [23] וּבְזֶה מְקוּיָּיםᵇ הַתּוֹרָה שֶׁנֶּאֱמַר
וְאַבְרָהָם הֶאֱמִין בְּיַהְוֶה וַיַּחְשְׁבֶהָ לּוֹ צְדָקָה

ᵃ Ms. reads "אבותינו" – probably a mistake written in anticipation of the
common phrase "אבותינו אברהם יצחק ויעקב".

ᵇ Crossed out and replaced with "ממלא" above line – in same script as main
text.

18 [19] You,[a] you believe that Yahweh is one – you do good; the satans[b] also believe so, and tremble. 19 [20] But do you want to know[c] that[d] the faith without works is dead? 20 [21] Was not our [father] Avraham[e] justified[f] by his works, when[g] he brought his son as an offering on the altar? 21 [22] And by this, you yourself are able to see that the faith performed[h] in his works – and by the works, the faith was made complete. 22 [23] And by this the Torah[i] was established[j] – which was spoken:[k] "And Avraham believed in Yahweh, and he reckoned[l] it to him as righteousness."

---

[a] "You" is singular throughout this paragraph, speaking to each person individually.

[b] The Hebrew word "שטן" (satan) literally means "adversary" or "accuser." If it has the definite article (The Adversary) it is normally used as a title (e.g. Zech. 3:1; Job 1:6-11; Mat. 4:1; Mark 1:13, etc.) and is transliterated as 'Ha-Satan'; however, 'satan' (usually without the article, or plural) is used for 'enemy/adversary' (e.g. 1 Sam. 29:4; 2 Sam. 19:23(22); 1 Kin. 5:18(5:4), 11:14; Mat. 16:23, etc.) or as a synonym of 'demon' (e.g. Mat. 8:31; Mark 3:23; Rev. 18:2, etc.).

[c] Or "are you willing to realize."

[d] Or "how."

[e] The Hebrew name for 'Abraham.'

[f] Or "Did not Avraham our [father] justify himself."

[g] Or "because."

[h] Or "worked."

[i] When Torah is used as a name, it can refer specifically to the written law (as covenant stipulations), but also more generally to the first five books of the Bible (the Pentateuch), or sometimes even to the entire Old Testament.

[j] Crossed out in ms. and replaced with "fulfilled" above line – in same script as main text.

[k] Lit. "said."

[l] Or "counted it for him."

23 [24] [[ ]^a וְעַכְשָׁיו יְכוֹלִים אַתֶּם לִרְאוֹת שֶׁהָאָדָם נִצְטַדֵּק עַל
יַד הַמַּעֲשִׂים וְלֹא לְבַד עַל יַד הָאֱמוּנָה 24 [25] (159a) וְכַדּוֹמֶה לָזֶה
רָחָב הַזּוֹנָה הֲלֹא הִיא נִצְטַדֵּק עַל יַד הַמַּעֲשִׂים כֵּיוָן שֶׁלָּקְחָתָה^b
הַמְרַגְּלִים וַתִּטְמְנֵם 25 [26] כִּי כְּמוֹ שֶׁהַגּוּף בְּלִי רוּחַ הוּא מֵת כָּךְ
הָאֱמוּנָה בְּלִי מַעֲשִׂים הוּא מֵת

פֶּרֶק ג'

אַחִים אֲהוּבִים אַל תִּהְיוּ כָּל אֶחָד בַּעַל מְלַמֵּד וּדְעוּ שֶׁהָעוֹנֶשׁ
יִהְיֶה יוֹתֵר גָּדוֹל 2 כִּי אָנוּ חוֹטְאִים בְּהַרְבֵּה דְּבָרִים וּמִי שֶׁלֹּא
חָטָא בְּשׁוּם דָּבָר הוּא אִישׁ קָדוֹשׁ וְיוּכַל לַרְסֹת^c אֶת כָּל הַגּוּף
3 וּרְאֵה שֶׁאָנוּ מְנַהֲגִים^d אֶת הַסּוּסִים בְּרֶסֶן כְּדֵי לְהַנְהִיג
אוֹתָם כִּרְצוֹנֵינוּ 4 וְגַם הַסְּפִינוֹת אַף עַל פִּי שֶׁהֵמָּה גְּדוֹלִים
וְהוֹלְכִים בְּחוֹזֶק הָרוּחַ

---

^a Crossed-out letters.

^b Or "שֶׁלָּקְחָתָּה". Although "לקחתה" looks like a second person masculine singular (2ms) verb, it is actually third person feminine singular (3fs), formed on analogy with III-ה verbs. In Mishnaic Hebrew, the use of "תה" at the end of III-ה 'perfect' 3fs verbs was also extended to some III-א verbs, which resulted in spellings where 3fs and 2ms 'perfect' verbs can look identical. See e.g. "קראתה" for "קראה" (Mishnah Yevamot 12:3, mss. Kaufmann and Parma); "יצאתה" for "יצאה" (Mishnah Arachin 7:5, Kaufmann ms.). In the Hebrew Gospels, this phenomenon is also found in II-Vowel verbs, e.g. "קמתה" for "קמה" (Luke 8:55, Vat. Ebr. 100 et al.); "רצתה" for "רצה" (John 11:20, Vat. Ebr. 100 et al.); "שקמתה" for "שקמה" (John 11:31, Vat. Ebr. 100 et al.). Here in the Hebrew Epistle of Ya'aqov, this same phenomenon has simply been extended to the root "לקח."

^c This is a Qal 'infinitive construct' from the root "רסן" with "ל" preposition.

^d Or possibly "מַנְהִיגִים".

23 [24] And now you[a] are able to see that man is justified[b] by the[c] works, and not by the faith alone. 24 [25] (159a) And like this – Rachav[d] the harlot – was she not justified[e] by the works when[f] she received the spies and hid them? 25 [26] For as the body without ruach[g] is dead, so the faith without works is dead.

3:1 Beloved brothers, not every one of you[h] must be an expert teacher;[i] and know[j] that the punishment will be greater.[k] 2 For we sin in many words.[l] But he who does not sin in any word,[m] he is a set-apart man, and able to bridle the whole body. 3 And look,[n] we steer[o] the horses with a bridle, to lead them according to our will. 4 And also the ships, although they are great, and go by the force of the wind[p] –

---

[a] Plural.

[b] Or "justifies himself."

[c] Or "his."

[d] The Hebrew name for 'Rahab.'

[e] Or "did she not justify herself."

[f] Or "because."

[g] The Hebrew word for "spirit," "breath" or "wind." (See glossary for more information.)

[h] Lit. "you [plural] must not be everyone an expert teacher."

[i] Hebrew "בעל מלמד" – lit. "a master of teaching."

[j] Plural imperative.

[k] Or "exceedingly great."

[l] Or "in many things" – probably used here with a double meaning.

[m] Or "any thing" – probably used here with a double meaning.

[n] Or "behold."

[o] Or "guide" or "direct."

[p] Or "sail by means of strong wind."

אַף עַל פִּי כֵן ^a מִנְהָגִים^b עַל יַד הֲגֵא קְטַנָּה שֶׁהִיא בְּיַד
הַמַּלְאָךְ ؛ כָּךְ הַלָּשׁוֹן הִיא אֵיבֶר קְטַנָּה וּפוֹעֶלֶת דְּבָרִים
גְּדוֹלִים רְאֵה אֵשׁ קָטָן מְבַעֵר יַעַר גָּדוֹל ؛ וְגַם הַלָּשׁוֹן הִיא
כְּמוֹ אֵשׁ עוֹלָם מְלוֹאָה בַּעֲווֹלוֹת כָּךְ הַלָּשׁוֹן בְּאֵיבְרוֹתֵינוּ
וּמַחֲטִיא אֶת כָּל הַגּוּף וּמַבְהִיר^c אוֹתָנוּ בַּהֲלִיכָתֵינוּ בְּאִם
שֶׁהִיא נִבְהָר^d מִגֵּיהִנֹּם^e

---

^a Ms. uses abbreviation "אעפ"כ" – could also possibly be read as
"אף על פי כך" (same meaning).

^b Or possibly "מֶנְהָגִים".

^c Alternative spelling for "וּמַבְעִיר".

^d Alternative spelling for "נִבְעָר".

^e Alternative spelling for "גיא הנם". The full title found in the Tanach is
"גיא בן הנם".

yet[a] they are steered[b] by a small rudder which is under the power of[c] the messenger.[d]

5 So the tongue is a small member, and makes great words.[e] Look,[f] a small fire kindles a great forest! 6 And also the tongue is like an eternal fire, full of iniquities; so is the tongue among our members, and *it* causes the whole body to sin, and kindles us in our walk,[g] if it is kindled from Gei-Hinnom.[h]

---

[a] Lit. "although it is so."

[b] Or "guided" or "directed."

[c] Lit. "in the hand of" – a frequent expression in Hebrew. Here it possibly alludes to the power/authority of the messenger's tongue, which steers the ship by bringing instructions to the helmsman (compare below footnote).

[d] The helmsman had to receive his steering instructions from the captain/officers, often via a messenger (the helmsman was usually positioned away from the captain). See e.g. Jonah chapter 1, where the captain came to speak with Jonah during the crisis of the storm – he was not the person physically steering the ship.

[e] Or "does great things."

[f] Or "behold."

[g] Or "behavior" or "conduct." The Hebrew root-word "הלך" (*halach*) is often used idiomatically in the Tanach, and can refer to the way one lives and behaves, as well as to one's attitudes. See e.g. 1 Kin. 9:4 (to walk before Yahweh in integrity means to do everything Yahweh has commanded and to keep his statutes and judgments); Ex. 16:4 and Deu. 8:6 (to walk in Yahweh's Torah/ways means to live out/do Yahweh's will/commandments); Deu. 4:3, 6:14, 8:19 (to walk after other gods means to follow/serve/seek other gods); Deu. 13:5(4) (to walk after Yahweh means to follow Yahweh, to keep his commandments and to obey his voice); Gen. 5:22-24, 6:9, (to walk with Yahweh means to live in a close relationship with Yahweh, being righteous and blameless); Mic. 6:8 (to walk humbly with Elohim means to be humble before Elohim, to do justice and to perform steadfast kindness); Mic. 2:3 and Dan. 4:34(37) (to walk in pride means to be proud and do arrogant things), etc.

[h] Lit. "The valley of Hinnom." This Hebrew word is transliterated into Greek as '*Gehenna*,' and is inaccurately translated as 'Hell.' This is a literal valley right next to Jerusalem ordained for future punishment. See Mat. 25:41-46 in the HebrewGospels.com version: "And then he will say to those who are on the

, כִּי הַטֶּבַע מִכָּל הַבְּהֵמוֹת וְהָעוֹפוֹת וְהַנְּחָשִׁים שֶׁהֵמָּה
בַּיַּבָּשָׁה אוֹ בַּיָּם הִיא כְּמוֹ הַטֶּבַע שֶׁל הָאָדָם , אֲבָל הַלָּשׁוֹן
לֹא יוּכַל שׁוּם אָדָם לָרֶסֶת כִּי הִיא רַע וּמְלוּאָה בְּסַם הַמָּוֶת ,
עַל יַד הַלָּשׁוֹן מְשַׁבְּחִים אָנוּ לְיַהְוֶה הָאָב וְעַל יַד זֹאת[a]
מְקַלְלִים אָנוּ לְהָאָדָם שֶׁהוּא בְּצֶלֶם אֱלֹהִים 10 מִפִּי אֶחָד יָצֵא
שֶׁבַח וּקְלָלוֹת וְאַל תִּהְיֶה כָּךְ אַחִים אֲהוּבִים 11 וְכִי יֵשׁ מַעְיָין
שֶׁיֵּשׁ בָּהּ מַיִם מְלוּחִים וּמְתוּקִים 12 אוֹ יוּכַל עֵץ[b] שֶׁל תְּמָרִים[c]
לִיתֵּן[d] שֶׁמֶן אוֹ גֶּפֶן תְּאֵנִים כָּךְ הַמַּעְיָין לֹא יוּכַל לִיתֵּן מַיִם
מְלוּחִים וּמְתוּקִים

---

[a] Hebrew ms. has abbreviation "וע"יז", which could also be read "וְעַל יַד זֶה" (masculine). Note that "לשון" is sometimes referred to as masculine in Hebrew, e.g. Ps. 22:16; Job 27:4; Lam. 4:4. Compare also verse 6, where several masculine verbs are used with "לשון".

[b] Note that a date palm is also considered an "עץ". See e.g. Joel 1:12.

[c] Crossed out and replaced with "תאנים" – in same/similar script as main text.

[d] This is an alternative form of the 'infinitive construct' with "ל" preposition (root: "נתן"). Normally spelled "לתת" in the Tanach.

7 For the nature of all the animals, and the birds, and the serpents,[a] which are on the dry land or in the sea, is like the nature of man.[b] 8 But the tongue, no[c] man is able to bridle, for it is evil and is full of the poison of death. 9 With the tongue we praise Yahweh the Father, and with it we curse[d] the man who is[e] in the image of Elohim.[f] 10 From one mouth there comes out praise and curses; but it must not be so, beloved brothers. 11 For is there indeed a fountain which has in it salt and sweet waters? 12 Or is a tree of dates[g] able to give oil,[h] or a vine – figs? So[i] the fountain is not able to give salt and sweet waters.

---

left side... go into the fire of Gei-Hinnom, which is prepared for Ha-Satan and his messengers... And these will go into the fire of Gei-Hinnom, but the righteous ones will go into everlasting light." To learn more about the Biblical definition of 'Gei-Hinnom,' see Jer. 7:30-33, Is. 30:33, 66:24, etc.

[a] Or possibly 'reptiles.'

[b] Possibly means that the nature of all (i.e. the greatest majority of) animals allows them to be taught and trained just like humans can be taught and trained. The Greek version paraphrases and states that all animals have been tamed by man.

[c] Hebrew often uses "no" or "not any" or "all" to refer to the majority. (Compare above footnote.)

[d] Or "speak with contempt of" or "declare insignificant."

[e] Or possibly "who was *made* in the image of Elohim."

[f] Usually translated as 'God.' In Hebrew however, the word 'luck' or 'fortune' is pronounced as "*gad*" and sometimes as "*god*" (medieval) – see e.g. Gen. 30:10-11; Josh. 11:17; Isa. 65:11. Therefore we prefer not to use 'God.'

[g] Or "a date palm." The word for "dates" in the Hebrew ms. is crossed out and replaced with "figs" (in the same/similar script as main text).

[h] Most seeds contain a low percentage of oil, which is hard to extract. However, olive oil is easily extracted from the flesh of the fruit, which contains a large percentage of oil. The Tanach even refers to "olive trees" as "עץ שמן" ('ets shemen) – "trees of oil," with the same Hebrew word used here for 'oil.' Thus, it is evident that James is speaking of olive oil specifically. The Greek translation even replaced the term 'oil' with 'olives' to avoid confusion.

[i] Or "Thus" or "Even so."

13 מִי שֶׁהוּא חָכָם וְנָבוֹן בָּכֶם מַרְאֶה לִי הֲלִיכָתוֹ הַטּוֹב בְּחָכְמָה 14 אֲבָל בְּאִם שֶׁיֵּשׁ בִּלְבַבְכֶם קִנְאָה וְשִׂנְאָה אַל תִּתְפָּאֲרוּ וְאַל תְּשַׁקְּרוּ כְּנֶגֶד הָאֱמֶת 15 כִּי זֶה אֵינוֹ חָכְמָה שֶׁבָּא מִלְמַעְלָה רַק מֵהָאֲדָמָה מֵהָאָדָם וּמֵהַשְּׂטָנִים 16 כִּי בְּמִי שֶׁיֵּשׁ קִנְאָה וְשִׂנְאָה בָּזֶה יֵשׁ הַרְבֵּה דְּבָרִים רָעִים 17 אֲבָל הַחָכְמָה מִלְמַעְלָה הִיא לְכַתְּחִילָה נָקִי וְאַחַר כָּךְ[a] שָׁלוֹם וּבְנַחַת וְיוּכַל לְפַיְּיסָה[b] וּמָהִיר לִשְׁמוֹעַ מָלֵא רַחֲמִים וְאַחֲרִית לְטוֹבָה וְלֹא מַשְׂאוּי[c] פָּנִים וַחֲנִיפוֹת

---

[a] Ms. uses abbreviation "ואח"כ". Could also be read as "ואחרי כן" (same meaning).

[b] Or possibly "לְפַיְּיסָה".

[c] Or possibly "מַשְׂאוּי" or "מַשָׂאוּי" or "מַשָׂאוּי" (alternative pronunciations). The lexical form is often spelled "משוא".

13 Whosoever is wise and understanding among you, let him show me his good walk[a] with wisdom. 14 But if there be jealousy and hatred **in your hearts**, do not boast and do not lie against the truth. 15 For this is not wisdom which comes from above; but from the earth, from the man, and from the satans. 16 For in whomsoever there is jealousy and hatred, in him[b] there are many evil things.[c]

17 But the wisdom from above is firstly[d] pure;[e] and afterwards shalom,[f] and with rest, and is able to reconcile,[g] and quick to listen, full of mercy; and lastly *it* is to[h] goodness[i] and not *to* partiality[j] or flattery.[k]

---

[a] Or "behavior" or "conduct." The Hebrew root-word "הלך" (*halach*) is often used idiomatically in the Tanach, and can refer to the way one lives and behaves, as well as to one's attitudes. See e.g. 1 Kin. 9:4 (to walk before Yahweh in integrity means to do everything Yahweh has commanded and to keep his statutes and judgments); Ex. 16:4 and Deu. 8:6 (to walk in Yahweh's Torah/ways means to live out/do Yahweh's will/commandments); Deu. 4:3, 6:14, 8:19 (to walk after other gods means to follow/serve/seek other gods); Deu. 13:5(4) (to walk after Yahweh means to follow Yahweh, to keep his commandments and to obey his voice); Gen. 5:22-24, 6:9, (to walk with Yahweh means to live in a close relationship with Yahweh, being righteous and blameless); Mic. 6:8 (to walk humbly with Elohim means to be humble before Elohim, to do justice and to perform steadfast kindness); Mic. 2:3 and Dan. 4:34(37) (to walk in pride means to be proud and do arrogant things), etc.

[b] Lit. "this *one*," but often means 'he' or 'him.'

[c] Or "words" – continuing the theme of the "tongue."

[d] Lit. "at the first."

[e] Or "innocent" or "blameless."

[f] Meaning "complete" or "peaceful."

[g] Or "to make peace."

[h] Or "it leads to goodness" or "it causes goodness."

[i] Or "that which is good."

[j] Lit. "lifting up faces" – i.e. to respect/favor a particular individual more than others. Compare e.g. Lev. 19:15; Deu. 10:17; Pro. 18:5.

[k] Or "hypocrisy."

18 אֲבָל הַפֵּירוֹת מֵהַצִּידְקוּת נִזְרַעַת[a] בְּשָׁלוֹם לְאֵילֶה הַמְּקַיְּימִים הַשָּׁלוֹם

פֶּרֶק ד'

1 וּבִשְׁבִיל מָה בָּא מִלְחָמָה בְּתוֹכֵיכֶם[b] הֲלֹא בִּשְׁבִיל חֲמֵדֹתֵיכֶם הַלּוֹחֲמִים בְּאֵיבְרֵתֵיכֶם 2 וְאַתֶּם [מִתְאַוִּים][c] וְאֵינוּ[d] מְקַבְּלִים וְנוֹקֵם וְנוֹטֵר וְאֵינוּ מַרְוִויחַ בָּזֶה וְהַכֹּל בִּשְׁבִיל מָה מִפְּנֵי שֶׁאַתֶּם אֵינוּ מִתְפַּלְלִים 3 וְאַתֶּם עוֹשִׂים תְּפִילָה וְלֹא נַעֲנָה בִּשְׁבִיל שֶׁאַתֶּם מִתְפַּלְלִים בְּרָעָה 4 הַנּוֹאֵף וְהַנּוֹאֶפֶת הֲלֹא אַתֶּם יוֹדְעִים שֶׁמִּי שֶׁאוֹהֵב עוֹלָם הַזֶּה הוּא שׂוֹנֵא מִיַּהְוֶה וּמִי שֶׁרוֹצֶה לִהְיוֹת אוֹהֵב לָעוֹלָם הַזֶּה הוּא יִהְיֶה שׂוֹנֵא לַיַהְוֶה

---

[a] Or possibly "נִזְרָעֹת" – but note that singular passive verbs are sometimes used with plural subjects. See e.g. Gen. 35:26, 46:22; Ex. 27:7, 35:24; 2 Sam. 21:10; 1 Kin. 8:26, etc.

[b] In the Tanach, a number of prepositions take a 'plural' form when a suffix is attached, e.g. "עֲלֵיכֶם" (Ex. 5:21); "אַחֲרֵיהֶם" (Gen. 41:23). In the Hebrew Revelation, James and Jude, the 'plural' form is used with a wider range of prepositions whenever a second person suffix is attached. Compare also footnote on chapter 1:3 and 2:8.

[c] Ms. has "מתאויים" – probably a spelling mistake for "מתאווים".

[d] In the Hebrew Revelation and James, "אינו" or "אינה" is generally used instead of "אין". The "ו" or "ה" at the end does not always represent a third person singular pronominal suffix.

₁₈ But the fruits of righteousness are sown in shalom^a for^b those who establish^c the shalom.

4:₁ And why^d does war^e happen^f in your midst?^g Is it not because of your desires^h which fight in your members?ⁱ ₂ So you desire,^j but do not receive; and *he*^k who takes revenge and stays angry^l does not profit by it. And why all *this*? – Because you^m do not pray, ₃ *and* when you do a prayer, it is not answered because you pray wrongly.ⁿ

₄ O adulterer and adulteress, do you not know that whosoever loves this world, he hates Yahweh? So, whosoever wants to be a lover^o of this world, **he** will be a hater^p of Yahweh.

------

^a 'Shalom' means "wholeness," "completeness," "wellbeing" or "peace." 'Shalom' was also used as a greeting.

^b Or possibly 'by.'

^c Or "perform."

^d Lit. "because of what."

^e Or "fighting" – Hebrew text uses same root-word twice in this verse, and repeats it again in verse 7.

^f Lit. "come."

^g Or "among you."

^h Or "lusts."

ⁱ I.e. "body parts" – could also refer to one's inner parts, and possibly to members of the assembly/community.

^j Or "covet."

^k Verbs are singular in the second half of this sentence.

^l Or "bears a grudge" – compare Lev. 19:18, where the same Hebrew words are used. In Mat. 22:39 Yeshua referred to Lev. 19:18 as the second greatest command in the Torah.

^m Plural.

ⁿ Lit. "in evil."

^o Or "friend."

^p Or "enemy."

‭5‬ אוֹ אַתֶּם מְחַשְּׁבְתֶּם[a] שֶׁהַתּוֹרָה אֹמֵר בְּחִנָּם הָרוּחַ שֶׁדָּר בְּתוֹכֵיכֶם[b] הוּא מִתְאַוֶּה כְּנֶגֶד הַצִּיּוֹת[c] יַהְוֶה ‭6‬ וְנוֹתֵן הַרְבֵּה חֶסֶד כֵּיָן שֶׁהַתּוֹרָה אֹמֵר שֶׁיַּהְוֶה מַגְבִּיהַּ אֶת הַשְּׁפָלִים וּמַשְׁפִּיל אֶת הָרָמִים[d] ‭7‬ וְעַכְשָׁיו תִּהְיוּ מוּכְנָעִים לְיַהְוֶה וְתִלָּחֲמוּ[e] כְּנֶגֶד הַשְּׂטָנִים תִּבְרְחוּ[f] מִמְּכֶם

---

[a] This is either a participle with a 'perfect' ending (such mixed forms do occasionally occur in the Tanach, e.g. "משתחויתם" in Ezek. 8:16; see also "תבאתי" in 1 Sam. 25:34 (Ketiv), which looks like a combination of the perfect "באת" and imperfect "תבאי"); or else this is a contraction of "מה חשבתם" and should be pointed as "מֶחֲשַׁבְתֶּם" (See e.g. "מתלאה", Mal. 1:13). Compare also Jude v. 21, and Rev. 16:9.

[b] See footnote on chapter 4:1.

[c] "הציוות"– Probably an alternative word/spelling for "הַצַּוֹּת". Alternatively, "הציוות" could possibly be a spelling mistake for "הַצִּיּוֹת".

[d] See Ezek. 17:24 and 2 Sam. 22:28.

[e] Or possibly "וְתִלְחֲמוּ" – but compare "הלוחמים" in verse 1.

[f] For the use of "ת" instead of "י", see footnote on chapter 1:4.

₅ Or do you think that the Torah says in vain *that* the ruach[a] which dwells inside you,[b] it desires[c] against the commandments of Yahweh?[d]

₆ Yet *he* gives much steadfast love, for the Torah says that Yahweh exalts the humble ones, and humiliates the proud[e] ones.[f] ₇ Therefore you must be humble[g] before Yahweh, and fight against the satans[h] – **they** will flee away from you.

---

[a] The Hebrew word for "spirit," "breath" or "wind." Apart from these basic uses, ruach can also refer to a person's emotions, will or attitude (e.g. Gen. 26:35, 41:8; Josh. 2:11; Judg. 8:3; Is. 57:15; Ps. 32:2; Job 21:4; Pro. 16:18). See glossary for more information.

[b] James specifically addresses people who love this world (see also "adulterer and adulteress" in v. 4). Thus, it is not Yahweh's Spirit which desires against his own commandments, but e.g. the spirit of a rebellious human being (Ps. 78:8,10), the "spirit of the world" (1 Cor. 2:12), the "spirit of fornication" (Hos. 4:12-13), etc. On the contrary, Yahweh's Spirit enables those who serve him to obey his commandments (Ezek. 36:26-27; Rom. 8:4-9).

[c] Or "covets."

[d] This is not a direct quote from the Torah, but a principle found in the Torah and throughout the Tanach. See e.g. Ps. 78:8,10 (their spirit was unfaithful and they refused to keep Yahweh's Torah); Gen. 6:5 and 8:21 ("heart" and "ruach" are synonyms, e.g. Ps. 78:8); Pro. 21:10 ("nephesh" and "ruach" can be synonymous, see glossary); Deu. 1:26-44 (when Yahweh commanded them to go, they wanted to stay; when Yahweh commanded them to stay, they wanted to go ("ruach" is connected to a person's will/desires)); Deu. 31:27 (they were stubborn and rebellious, they refused to obey Yahweh's commandments).

[e] Lit. "high" or "exalted" – but from a different root-word than the word "exalts" in first half of verse.

[f] See Ezek. 17:24 and 2 Sam. 22:28.

[g] Lit. "be humbled to" – or possibly 'you must humble yourselves.'

[h] The Hebrew word "שטן" (satan) literally means "adversary" or "accuser." If it has the definite article (The Adversary) it is normally used as a title (e.g. Zech. 3:1; Job 1:6-11; Mat. 4:1; Mark 1:13, etc.) and is transliterated as 'Ha-Satan';

8 וּמְקָרְבִים[a] אֶתְכֶם לַיהוָה (159b) יְקָרֵב הוּא לָכֶם וּתְטַהֲרוּ אֶת יְדֵיכֶם הַחוֹטְאִים וְתַעֲשׂוּ [לְבַבְכֶם][b] נָקִי , וּתְנַשְּׂאוּ סְבָלוֹת[c] וּבְכוּ וּ[מִ]צְטַחֲקֵיכֶם[d] תִּתְהַפֵּךְ לִבְכִיָּה וְשִׂמְחָתֵיכֶם[e] לְיָגוֹן 10 מַכְנִיעִים אֶתְכֶם לִפְנֵי יַהְוֶה יִשְׁמַע הוּא לָכֶם 11 אַחִים אֲהוּבִים אַל תֵּלְכוּ רָכִיל בֵּינֵיכֶם כִּי מִי שֶׁהוֹלֵךְ רָכִיל בְּאָחִיו הוּא רָכִיל בַּדָּת[f] וְאִם אַתָּה תַּעֲשֶׂה כֵּן אֵין אַתָּה מְקַיֵּים אֶת הַדָּת 12 וְיֵשׁ לְבַד אֶחָד שֶׁנּוֹתֵן הַדָּת שֶׁיּוּכַל לַעֲנוֹשׁ וְלִמְחוֹל אֲבָל מִי אַתָּה לִשְׁפּוֹט אֶת הָאֲחֵרִים

---

[a] Or possibly "וּמַקְרִבִים".

[b] Ms. has "לבבבכם" – either a scribal mistake or else possibly an unusual medieval spelling.

[c] Or possibly "סְבָלוֹת".

[d] Ms. has "ותצחקיכם" – probably a scribal mistake. See also footnote on chapter 1:3.

[e] See footnote on chapter 1:3.

[f] See Lev. 19:16-17.

8 If[a] you bring yourselves[b] near to Yahweh, (159b) he himself will draw near to you. So, cleanse your hands,[c] o sinners, and make your hearts pure! 9 And take up[d] *your* burdens[e] and weep! And let your laughter be turned into weeping, and your joy into grief. 10 Humble yourselves before Yahweh, he himself will hear[f] you.

11 Beloved brothers, do not go about with slander among yourselves, for whosoever goes about as a slanderer[g] against his brother, is a slanderer against the law;[h] and if **you**[i] do so, you do not establish[j] the law. 12 And there is only one who gives the law, who is able to punish[k] and to forgive; but who are you to judge the others?

---

however, 'satan' (usually without the article, or plural) is used for 'enemy/adversary' (e.g. 1 Sam. 29:4; 2 Sam. 19:23(22); 1 Kin. 5:18(5:4), 11:14; Mat. 16:23, etc.) or as a synonym of 'demon' (e.g. Mat. 8:31; Mark 3:23; Rev. 18:2, etc.).

[a] Or "When."

[b] Or "draw near."

[c] Compare Ps. 24:4 and 73:13. The expression "your hands" means "what you do" or "your deeds." See also Ps. 18:21-22(20-21) and Job 17:9 ("clean of hands" means "righteous"); Ezek. 23:37 and Is. 1:15-16 ("your hands are full of blood" means "you commit bloodshed").

[d] Or possibly "bear."

[e] Or possibly "longsuffering."

[f] Hebrew "שמע" (*shama'*) means to hear and act upon.

[g] Or "with slander."

[h] It is "against the law" to slander. See e.g. Lev. 19:16-17: "You must not go about as a slanderer against your people; you must not stand against the blood of your fellow; I am Yahweh. You must not hate your brother in your heart... " (Slander is associated with false witness and hatred.)

[i] Singular.

[j] Or "perform."

[k] Or "condemn."

וְעַכְשָׁיו הַאִם שֶׁאַתֶּם אוֹמְרִים הַיּוֹם אוֹ מָחָר רוֹצִים אָנוּ 13
לֵילֵךְ[a] לַמָּקוֹם אוֹ לָעִיר הַזֹּאת וְרוֹצִים אָנוּ לַעֲמוֹד שָׁם אֶחָד
שָׁנָה וְלַעֲשׂוֹת מַשָּׂא וּמַתָּן וּלְהַרְוִיחַ 14 וְאַתֶּם לֹא יוֹדְעִים מַה
שֶׁיּוּכַל לִהְיוֹת לְמָחָר כִּי מַה יֵּשׁ חַיּוֹתֵיכֶם הֲלֹא רוּחַ הוּא
לִזְמַן מוּעָט וְאַחַר כָּךְ הוּא הוֹלֵךְ 15 וְאַתֶּם צְרִיכֶם[b] לוֹמַר
בְּאִם שֶׁיִּרְצֶה יַהְוֶה וְאָנוּ חַיִּים רוֹצִים אָנוּ לַעֲשׂוֹת זֹאת 16
אֲבָל עַכְשָׁיו אַתֶּם מִתְפָּאֲרִים בְּגַאֲוָתֵיכֶם[c] וְזֹאת הִיא לְרָעָה 17
כִּי מִי שֶׁיּוֹדֵעַ לַעֲשׂוֹת טוֹב וְאֵינָה עוֹשֶׂה לָזֶה נֶחְשָׁב לְחֵטְא

פֶּרֶק ה׳

וְעַכְשָׁיו הָעֲשִׁירִים צַעֲקוּ וּבְכוּ עַל הָרָעָה שֶׁיָּבֹא עֲלֵיכֶם 2 1
עֲשִׁירֹתֵיכֶם[d] רָקַב וְשִׂמְלֹתֵיכֶם הָיְתָה לְמַאֲכָל כָּעָשׁ 3
וְכַסְפֵּיכֶם[f] וּזְהָבֵיכֶם[g] יַחֲלוֹד וְזֶה [e]
יִהְיֶה לָכֶם לְעֵדוּת וְיֹאכַל אֶת בְּשַׂרְכֶם כְּמוֹ אֵשׁ וְאַתֶּם תְּקַבְּצוּ
עֲשִׁירוּת בְּאַחֲרִית הַיָּמִים

---

[a] This is an alternative form of the 'infinitive construct' with "ל" preposition (root: "הלך"). Spelled "ללכת" in the Tanach.

[b] Alternative spelling for "צריכים". Such 'defective' spellings of masculine plural nouns/participles are commonly found in the Tanach. See e.g. Gen. 1:21 (תנינם), 25:24 (תומם); Ex. 8:10 (חמרם); Lev. 10:16 (הנותרם). Compare also chapter 2:6 and Jude v. 12.

[c] Or possibly "בְּגַאֲוֹתֵיכֶם" or "בְּגֵאוֹתֵיכֶם" – but see footnote on chapter 1:3.

[d] Or possibly "עֲשִׁירֹתֵיכֶם" – but see footnote on chapter 1:3.

[e] Phrase crossed out by original scribe. (Scribe seems to have written from memory and made a mistake.)

[f] See footnote on chapter 1:3.

[g] See footnote on chapter 1:3.

₁₃ And now, do you say, "Today or tomorrow we want to go to that ᵃ place or to this city, and we want to stay there one year and do business,ᵇ and make profit" – ₁₄ while you do not *even* know what is able to happen tomorrow? For what are your lives? Is it not a ruach for a little time, and afterwards it goes away? ₁₅ But you need ᶜ to say: "If Yahweh wants, and we are alive, we want to do this." ₁₆ But now you boast in your pride, and this leads to evil.ᵈ ₁₇ For whosoever knows to do good, and does not do *it*, for him ᵉ it will be reckoned as sin.

5:₁ And now,ᶠ o rich ones, cry out and weep about ᵍ the evil ʰ that will come upon you. ₂ Your riches have rotted, and your clothes became food as *for* the moth. ₃ And your silver and your gold will rust, and this will be a testimony against you; and it will eat your flesh as fire *does*, for **you** will gather riches in the last days: ⁱ

ᵃ Lit. "the."

ᵇ Or "trading" – Lit. "carrying/taking and giving."

ᶜ Or "you should say."

ᵈ Or possibly 'guilt.'

ᵉ Lit. "this *one*," but often means 'he' or 'him.'

ᶠ Or "Therefore."

ᵍ Or "over."

ʰ Or "calamity" or "disaster."

ⁱ Lit. "the end of the days."

₄ רְאֵה פְּעוּלַת שָׂכִיר שֶׁתָּלִין אֶצְלֶיךָ ᵃ צוֹעֵק לְפָנַי וְצַעֲקוֹתֵיהֶם בָּא לִפְנֵי אָזְנַיִם מֵהָאָדוֹן [צְבָאוֹת] ᵇ ₅ וְהָיָה לָכֶם תַּאֲווֹת עוֹלָם הַזֶּה וְשָׂמְחוּ לְקוֹל עוּגָב ᶜ ₆ וְאַתֶּם מְחַיְּיבִים לְהַצֶּדֶק ᵈ וַתָּמִיתוּ אוֹתוֹ וְהוּא לֹא מִיחָה לָכֶם ₇ וְעַכְשָׁיו אַחִים אֲהוּבִים תִּהְיֶה לָכֶם תִּקְוָה עַל הֶעָתִיד מֵהָאָדוֹן רְאֵה בַּעַל הַשָּׂדֶה מְצַפֶּה עַל הַפֵּירוֹת הָאָרֶץ וְתִקְוָתוֹ הִיא עַל הַיּוֹרֶה וּמַלְקוֹשׁ ₈ וְאַף אַתֶּם חַזְּקוּ לְבַבְכֶם

ᵃ See footnote on chapter 4:1.

ᵇ Spelling based on note in margin of ms.

ᶜ Quoted from Job 21:12.

ᵈ Or possibly "לְהַצַּדִּק".

4 Look!^a – The wages of *the* hired laborer^b that remains with you^c overnight,^d cries^e out before me; and their outcries have come before the ears of Ha-Adon^f Tseva'ot.^g **5** And you have had the desires^h of this world, "and they rejoiced at *the* sound of a flute."ⁱ **6** And you declared the righteous guilty and killed him; and he did not protest against^j you.

7 Therefore beloved brothers, you must have hope because of the future^k of Ha-Adon. Look,^l the owner of the field^m waitsⁿ for the fruits of the earth; and his hope^o is on the early rain and latter rain. **8** So also you, make your hearts strong! –

---

^a Or "Behold!"

^b Or "hireling."

^c Singular – addresses people individually.

^d Compare Lev. 19:13: "...the wages of the hired laborer must not remain with you overnight until the morning."

^e Singular in Hebrew ("wages" is singular in Hebrew).

^f Or possibly "the Adon of."

^g "Tseva'ot" means "armies" and is used in various titles to stress the power of Yahweh.

^h Or "lusts."

ⁱ Quoted from Job 21:12. The Hebrew word for "flute" which is used here as well as in Job 21 is from the root "עגב" (*agav*) which means to "lust after."

^j Or "he did not hinder/prevent you." Take note that the "righteous" one mentioned here in verse 6 is singular, and likely refers to Yeshua who "did not open his mouth" against his unjust condemnation and the false accusations brought against him. Compare e.g. Is. 53:7-8 and Act. 8:32-35; Mat. 26:59-63, 27:12-14, etc.

^k Or "future *coming*."

^l Or "Behold."

^m Or "farmer."

ⁿ Or "looks with expectation" or "waits upon."

^o Or "his expectation."

כִּי הֶעָתִיד מֵהָאָדוֹן קְרוֹבָה , אַל תֵּאָנְחוּ כְּנֶגְדֵיכֶם[a] אַחִים
אֲהוּבִים כְּדֵי שֶׁלֹּא תָּבוֹאוּ לִידֵי תַּקָּלָה[b] כִּי הַשּׁוֹפֵט עוֹמֵד
לִפְנֵי הַפֶּתַח 10 אַחִים אֲהוּבִים קְחוּ לָכֶם לְמָשָׁל הַצָּעָרוֹת
וְהַסִּיבְלוּת מֵהַנְּבִיאִים שֶׁדִּבְּרוּ לָכֶם בְּשֵׁם הָאָדוֹן 11 רְאוּ
אֲנַחְנוּ מְשַׁבְּחִים לְאֵילוּ שֶׁסָּבְלוּ וְהַסִּיבְלוּת מֵאִיּוֹב שְׁמַעְתֶּם
וְהַסּוֹף מֵהָאָדוֹן רְאִיתֶם כִּי הָאָדוֹן הוּא אֵל רַחֲמִים וְרַב חֶסֶד
12 אֲבָל מִקּוֹדֶם כֹּל אַחִים אֲהוּבִים אַל תִּשָּׁבְעוּ לֹא בַּשָּׁמַיִם
אוֹ בָּאָרֶץ אוֹ בְּשׁוּם שְׁבוּעָה

---

[a] See footnote on chapter 4:1.
[b] Or possibly "תְּקָלָה".

For the future[a] of Ha-Adon is near. ₉ Do not sigh[b] against one another,[c] beloved brothers, that you do not come under control of a snare,[d] for the judge is standing before the door.

₁₀ Beloved brothers, take as a parable for yourselves, the sufferings and the endurance[e] of the prophets who spoke to you in the name of Ha-Adon. ₁₁ Look,[f] we commend those who have endured:[g] for you have heard of the **endurance**[h] **of 'Iyov,**[i] and you have seen the **end** *goal* **of Ha-Adon** – that[j] Ha-Adon is an El[k] of mercies,[l] and great of steadfast-love.

₁₂ But first of all,[m] beloved brothers, you must not swear[n] – not by the heavens or by the earth or by any oath;

---

[a] Or "future *coming*."

[b] Or "groan" or "grumble."

[c] Lit. "yourselves."

[d] Or "stumbling block."

[e] Or "patience" or "longsuffering."

[f] Or "behold."

[g] Or "endured suffering."

[h] Or "longsuffering."

[i] The Hebrew name for 'Job.'

[j] Or "for."

[k] 'El' (similar to 'Elohim') is usually translated as 'God.' In Hebrew however, the word 'luck' or 'fortune' is pronounced as "*gad*" and sometimes as "*god*" (medieval) – see e.g. Gen. 30:10-11; Josh. 11:17; Isa. 65:11. Therefore we prefer not to use 'God.'

[l] Or "compassion."

[m] Or possibly "before all *of this*."

[n] The Torah commands: "Yahweh your Elohim you must fear, and him you must serve and **by his name you must swear**" (Deu. 6:13). Whenever "swear" is condemned or used negatively in the Tanach it always refers to swearing **falsely**. See e.g. Zec. 5:3-4; Eccl. 9:2.

אֲבָל דִּיבּוּרָתֵיכֶם[a] תִּהְיֶה הֵן הֵן וְלָאו[b] לָאו כְּדֵי שֶׁלֹּא תִּכָּשְׁלוּ[c]
13 וְאִם אֶחָד בָּכֶם סוֹבֵל אֵיזֶה דָּבָר הוּא צָרִיךְ לְהִתְפַּלֵּל[d] וְאִם
אֶחָד בָּכֶם בְּטוֹב לֵב זֶה צָרִיךְ לְזַמֵּר תְּהִילִים 14 וְאִם אֶחָד
חוֹלֶה צָרִיךְ לִקְרֹא לוֹ הַזְּקֵנִים מֵהָעֵדָה וְהֵם תַּעֲשׂוּ[e] תְּפִילָה
בִּשְׁבִילוֹ [   ][f] וּמוֹשְׁחִים אוֹתוֹ בַּשֶּׁמֶן בְּשֵׁם הָאָדוֹן 15
וְהַתְּפִילָה מֵהָאֱמוּנָה יַעֲזוֹר לְהַחוֹלֶה וְהָאָדוֹן יָקוּם[g] אוֹתוֹ
וְאִם שֶׁחָטָא יִמְחוֹל לוֹ הַחֲטָאִים 16 וְהִתְוַדּוּ אֶת חַטֹּאתָם
אֶחָד לְאֶחָד וְכָל אֶחָד יַעֲשֶׂה תְּפִילָה בִּשְׁבִיל חֲבֵירוֹ כִּי קָרוֹב
יַהְוֶה לְכָל קֹרְאָיו לְכֹל אֲשֶׁר יִקְרָאֵהוּ בֶּאֱמֶת[h] 17 וְגַם אֵלִיָּהוּ
הַנָּבִיא הָיָה אָדָם כָּמוֹנוּ וְעָשָׂה תְּפִילָה שֶׁלֹּא יָבֹא גֶּשֶׁם וְלֹא
בָּא גֶּשֶׁם עַל הָאָרֶץ שְׁלֹשָׁה [   ][i] שָׁנִים וָחֵצִי

---

[a] See footnote on chapter 1:3.

[b] Same meaning as "לא", also attested more than 140 times in the Mishnah.

[c] Or possibly "תִּכָּשְׁלוּ".

[d] Alternative spelling for "להתפלל" – see footnote on chapter 1:5.

[e] For the use of "ת" instead of "י", see footnote on chapter 1:4.

[f] Crossed-out letters.

[g] Although this could possibly be a scribal mistake for "יָקִים", take note that similarly, the word "שוב" in the Qal conjugation is also sometimes used with a causative meaning in the Tanach! See e.g. Nah. 2:3; Ps. 85:5; Deu. 30:3; Jer. 29:14, 30:3, 30:18, 31:23, 33:26 (Ketiv); Joel 4:1 (Ketiv), etc. Compare also "לעמוד" in Jude v. 24.

[h] Quoted from Ps. 145:18.

[i] Crossed-out (repeated) word.

but let your speech be: "Yes, yes," and "No, no"[a] – in order that you do not stumble.

13 And if one among you endures[b] something, he must pray; and if one among you is with goodness of heart,[c] this one must sing psalms.[d] 14 And if one is sick, he must call the elders of the assembly to him. And **they** must do a prayer for him and anoint him with oil in the name of Ha-Adon. 15 And the prayer of the faith will support the sick one, and Ha-Adon will raise him up; and if he had sinned, he will forgive him the sins. 16 And let them confess their sins one to another, and let everyone do a prayer for his fellow,[e] for "Yahweh is close to all who call upon him, to all who call upon him in truth."[f]

17 And also Eliyahu[g] the prophet was a man just like us, and he did a prayer[h] that rain should not come, and rain did not come on the land,[i] three and a half years.

---

[a] Meaning "let 'yes' be 'yes' and 'no' be 'no'" – i.e. do not even lie in everyday speech.

[b] Or "suffers."

[c] Meaning "is glad." Compare e.g. 1 Kin. 8:66; Is. 65:14; Pro. 15:15, etc.

[d] Or "praises" or "songs of praise."

[e] Or "companion." - Meaning "let them pray one for another."

[f] Quoted from Ps. 145:18.

[g] The Hebrew name for 'Elijah.'

[h] This does not mean that people may claim anything they want, and that they will receive it by simply believing 'hard' enough. Compare 1 Kin. 17-18. Yahweh first prophesied through Elijah that there would be no rain (1 Kin. 17:1), then Elijah prayed that it would happen (Jas. 5:17) and it did. Years later, Yahweh told him that it would rain (1 Kin. 18:1), he prayed that it would happen (1 Kin. 18:42; Jas. 5:18) and it did. Elijah did not make this up himself. If Yahweh gives a prophecy, one can pray for its fulfillment with faith and confidence in **Elohim**, and not in oneself.

[i] Or 'earth' – probably refers to a wider region than the land of Israel, but not necessarily the entire world. Compare e.g. Jer. 25:11.

18 וְאַחַר כָּךְ[a] עָשָׂה תְּפִילָה שֶׁיָּבֹא גֶשֶׁם וְנָתַן הַשָּׁמַיִם אֶת מֵימָם וְהָאָרֶץ אֶת פִּרְיָהּ 19 אַחִים בְּאִם שֶׁאֶחָד בָּכֶם יֵלֵךְ מִדֶּרֶךְ הַטּוֹב לָרַע וְאֶחָד מוֹנֵעַ אוֹתוֹ 20 דְּעוּ מִי שֶׁמְּהַפֵּךְ אוֹתוֹ מֵרִשְׁעָתוֹ (160a) זֶה מַצִּיל נְשָׁמָה אֶחָד מֵהַמָּוֶת וּמְכַפֵּר לְהַרְבֵּה עֲוֹנוֹת

---

[a] Ms. has abbreviation "ואח"כ". Could also be read as "ואחרי כן" (same meaning).

18 And afterwards he did a prayer that rain should come, so the heavens gave their waters and the earth its fruit.

19 Brothers, if one among you wants to go[a] from the good way to the evil, and someone restrains[b] him – 20 know[c] *that* whosoever turns him back from his wickedness, (160a) he[d] will deliver a neshamah[e] from the death and make atonement for many iniquities.

_____

[a] Lit. "would go."
[b] Or "holds him back" or possibly "brings him back."
[c] Plural imperative.
[d] Lit. "this *one*," but often means 'he' or 'him.'
[e] The Hebrew word for "blowing/breath," "soul" or "spirit." (See glossary for more information.)

The Hebrew Epistle of Jude

אגרת יהודה

Based on Ms. Oo.1.32 from the Cambridge University Library. Also supported by Ms. Gaster 1616 from the Manchester University Library.

Version 2.2 © April 2024

Introduction

In merely one chapter, Jude (Yehudah) mentions at least ten events[a] from the Old Testament time period, and lists the names of nine persons[b] and four places[c] known from the Old Testament! It should be obvious to any reader that Yehudah used the Old Testament scriptures as the basis of his epistle.

Consistent with the theme of Old Testament examples, the Hebrew version of Jude v. 4 seems to discuss unbelievers in **Old Testament** times while the Greek version strictly refers to unbelievers in **New Testament** times!

Jude v. 4:

<u>Translated from Oo.1.32</u>: "For some sons of man **came in among them** – of those who were already written up[d] for this condemnation[e] – and they were wicked ones, and

---

[a] 1. Faith given to the set-apart ones (see e.g. Gen. 15:6; Ex. 14:31; Num. 14:11; Heb. 11, etc.); 2. People brought out of Egypt; 3. Unbelievers destroyed; 4. Angels that sinned were cast down; 5. Sodom and Gomorrah destroyed; 6. Moses' burial; 7. Cain (and Abel); 8. Balaam tempted by profit; 9. Rebellion of Korah; 10. Enoch who prophesied.

[b] 1. Yahweh; 2. Michael; 3. Satan; 4. Moses; 5. Cain; 6. Balaam; 7. Korah; 8. Enoch; 9. Adam.

[c] 1. Egypt; 2. Sodom; 3. Gomorrah; 4. Gei-Hinnom (the valley of Hinnom, see also glossary).

[d] Or "recorded."

[e] Or "punishment."

hindered [a] the steadfast-love of Yahweh [b] in arrogance, [c] and **they did not believe in Y   and in his Mashiach**." [d]

<u>Translated from Greek</u> (ESV): "For certain people **have crept in unnoticed** who long ago were designated for this condemnation, ungodly people, who pervert the grace of our God into sensuality and deny **our** only **Master and Lord, Jesus Christ**."

In the context of the numerous Old Testament examples used by Yehudah, it is possible that "among **them**" in verse four refers to people who lived in the Old Testament time period.

On the other hand, The Greek version omits the phrase "among **them**," and reads "**our** only Master and Lord, **Jesus Christ**" instead of "Y   and **his Mashiach**." Thus, there is no hint from the Greek version that people in the Old Testament could believe in the Messiah! [e]

------

[a] Or "invalidated."

[b] The manuscript uses the Hebrew abbreviation 'ה' (he) for "Ha-Shem," which literally means 'The Name.' For further discussion on this abbreviation 'ה', see pp. 62-69. Our translations employ 'The Name' Yahweh in every instance indicated by the Hebrew manuscripts. The only grammatically possible pronunciation of יהוה, from which all other abbreviations/contractions of the Name can be formed, is   with emphasis on the second syllable. For more information, see HebrewGospels.com/yhwh.

[c] Or "presumptuously hindered the steadfast-love of Yahweh."

[d] All emphasis throughout introductory sections was added for clarity. However, in the transcript/translation section, emphasis in the English translation reflects emphasis in the Hebrew text.

[e] According to the Hebrew Gospel of John (1:36, HebrewGospels.com version) Yeshua Mashiach is "the Messenger of Yahweh." The Messenger (or 'Angel') of Yahweh [Yahweh's Mashiach] was known in the Old Testament, and led the Israelites through the wilderness and into the promised land (Ex. 3:2-6, 14:19, 23:20-23; Num. 20:16; Judg. 2:1-4). In Ex. 3:2-4, 3:7, 3:16 and Judg. 6:11-14 the 'messenger of Yahweh' is also called 'Yahweh' (i.e. Yahweh the Son). See footnote on p. 45 for a related discussion.

Furthermore, the Hebrew version of Yehudah quotes a whole verse from the Hebrew Old Testament where the Greek version does not quote from the Old Testament at all!

Jude v. 16:

Translated from Oo.1.32 (quoted from Ps. 5:10(9)): "For there is no steadfastness in his[a] mouth,[b] their inside is destruction, their throat is an open grave, they flatter with their tongue."

Translated from Greek: "These are grumblers, discontented, going with their own lusts; and their mouth speaks proud things, flattering people for the sake of gain."

Having seen these differences between the Hebrew and Greek versions of Jude, we need to ask the next question: Is the Hebrew or Greek version of Yehudah the original? We will discuss this below in "Evidence of Authenticity and Interesting Readings."

---

[a] Could mean "their" (collective use).
[b] Or "there is nothing steadfast/right in what they say."

Evidence of Authenticity and Interesting Readings

Below we will examine a few amazing differences between the Hebrew and Greek versions of Jude, which indicate that the Hebrew version is authentic, while the Greek version is a translation thereof.

Hebrew keyword repetition

Although short, the Epistle of Jude (Yehudah) contains several sections and topics of discussion. These sections are sometimes linked together by the repetition of some key word which is repeated in both sections. Below is an example:

Jude v. 19-20:

Warning: "And these are in the flesh, and not in the **Ruach**." [a, b]

Exhortation: "But you, beloved brothers, strengthen yourselves in your faith by **Ruach** Ha-Qodesh." [c, d]

The keyword 'Ruach' (Spirit) beautifully links these two verses and two sections together. Though the above theme is also visible in the Greek version of Jude, below we will study an example where the keyword theme was lost in the Greek version and only preserved in the **Hebrew** version:

---

[a] Or "Spirit."
[b] Translated from Oo.1.32.
[c] Meaning "the Set-Apart Spirit."
[d] Translated from Oo.1.32.

Jude v. 23-24:

Exhortation (from Hebrew): "...but, keep a distance[a] from the **sinners**!"[b]

Conclusion (from Hebrew): "But he who is able to keep you without doubting and to set you before Ha-Adon without any **sin**..."[c]

Here the Hebrew version has a clear theme and link between these two sections in the Epistle of Jude, but in the **Greek version** the link is rather **vague**:

Jude v. 23-24:

Exhortation (from Greek): "hating even the garment **stained by the flesh**."[d]

Conclusion (from Greek): "Now to him who is able to keep you from stumbling and to present you **blameless**..."[e]

This theme is not nearly as clear nor impressive in the Greek text as in the Hebrew. The Hebrew version uses the same root word (חטא) in both verses, while the Greek version does not.

Greek translators often rendered the same repeated Hebrew word with different synonyms, in order to create a translation which sounds elegant and avoids monotony.[f] Although the Hebrew language exhibits an abundance of synonyms (that even Greek

---

[a] Or "stay away."
[b] Translated from Oo.1.32.
[c] Translated from Oo.1.32.
[d] Quoted from the ESV.
[e] Quoted from the ESV.
[f] Apart from the example given below, compare also Ps. 17:14, 25:3, 45:4-5, 56:8, etc. in Hebrew vs. Septuagint Greek. See also footnote on pp. 245-246.

translators struggled to convey in translation)[a] the repetition of a Hebrew keyword was often used to gain one's attention, place emphasis on a specific topic and to drive the point home. Below is an example from the Hebrew Masoretic Text vs. Septuagint Greek translation:

Psalm 9:10:

Hebrew Masoretic Text:

"וִיהִי יהוה מִשְׂגָּב לַדָּךְ מִשְׂגָּב לְעִתּוֹת בַּצָּרָה:"

= "And Y   will be a **refuge** to the poor, a **refuge** in times of distress."[b]

Greek Septuagint: "καὶ ἐγένετο κύριος καταφυγὴ τῷ πένητι βοηθὸς ἐν εὐκαιρίαις ἐν θλίψει"

= "And *the* Lord was[c] a **refuge** for the poor, a **helper** in times of distress."[d]

In the above example, the original Hebrew text repeats the keyword 'refuge,' while the Greek translation elegantly but inaccurately changes the second occurrence of 'refuge' to 'helper.'

A similar example can be seen in Jude v. 8-10, where the Hebrew version repeats the same word for "despise" twice in the section

---

[a] E.g. the Hebrew Masoretic Text uses seven synonyms for "anger" in the Book of Psalms (אַף, חֵמָה, חָרוֹן, עֶבְרָה, זַעַם, כַּעַס, קֶצֶף) but the Greek Septuagint translator(s) used only two synonyms for "anger" (θυμοσ and οργη, including compound forms) to translate these seven Hebrew words. Ps. 78:49 is a good example which illustrates that the Greek translator(s) could not match the number of synonyms used in the original Hebrew.

[b] Lit. "at times in the distress."

[c] Or "is."

[d] Lit. "in times in distress."

about cursing/blasphemy, while the Greek version eliminates the repetition by using two different Greek words:

Jude v. 8-10:

Translated from Oo.1.32: "And likewise those who **despise** the authority, and curse... these *people* curse while they know nothing, and also what they do know, they **despise**."

Translated from Greek: "But likewise also these... **despise**[a] authority, and blaspheme... these *people* blaspheme whatever they do not know, and what they do know... in these things they **corrupt themselves**."

The fact that the Hebrew preserves such repeated keywords which were lost in the Greek version, is an important indication that the Hebrew version is the original, while the Greek version is an interpreted translation.

Explicit subject gapping

Another good proof for the authenticity of this Hebrew version of Jude is 'gapping.' Although there are many[b] kinds of gapping in the Hebrew language, we want to discuss one particular type here, called 'explicit subject gapping.'[c]

Explicit subject gapping is very common in the Hebrew Old Testament. For example, a sentence (or paragraph) speaking of two or more persons, will only name each person once (or perhaps twice), and afterwards simply refer to "he," "she," or "they," etc., without repeating the name(s). We also do this in English to some

---

[a] Or "reject."
[b] E.g. gapping of explicit subject, gapping of explicit object, verb gapping, preposition gapping, etc.
[c] Or 'gapping of explicit subject.' 'Gapping' is also known by the term 'ellipsis.'

degree, but not as much as they liked to do this in ancient/biblical Hebrew. In the Hebrew Old Testament this is done to the extent that one often needs to pay close attention to the context, to determine exactly who the "he... he... he... he..." is referring to – the subject often changes without any warning. We say that the explicit subject is '**gapped**,' or 'understood by context.'

In cases where confusion is very likely to occur, translators often inserted the implied explicit subject to help their readers understand the text without any difficulty.

Thus, if we compare two texts of the Bible in different languages, and find multiple and consistent examples of **gapping** in the one, and **supplied** subjects/objects in the other, we know that the less interpretive version is closer to the original. (This argument is especially strong in contexts where confusion is likely to occur if the subjects/objects are not stated explicitly.)[a] Let's first look at an example from the Hebrew Old Testament vs. the Greek Septuagint translation of the Old Testament, and then move on to an example in Jude:

Genesis 12:7:

Hebrew Masoretic Text:

"וַיֵּרָא יהוה אֶל־אַבְרָם וַיֹּאמֶר לְזַרְעֲךָ אֶתֵּן אֶת־הָאָרֶץ הַזֹּאת וַיִּבֶן שָׁם מִזְבֵּחַ..."

= "Then Y٤٠   appeared to Avram[b] and said, 'To your seed will I give this land.' And there **he built** an altar..."

---

[a] Translators always strive to remove any possible ambiguity from their translations. If the resultant translation could cause confusion, translators would not leave out the explicit subject if it existed in the original text.
[b] The Hebrew name for 'Abram.'

The explicit subject of the Hebrew verb "יִּבֶן" (he built) is **not** written in the Hebrew Bible, it is only **understood by context**. The explicit subject "Avram" is **gapped** in the second part of this verse. Because the subject is not explicitly stated in the second part of this verse, the reader might think that the pronoun "**he**" refers to Yahweh, as Yahweh is the last named subject[a] in the narrative. But from the context it is clear that it was Avram who built the altar and not Yahweh.

For easier reading and to remove any ambiguity, the Septuagint translators **supplied** (inserted) the explicit subject "Avram" in their Greek translation:

Genesis 12:7:

<u>Greek Septuagint</u>: "καὶ ὤφθη κύριος τῷ αβραμ καὶ εἶπεν αὐτῷ τῷ σπέρματί σου δώσω τὴν γῆν ταύτην. καὶ ᾠκοδόμησεν ἐκεῖ αβραμ θυσιαστήριον"

= "And *the* Lord appeared to Abram and said to him, 'To your seed I will give this land.' And there **Abram** built an altar..."

In the Septuagint Greek translation, the explicit subject "Avram" (Abram) was inserted in the second part of this verse to avoid any possible confusion. The fact that the Hebrew version has the explicit subject gapped while the Greek Septuagint has it written, clearly shows that the Hebrew is the original version and the Greek is the second-hand, interpreted translation.

Now, here is a similar example from the Hebrew vs. Greek versions of Jude:

---

[a] Although the name Abram occurs in this verse, he is only mentioned as an indirect object (the one to whom Yahweh appeared).

Jude v. 5:

Oo.1.32:

"אבל אני רוצה להודיע לכם זאת שזה שהוציא את עמו
ממצרים..."

= "But I want to make this known to you, that **he**[a] who brought his people out of Mitsrayim..."[b]

The Hebrew version of Jude v. 5 does not state the explicit subject but only refers to "**he**"[c] who brought them out of Egypt. One could then read the context and hypothesize whether the "**he**" specifically refers to Y   , or whether it specifically refers to his Messiah, as both are mentioned in the context:

Jude v. 4: "...they did not believe in **Y**   and in **his Mashiach**."

Jude v. 5: "But I want to make this known to you, that **he** who brought his people out of Mitsrayim..."

Who is the explicit subject of verse 5, is it "**Y**   or "**his Mashiach**"? The answer is not stated[d] explicitly in the Hebrew version of Jude, and this is typical of original Hebrew documents.

In this verse, various Greek translators/copyists of Jude inserted an explicit subject in an attempt to lessen the ambiguity. But

---

[a] Lit. "this *one*," but often means 'he' or 'him.'

[b] The Hebrew name for 'Egypt.'

[c] Lit. "this *one*," but often means 'he' or 'him.'

[d] A good answer based on the context of verses 1 - 5 would probably be that Yahweh brought them out of Egypt by his Messiah (the immediate context in the Hebrew version mentions both Yahweh and his Messiah). Still, there is no answer as to which name or title is the implied subject of verse 5.

incredibly, the Greek manuscripts do not even agree among themselves as to the explicit subject!

Many Greek manuscripts read[a] "κυριος" (Lord),[b] but quite a few read "ιησους" (Jesus),[c] while yet others read "θεος" (God)![d] The very oldest Greek manuscript of Jude v. 5 reads "θεος χριστος" (God Christ)[e] and some late copies read "κυριος ιησους"[f] (Lord Jesus).[g]

Which Greek reading is correct? Scholars argue back and forth about this issue.[h] Because Greek manuscripts contain so much

---

[a] Take note that Greek abbreviations like "κ̅ς̅" for "κυριος" are spelled out here for easy reading.

[b] "κυριος" (or "ο κυριος") is attested in e.g. Codex Sinaiticus, 018, 020, 044, 18, 35, 307, 436, 642, 1175, 1448, Byzantine MT, Textus Receptus, etc.

[c] "ιησους" (or "ο ιησους") is attested in e.g. Codex Alexandrinus, Codex Vaticanus, 33, 81, 88, 323, 424 (corrector), 665, 915, 1241, 1739, etc.

[d] "ο θεος" is attested in e.g. Codex Ephreami (corrector), 5, 442, 621, 623, 1243, 1845.

[e] "θεος χριστος" is attested in P72 – the oldest known copy of Jude v. 5.

[f] "κυριος ιησους" (or "ο κυριος ιησους") is attested in manuscripts 1735, L241, L591, L1178. See e.g. Tommy Wasserman, *The Epistle of Jude: Its Text and Transmission*, Almqvist and Wiksell, 2006, p 262.

[g] The reading "κυριος ιησους" (Lord Jesus) is most likely a compilation of the readings "κυριος" and "ιησους" found in various early Greek mss. However, P72 employs a compound subject "θεος χριστος" (God Christ), which cannot be a compilation from any known Greek manuscripts (no other Greek ms. reads "χριστος"). This unique reading was possibly derived from the immediate context (v. 4) which refers to both Yahweh and his Messiah in the Hebrew version. (Note that Yahweh was often translated as Theos (see pp. 62-69); and Christos is the standard Greek translation for the Hebrew word Mashiach.)

[h] E.g. "Some scholars support κύριος (Bauckham, *Relatives of Jesus*, 308–9; Landon, *A Text-Critical Study of the Epistle of Jude*, 75–76), especially on internal grounds (א Ψ, C*, 630, 1505, etc.)... Supporting Ἰησοῦς are Wikgren, 148–49; Osburn, *The Text of Jude 5*, 111–15; C. Bigg, *The Epistles of St. Peter and St. Jude*, 1901, 328; Bauckham, *Jude, 2 Peter*, 49." – Thomas R. Schreiner, *1, 2 Peter, Jude, The New American Commentary*, Broadman and Holman, 2007, p. 444 (footnote). See also Bruce Manning Metzger, *A Textual*

variation in this verse, some scholars[a] have even hypothesized that the explicit subject was not written in the 'original Greek' text, but was later filled in differently by various copyists. However, no such 'original Greek' manuscript has ever been found to settle the argument.

It turns out that this textual problem in Jude is not solved by any Greek manuscript,[b] but rather it is solved and settled by the Hebrew version: The original **Hebrew** version had no explicit subject stated, and various Greek translators/copyists inserted different subjects in their Greek manuscripts as they saw fit.

Not one of the various Greek or Greek-based readings is the original – the Hebrew reading is the original! The Latin Vulgate and the Syriac Peshitta also have the explicit subject inserted based on various Greek readings, and only the Hebrew version preserves the original uninterpreted reading.

Explicit object gapping

Explicit object gapping works just like explicit subject gapping, but the word/phrase in question is the object of the sentence rather than the subject.

Commentary on the Greek New Testament, United Bible Societies, 2nd ed., 1994, p. 657.

[a] E.g. "The best attested reading Ἰησοῦς can only be a blunder. It seems probable that the original text had only ὁ..." – Fenton John Anthony Hort, *The New Testament in the Original Greek, Appendix I, Notes on Select Readings,* Macmillan, 1882, p. 106 (appendix).

[b] The Revised Standard Version (RSV) does read "he who saved..." – however, this was only a textual emendation with no supporting manuscript evidence. The RSV footnote states that "Ancient authorities read *Jesus* or *the Lord* or *God.* The updated New Revised Standard Version removed the emendation and reads "the Lord."

Let's first discuss one such example in the Hebrew Tanach, compared against the Septuagint Greek translation:

Genesis 14:17-19:

<u>Hebrew Masoretic Text:</u>

"וַיֵּצֵא מֶלֶךְ־סְדֹם... וּמַלְכִּי־צֶדֶק מֶלֶךְ שָׁלֵם הוֹצִיא לֶחֶם וָיָיִן וְהוּא כֹהֵן לְאֵל עֶלְיוֹן: וַיְבָרֲכֵהוּ וַיֹּאמַר..."

= "Then the king of Sedom came out... And Malki-Tsedeq the king of Shalem brought out bread and wine (and he is priest of [a] El Elyon). And he blessed **him** and said..."

The explicit object of the Hebrew verb "וַיְבָרֲכֵהוּ" (he blessed him) is **not** written in the Hebrew Bible, it can only be known with certainty by reading the whole context. Because the explicit object "Abram" is gapped in the first part of verse 19, a person reading the narrative up to the point quoted above, might think that the pronoun "**him**" refers to the king of Sodom (mentioned in verse 17), or even to El Elyon (the most recent name/title in the narrative). However, when reading further, the context clearly shows that Abram is the person who was blessed in verse 19.

To ensure that no misunderstanding could occur, the Greek translators or scribes **supplied** (inserted) the explicit object "Abram" in their translation:

Genesis 14:17-19:

<u>Greek Septuagint:</u> "Ἐξῆλθεν δὲ βασιλεὺς Σοδομων... καὶ Μελχισεδεκ βασιλεὺς Σαλημ ἐξήνεγκεν ἄρτους καὶ οἶνον· ἦν δὲ ἱερεὺς τοῦ θεοῦ τοῦ ὑψίστου. καὶ ηὐλόγησεν τὸν Αβραμ καὶ εἶπεν..."

---

[a] Or "to."

= "And the king of Sodom came out... And Melchizedek the king of Salem brought out loaves and wine (and he was priest of God Most High). And he blessed **Abram** and said..."

The fact that the Hebrew version has the explicit object gapped while the Greek Septuagint has it written, shows very clearly that the Hebrew is the original, unedited text, and that the Greek Septuagint is a second-hand, interpreted translation.[a]

Now, let's investigate a similar example of explicit object gapping in the Hebrew epistle of Jude, contrasted with the Greek version:

Jude v. 25:

Oo.1.32:

"לזה תהיה כבוד ותפארת ומלכות מעולם ועד עולם אמן"

= "to **him**[b] be honor and glory and kingship, from everlasting and unto everlasting,[c] amein!"[d]

Byzantine Greek: "μόνῳ σοφῷ Θεῷ σωτῆρι ἡμῶν, δόξα καὶ μεγαλωσύνη, κράτος καὶ ἐξουσία, καὶ νῦν καὶ εἰς πάντας τοὺς αἰῶνας. ἀμήν."

---

[a] Note that this argument is especially strong in a context where confusion is likely to occur if the object is gapped (as in the example from Gen. 14 shown above). If there is no ambiguity, translators would not be inclined to add an explanation.

[b] Lit. "this *one*," but often means 'he' or 'him.'

[c] A Hebrew idiom which often means "forever and ever" – see e.g. Jer. 7:7, 25:5; 1 Chr. 16:36; Neh. 9:5; Ps. 41:14(13), 103:17, 106:48.

[d] When the Hebrew word "אמן" (*amein*) is used adverbially, it means "surely" or "truly."

= "to **the only wise God our Saviour**, be glory and majesty, dominion and authority, both now and throughout all eternity. Amen."

The Greek version supplies the explicit subject "**the only wise God our Saviour**" where the Hebrew has it gapped and simply reads "him." [a] Again, discrepancies exist between various Greek manuscripts as to the exact wording of this verse:

Jude v. 25:

<u>Byzantine MT</u>: "μόνῳ σοφῷ θεῷ σωτῆρι ἡμῶν"

= "to the only wise God our Saviour"

<u>Miniscule 1175</u>: "μονω σοφω σωτηρι ημων"

= "to the Only Wise, our Saviour" [b]

<u>Several famous Greek manuscripts</u>: [c] "μονω θεω σωτηρι ημων δια ιησου χριστου του κυριου ημων"

= "to the only God our Saviour through Jesus Christ our Lord"

<u>Papyrus 72</u>: "μονω θεω ημων αυτω δοξα... δια ιησου χριστου του κυριου [d] ημων αυτω δοξα"

= "to our only God, to him be glory... through Jesus Christ our Lord, to him be glory"

---

[a] Lit. "this *one*," but often means 'he' or 'him.'
[b] Or possibly "to our only wise Saviour."
[c] E.g. Codex Sinaiticus, Codex Alexandrinus, Codex Vaticanus, etc. The Syriac Peshitta and Latin Vulgate also use very similar wording.
[d] Ms. reads "κυω̅" – indicating that the "ω" is simply a mistake.

These variants obviously represent the interpretation of various translators/editors.[a]

The Hebrew reading simply has "him," and various interpreters/translators supplied the explicit subject as they thought best. The Syriac Peshitta and the Latin vulgate also insert the explicit object, based on the Greek.

This again shows the uninterpreted Hebrew reading to be the original,[b] and the various differing Greek and Greek-based readings to be interpreted, second-hand translations.

As with the Hebrew Revelation and James, this Hebrew version of Jude shows a surprising amount of authenticity which cannot be reclaimed from the Greek, Aramaic or Latin versions. Therefore, we can conclude that this Hebrew textual tradition has preserved the original text of the Epistle of Jude more accurately than the Greek, Aramaic and Latin versions.

These unique readings and important examples of gapping in the Hebrew version indicate that the Greek text of Jude was translated from the original Hebrew text, with added interpretations and expansions.

---

[a] Clearly, the different Greek readings cannot all be the original. So, how did these different Greek readings originate? If an explicit object was written in the so-called 'Original Greek' version, one would not expect such extended variations to occur in later copies. But if, on the other hand, the original version did not state the explicit subject, it is foreseeable that various scribes/translators would attempt to clear up the ambiguity – and of course, they would come up with various different wordings. Unfortunate for proponents of Greek primacy of the Epistle of Jude, there are no known Greek manuscripts which have the explicit object gapped in Jude v. 25.

[b] The Hebrew reading of Jude v. 25 in Oo.1.32 is the only version which can be regarded as the base text from which all other versions could have originated.

This page is intentionally left blank.

אִיגֶּרֶת יְהוּדָה

1 (160a)^a יְהוּדָה עֶבֶד מִיֵשׁוּעַ^b הַמָּשִׁיחַ אֲבָל אָח אֶחָד מִן יַעֲקֹב הַשָּׁלִיחַ הַמְקוּדָּשִׁים בְּיַהְוֶה^c הָאָב וְנִסְתָּרִים בְּיֵשׁוּעַ הַמָּשִׁיחַ 2 יַהְוֶה יִתֵּן לָכֶם הַרְבֵּה אַהֲבָה וְחֶסֶד וְשָׁלוֹם וְרַחֲמִים 3 אַחִים אֲהוּבִים אַחַר שֶׁרָצִיתִי לִכְתּוֹב לָכֶם מִקְדוּשָׁתֵינוּ

---

^a The number stated in brackets is the corresponding folio number of Oo.1.32 on which this Hebrew transcript is based.

^b The short rabbinic spelling "ישו" used in the ms. was replaced with the full spelling "ישוע". See footnotes on p. 6 for more information.

^c The Hebrew manuscript uses an abbreviation "ה׳" for "השם". It was common practice for many scribes to write 'Ha-Shem' or some abbreviation rather than writing the full name "יהוה". For further evidence that this abbreviation for 'Ha-Shem' actually represents the name YHWH, see footnotes on Jas. 1:1 and Rev. 1:1. For a full justification that the true pronunciation of the Name is "יַהְוֶה", based on the Masoretic Text, see HebrewGospels.com/yhwh.

The Letter of Yehudah

1:1 (160a) Yehudah,[a] a servant of Yeshua[b] Ha-Mashiach[c] but a brother of Ya'aqov[d] the sent one, *to* those who are set apart in `ʾʿ     ʾ)`[e] the Father and hidden[f] in[g] Yeshua Ha-Mashiach. ₂ May Y̅⁻᾿   ᾿ give you much love and faithful kindness[h] and shalom and mercy.

₃ Beloved brothers, after I wanted to write to you about our set-apartness, [i]

---

[a] The Hebrew name for 'Jude' or 'Judah.'

[b] The Hebrew name for 'Jesus' – meaning 'Yahweh is Salvation.'

[c] Or "The Messiah." The Hebrew word "משיח" (*mashiach*) was translated into the Greek *'christos'* but should be clearly distinguished from the Catholic symbolic 'Christ.' Literal meaning: "anointed one," usually referring to someone anointed as king of Israel, or as priest or prophet. However, when used as a name, it refers to the Son of Yahweh, whom he anointed as the ultimate King of Israel, the Everlasting High Priest, and the Prophet who would speak Yahweh's words to his people – and if anyone disobeys him, Yahweh himself will require it of him. See Deu. 18:18-19 and Acts 3:22-23.

[d] The Hebrew name for 'James' or 'Jacob.'

[e] The manuscript uses the Hebrew abbreviation "הׄ" for 'Ha-Shem,' which literally means "The Name." Today still, many Jews will read "Ha-Shem" when they see the Creator's Hebrew name יהוה. For further discussion on this abbreviation 'הׄ', see pp. 62-69. Our translations employ 'The Name' Yahweh in every instance indicated by the Hebrew manuscripts. The only grammatically possible pronunciation of יהוה, from which all other abbreviations/contractions of the Name can be formed, is "Yah-weh" – with emphasis on the second syllable. For more information, see HebrewGospels.com/yhwh.

[f] Or "concealed." Compare e.g. Ps. 32:7, Ps. 61:5(4), where the same Hebrew root-word is used for "hiding place" or "shelter."

[g] Or "set-apart by Yahweh the Father and hidden by Yeshua."

[h] Hebrew "חסד" (*chesed*) – could also be translated as "steadfast love" or "faithfulness."

[i] Or "sanctification."

מָצָאתִי לְצֹרֶךְ לְהוֹכִיחַ לָכֶם בִּכְתָבִים[a] שֶׁתִּתְחַזְּקוּ אֶתְכֶם
בָּאֱמוּנָה שֶׁנוּתַּן[b] לַקְּדוֹשִׁים ‚ 4 כִּי אֵיזֶה בְּנֵי אָדָם בָּאִים בֵּנֵיהֶם
מִן אוֹתָם שֶׁנִּכְתָּבִים כְּבָר לָזֹאת הָעוֹנֶשׁ וְהֵמָּה רְשָׁעִים
וּמְעַכְּבִים הַחֶסֶד מִיַּהְוֶה בְּמֵזִיד וְאֵינָם מַאֲמִינִים בְּיַהְוֶה
וּבִמְשִׁיחוֹ ‚ 5 אֲבָל אֲנִי רוֹצֶה לְהוֹדִיעַ לָכֶם זֹאת שֶׁזֶּה[c] שֶׁהוֹצִיא
אֶת עַמּוֹ מִמִּצְרַיִם הֵמִית שְׁנֵי פְּעָמִים לְהָאֵינוֹ[e,d] מַאֲמִינִים ‚ 6
וְגַם הַמַּלְאָכִים שֶׁחָטְאוּ

---

[a] Or possibly "בַּכְּתָבִים".

[b] Note that masculine verbs are occasionally used with feminine subjects in Hebrew. See e.g. Judg. 21:21; 1 Sam. 25:27; 1 Kin. 22:36; Dan. 8:9; Neh. 6:9, 13:19; 2 Chr. 15:7, 20:37, etc.

[c] Margin reads "שזה" – in different script than main text. (There is no difference between the note and the word in main text, except for the script.)

[d] Or possibly "לְהָאֵינוּ" (alternative pronunciation). Also note that in the Hebrew Revelation and James, "אינו" or "אינה" is generally used instead of "אין". The "ו" or "ה" at the end does not always represent a third person singular pronominal suffix.

[e] Note that the definite article is often not merged with the inseparable prepositions in the Hebrew Revelation, James and Jude. This also happens occasionally in the Tanach, e.g. Gen. 39:11; Deu. 6:24; 1 Sam. 9:13, 13:21; Jer. 44:22; Ezek. 40:25, 47:22; Ps. 36:6; Eccl. 8:1; Ezra 9:7, 9:15; Neh. 5:11, 9:10, 9:19, 12:38; 2 Chr. 10:7, 25:10, 29:27, etc.

I found it necessary to rebuke you in writing[a] that you should strengthen yourselves in the faith[b] which was given to the set-apart ones. ₄ For some sons of man[c] came in among them – of those who were already written up[d] for this condemnation[e] – and they were wicked ones, and hindered[f] the steadfast-love of Y   in arrogance,[g] and they did not believe in Yᵉ'   and in his Mashiach.

₅ But I want to make this known to you, that he[h] who brought his people out of Mitsrayim,[i] killed those who did not believe, **two times**.[j] ₆ And also the messengers[k] who sinned,

---

[a] Lit. "by writings" (plural). Could also possibly refer to the "writings" or "scriptures" – on which Jude based his epistle.

[b] Lit. "faithfulness." Hebrew "אמונה" (*emunah*) – refers to both believing and doing (being faithful). See e.g. James 2:19-25[20-26]; 2 Chr. 19:9; 2 Kin. 12:16(15); Is. 59:4; Hos. 2:22(20); Ps. 33:4, 143:1, etc.

[c] Or "descendants of Adam," meaning "people" or "humans."

[d] Or "recorded."

[e] Or "punishment."

[f] Or "invalidated."

[g] Or "presumptuously hindered the steadfast-love of Yahweh."

[h] Lit. "this *one*," but often means 'he' or 'him.'

[i] The Hebrew name for 'Egypt.'

[j] Possibly refers to the second death, see v. 6-7 ("future day of judgment... the fire of Gei-Hinnom for ever") and compare Rev. 2:10[11], 20:6, 20:14, 21:8. Could also possibly refer to the rebellion of Korah (v. 11, see also Num. 16) in which Yahweh (i) killed more than 250 leaders, and (ii) the next day killed 14700 people who complained about this judgment.

[k] Plural of Hebrew "מלאך" (*mal'ach*). Used for both human and heavenly messengers. The English word 'angel' is not really a translation – only a transliteration of the Greek '*aggelos*' (messenger). Besides, the average person reading 'angel' would probably envisage some female figure with wings. Heavenly '*mal'achim*' or messengers are distinct from the cherubim; they do not have wings and appear as men. ('Angels' and 'men' are used interchangeably – see e.g. Gen. 18. Compare Mat. 28:2-5 and John 20:12 vs. Mark 16:5 and Luke 24:4, also see Heb. 13:2.) Ironically, the 'angels' depicted in many Christian books look more like the evil spirits described in Zec. 5:9.

וְנֶחְדְּפוּ^a מִלְמַעְלָה הֵמָּה נִסְתָּרִים בַּחוֹשֶׁךְ עַד הַיּוֹם^b הַדִּין
הֶעָתִיד , וְגַם הַמְּקוֹמוֹת סְדוֹם וַעֲמוֹרָה וְכַדּוֹמֶה לָזֶה בָּאִים
לְמָשָׁל וְסוֹבְלִים לְעַד אֵשׁ שֶׁל גֵּיהִנֹּם^c ₈ וְכַדּוֹמֶה לָזֶה אֵילוּ
שֶׁמְּבַזִּים הַשְּׂרָרוּת וּמְקַלְלִים לַמַּלְכוּת , אֲבָל הַמַּלְאָךְ מִיכָאֵל
בְּשָׁעָה שֶׁחוֹלֵק עִם הַשָּׂטָן בִּשְׁבִיל הַקֶּבֶר שֶׁל מֹשֶׁה אֲפִילוּ
הָכֵי לֹא קִלֵּל אוֹתוֹ רַק אָמַר לוֹ

---

^a Alternative spelling for "ונהדפו".

^b Note that this word has the definite article and is still in construct state based on context. This phenomenon is very common in the Hebrew Revelation, James and Jude, and also occurs in the Tanach – see e.g. Judg. 16:14; 1 Kin. 14:24; 2 Kin. 16:14, 23:17; Jer. 25:26; 1 Chr. 9:26, etc.

^c Alternative spelling for "גיא הנם". The full title found in the Tanach is "גיא בן הנם".

and were thrust down from above, they are being hidden in darkness until the future day of judgment. ₇ And also the places Sedom ᵃ and ʾAmorah, ᵇ who have likewise ᶜ become a proverb, ᵈ and are bearing ᵉ *the* fire of Gei-Hinnom ᶠ **for ever**.

₈ And likewise ᵍ those who despise the authority, ʰ and curse ⁱ the kingship. ʲ ₉ But the messenger Michael, ᵏ while disputing with Ha-Satan ˡ because of the grave of Mosheh, ᵐ did not even ⁿ curse him but said to him,

---

ᵃ The Hebrew name for 'Sodom.'

ᵇ The Hebrew name for 'Gomorrah.'

ᶜ Lit. "like this."

ᵈ Or "parable."

ᵉ Or "suffering."

ᶠ Lit. "The valley of Hinnom." This Hebrew word is transliterated into Greek as *'Gehenna,'* and is inaccurately translated as 'Hell.' This is a literal valley right next to Jerusalem ordained for future punishment. See Mat. 25:41-46 in the HebrewGospels.com version: "And then he will say to those who are on the left side... go into the fire of Gei-Hinnom, which is prepared for Ha-Satan and his messengers... And these will go into the fire of Gei-Hinnom, but the righteous ones will go into everlasting light." To learn more about the Biblical definition of *'Gei-Hinnom,'* see Jer. 7:30-33, Is. 30:33, 66:24, etc.

ᵍ Lit. "like this."

ʰ Or "rulership."

ⁱ Or "speak with contempt of" or "declare insignificant." In context this is a synonym of "despise."

ʲ Could mean 'authority of the king.'

ᵏ Pronounced "Mi-cha-el" in Hebrew.

ˡ The Hebrew word "שׂטן" (*satan*) literally means "adversary" or "accuser." If it has the definite article (The Adversary) it is normally used as a title (e.g. Zech. 3:1; Job 1:6-11; Mat. 4:1; Mark 1:13, etc.) and is transliterated as *'Ha-Satan'*; however, *'satan'* (usually without the article, or plural) is used for 'enemy/adversary' (e.g. 1 Sam. 29:4; 2 Sam. 19:23(22); 1 Kin. 5:18(5:4), 11:14; Mat. 16:23, etc.) or as a synonym of 'demon' (e.g. Mat. 8:31; Mark 3:23; Rev. 18:2, etc.).

ᵐ The Hebrew name for 'Moses.'

ⁿ Lit. "even so did not curse him."

הָאָדוֹן יַעֲנוּשׁ אוֹתְךָ 10 אֲבָל אֵילוּ מְקַלְלִים וְלֹא יוֹדְעִים שׁוּם
דָּבָר וְאַף מַה שֶׁיּוֹדְעִים הֵמָּה מְבַזִּים 11 וְאוֹי לָהֶם כִּי הֵמָּה
הוֹלְכִים עַל הַדֶּרֶךְ שֶׁל קַיִן וְנוֹפְלִים בַּנִּסָּיוֹן שֶׁל בִּלְעָם
בִּשְׁבִיל אֵיזֶה רְוָוחִים וְנֶהֱרָגִים בִּשְׁבִיל הַמַּחֲלוֹקֶת שֶׁל קֹרַח 12
וְהֵמָּה בַּעֲלֵי גֵּיאוּת עִם מַתְּנוֹתֵיכֶם וְהֵמָּה כַּעֲנָנִים בְּלִי מַיִם
שֶׁהוֹלְכִים בָּרוּחַ וְאִילָנוֹת[a] שֶׁאֵינָם נוֹשְׂאִם[b] פֵּירוֹת 13 וּכְמוֹ
גַּלֵּי הַיָּם שֶׁזּוֹרְקִים לַחוּץ רֶפֶשׁ וְטִיט 14 וְגַם מִזֹּאת נִיבָּא חֲנוֹךְ
הַשְּׁבִיעָה מֵאָדָם וְאָמַר רְאֵה הָאָדוֹן יָבֹא עִם אַלְפֵי אֲלָפִים
רִבְבוֹת קְדוֹשִׁים 15 לַעֲשׂוֹת מִשְׁפָּט לָרְשָׁעִים בִּשְׁבִיל
מַעֲשֵׂיהֶם הָרָעִים 16 כִּי אֵין בְּפִיהוּ נְכוֹנָה קִרְבָּם הַוּוֹת קֶבֶר
פָּתוּחַ גְּרוֹנָם לְשׁוֹנָם יַחֲלִיקוּן[c]

---

[a] Could also be pointed with a Dagesh as "וְאִילָנּוֹת".

[b] Alternative spelling for "נושאים". Such 'defective' spellings of masculine plural nouns/participles are commonly found in the Tanach, especially if the word already contains a vowel letter "י" or "ו". See e.g. Gen. 1:21 (תנינם), 25:24 (תומם); Ex. 8:10 (חמרם); Lev. 10:16 (הנותרם). Compare also Jas. 2:6 and 4:15.

[c] Quoted from Ps. 5:10.

"Ha-Adon[a] condemns[b] you." 10 But these *people* curse while they know nothing, and also what they do know,[c] they despise.

11 And woe to them! – For they are walking on the way of Qayin,[d] and are falling into the temptation of Bil'am[e] because of some profit, and are being killed because of the dispute[f] of Qorach.[g] 12 And they are prideful[h] with your gifts; and[i] they are like clouds without water which go with the wind, and trees that do not bear fruit, 13 and like the waves of the sea that throw out mire and mud.

14 And Chanoch,[j] the seventh from Adam, also prophesied about **this**, and said, "Look![k] – Ha-Adon will come with thousands of thousands, ten thousands of set-apart ones, 15 to execute judgment on the wicked ones because of their evil deeds." 16 "For there is no steadfastness in his[l] mouth,[m] their inside is destruction,[n] their throat is an open grave, they flatter with their tongue."[o]

---

[a] Or "The Lord" – Adon is the Hebrew word for 'lord' or 'master.'
[b] Or "Ha-Adon, he will punish you."
[c] Likely refers to people who know the Torah (Yahweh's instructions/law) but refuse to obey. See e.g. Rom. 1:32.
[d] The Hebrew name for 'Cain.'
[e] The Hebrew name for 'Balaam.'
[f] Or "division" – probably used with a double meaning. (See Num. 16.)
[g] The Hebrew name for 'Korah.'
[h] Or "proud" – lit. "owners of pride."
[i] Or "but."
[j] The Hebrew name for 'Enoch.'
[k] Or "behold."
[l] Could mean "their" (collective use).
[m] Or "there is nothing steadfast/right in what they say." – Meaning that they always tell lies, compare John 8:44.
[n] Lit. "destructions" (plural).
[o] Quoted from Ps. 5:10(9).

17 אֲבָל אַתֶּם אַחִים אֲהוּבִים תִּזְכְּרוּ בְּהַדִּבּוּר שֶׁנֶּאֱמַר
מִכַּתְּחִילָה מֵהַשְּׁלוּחִים[a] מֵאֲדוֹנֵינוּ יֵשׁוּעַ הַמָּשִׁיחַ 18 שֶׁאָמְרוּ
לָכֶם כִּי בְּאַחֲרִית הַיָּמִים יִהְיוּ אֶצְלֵיכֶם[b] לֵצָנִים שֶׁהוֹלְכִים
אַחֲרֵי תַאֲווֹתֵיהֶם 19 וְאֵילוּ הֵמָּה בַּבָּשָׂר וְלֹא בָרוּחַ 20 אֲבָל
אַתֶּם אַחִים אֲהוּבִים חַזְּקוּ אֶתְכֶם בֶּאֱמוּנָתֵיכֶם[c] עַל יַד הָרוּחַ
הַקּוֹדֶשׁ 21 וְתַעַמְדוּ בְּאַהֲבַת יַהְוֶה וּתְצַפִּים[d] עַל הָרַחֲמִים
מֵאֲדוֹנֵינוּ יֵשׁוּעַ לְחַיִּים (160b) לָעַד

---

[a] Based on the color manuscript photos, it seems that the scribe might have written "מהשליחים", and then changed it to "מהשלוחים".

[b] In the Tanach, a number of prepositions take a 'plural' form when a suffix is attached, e.g. "עֲלֵיכֶם" (Ex. 5:21); "אַחֲרֵיהֶם" (Gen. 41:23). In the Hebrew Revelation, James and Jude, the 'plural' form is used with a wider range of prepositions whenever a second person suffix is attached. Compare also footnote on verse 20.

[c] In the Tanach, second person plural suffixes are normally attached to feminine plural nouns with a "יְ" helping vowel, e.g. "בְּנֹתֵיכֶם" (Ex. 3:22); "חַטֹּאתֵיכֶם" (Amos 5:12). In the Hebrew Revelation, James and Jude, the use of such helping vowels between the noun and suffix has been extended to singular nouns as well (the "יְ" does not make the noun plural). This is also rarely attested in the Tanach, e.g. "שְׁבוּתֵיכֶם" (Zeph. 3:20) and similarly (with plural-like form) "מִשְׁנְאָתֶיךָ" (Ezek. 35:11). Compare also footnote on verse 18.

[d] This is either an 'imperfect' verb with a participle ending (such mixed forms do occasionally occur in the Tanach, e.g. "משתחויתם" in Ezek. 8:16; see also "תבאתי" in 1 Sam. 25:34 (Ketiv), which looks like a combination of the perfect "באת" and imperfect "תבאי"); or else this could possibly be a mistake for "מְצַפִּים" or "תְּצַפּוּ". Compare also Jas. 4:5 and Rev. 16:9.

17 But you, beloved brothers, you must remember the word which was said from the beginning by the sent ones of our Adon Yeshua Ha-Mashiach, 18 that they said to you that, "In the last days[a] there will be scoffers beside[b] you, who walk after their desires."[c] 19 And these are in the flesh, and not in the Ruach.[d]

20 But you, beloved brothers, strengthen yourselves in your faith[e] by Ruach Ha-Qodesh.[f] 21 And stand[g] in the love of Y‧ ‧ and wait[h] on the mercies of our Adon Yeshua for eternal life,[i]

---

[a] Lit. "At the end of the days."
[b] Or "near" or "alongside."
[c] Or "their *own* lusts."
[d] The Hebrew word for "spirit," "breath" or "wind." (See glossary for more information.)
[e] Lit. "faithfulness." Hebrew "אמונה" (*emunah*) – refers to both believing and doing (being faithful). See e.g. James 2:19-25[20-26]; 2 Chr. 19:9; 2 Kin. 12:16(15); Is. 59:4; Hos. 2:22(20); Ps. 33:4, 143:1, etc.
[f] Meaning "the Set-Apart Spirit."
[g] Or "continue."
[h] Or "look with expectation" or "look with hope."
[i] Lit. "for life for ever."

‬₂₂ וְגַם אַתֶּם תִּהְיוּ רַחֲמִים‪ᵃ‬ [ ] ‪ᵇ‬ ₂₃ אֵיזֶה מִכֶּם בְּמַעֲשִׂים
טוֹבִים וְתִרְחֲקוּ מִן הַחַטָּאִים ₂₄ אֲבָל זֶה שֶׁיּוּכַל לִשְׁמֹר
אֶתְכֶם בְּלִי סָפֵק וְלַעֲמוֹד‪ᶜ‬ אֶתְכֶם לִפְנֵי הָאָדוֹן בְּלִי שׁוּם
חֵטְא ₂₅ לָזֶה תִּהְיֶה כָּבוֹד וְתִפְאֶרֶת וּמַלְכוּת מֵעוֹלָם וְעַד
עוֹלָם אָמֵן

ᵃ Possibly a mistake for "רַחֲמָנִים".

ᵇ Crossed-out letters.

ᶜ Although this could possibly be a mistake for "ולהעמיד" = "וְלַעֲמִיד",
compare a similar use of a Qal verb with causative meaning in Jas. 5:15.

(160b) 22 and also you yourselves must be merciful. 23 Indeed, some of you are with[a] good deeds, but, keep a distance[b] from the sinners![c]

24 But he[d] who is able to keep you without doubting and to set you before Ha-Adon without any sin, 25 to him[e] be honor and glory and kingship, from everlasting and unto everlasting,[f] amein![g]

---

[a] Or "some of you do have."

[b] Or "stay away."

[c] Or "But those of you who are with good deeds, you must keep a distance from the sinners."

[d] Lit. "this *one*," but often means 'he' or 'him.'

[e] Lit. "this *one*," but often means 'he' or 'him.'

[f] A Hebrew idiom which often means "forever and ever" – see e.g. Jer. 7:7, 25:5; 1 Chr. 16:36; Neh. 9:5; Ps. 41:14(13), 103:17, 106:48.

[g] When the Hebrew word "אמן" (*amein*) is used adverbially, it means "surely" or "truly."

Glossary

Adon   (Pl. *'adonim'*) Standard Hebrew word for 'lord' or 'master.'

Amein   Hebrew pronunciation of 'Amen.' When the Hebrew word "אמן" (*amein*) is used adverbially, it means "surely" or "truly." When used as a title, it means "Sure," "Faithful" or "Truth."

Avraham   The Hebrew name for 'Abraham.'

Bavel   The Hebrew name for 'Babylon.'

Dawid   The Hebrew name for 'David.'

El   Usually translated as 'God.' In Hebrew however, the word 'luck' or 'fortune' is pronounced as "gad" and sometimes as "god" (medieval) – see e.g. Gen. 30:10-11; Josh. 11:17; Isa. 65:11. Therefore we prefer not to use 'God.'

Eloah   Similar to El, see above note.

Elohim   Plural of Eloah, with same meaning (see above).

Gei-Hinnom   Lit. "The valley of Hinnom." This Hebrew word is transliterated into Greek as *'Gehenna,'* and is inaccurately translated as 'Hell.' This is a literal valley right next to Jerusalem ordained for future punishment. See Mat. 25:41-46 in the HebrewGospels.com version: "And then he will say to those who are on the left side... go into the fire of Gei-Hinnom, which is prepared for Ha-Satan and his messengers... And these will go into the fire of Gei-Hinnom, but the righteous ones will go into everlasting light." To learn more about the Biblical definition of *'Gei-Hinnom,'* see Jer. 7:30-33, Is. 30:33, 66:24, etc.

Ha-Mashiach   Or "The Messiah." The Hebrew word "משיח" (*mashiach*) was translated into the Greek *'christos'* but should be clearly distinguished from the Catholic symbolic 'Christ.' Literal meaning: "anointed one," usually referring to someone anointed as king of Israel, or as priest or prophet. However, when used as a name, it refers to the Son of Yahweh, whom he anointed as the ultimate King of Israel, the Everlasting High Priest, and the Prophet who would speak Yahweh's words to his people – and if anyone disobeys him, Yahweh himself will require it of him. See Deu. 18:18-19 and Acts 3:22-23.

Ha-Satan The Hebrew word "שׂטן" (*satan*) literally means "adversary" or "accuser." If it has the definite article (The Adversary) it is normally used as a title (e.g. Zech. 3:1; Job 1:6-11; Mat. 4:1; Mark 1:13, etc.) and is transliterated as '*Ha-Satan*'; however, '*satan*' (usually without the article, or plural) is used for 'enemy/adversary' (e.g. 1 Sam. 29:4; 2 Sam. 19:23(22); 1 Kin. 5:18(5:4), 11:14; Mat. 16:23, etc.) or as a synonym of 'demon' (e.g. Mat. 8:31; Mark 3:23; Rev. 18:2, etc.).

Mashiach See "Ha-Mashiach."

Menorah (Pl. '*menorot.*') The Hebrew word for 'lampstand.'

Mitsrayim The Hebrew name for 'Egypt.'

Mosheh The Hebrew name for 'Moses.'

Nephesh (Pl. '*nephashot.*') Lit. "breath" (e.g. Job 11:20, 41:13), can mean 'person' (e.g. Gen. 12:5, 14:21, 46:18-27; Ex. 16:16; Lev. 17:15), 'life' (e.g. Gen. 19:17; Lev. 17:11), 'soul' (e.g. Ps. 49:16-20(15-19); Gen. 35:18; Ex. 30:16; Is. 10:18; Ezek. 18:4), etc. But take note that nephesh rarely (if ever) refers to the spirit of a human [which continues to exist after a person dies] (contrast ruach and neshamah). Biblically speaking, a nephesh can die (e.g. Num. 6:6, 9:6; Lev. 22:4; Ezek. 13:19). In the Hebrew Bible, nephesh often refers to a person's being [also for animals] or to a person's 'self' (e.g. Deu. 4:9; Num. 30:14; 1 Sam. 18:1; Gen. 1:20, 1:30, 12:13, 27:4); but is also often associated with a person's will, desire or feelings (e.g. Ex. 23:9; Lev. 26:15; Deu. 24:15; Judg. 16:16, 18:25, 2 Sam. 3:21; Is. 42:1, 55:2, Jer. 13:17, Ezek. 23:22, 24:21; Hos. 4:8; Zech. 11:8). It can also possibly refer to a person's throat [through which air is breathed] (e.g. Ps. 69:2(1), 124:4-5; Jon. 2:6).

Neshamah (Pl. '*neshamot.*') The Hebrew word for "blowing/breath," "soul" or "spirit." Neshamah is also specifically used to refer to a person's "spirit/soul" which continues to exist after a person dies (e.g. Rev. 6:9). Neshamah can overlap with nephesh [when referring to blowing/breath] (e.g. Gen. 2:7; Josh. 11:11); and with ruach [when referring to blowing/wind] (2 Sam. 22:16; Ps. 18:16; Job 4:9); and with ruach [when referring to spirit/breath] (e.g. Job. 27:3, 33:4, 34:14; Dan. 10:17); but note that neshamah is only used with reference to Yahweh and humans, there is no definite example where neshamah is used for animals. (Compare Deu. 20:16 vs. Josh. 11:14, which indicates that neshamah did not include the animals.) In contrast to neshamah, nephesh and ruach are used with reference to Yahweh, humans and animals.

Qadosh   Lit. "set-apart" (for a special purpose, usually for Yahweh). It may also be used with the connotation of "blessed."

Ruach   (Pl. *'ruchot.'*) The Hebrew word for "spirit," "breath" or "wind." Apart from these basic uses, ruach can also refer to a person's emotions, will or attitude (e.g. Gen. 26:35, 41:8; Josh. 2:11; Judg. 8:3; Is. 57:15; Ps. 32:2; Job 21:4; Pro. 16:18). It can overlap with nephesh [when meaning "breath"] (e.g. Gen. 7:15; Ex. 15:8; Is. 11:4; Jer. 10:14, 51:17; Ps. 33:6, 135:17; Job 12:10). Ruach can also refer to the "spirit" of a human, which continues to exist after a person dies, and can thus overlap with neshamah [when referring to "spirit/soul"] (e.g. Acts 7:59; John 19:30 (HebrewGospels.com version); Eccl. 3:21, 12:7; Num. 16:22, 27:16; Is. 57:16).

Ruach Ha-Qodesh   The Hebrew phrase for "the Set-Apart Spirit."

Ruchot   See "Ruach."

Satan   See "Ha-Satan."

Sedom   The Hebrew name for 'Sodom.'

Shalom   Lit. "wholeness," "completeness" or "well-being," can also mean 'peace.' *'Shalom'* is also used as a greeting.

She'ol   The place of the dead. To learn more about the Biblical definition of She'ol, see: Gen. 37:35, Num. 16:30-33, 1 Sam. 2:6, Is. 14:9-15, Ezek. 31:15-18, Jonah 2:3(2), etc.

Shophar   (Pl. *'shopharot.'*) The Hebrew word for "ram's horn" or "trumpet."

Tanach   *'Tanach'* is a Hebrew acronym for *'Torah, Nevi'im, Ketuvim,'* or in English, 'The Law, the Prophets, the Writings.' In other words, it refers to the entire so-called 'Old Testament.'

Torah   The Hebrew word *'torah'* means "instruction" or "law." The Creator established his perfect and everlasting Torah (instruction/law) as the basis of his covenant with his people. These instructions/laws were recorded by Mosheh in written form, and thus the Torah is also known as the 'Law of Moses,' although in reality it is Yahweh's law/instructions for his people. When Torah is used as a name, it can refer specifically to the written law (as covenant stipulations), but also more generally to the first five books of the Bible (the Pentateuch), or sometimes even to the entire Old Testament.

Ya'aqov   The Hebrew name for 'James' or 'Jacob.'

Yahweh   The manuscript uses the Hebrew abbreviation "הֿ" for '*Ha-Shem,*' which literally means "The Name." Today still, many Jews will read "*Ha-Shem*" when they see the Creator's Hebrew name יהוה. Our translations employ 'The Name' Yahweh in every instance indicated by the Hebrew manuscripts. As for pronunciation, the only grammatically possible pronunciation, from which all other abbreviations/contractions can be formed, is "*Yah-weh*" – with emphasis on the second syllable. For more information, see HebrewGospels.com/yhwh.

Yehudah   The Hebrew name for 'Jude,' 'Judah' or 'Judea.'

Yehudim   The Hebrew name for 'Jews.'

Yerushalayim   The Hebrew name for 'Jerusalem.'

Yeshua   The Hebrew name for 'Jesus.' '*Yeshua*' is short for '*Yehoshua,*' and means 'Yahweh is Salvation,' see Mat. 1:21.

Yisrael   The Hebrew name for 'Israel.'

Yochanan   The Hebrew name for 'John.'

Selected Bibliography

The following resources were found useful while preparing this book. However, we do not endorse the authors nor contents of the works listed below.

Alan E. Brooke, Norman McLean et al., *Critical Apparatus to the Cambridge Edition of the Greek Septuagint*, Electronic Text digitized by Matthew T. Williams and Nathan Smith, 2010.

Alexander Roberts, *Greek, the Language of Christ and His Apostles*, Longmans Green and Co., 1888.

— *A Short Proof that Greek was the Language of Christ*, Alexander Gardner Publishers, 1893.

Alfred Rahlfs, *Septuaginta*, 2nd ed., Deutsche Bibelgesellschaft, 2006.

A. T. Robertson, *A Grammar of the Greek New Testament in the Light of Historical Research*, Broadman Press, 1934.

Barbara Aland, Kurt Aland et al., *Novum Testamentum Graece, 28th revised edition*, Deutsche Bibelgesellschaft, 2012.

B. Blayney et al., *The Treasury of Scripture Knowledge*, Macdonald Publishing Company, 1982.

Bill Warren, *The Center for New Testament Textual Studies: NT Critical Apparatus*, 3rd ed. (CNTTS 3), the New Orleans Baptist Theological Seminary, 2021.

Bruce M. Metzger, *Manuscripts of the Greek Bible: An Introduction to Greek Paleography,* Oxford University Press, corrected ed., 1991.

— *A Textual Commentary on the Greek New Testament*, 2nd ed., United Bible Societies, 1994.

Chaim Rabin, *Hebrew and Aramaic in the first Century*, in *The Jewish People in the First Century*, vol. 2, Fortress Press, 1976.

Constantin von Tischendorf et al., *Novum Testamentum Graece,* Giesecke and Devrient, 1869–1894.

Craig A. Evans and Stanley E. Porter, *Dictionary of New Testament Background*, InterVarsity Press, 2000.

Daniel B Wallace, *Center for the Study of New Testament Manuscripts,* manuscripts.csntm.org.

Daniel Machiela, *A Handbook of the Aramaic Scrolls from the Qumran Caves*, Brill, 2023.

David J. A. Clines, *The Concise Dictionary of Classical Hebrew*, Sheffield Phoenix Press, 2009.

E. A. Sophocles, *A Catalog of Greek Verbs*, Huntington Hartford, 1844.

Earnest Klein, *A Comprehensive Etymological Dictionary of the Hebrew Language for Readers of English*, Carta Israel Map and Publishing Company, 1987.

Eep Talstra, *The ETCBC (WIVU) Linguistic Database*, the Free University of Amsterdam, Werkgroep Informatica, 2014.

Eldon Jay Epp and Gordon D. Fee, *Studies in the Theory and Method of New Testament Textual Criticism,* Eerdmans, 1993.

Eliezer Ben Yehudah, *Complete Dictionary of Ancient and Modern Hebrew* (17 volumes), Hozaa-La'Or Le Zecher Eliezer Ben-Yehuda, 1908-1958.

Emanuel Tov et al., *Textual Criticism of the Hebrew Bible,* 3rd ed., Fortress Press, 2012.

– *Textual Criticism of the Hebrew Bible, Qumran, Septuagint: Collected Essays*, vol. 3, Brill, 2015.

– *Hebrew Bible, Greek Bible, and Qumran, Collected Essays*, Mohr Siebeck, 2008.

– *The Nature and Background of Harmonizations in Biblical Manuscripts*, in *Journal for the Study of the Old Testament*, vol. 31, 1985.

– *The Harmonizing Character of the Septuagint of Genesis 1-11*, in *Die Septuaginta Text, Wirkung, Rezeption*, vol. 4, Mohr Siebeck, 2014.

– *The Greek and Hebrew Bible: Collected Essays on the Septuagint*, Brill, 1999.

– *The Text-Critical Use of the Septuagint in Biblical Research*, 3rd ed., Eisenbrauns, 2015.

– *The Revised CATSS Hebrew/Greek Parallel Text*, OakTree Software, 2009.

E. S. Drower and R. Macuch, *A Mandaic Dictionary*, Oxford University Press, 1963.

Evert Van Emde Boas et al., *Cambridge Grammar of Classical Greek*, Cambridge University Press, 2019.

F. H. A. Scrivener, *The New Testament in the Original Greek*, Cambridge University Press, 1881.

Franz J. Delitzsch, *The Books of the New Testament, Translated from the Greek Tongue to the Hebrew Tongue*, (various editions and publishers), 1877-1892.

F. W. Gesenius, *Gesenius' Hebrew Grammar: Second English Edition,* Clarendon Press, 1910.

Geoffrey Khan, *Encyclopedia of Hebrew Language and Linguistics*, 4 volumes, Brill, 2013.

George A. Kiraz, *Syriac New Testament Peshitta*, based on the SEDRA 3 database, OakTree Software, 2006.

– *Syriac Curetonianus Gospels*, OakTree Software, 2006.

– *Syriac Sinaiticus Gospels*, OakTree Software, 2006.

– *Analytical Lexicon of the Syriac New Testament*, Logos Research Systems, 2003.

George Gabel, *The Text of Hebrews in GA 1739, in Selected Other Greek Manuscripts, and in Works of Origen: Preliminary Quantitative Assessments,* in *The New Testament in Antiquity and Byzantium*, De Gruyter, 2019.

George Howard, *The Hebrew Gospel of Matthew*, Mercer University Press, 2005.

Gerhard Kittel et al., *Theological Dictionary of the New Testament*, Eerdmans, 1964.

G. K. Beale, *The Book of Revelation: A Commentary on the Greek Text, New International Greek Testament Commentary*, Eerdmans, 1999.

Grant R. Osborne, *Revelation: Baker Exegetical Commentary on the New Testament*, Baker Academic, 2002.

H. C. Hoskier, *Concerning the Text of the Apocalypse, Collations of All Existing Available Greek Documents*, Bernard Quaritch, 1929.

Henry Barclay Swete, *The Apocalypse of St. John*, 2d. ed., Macmillan, 1907.

– *The Old Testament in Greek According to the Septuagint*, Cambridge University Press, 1909.

H. J. Schonfield, *An Old Hebrew Text of St. Matthew's Gospel*, T. and T. Clark, 1927.

Isaac Salkinson and C. D. Ginsburg, *The New Testament, A New Translation from the Greek Tongue to the Hebrew Tongue*, The Society for Distributing Hebrew Scriptures, revised ed., 2004.

Jacob Elon Conner, *Christ Was Not a Jew*, independently published, 1936.

J. Alan Groves Center for Advanced Biblical Research, *Hebrew Masoretic Text with Westminster Hebrew Morphology*, 1991-2016.

J. A. L. Lee, *Translations of the Old Testament, Greek*, in *Handbook of Classical Rhetoric in the Hellenistic Period, 330 B.C.-A.D. 400*, ed. S. E. Porter, Brill, 2001.

James Barr, *Which Language did Jesus Speak? – Some Remarks of a Semitist*, University of Manchester, John Rylands Library, 1970.

Jean Carmignac, *The Birth of the Synoptic Gospels*, translated from French by Michael J. Wrenn, Franciscan Herald Press, 1987.

J. F. Elwolde, *Hebrew, Biblical and Jewish,* in *Encyclopedia of Language and Linguistics*, ed. K. Brown, vol. 5, Elsevier, 2006.

J. F. Walvoord and R. B. Zuk, *The Bible Knowledge Commentary: An Exposition of the Scriptures*, vol. 2, Victor Books, 1983.

J. K. Elliott, *A Bibliography of Greek New Testament Manuscripts,* 3rd ed., Brill, 2015.

J. M. Harden, *Dictionary of the Vulgate New Testament*, Macmillan, 1921.

John Gwynn, *The Apocalypse of St. John, in a Syriac Version Hitherto Unknown*, Hodges Figgis and Co., 1897.

Joseph Ezekiel, *A Handbook of Hebrew Abbreviations*, Anglo-Jewish and Vernacular Press, 1887.

Joseph H. Thayer, *Greek-English Lexicon of the New Testament*, American Book Company, 1889.

Juan Hernández Jr., *The Greek Text of Revelation,* in *The Oxford Handbook of the Book of Revelation*, Oxford University Press, 2020.

K. Elliger and W. Rudolph, *Biblia Hebraica Stuttgartensia*, Deutsche Bibelgesellschaft, 1977.

Kurt Aland and Barbara Aland, *The Text of the New Testament: An Introduction to the Critical Editions and to the Theory and Practice of Modern Textual Criticism*, Eerdmans, 1989.

L. Cowden Laughlin, *The Solecisms of the Apocalypse*, C. S. Robinson and Co., 1902

Leeor Gottlieb, *Targum Chronicles and its Place Among the Late Targums*, Brill, 2020.

– *Targums WordMap, The Equivalent Project*, Israel Science Foundation, OakTree Software, 2019.

Leon Vaganay, *An Introduction to New Testament Textual Criticism*, 2nd ed., University of Cambridge, 1991.

Ludwig Koehler and Walter Baumgartner, *The Hebrew and Aramaic Lexicon of the Old Testament*, Brill, 1994-2000.

Marcus Jastro, *A Dictionary of the Targumim, the Talmud Babli and Yerushalmi, and the Midrashic Literature*, 2 volumes, Luzac and Co., 1903.

Martin Abegg, *Kaufmann Mishna, Based Upon the Kaufmann A 50 Manuscript*, OakTree Software, 2009.

– *Judean Desert Manuscripts*, OakTree Software, 2016.

– *Qumran Non-Biblical Manuscripts*, OakTree Software, 1999-2009.

– *Dead Sea Scrolls Biblical Corpus*, OakTree Software, 2009.

Martin Abegg, Jerome Lund et al., *Syriac Peshitta (Old Testament)*, OakTree Software, 2022.

Martin Heide, *Die Syrische Apokalypse oder Offenbarung an Johannes. Kritische Edition der Harklensischen Textzeugen, Studien zum Text der Apokalypse II*, De Gruyter, 2017.

Maurice A. Robinson et al., *The New Testament in the Original Greek: Byzantine Textform*, Chilton Book Publishing, 2005.

– *Elzevir Textus Receptus (1624) with morphology*, Logos Research Systems, 2002.

M. H. Segal, *A Grammar of Mishnaic Hebrew*, Clarendon Press, 1980.

– *Mishnaic Hebrew and its Relation to Biblical Hebrew and to Aramaic*, in *The Jewish Quarterly Review*, 1908.

Michaele Tvveedale, *Biblia Sacra Juxta Vulgatam Clementinam,* The Bishops' Conference of England and Wales, 2005.

Miguel Pérez Fernández, *An Introductory Grammar of Rabbinic Hebrew*, Brill, 1997.

Nigel Turner, *Grammatical Insights into the New Testament*, T. and T. Clark, 1965.

Peter Malik, *P. Beatty III (P47): The Codex, its Scribe, and its Text*, Brill, 2017.

Philip W. Comfort, *The Text of the Earliest New Testament Greek Manuscripts*, 2nd ed., Tyndale House Publishers, 2009.

Ralph W. Klein, *Textual Criticism of the Old Testament, the Septuagint After Qumran,* Fortress Press, 1981.

Robert B. Y. Scott, *The Original Language of the Apocalypse*, The University of Toronto Press, 1928.

Robert Jamieson, A. R. Fausset et al., *A Commentary, Critical and Explanatory on the Whole Bible*, The S. S. Scranton Company, vol. 2, 1871.

Robertus Stephanus, *ΤΗΣ ΚΑΙΝΗΣ ΔΙΑΘΗΚΗΣ ΑΠΑΝΤΑ* (Stephanus' Textus Receptus), Lutetiae, 1550.

Robert Weber, Roger Gryson et al., *Biblia Sacra Luxta Vulgatam Versionem*, Deutsche Bibelgesellschaft, 1994.

Simon J. Kistemaker, *Exposition of the Book of Revelation*, *Baker New Testament Commentary*, Baker Book House, 2001.

Staffan Olofsson, *The LXX Version, A Guide to the Translation Technique of the Septuagint*, Almqvist and Wiksell Inernational, 1990.

– *Studying the Word Order of the Septuagint: Questions and Possibilities*, in *Scandinavian Journal of the Old Testament,* vol. 10(2), 1996.

Stefan Schorch, *The Samaritan Pentateuch, A Critical Edition Maior, vol. 1 Genesis,* De Gruyter, 2021.

– *The Samaritan Pentateuch, A Critical Edition Maior, vol. 3 Leviticus,* De Gruyter, 2018.

Stephen A. Kaufmann et al., *Targum Onkelos; Targum Johnathan; Targum Writings; Targum Neofiti; Targum Pseudo Johnathan; Targum Eshter Sheni; Targum Fragments; Targum Cairo Geniza,* The Complete Aramaic Lexicon (CAL) Project, OakTree Software, 2008-2014.

– *Targum Lexicon*, The Complete Aramaic Lexicon (CAL) Project, Logos Research Systems, 2005.

The Friedberg Jewish Manuscript Society, (transcriptions and/or photos of more than 100,000 Jewish manuscript fragments), fjms.genizah.org.

The International Collection of Digitized Hebrew Manuscripts (Ktiv), National Library of Israel, www.nli.org.il/en/discover/manuscripts/hebrew-manuscripts.

The Leon Levy Dead Sea Scrolls Digital Library, Israel Antiquities Authority, www.deadseascrolls.org.il

The Modern Hebrew New Testament, The Bible Society in Israel, 2010.

The New Testament Virtual Manuscript Room (INTF), University of Münster, ntvmr.uni-muenster.de.

The Oxford Textus Receptus: *Η ΚΑΙΝΗ ΔΙΑΘΗΚΗ, Novum Testamentum Accedunt Parallela S. Scripturae Loca Vetus Capitulorum Notatio Canones Eusebii*, Typographeo Clarendoniano, 1873.

Thomas R. Schreiner, *1, 2 Peter, Jude, The New American Commentary*, Broadman and Holman Publishers, 2007.

Tommy Wasserman, *The Epistle of Jude: Its Text and Transmission*, Almqvist and Wiksell, 2006.

William Arndt et al., *A Greek-English Lexicon of the New Testament and Other Early Christian Literature*, University of Chicago Press, 2000.

William D. Mounce, *Basics of Biblical Greek Grammar,* 2nd ed., 2003.

William L. Holladay, *A Concise Hebrew and Aramaic Lexicon of the Old Testament*, Brill, 1971.

William Whiston, *The Works of Josephus: Complete and Unabridged*, Hendrickson, 1996.

Yaacov Weinberger, Aviezri Fraenkel et al., *The Bar Ilan Responsa Project – The Largest Torah Literature Database*, www.responsa.co.il.

Yehudah v. 24-25: "But he who is able to keep you without doubting and to set you before Ha-Adon without any sin, to him be honor and glory and kingship, from everlasting and unto everlasting, amein!"

Made in the USA
Monee, IL
07 August 2024

e23d2351-97c6-4acc-a5ef-fe685dfcf4e1R01